Thank you for purchasing this book. It's designed to inspire your next tattoo.

There are many different weird and wonderful ai designs within this book, and I hope it helps the viewer in the process of choosing their next tattoo. These tattoo designs should be used as a guide or tool for the tattoo artist to create their own work from. If you discover a tattoo design that you like, (which I'm sure you will!) I would recommend that the tattoo artist you choose, adds his or her own creative style to the design, and makes it their own.

I hope you enjoy the design book as much as I enjoyed making it.

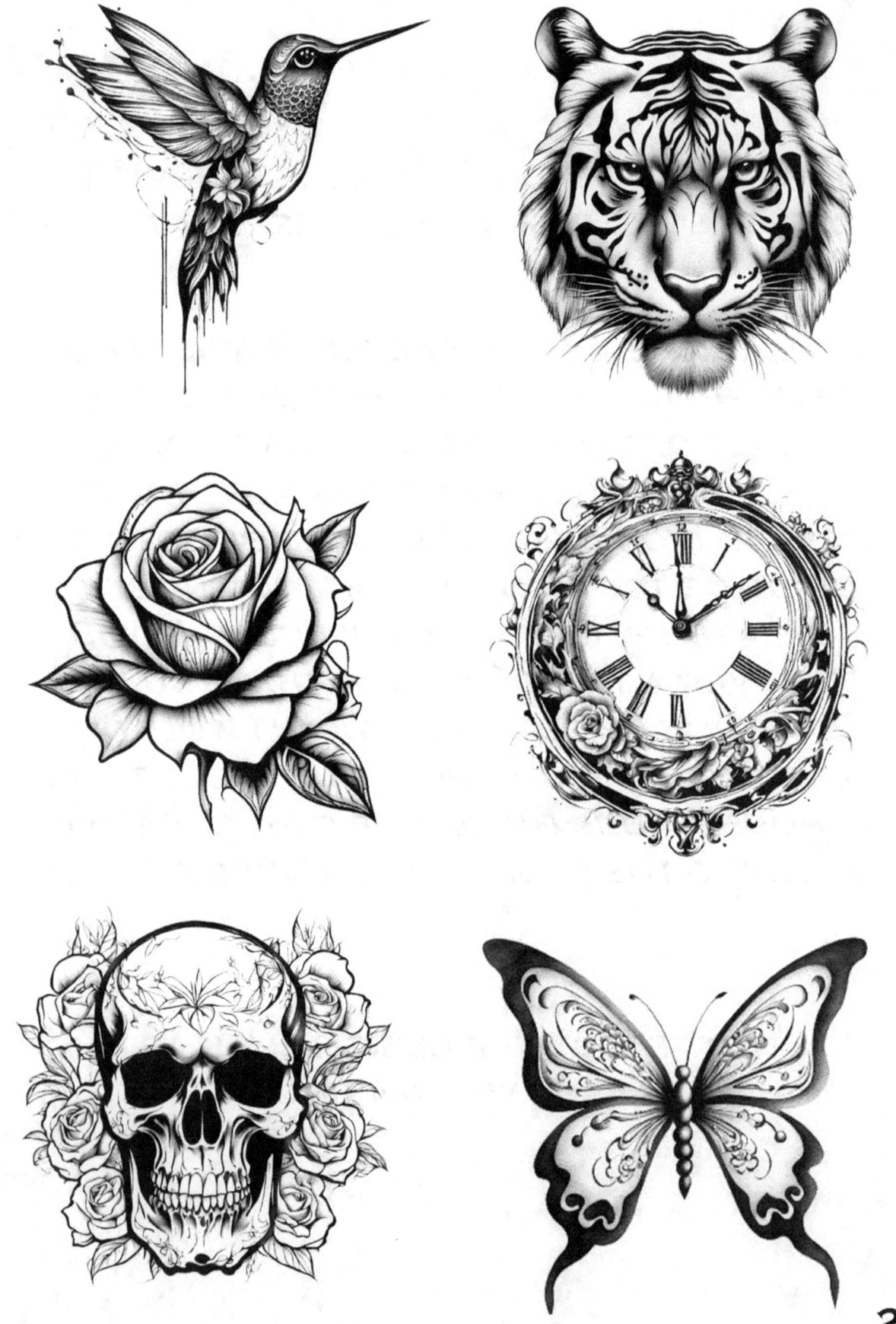

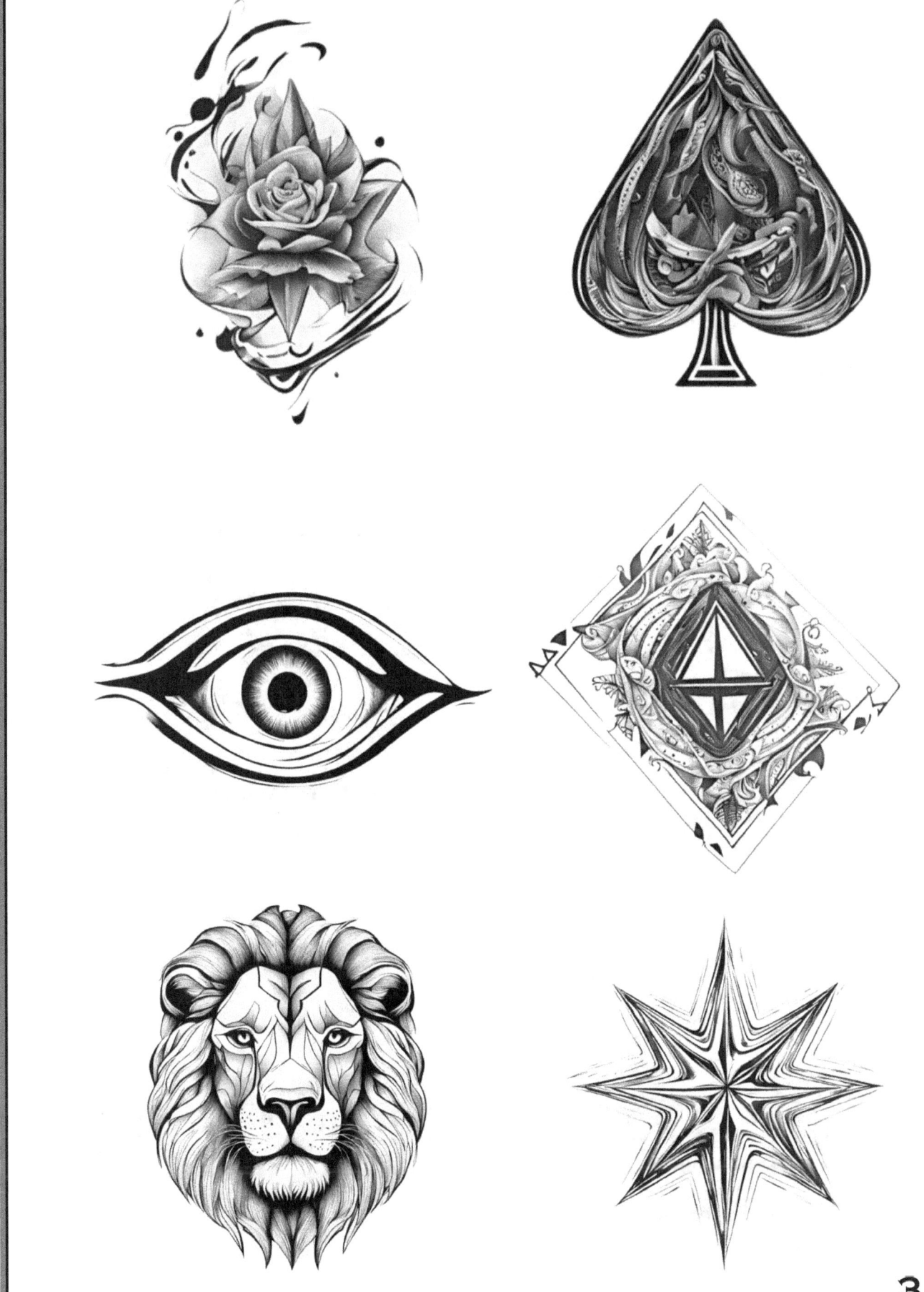

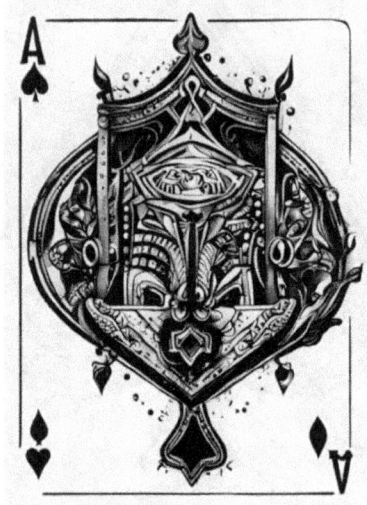
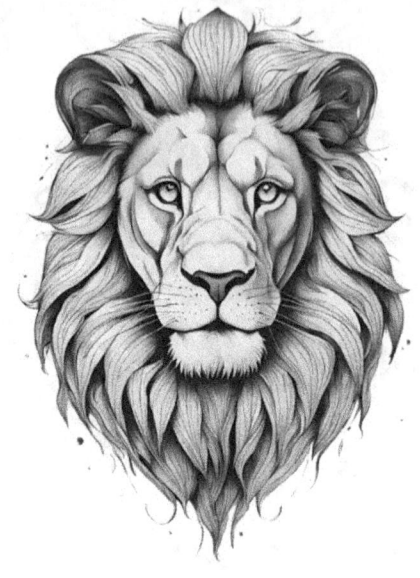
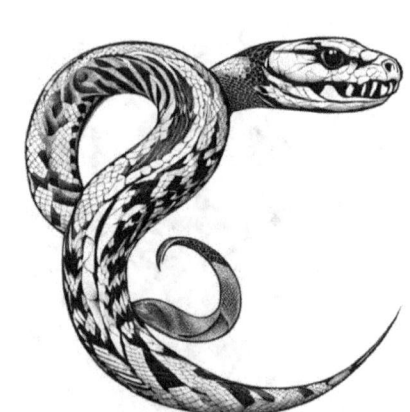
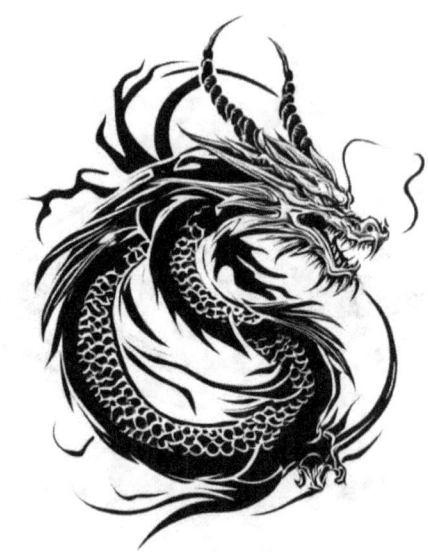
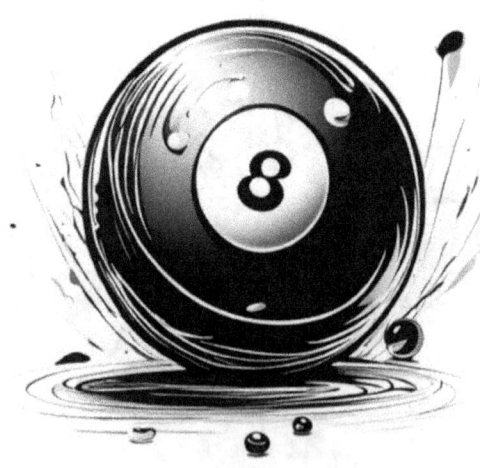
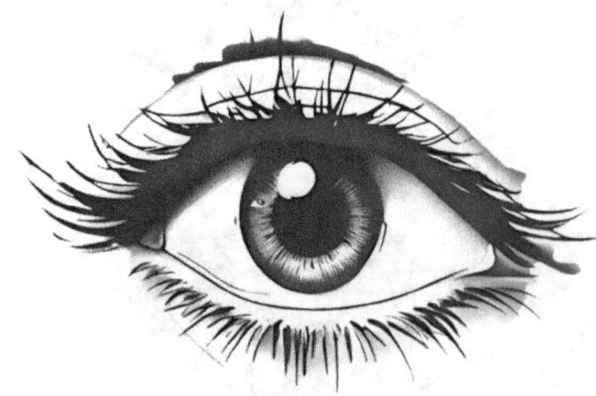

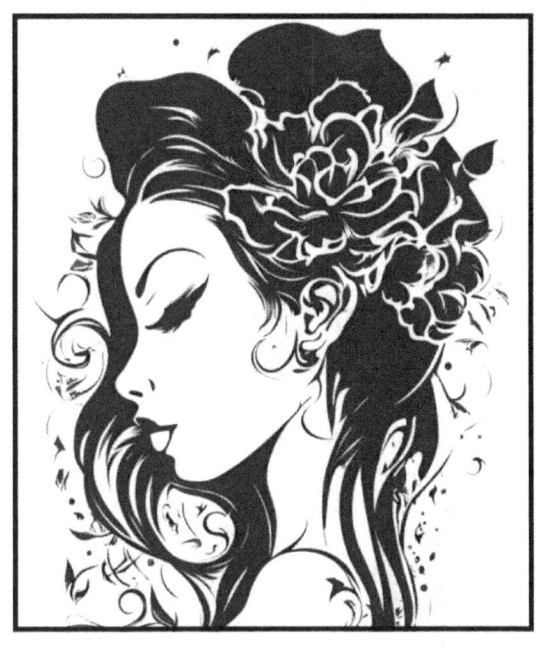
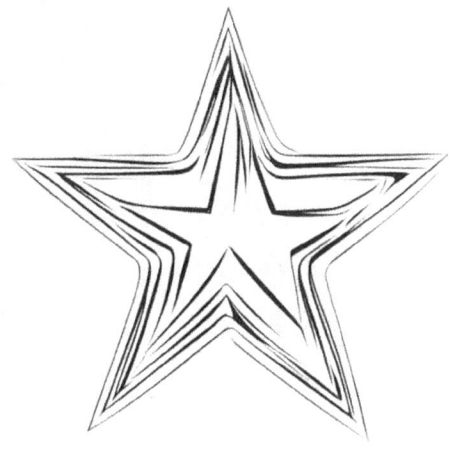
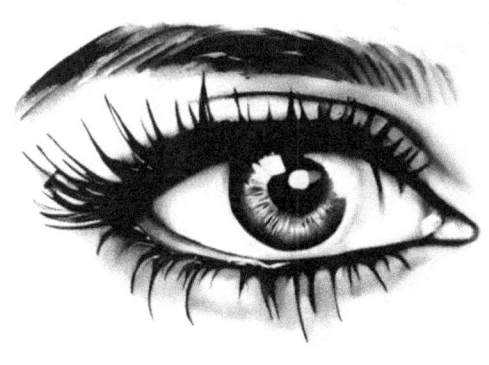
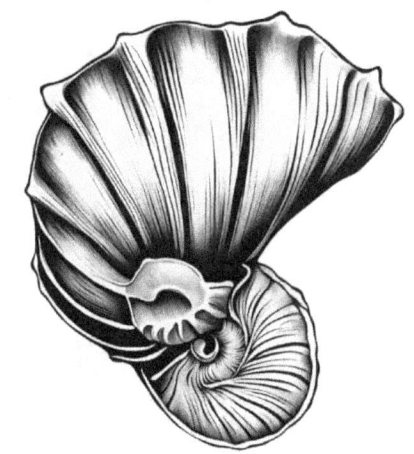
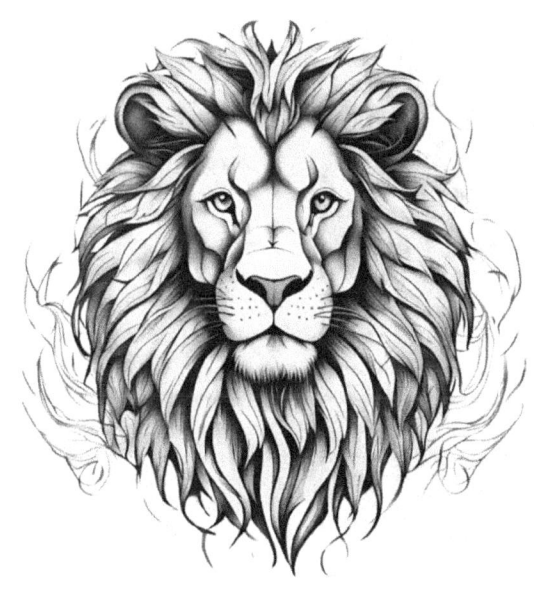
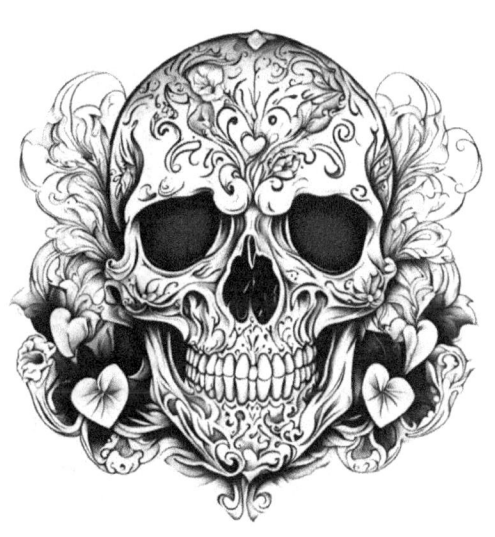

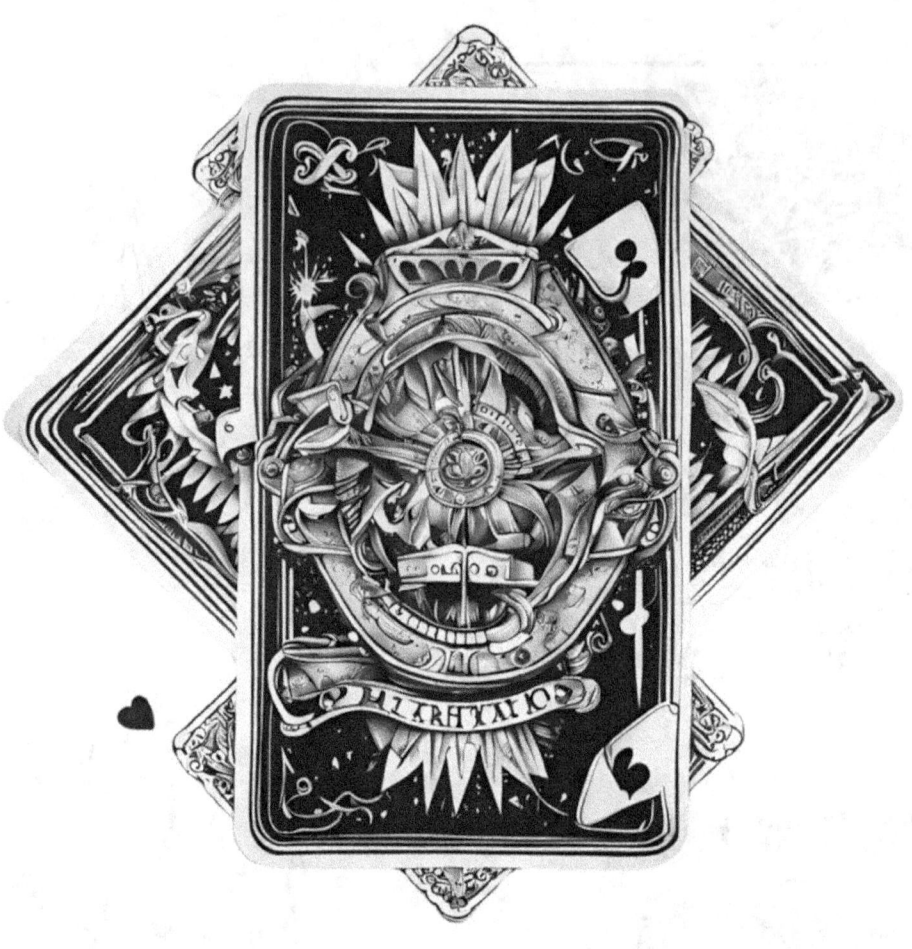
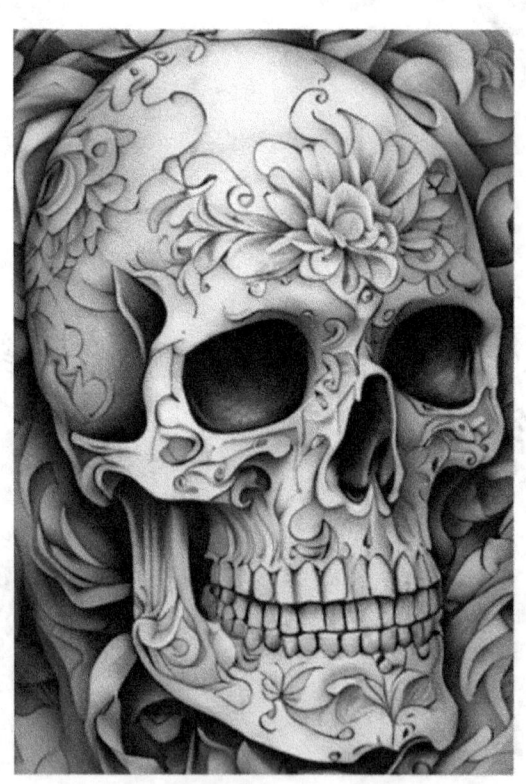

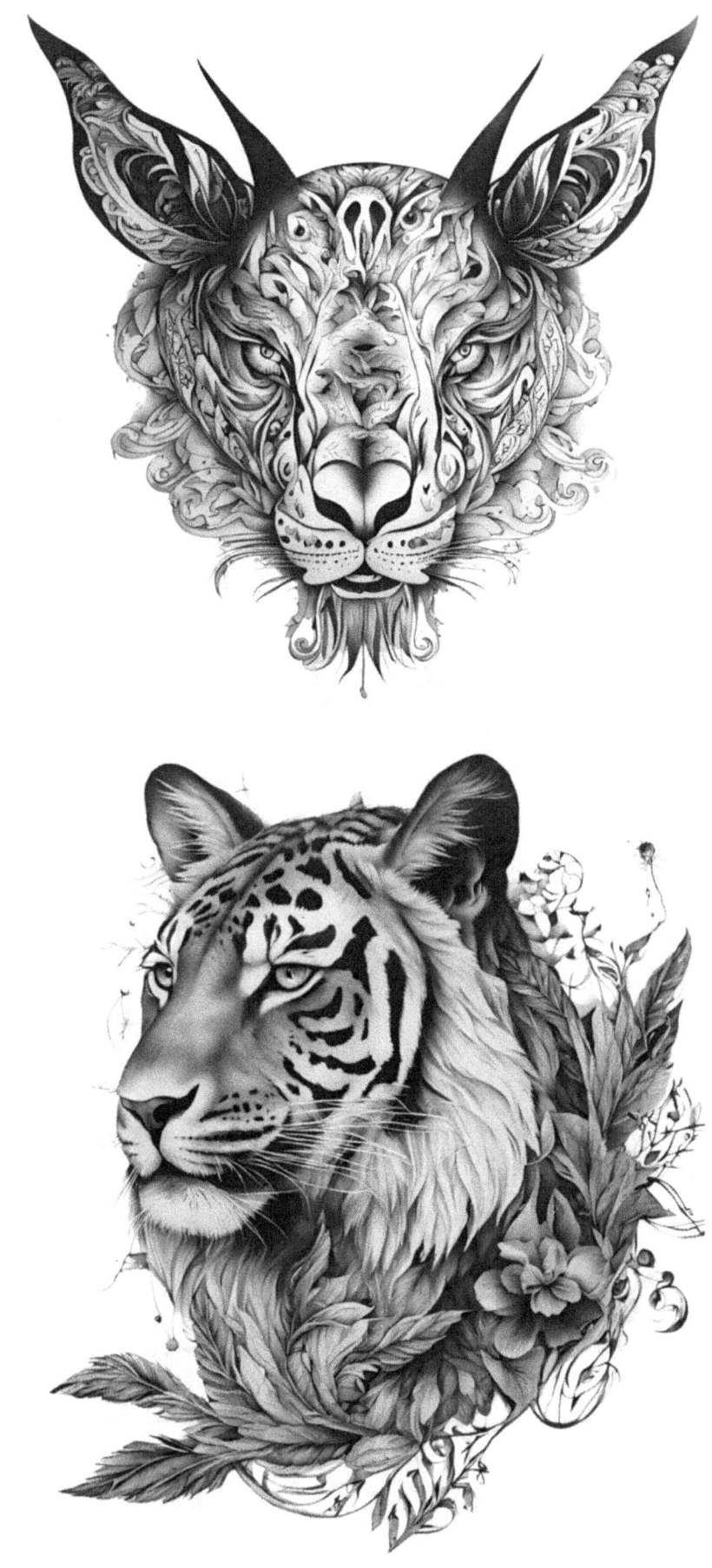

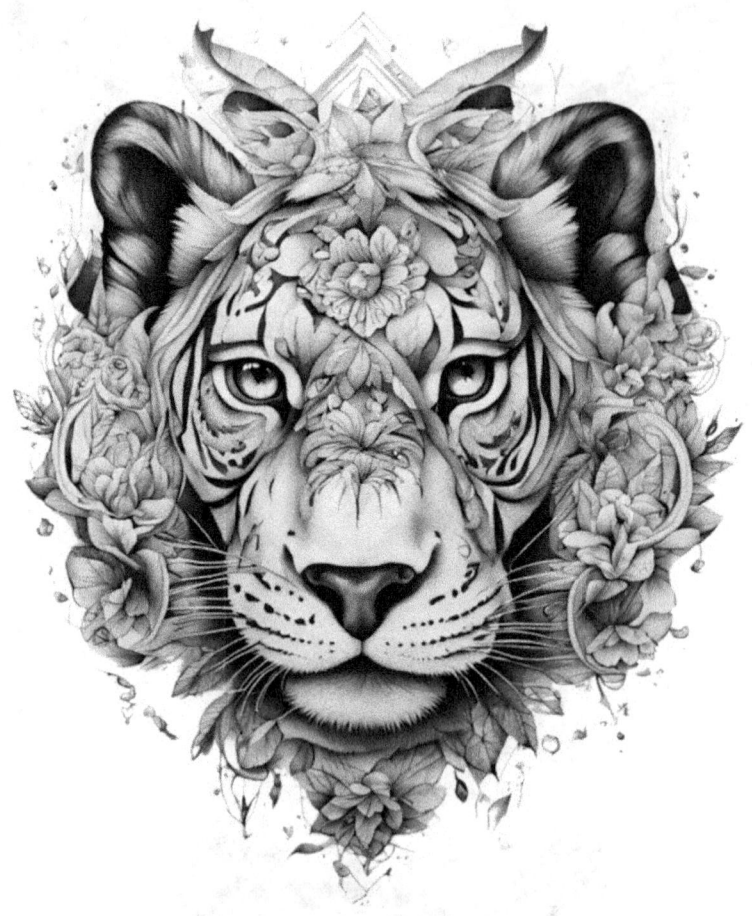
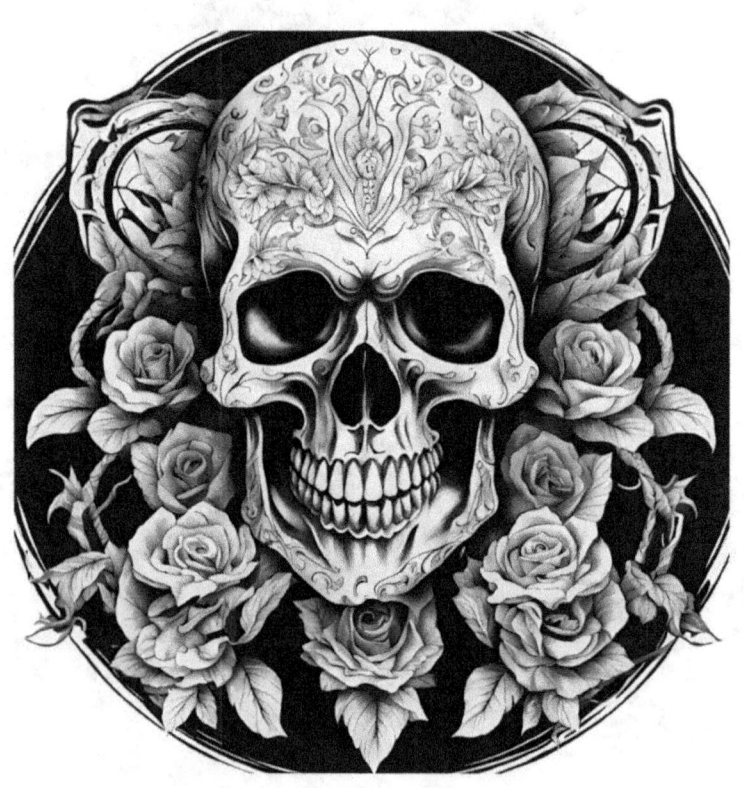

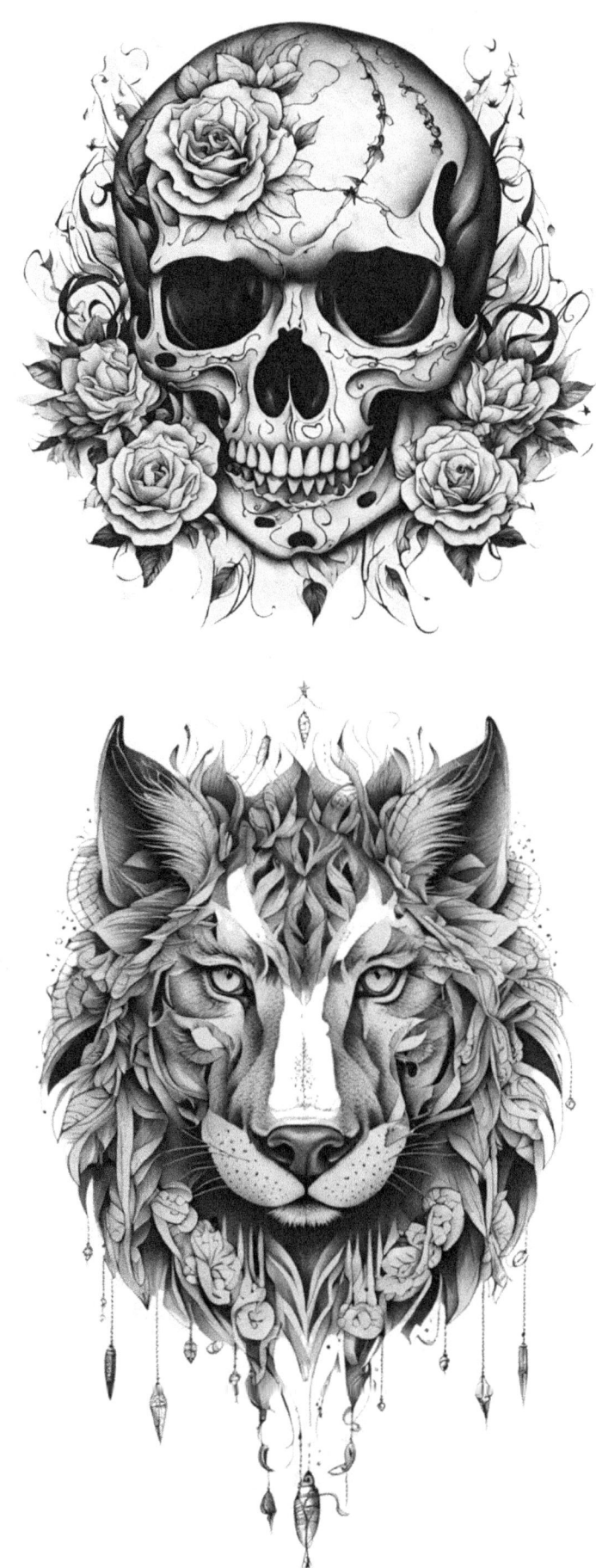

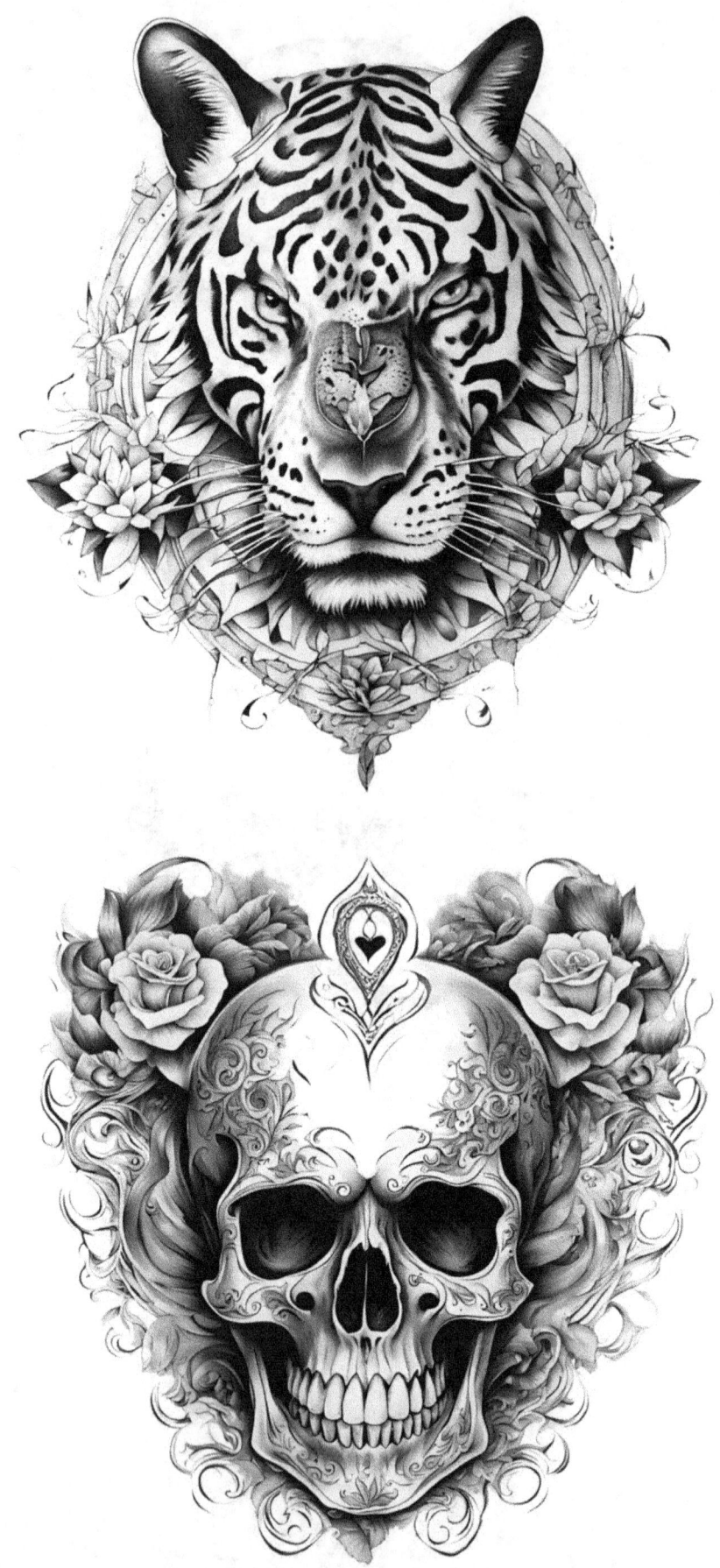

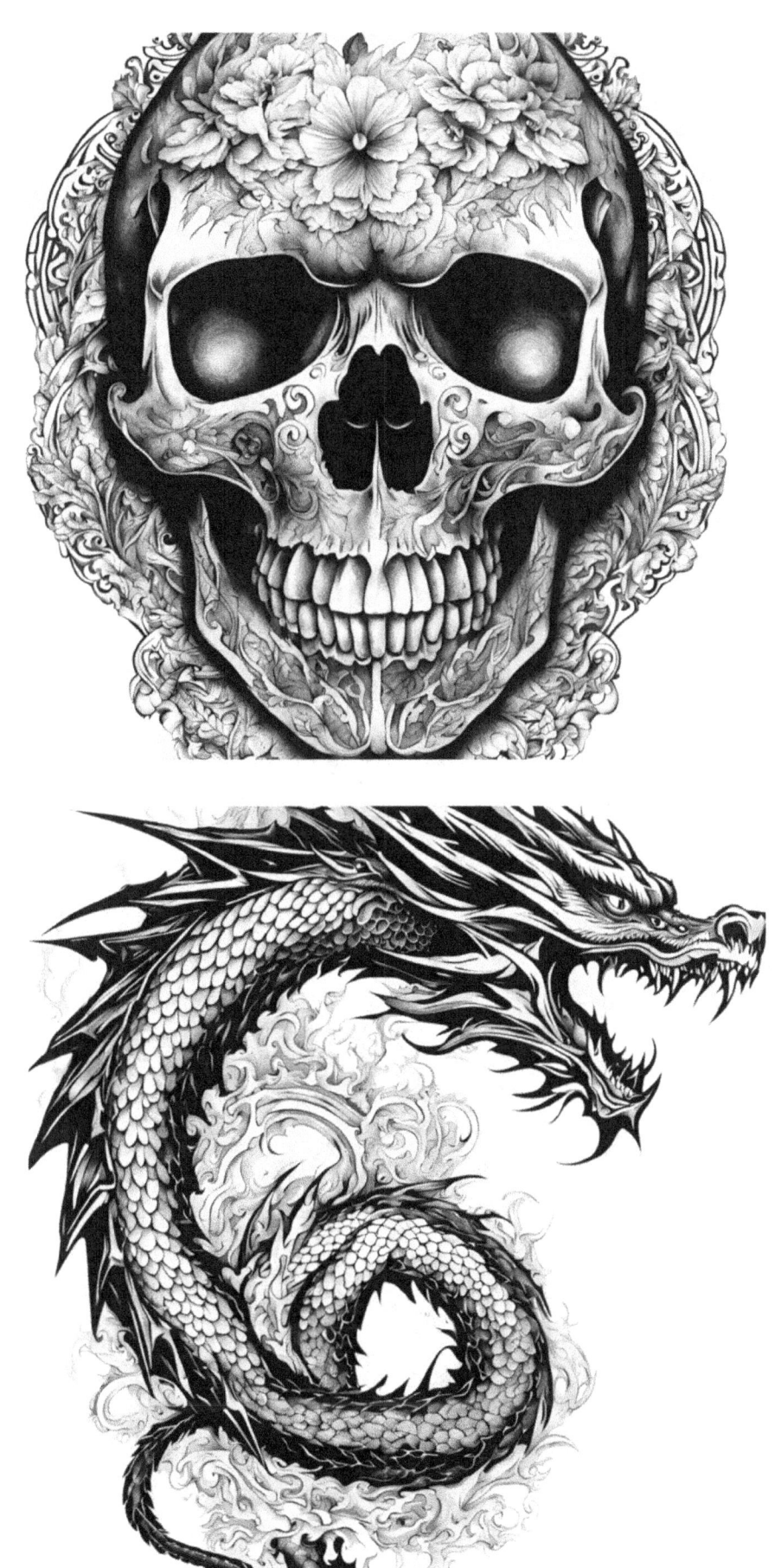

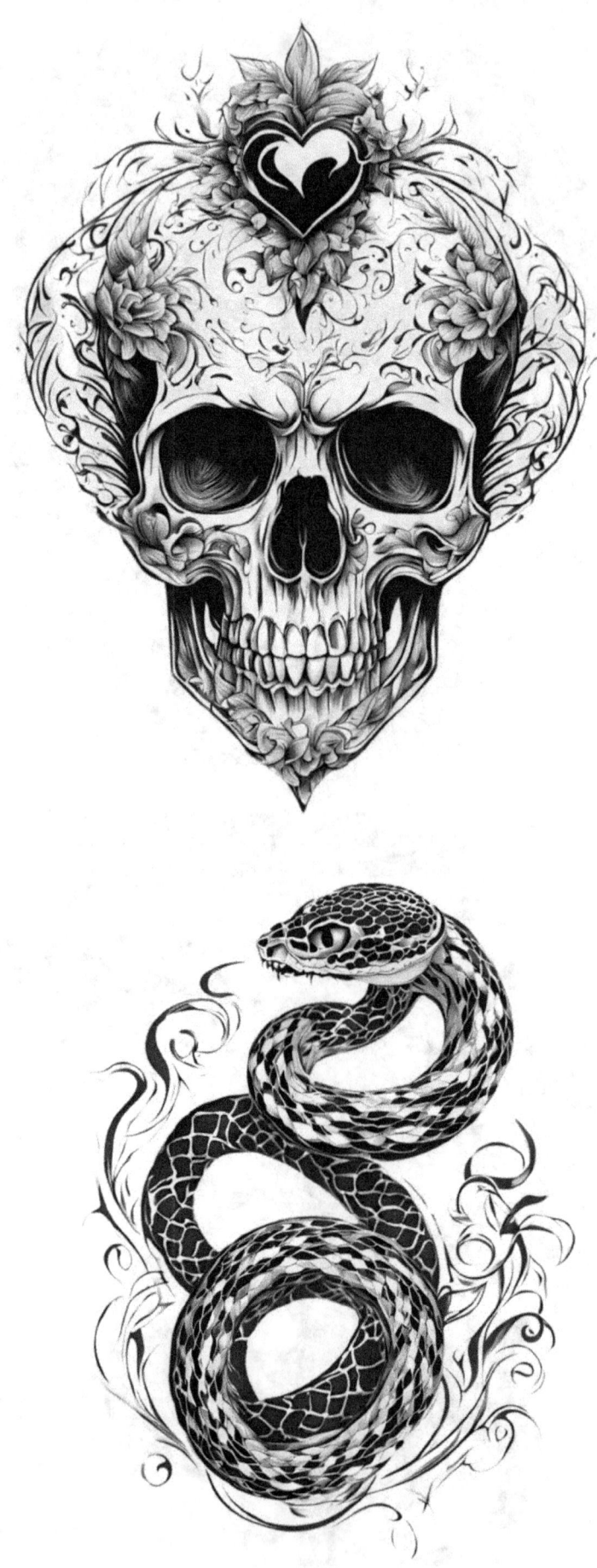

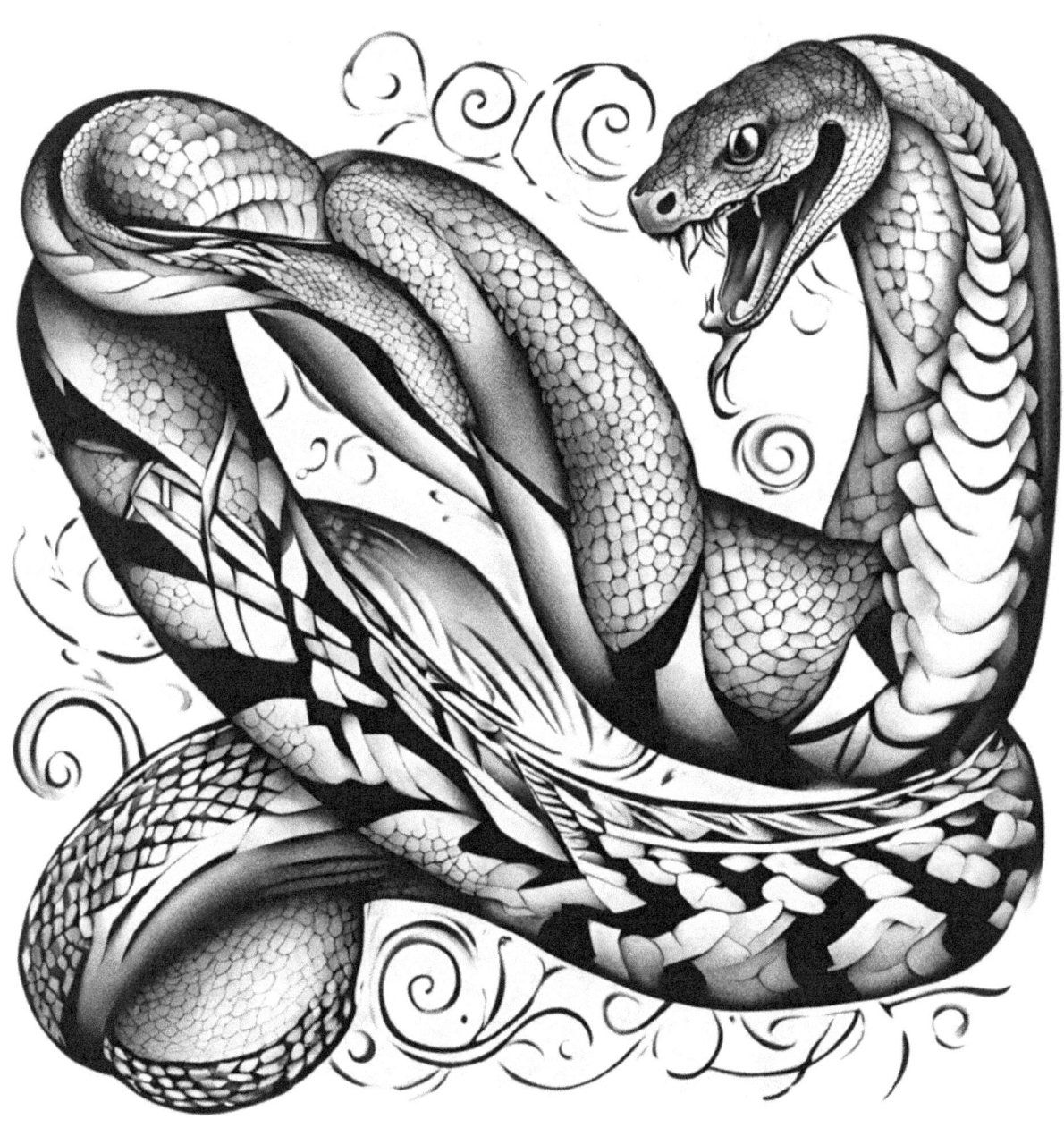

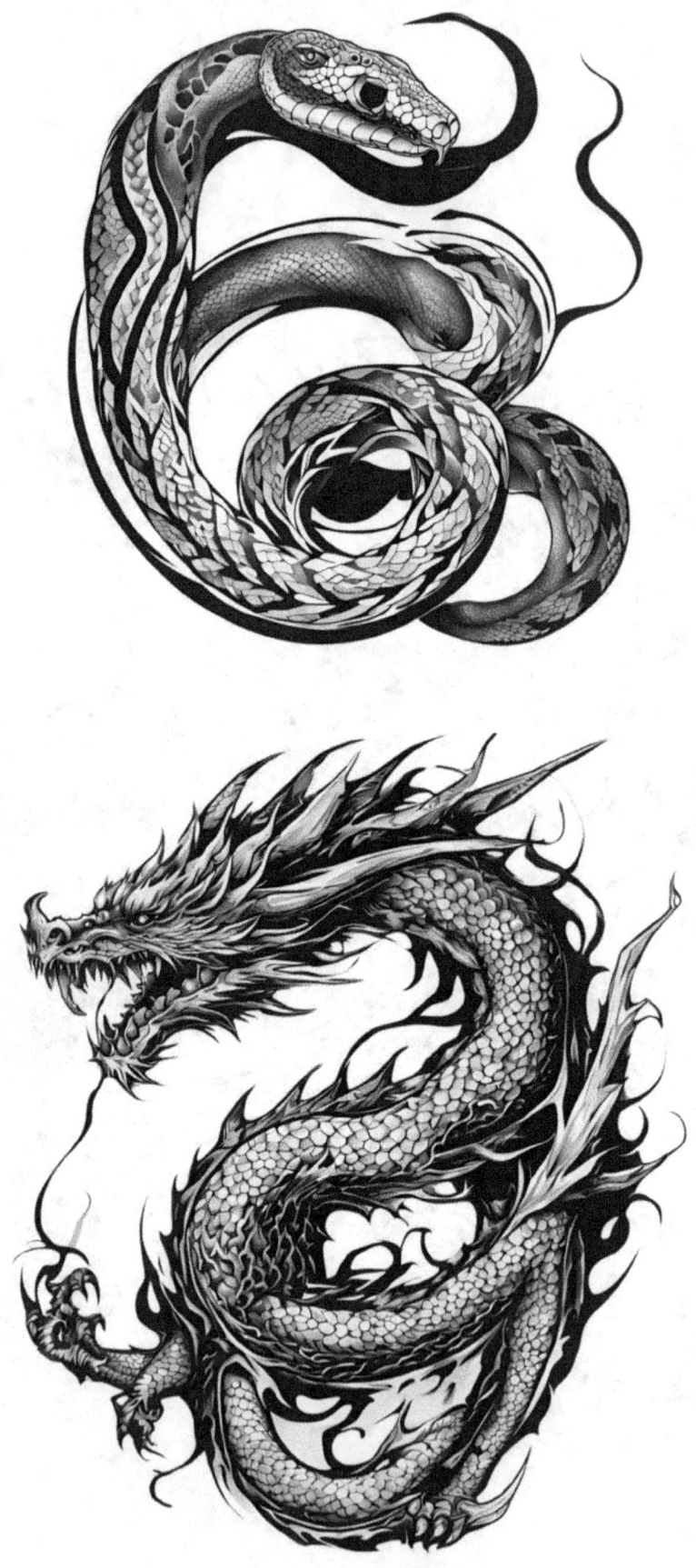

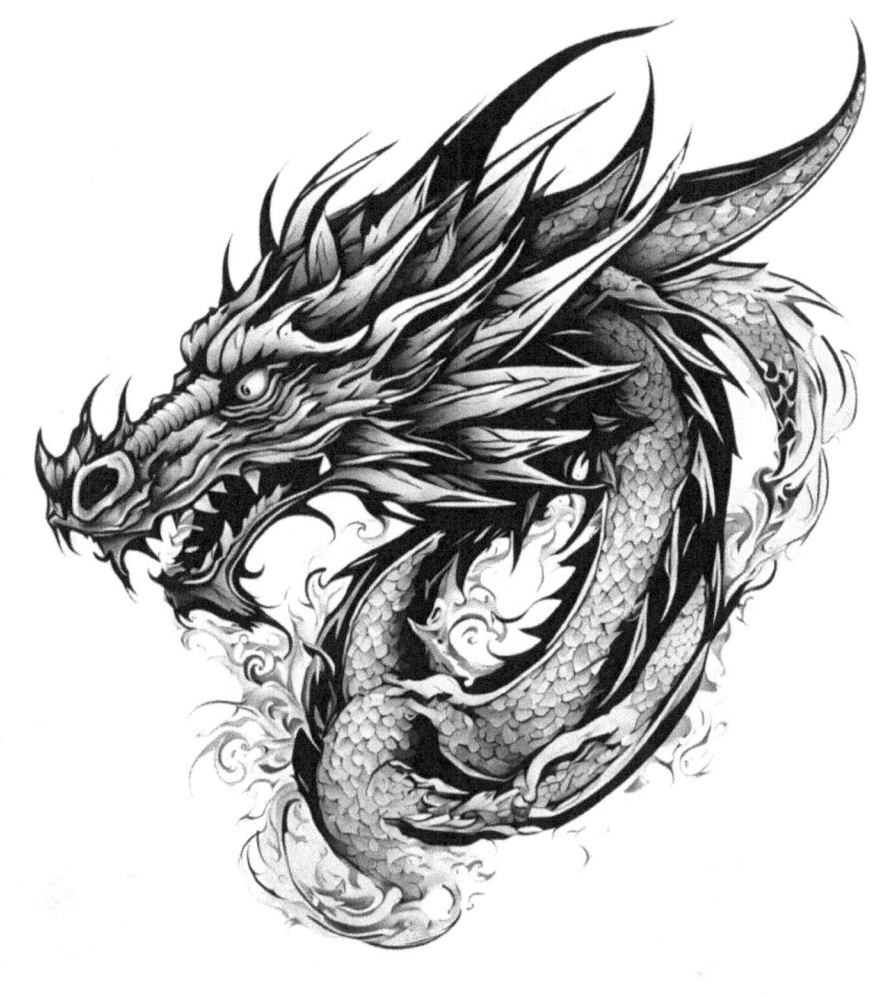
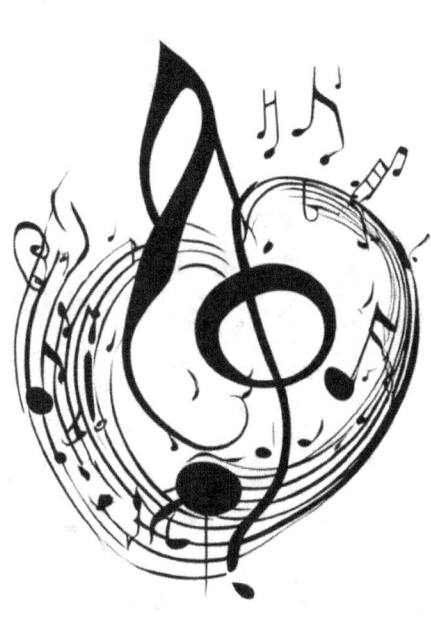
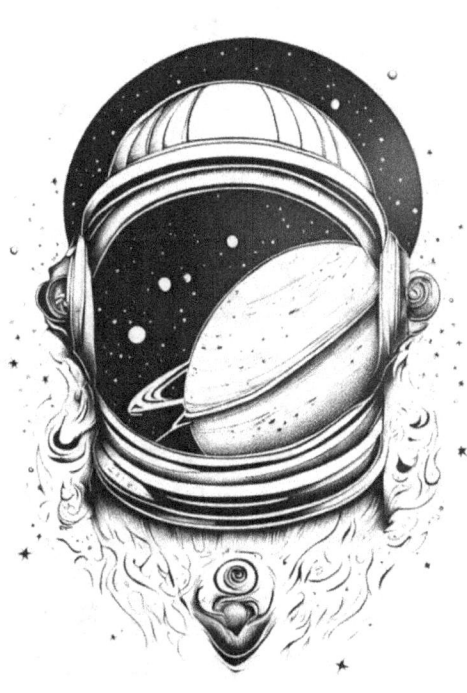

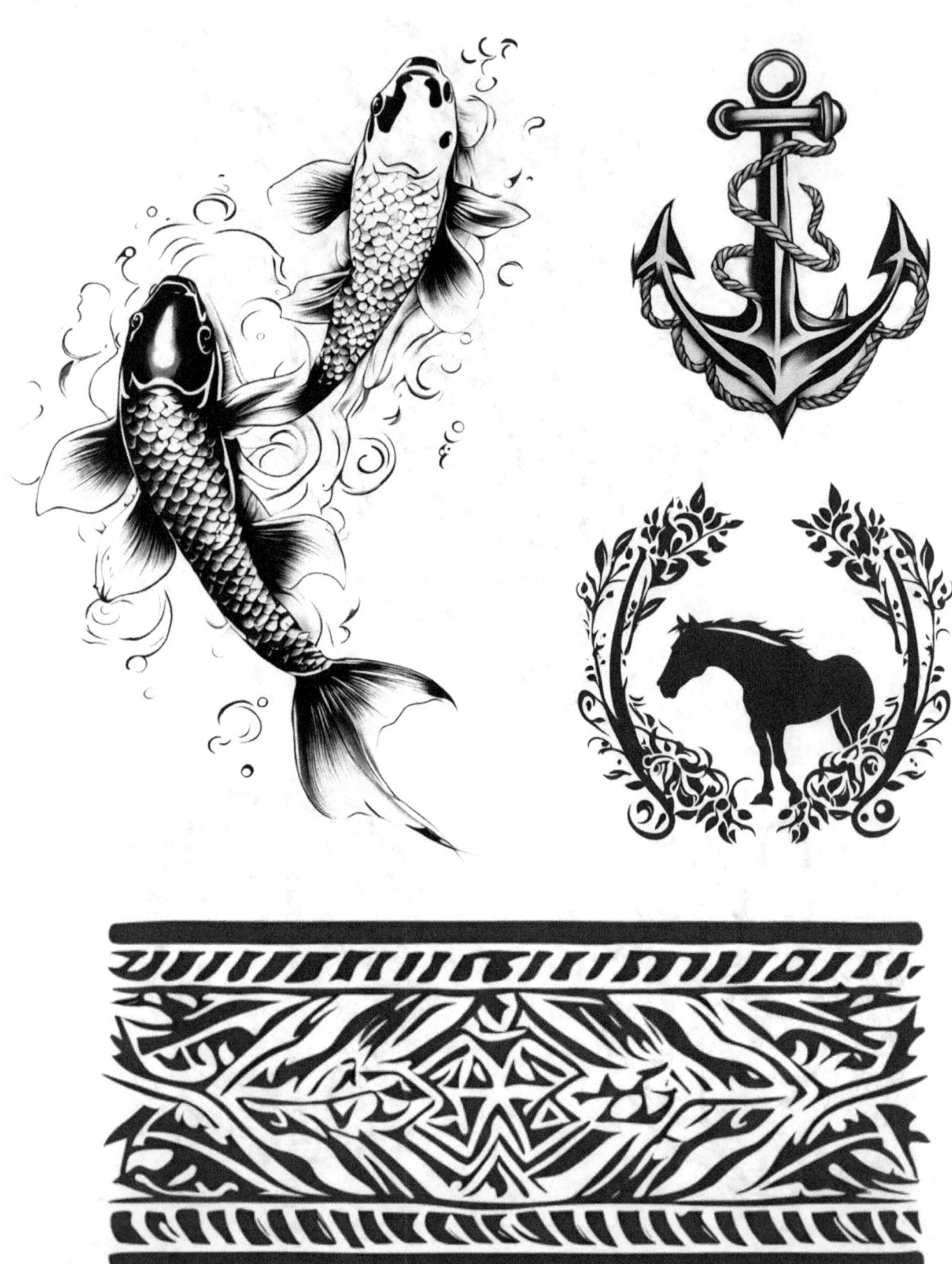

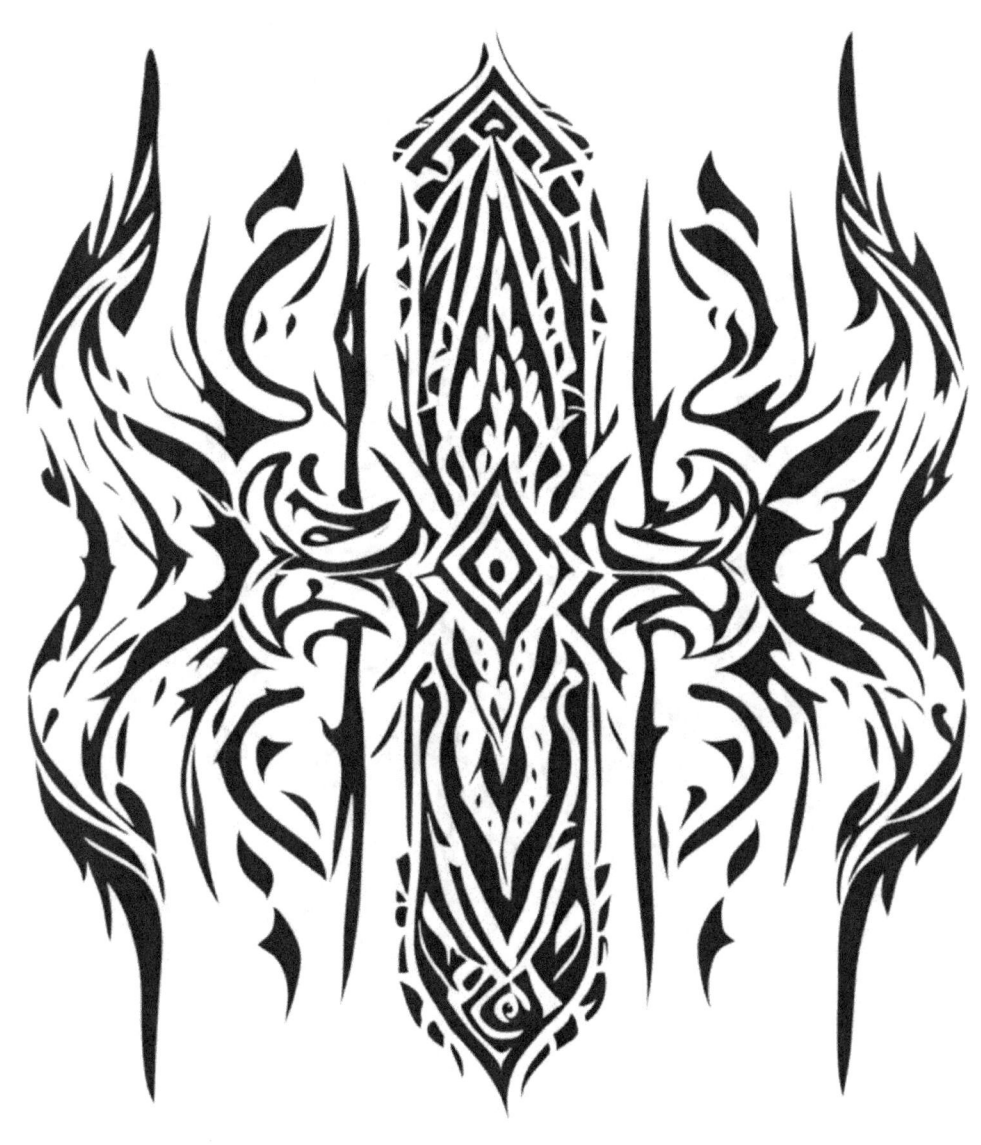
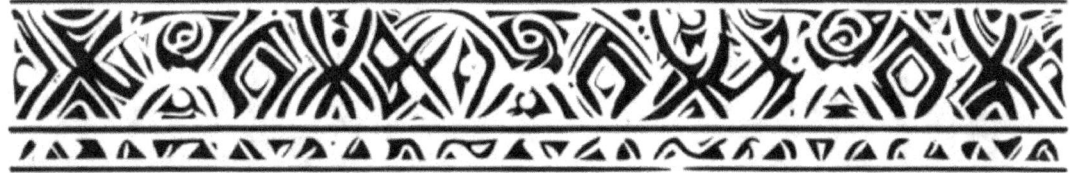

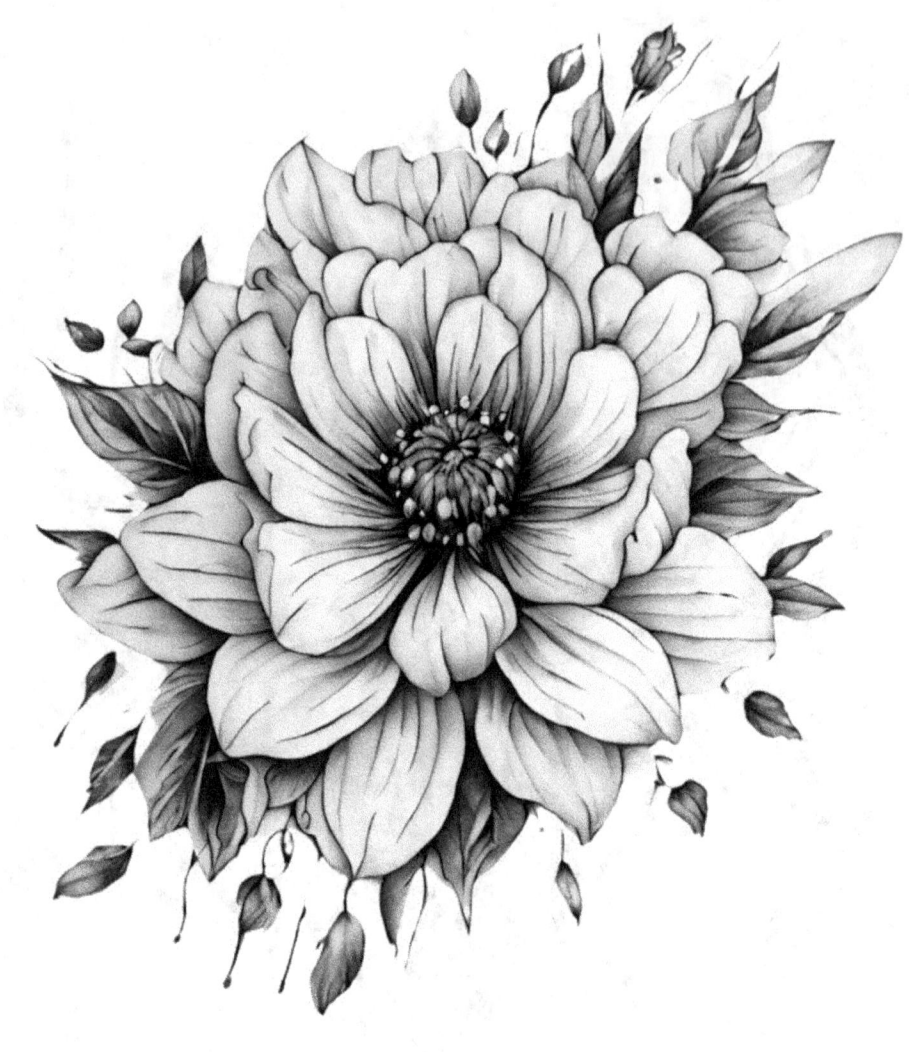
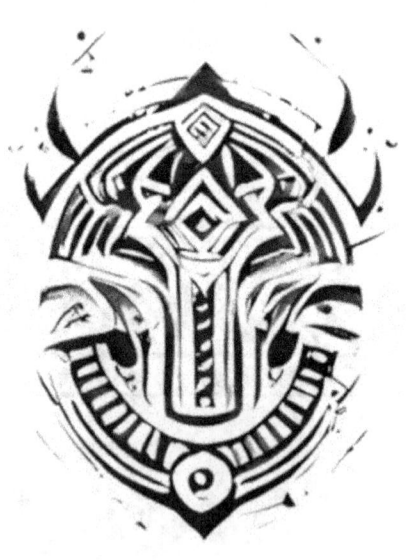
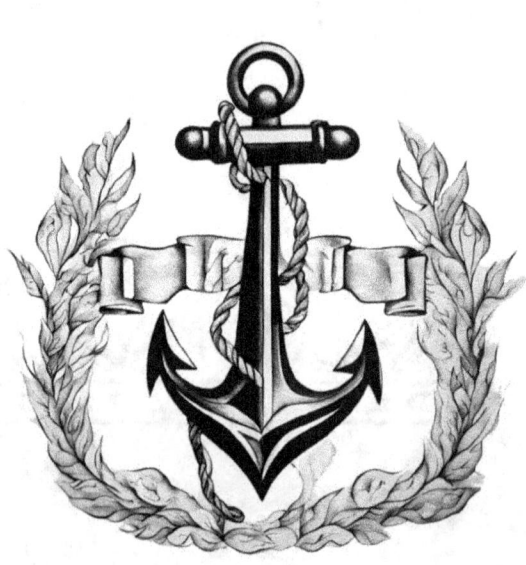

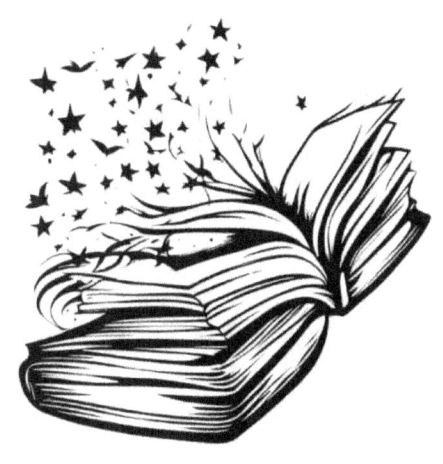
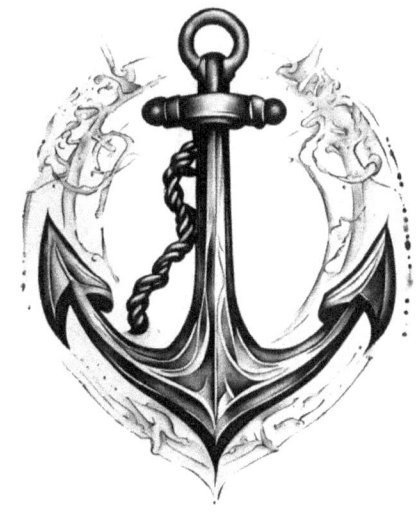
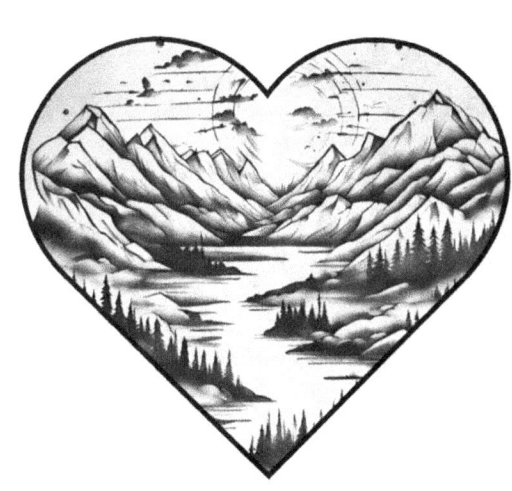
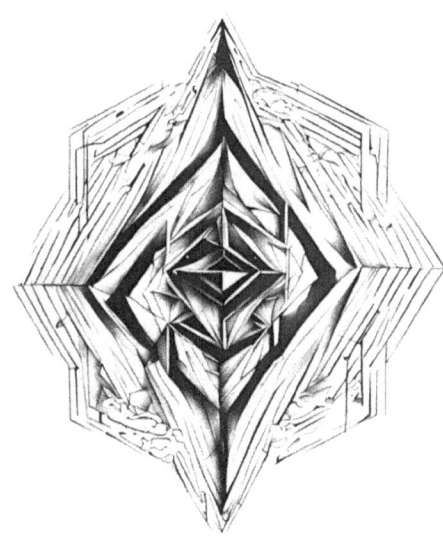
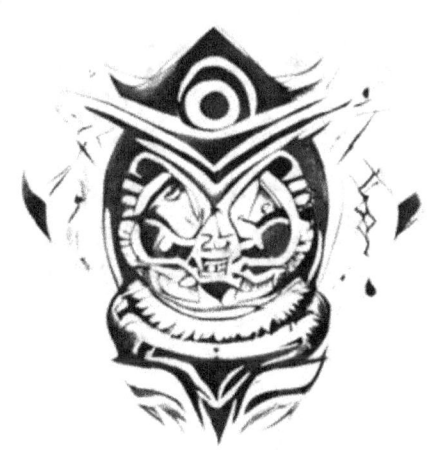
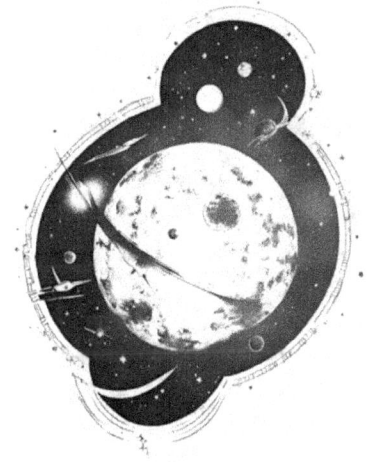

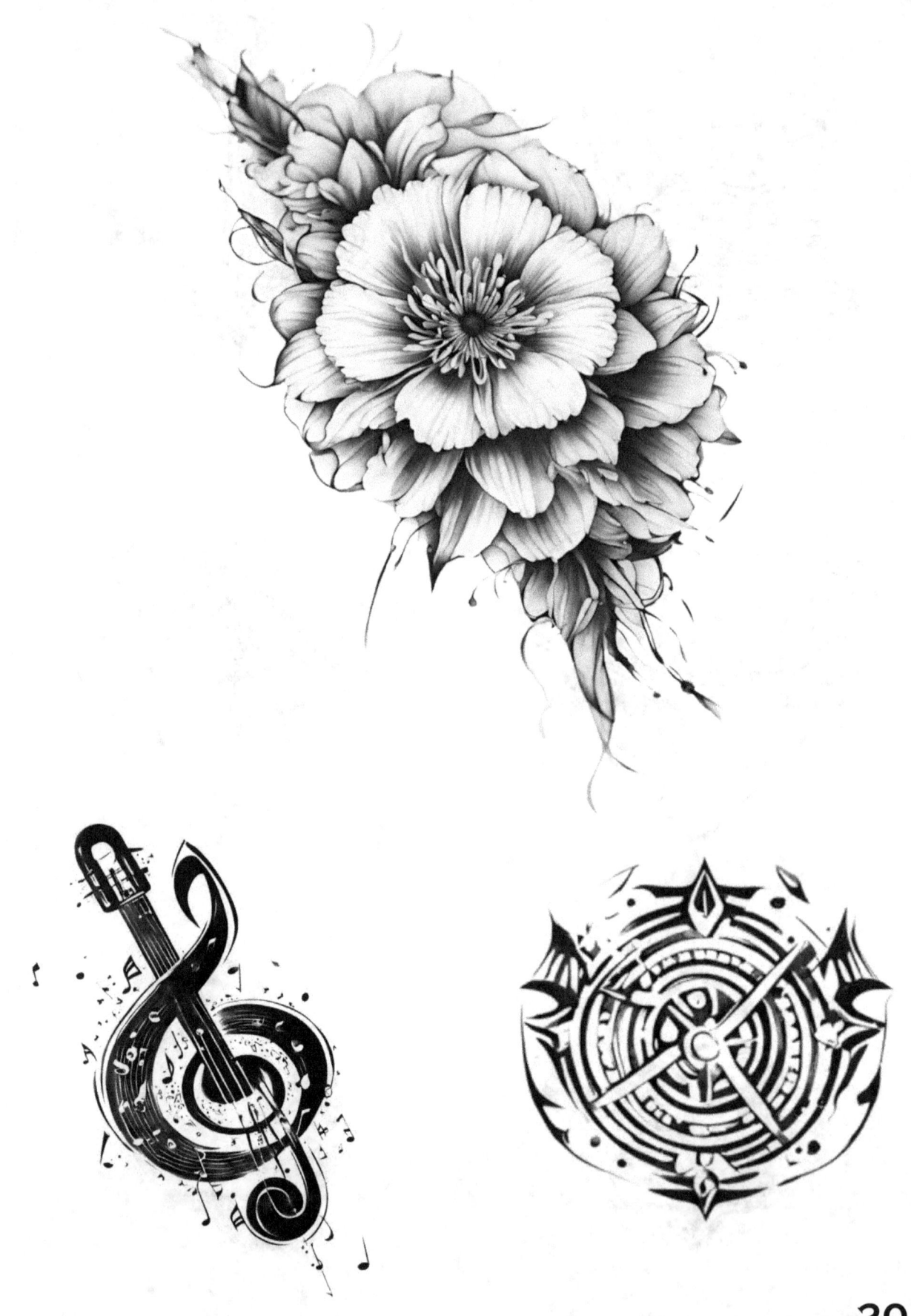

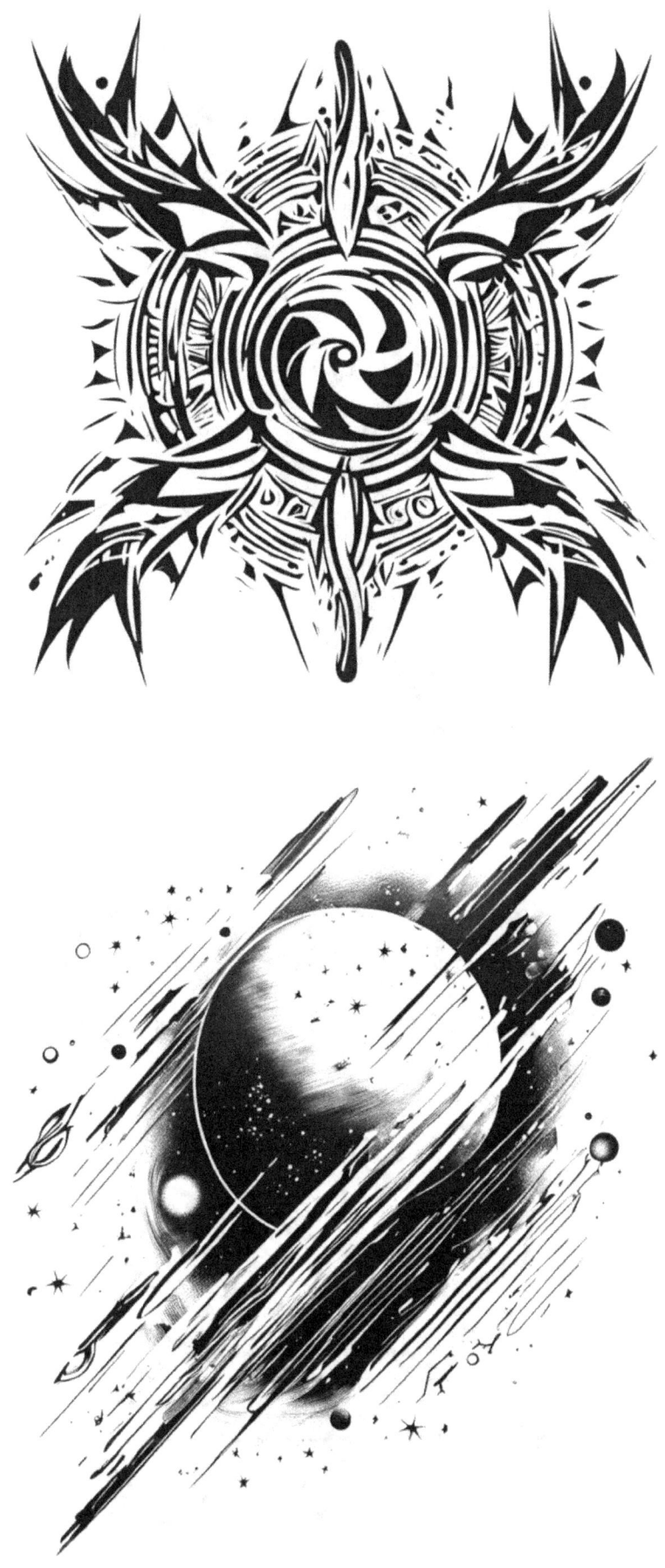

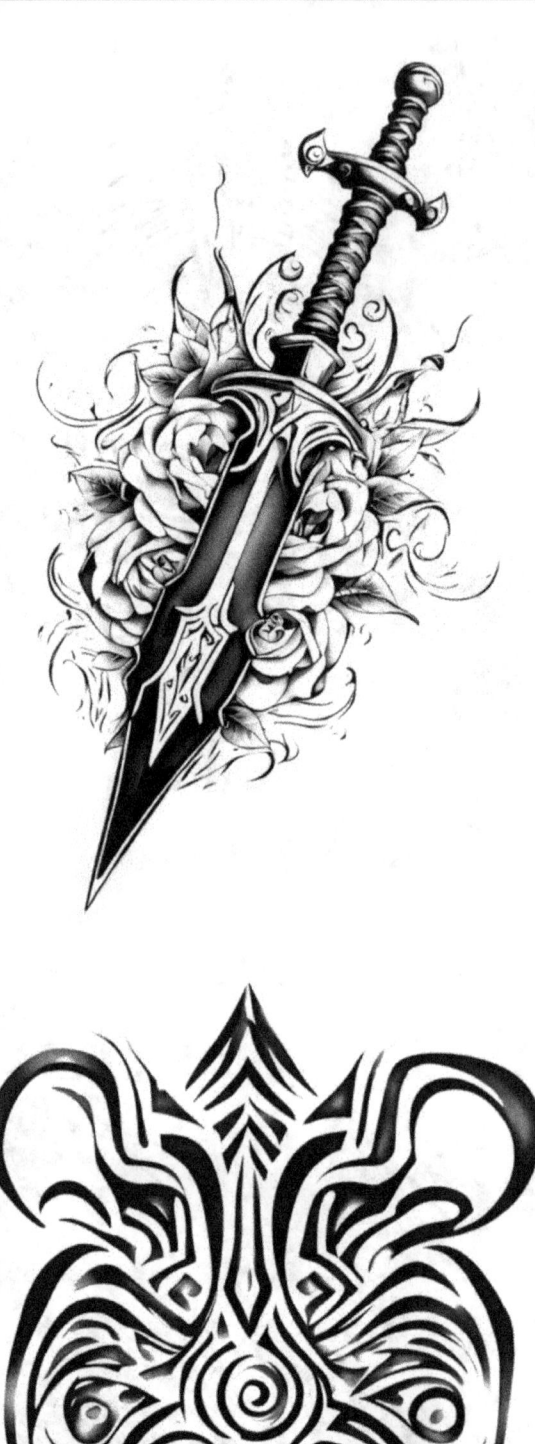

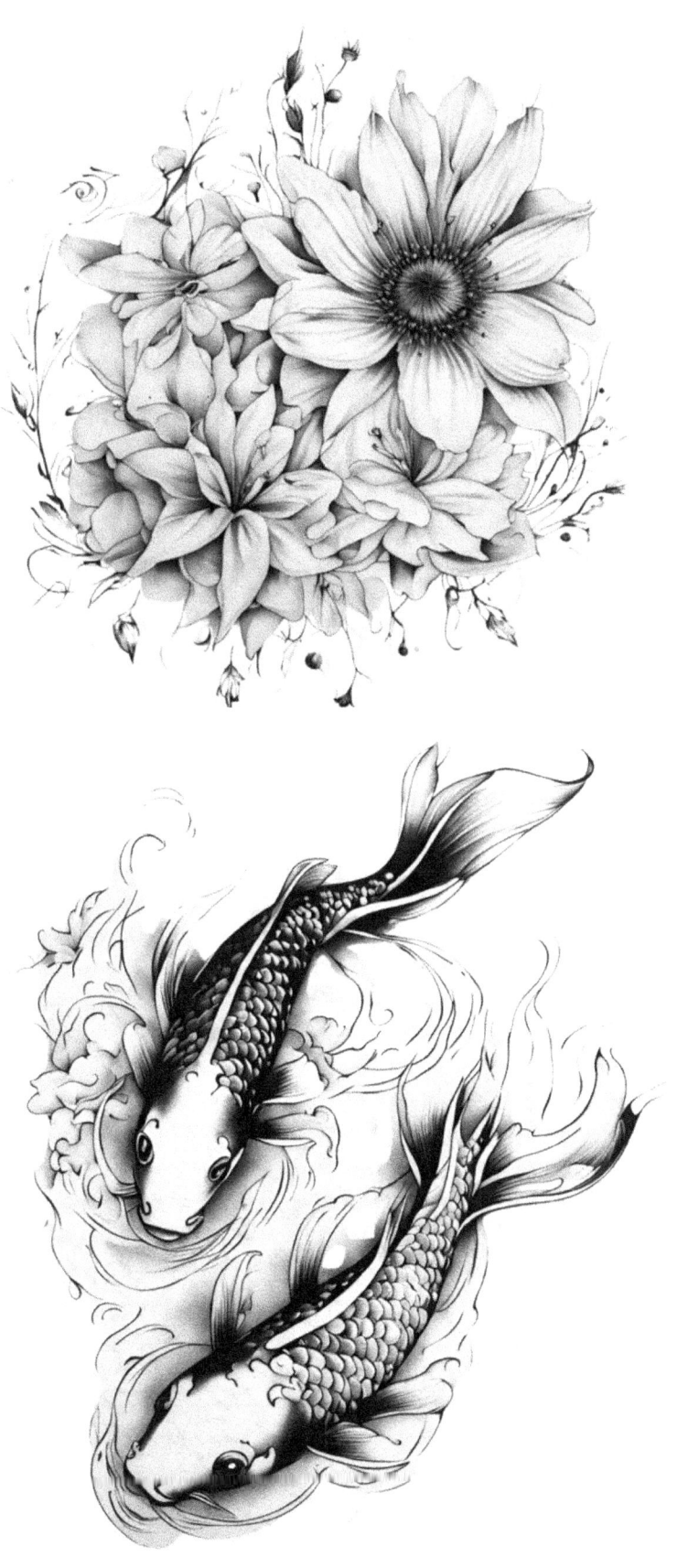

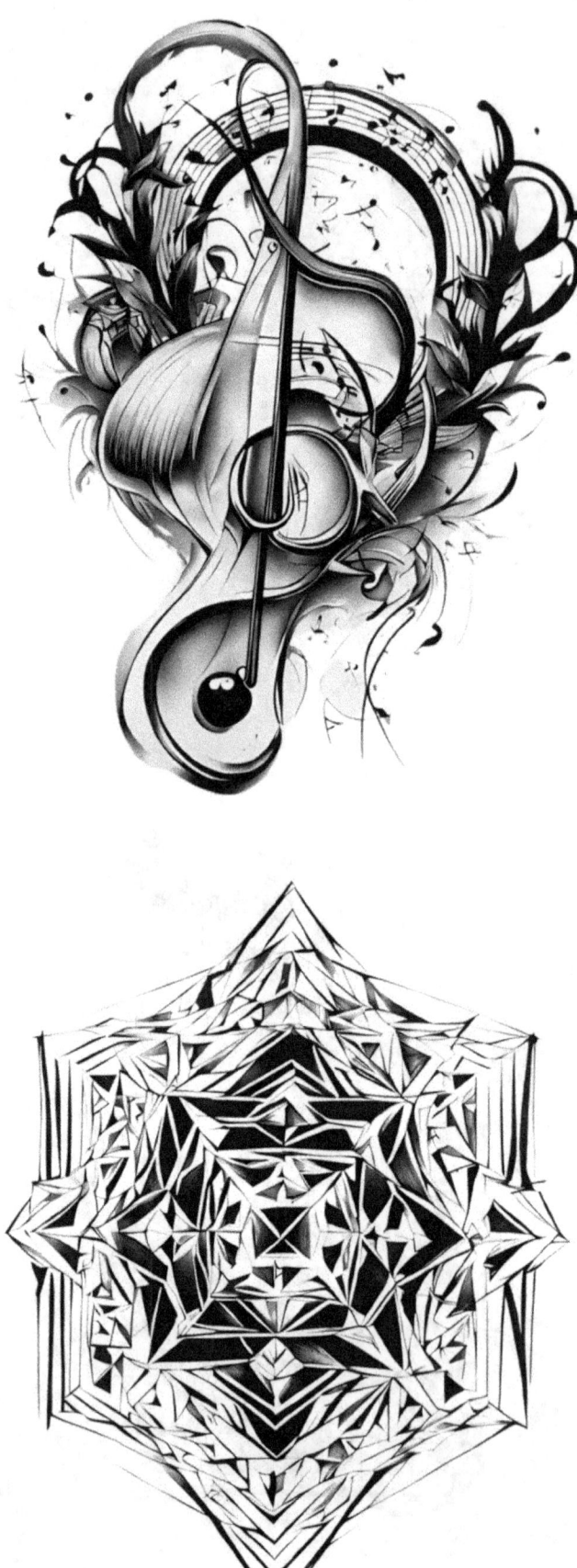

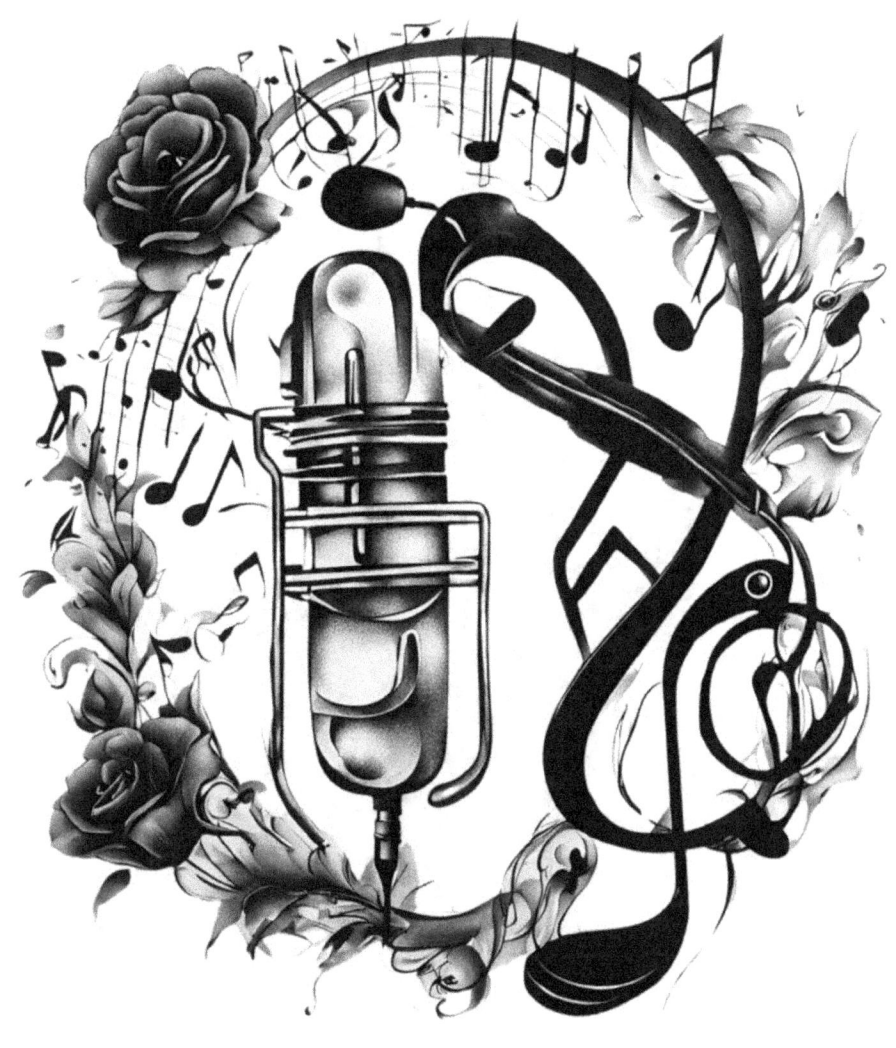
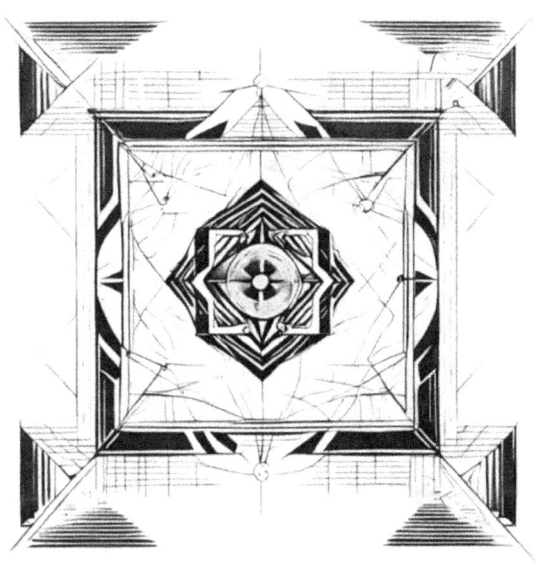
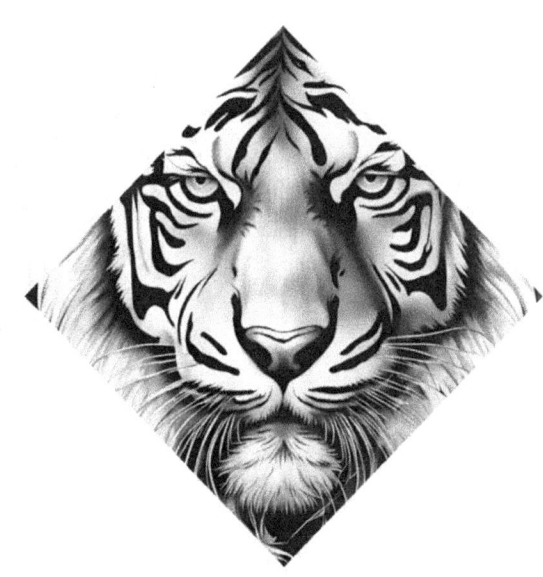

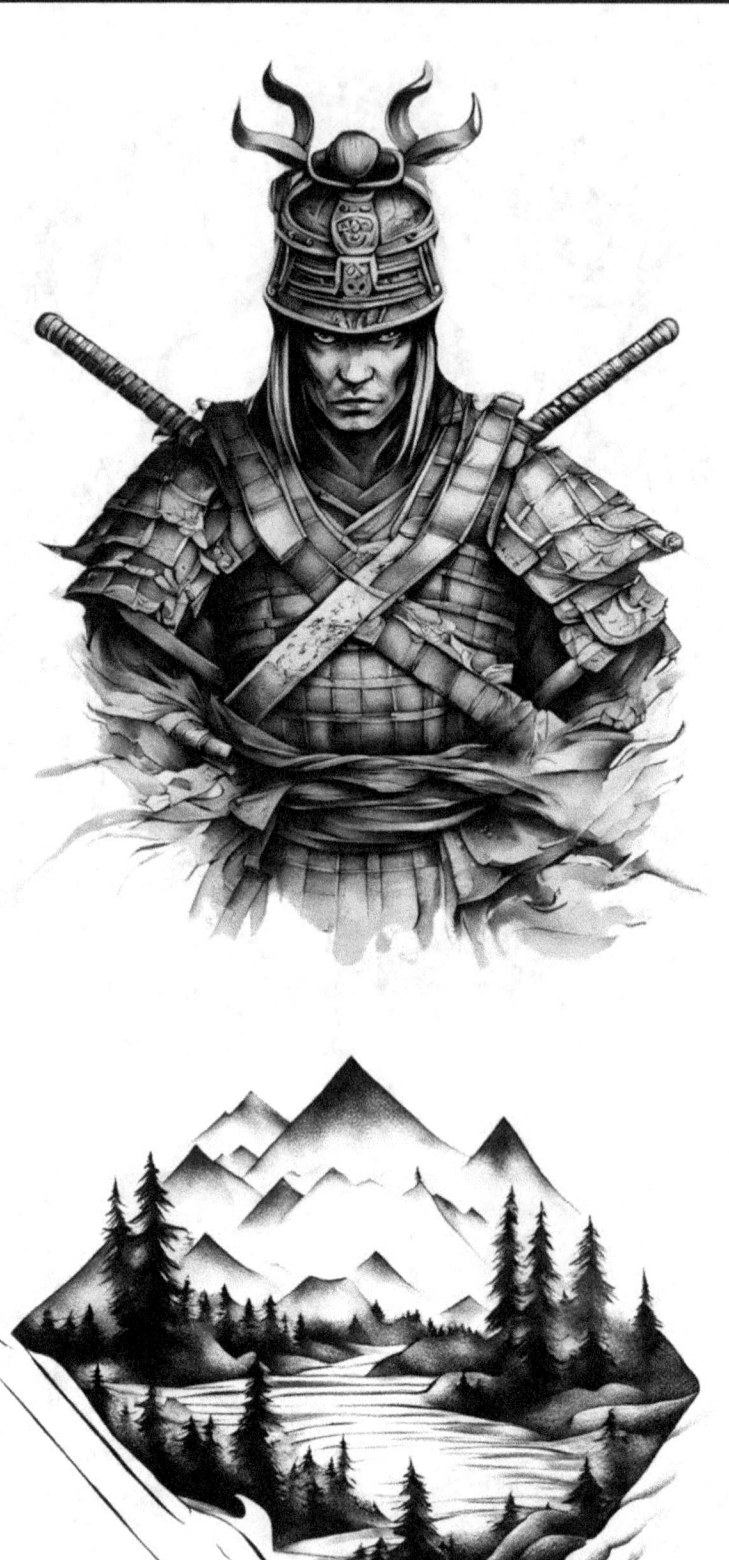

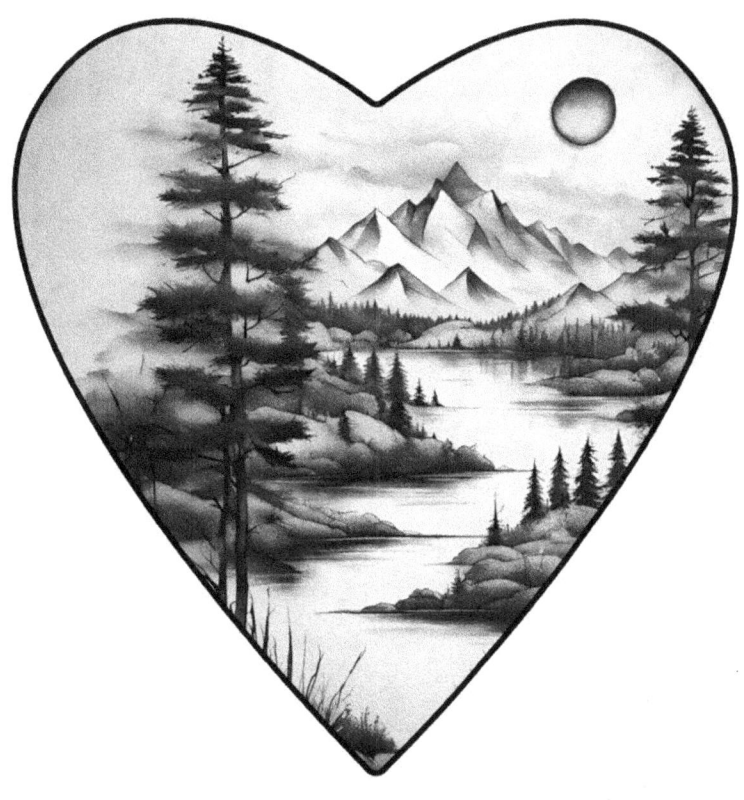
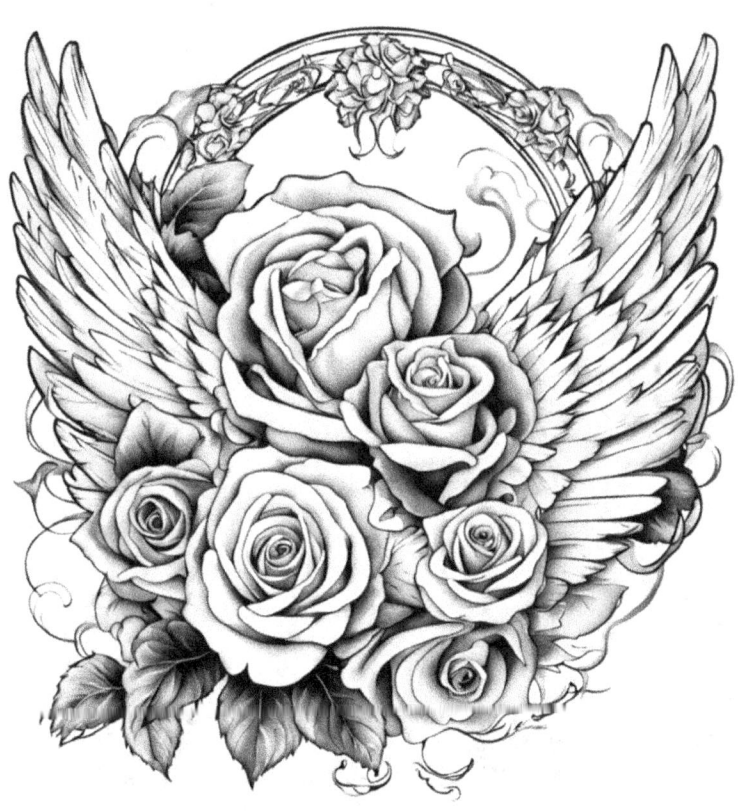

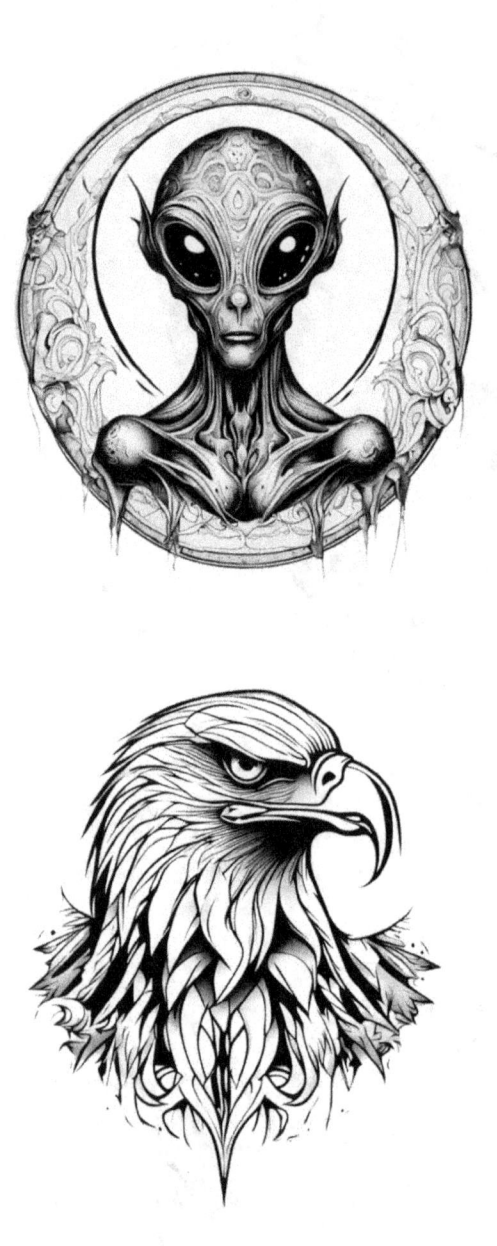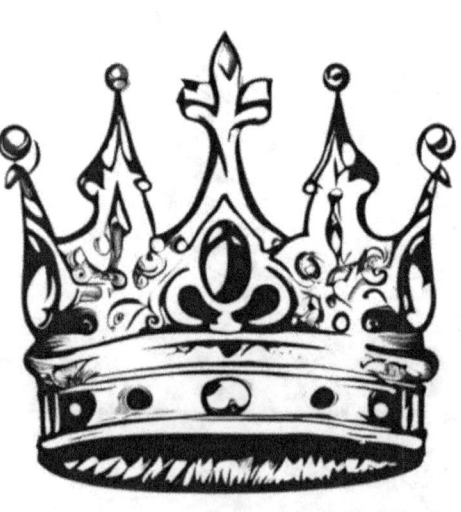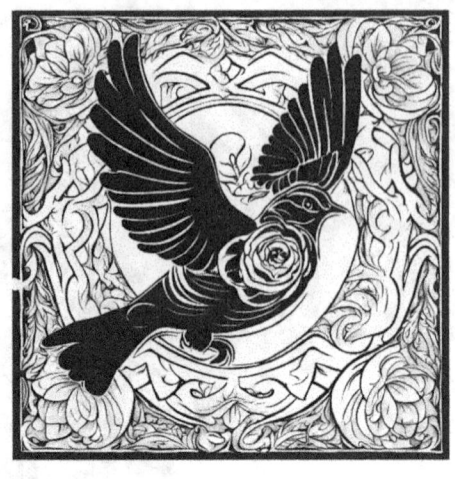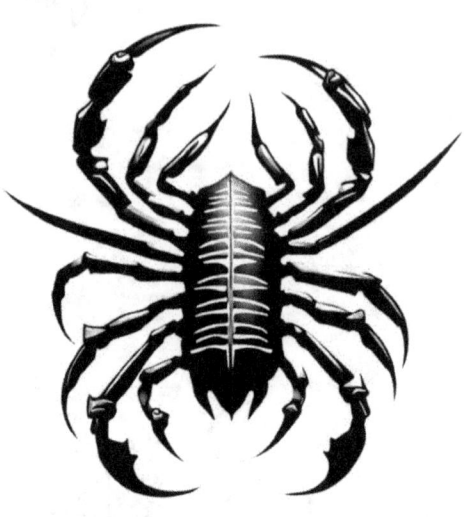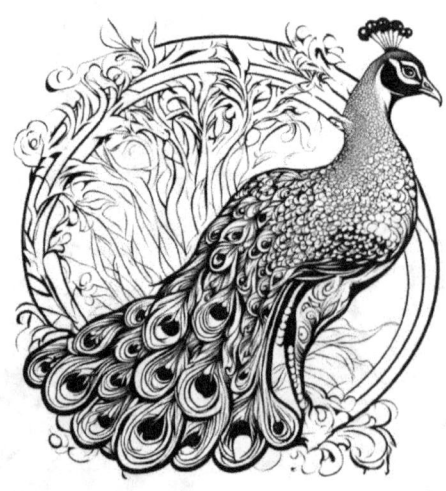

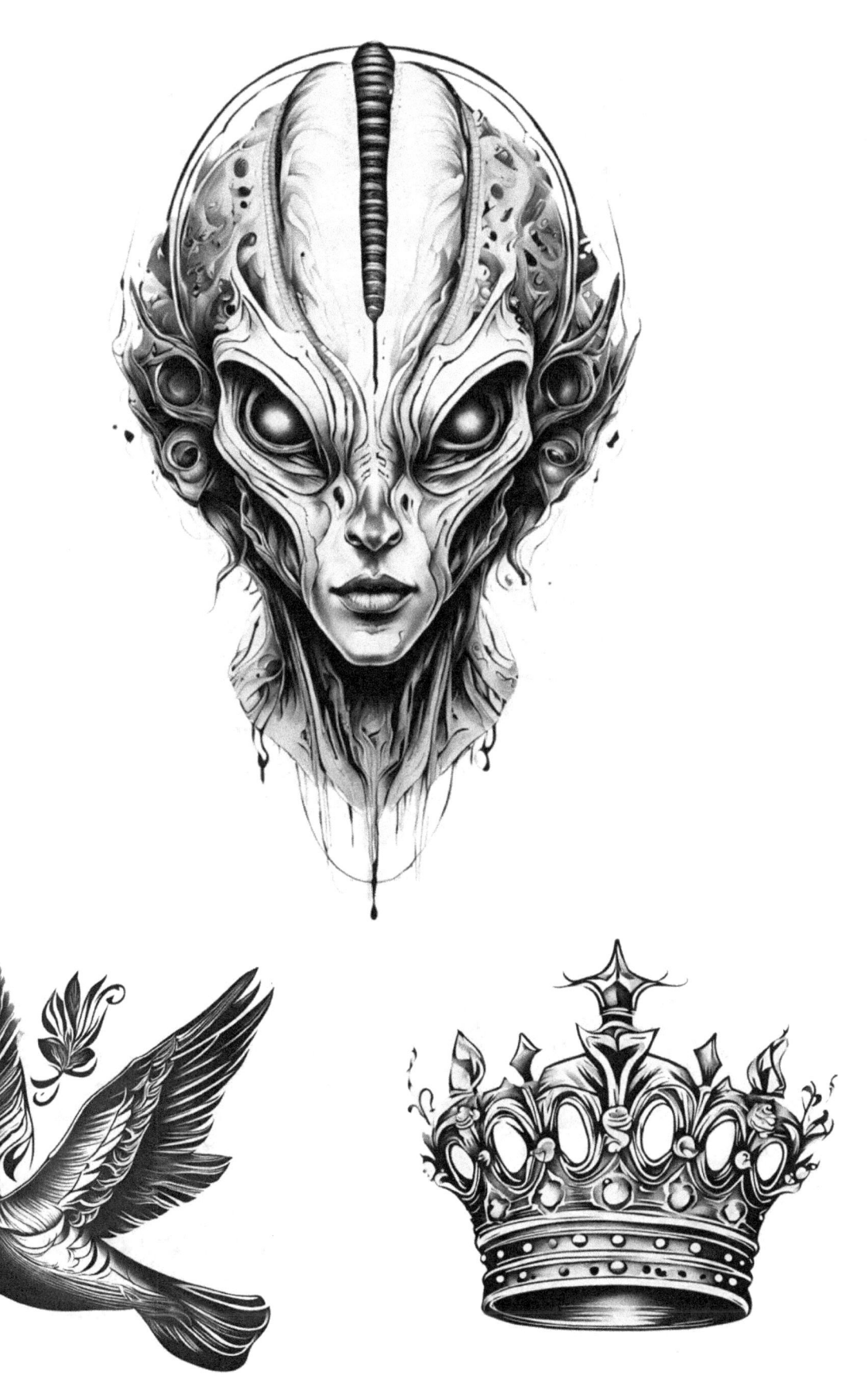

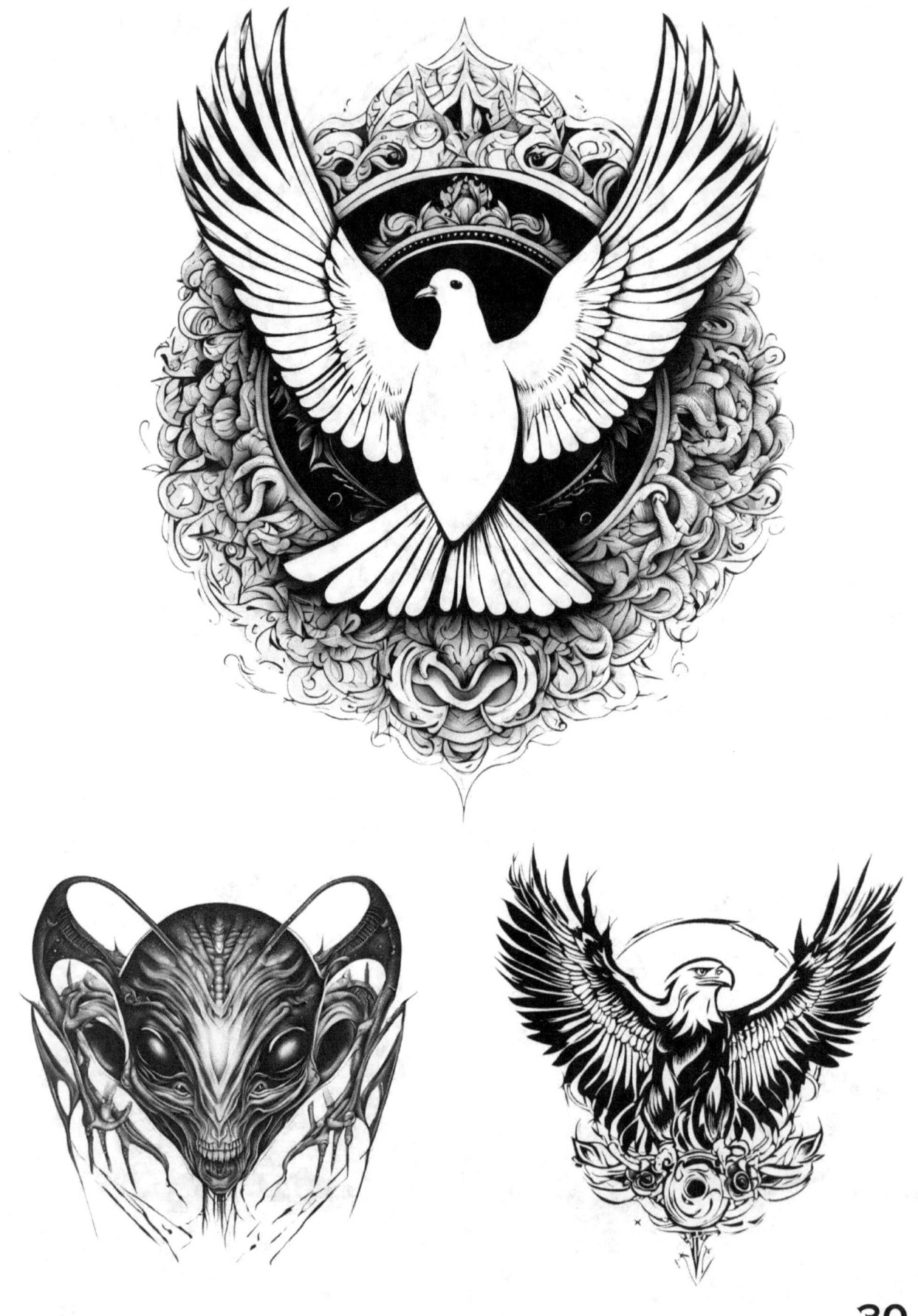

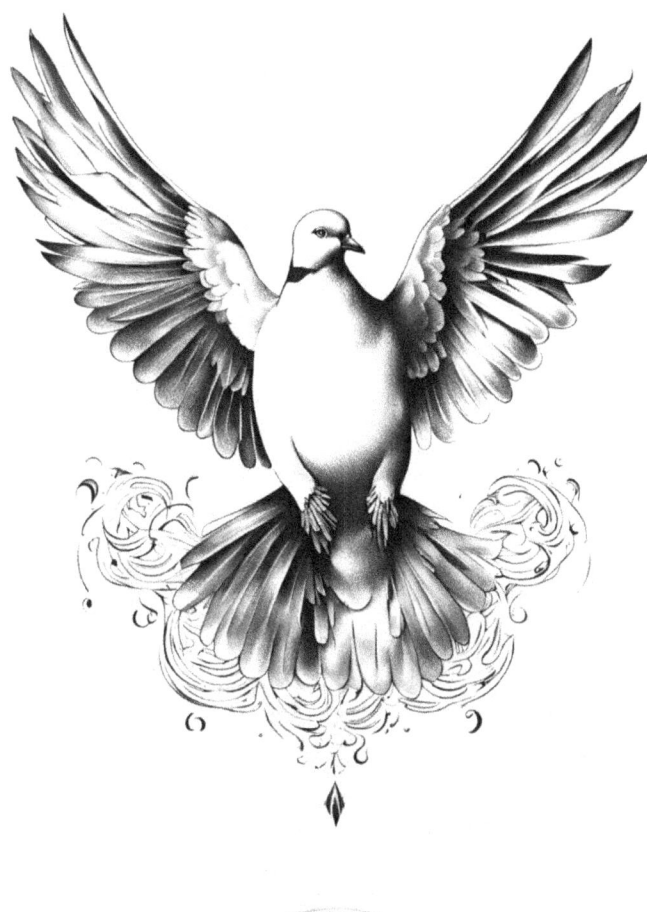
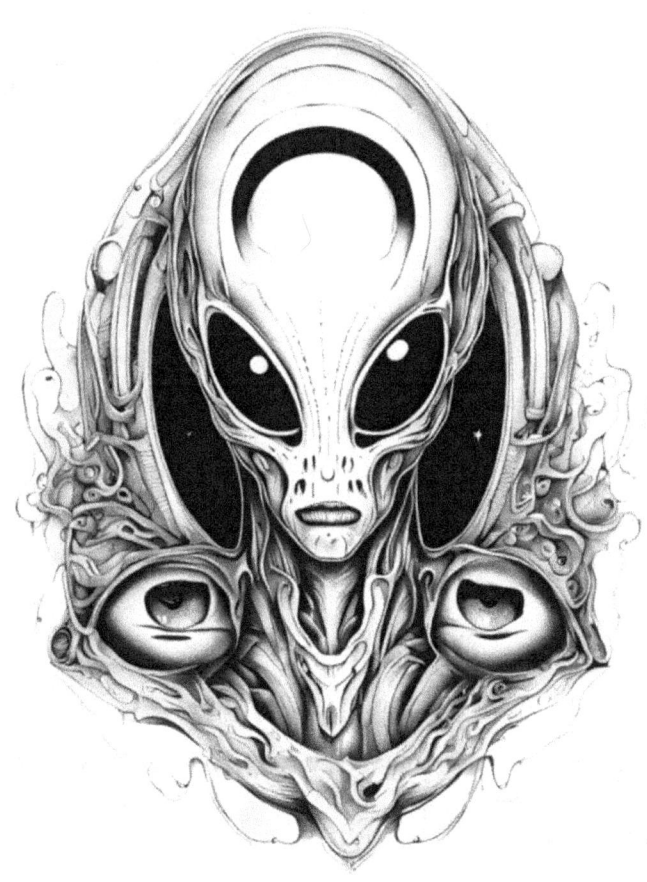

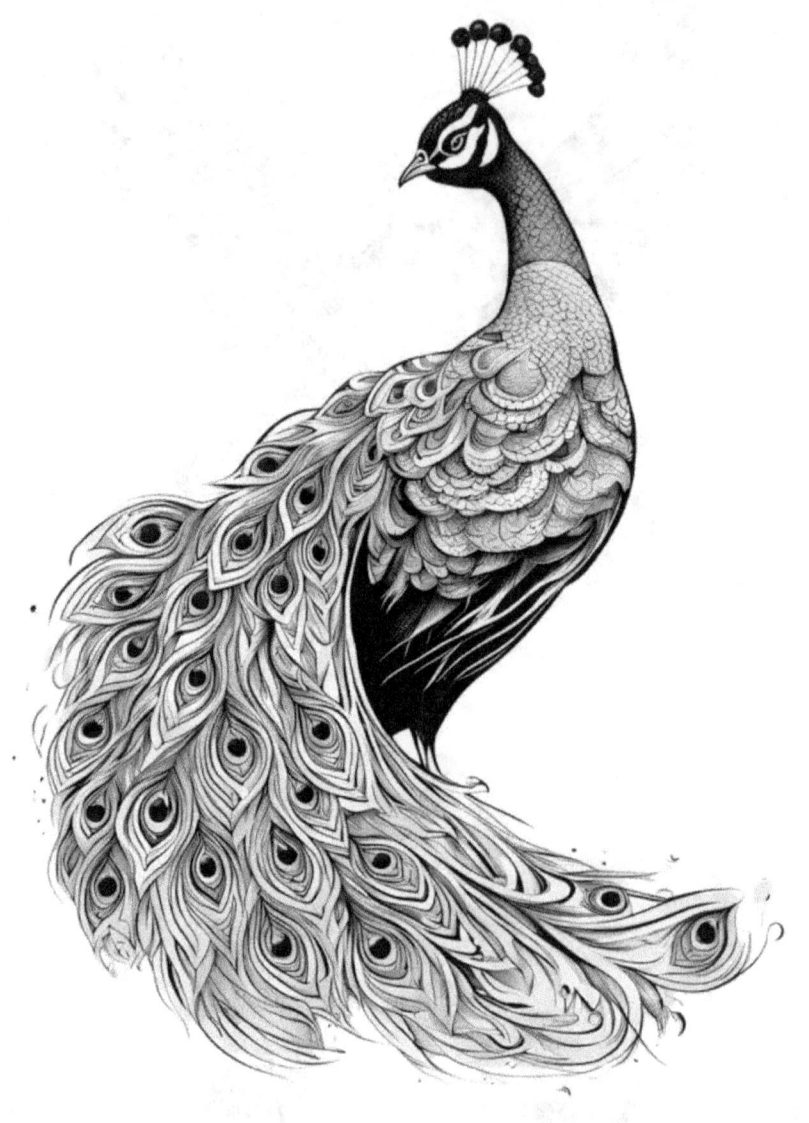
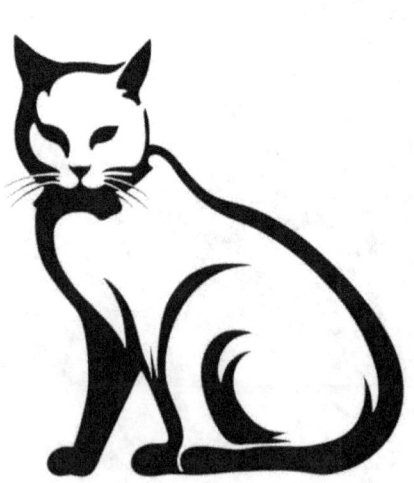
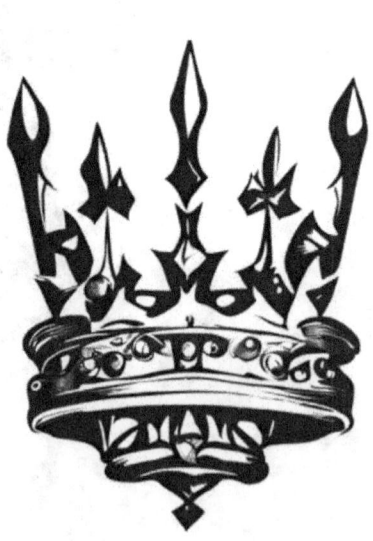

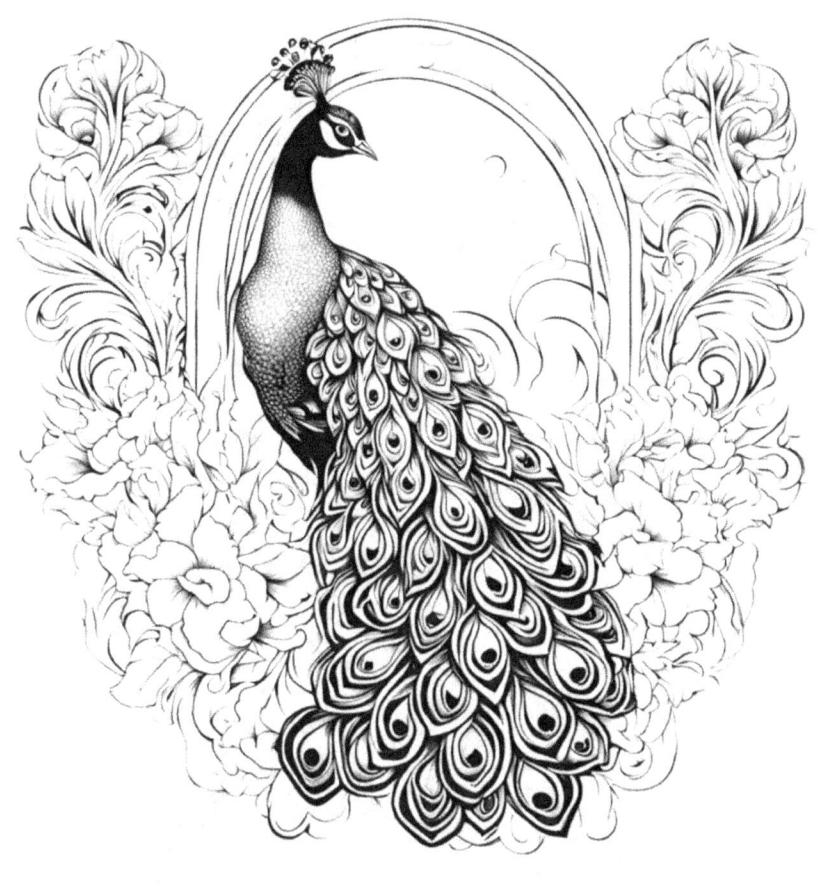
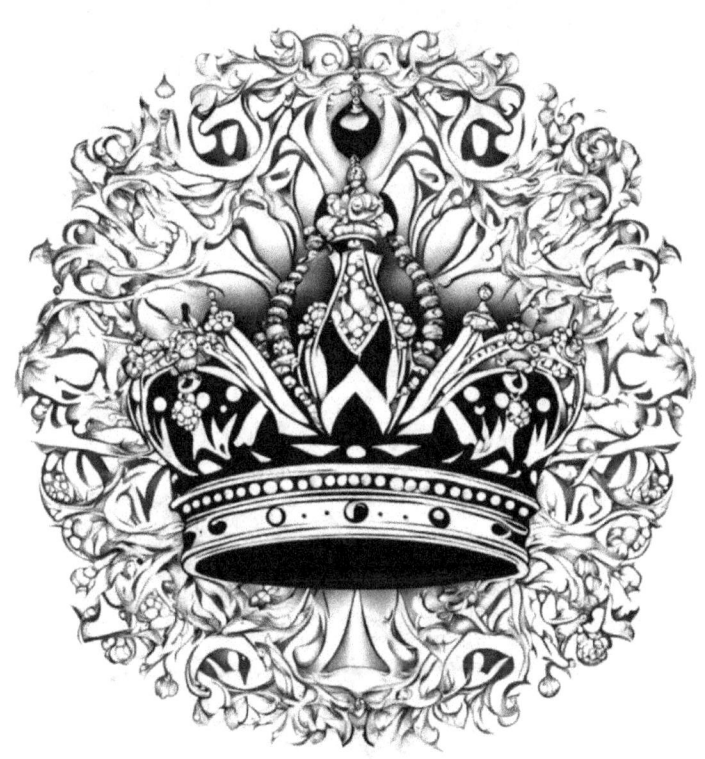

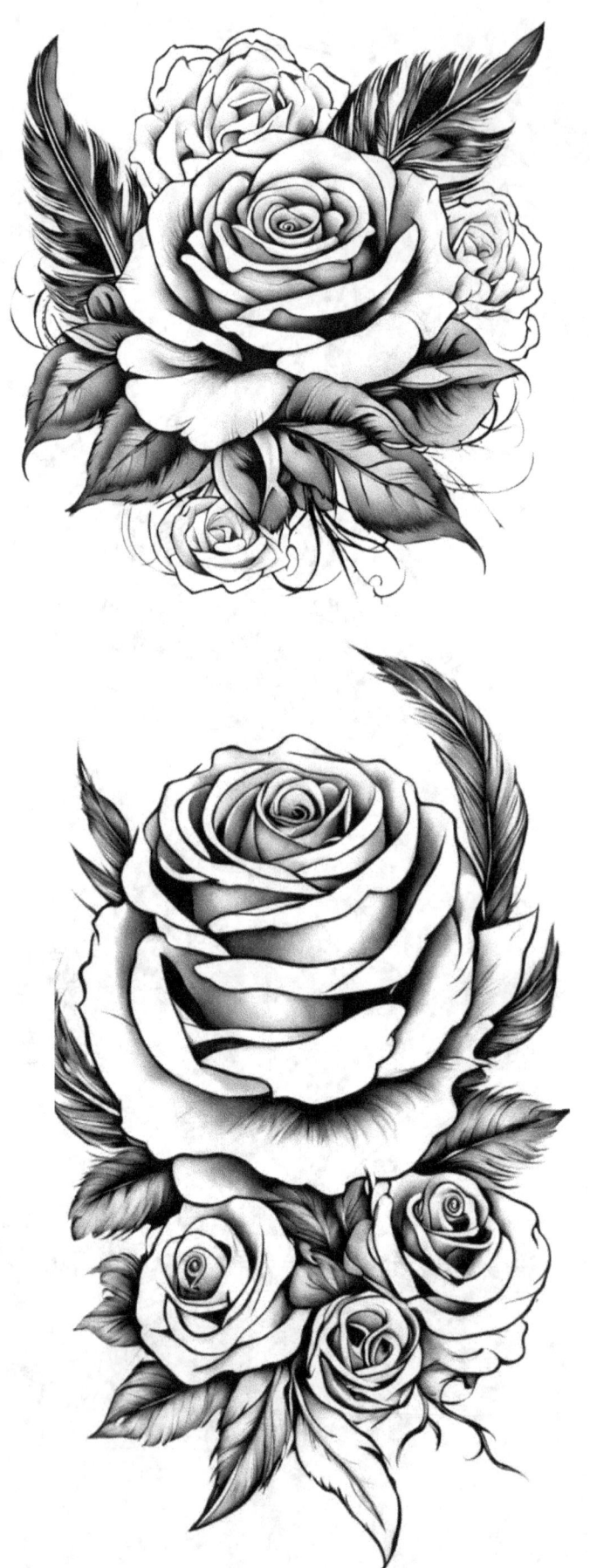

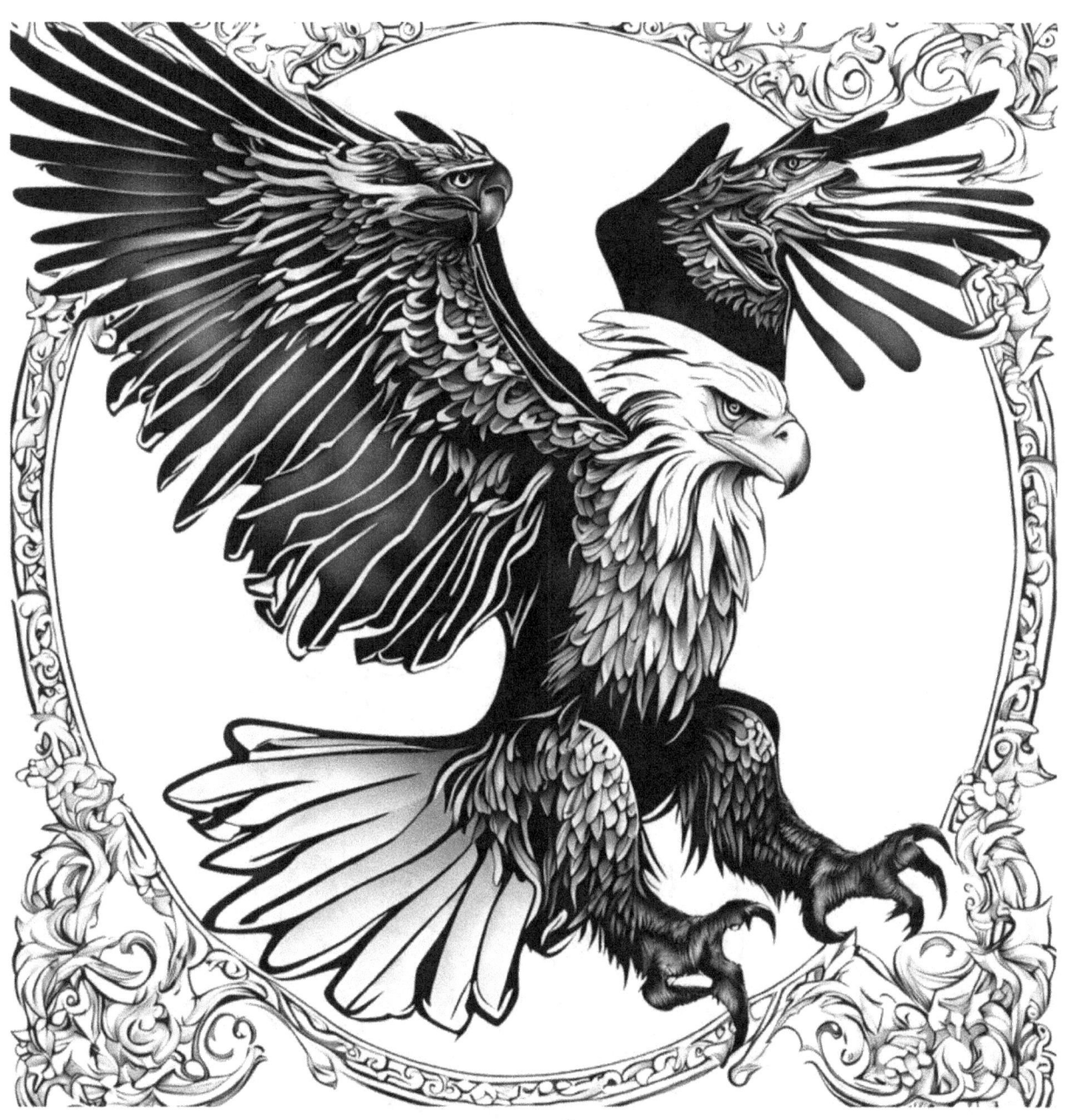

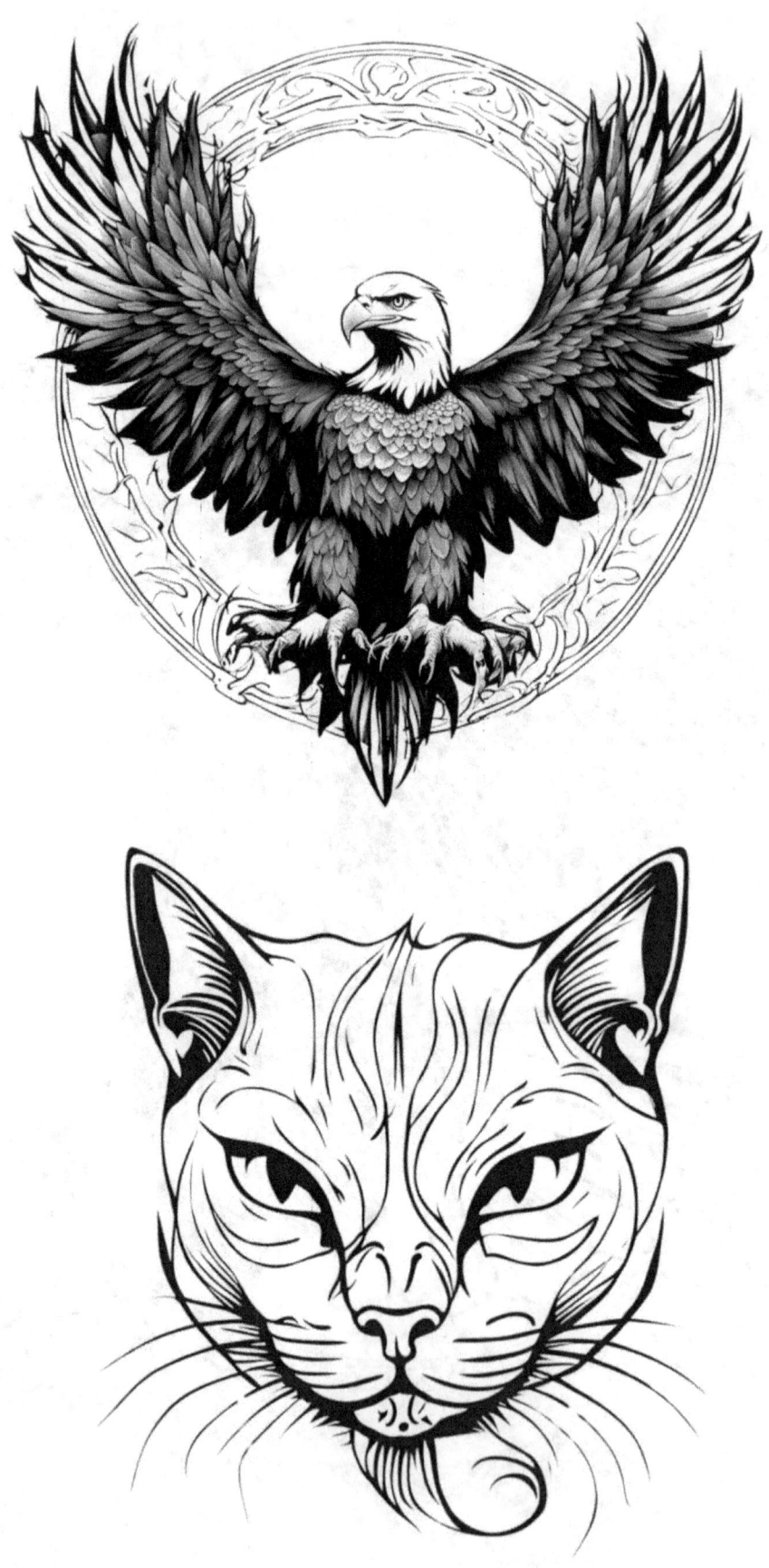

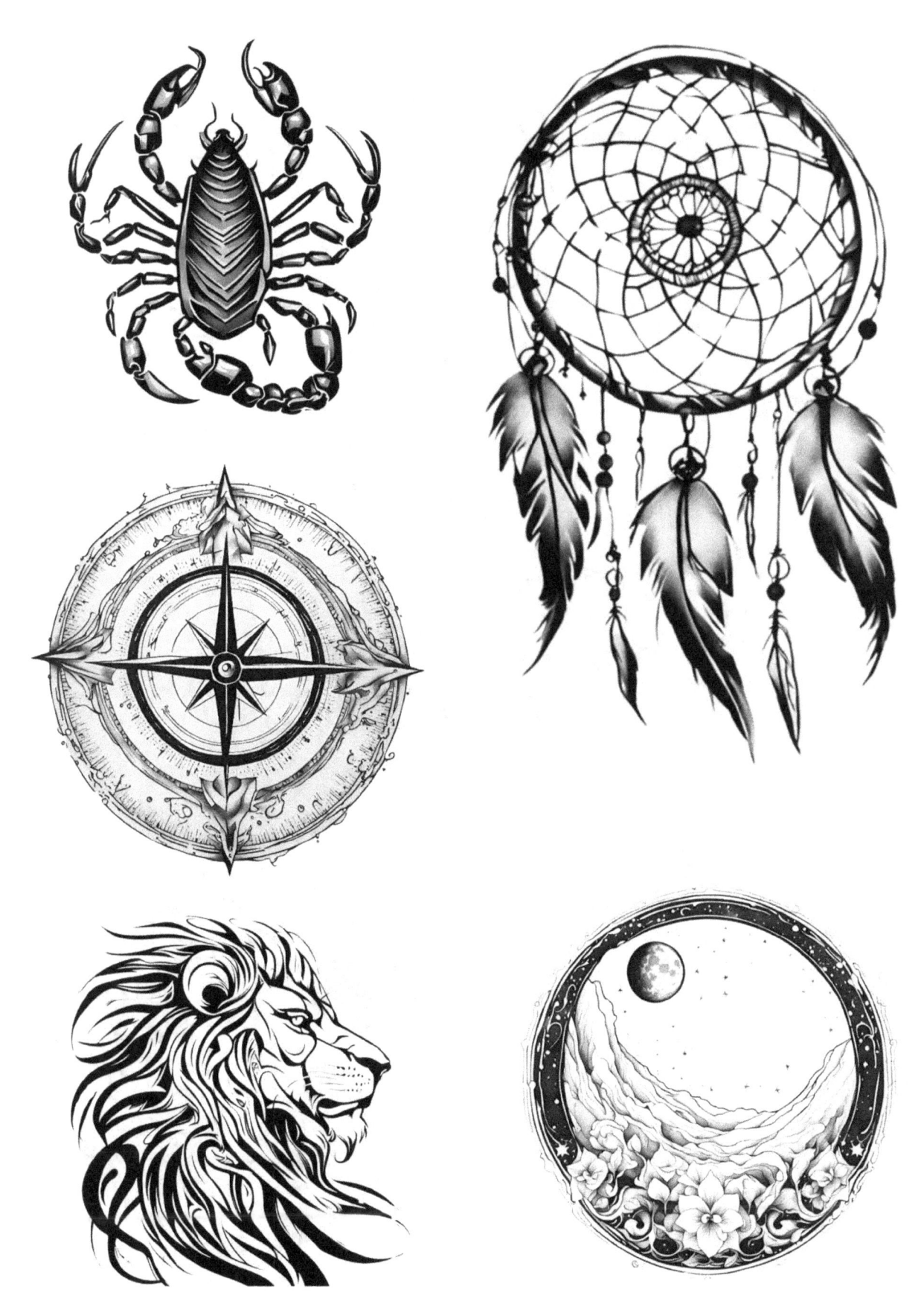

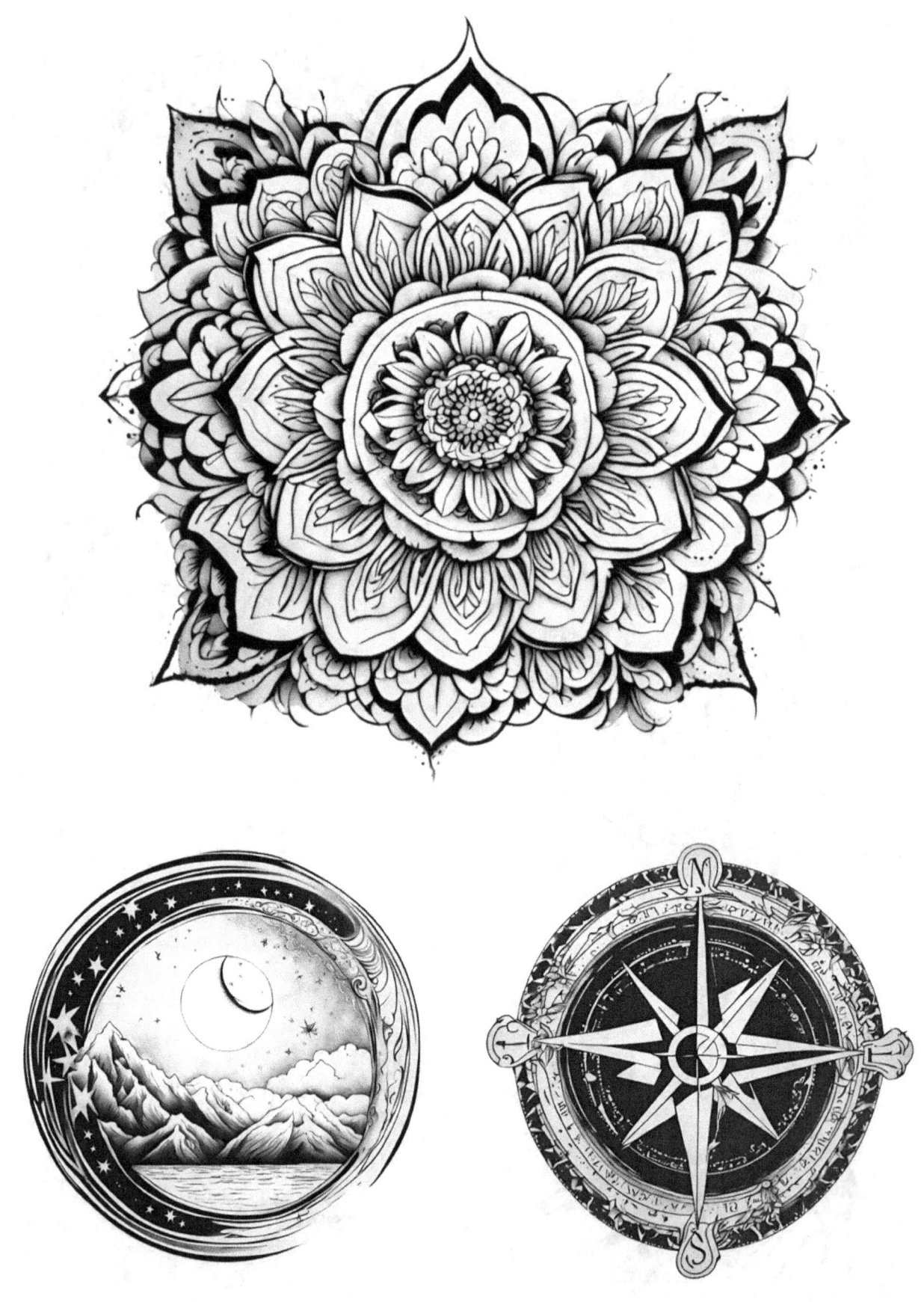

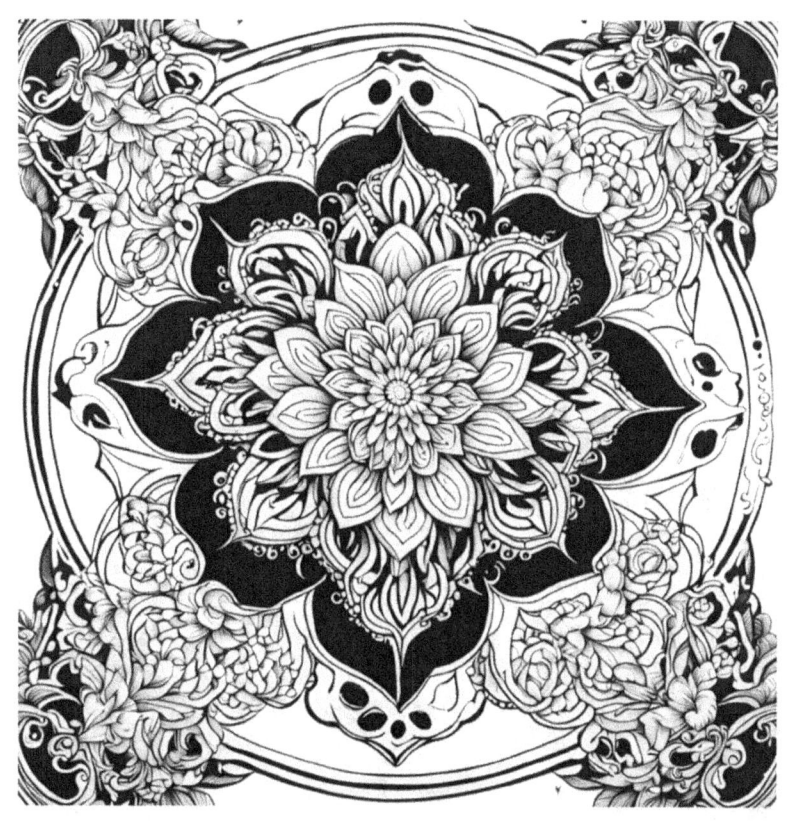
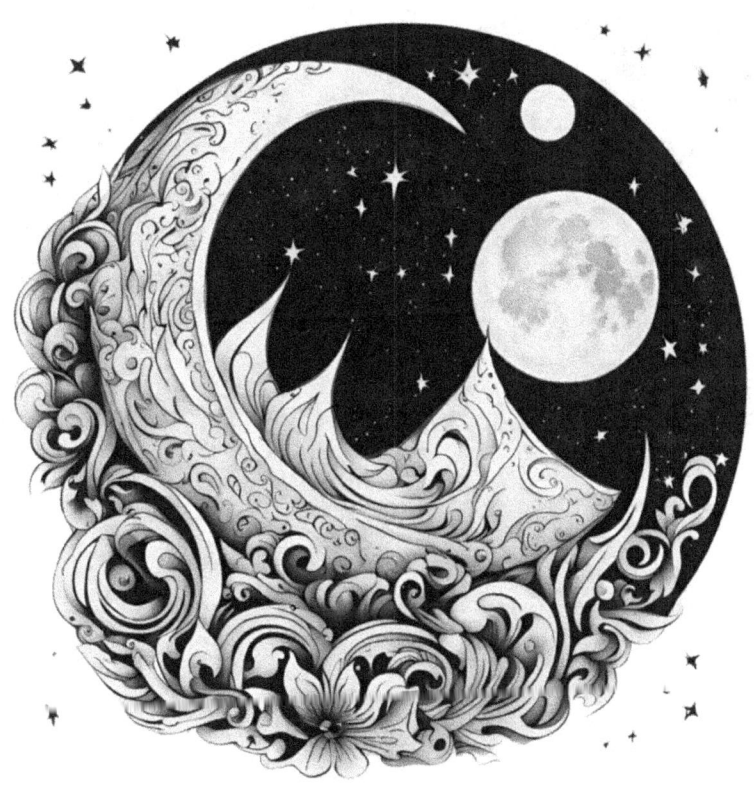

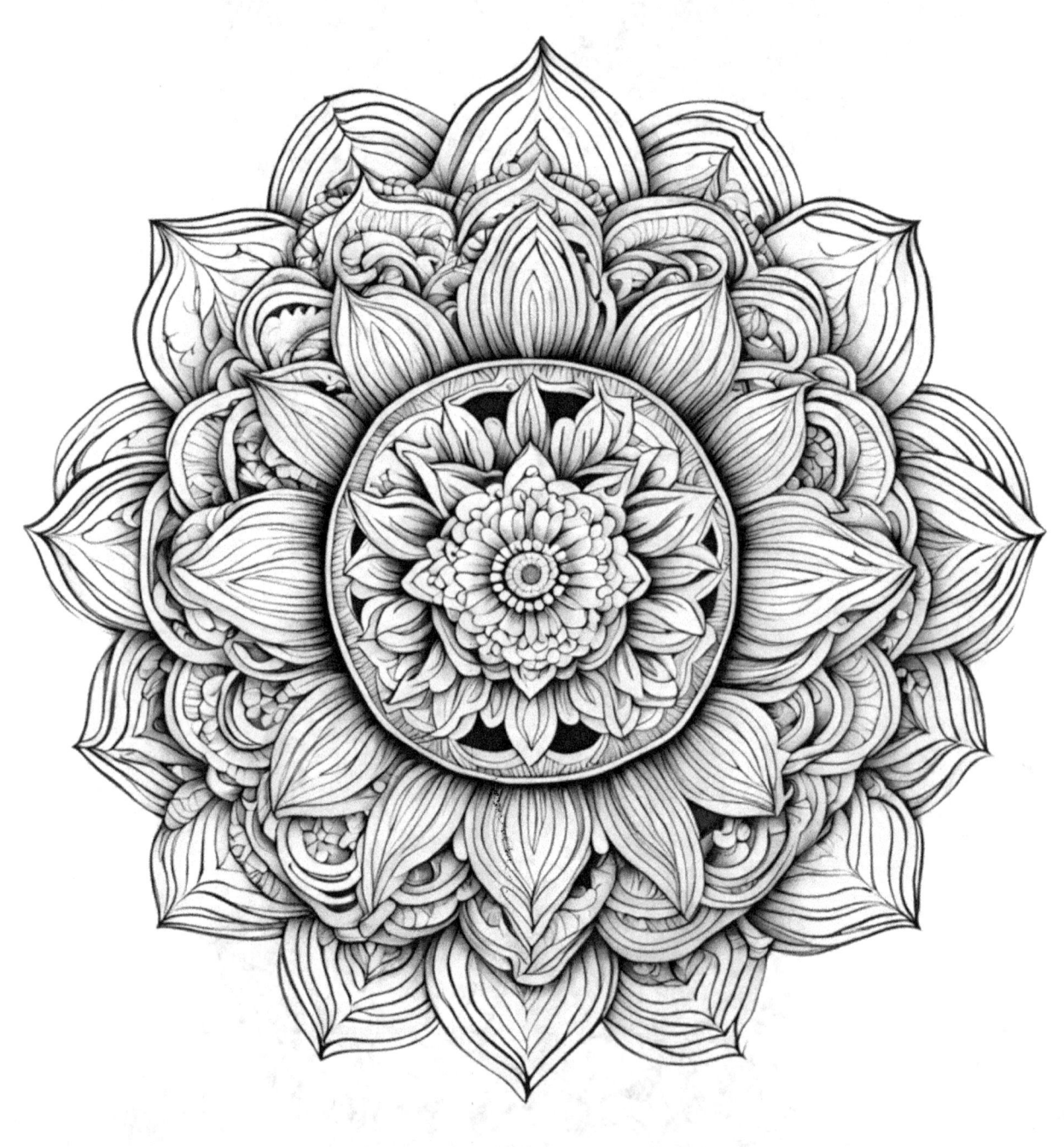

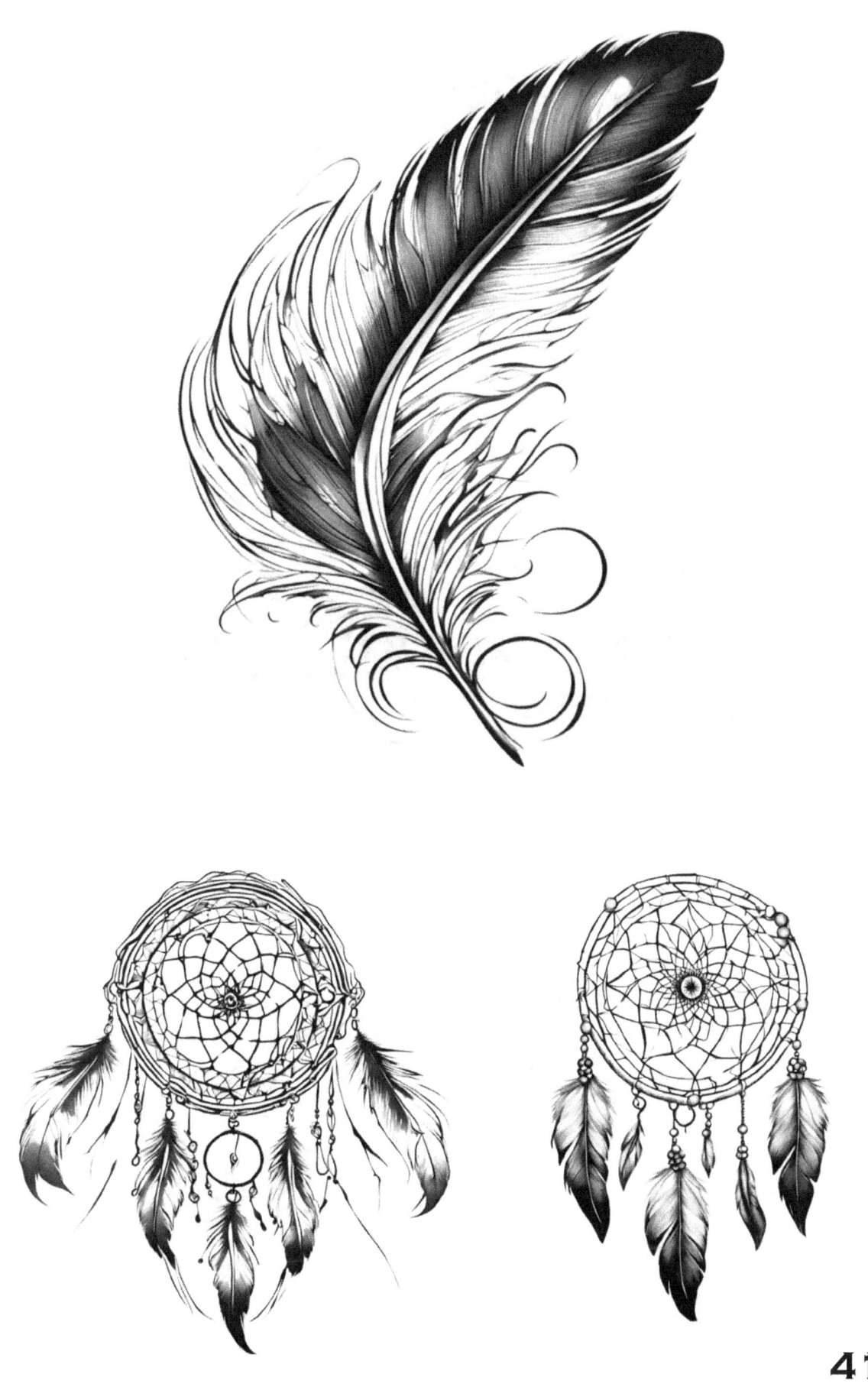

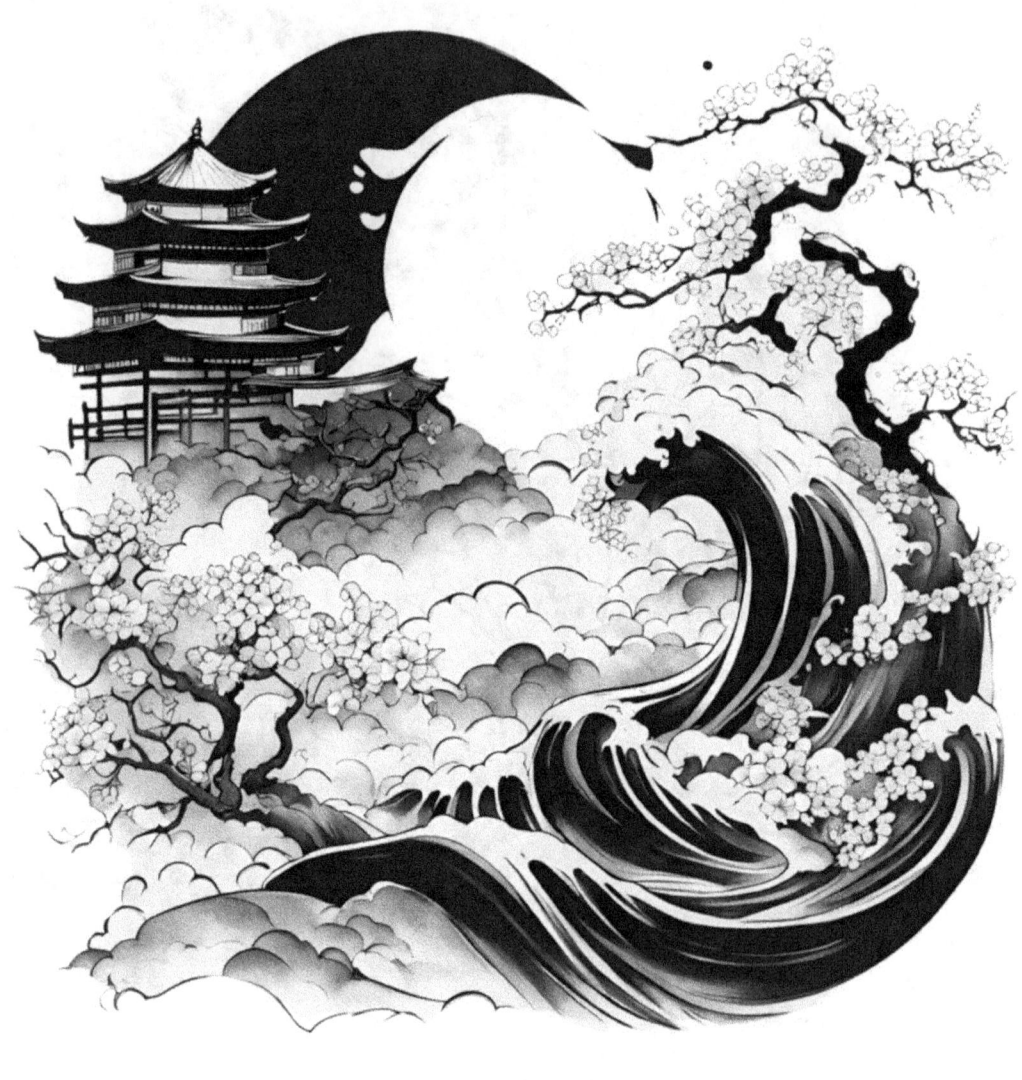

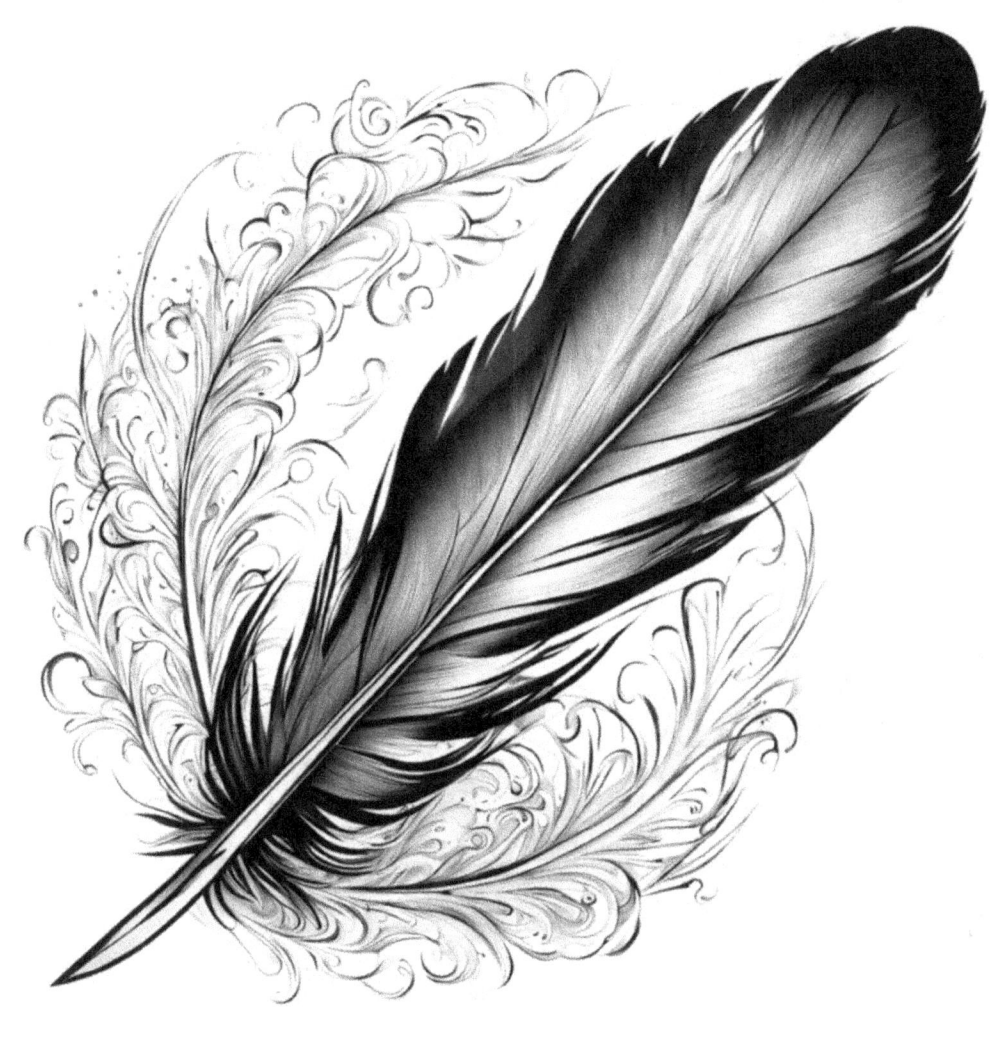
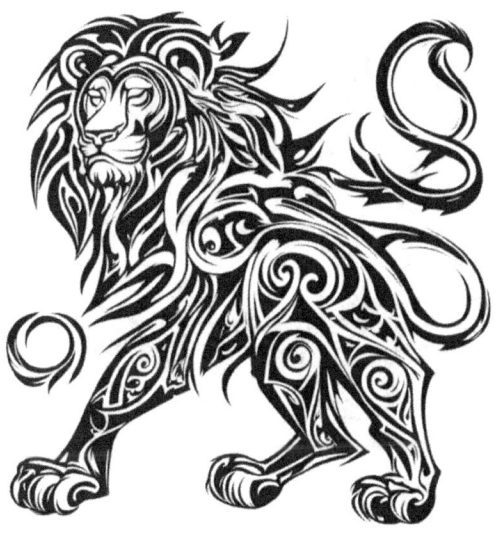
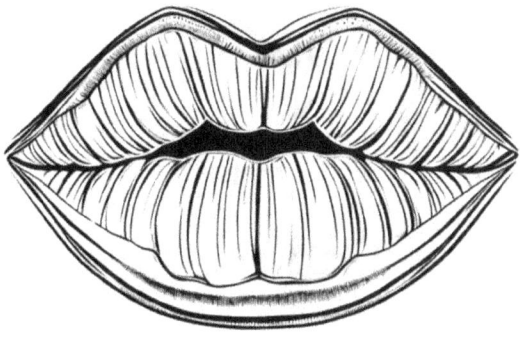

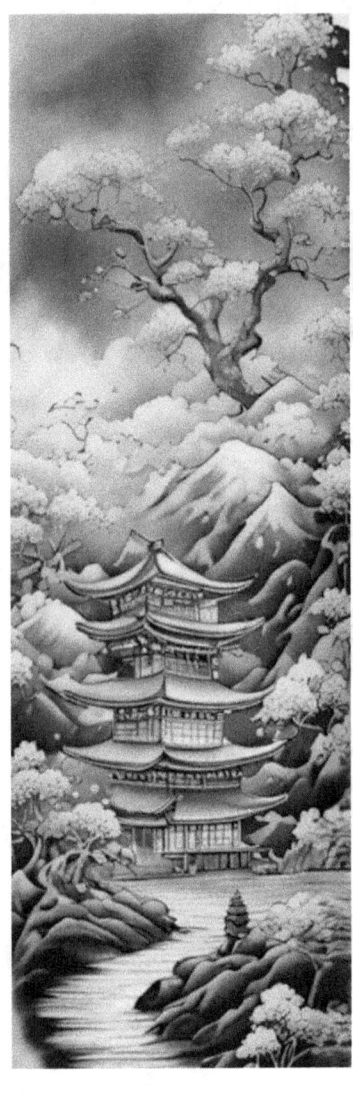
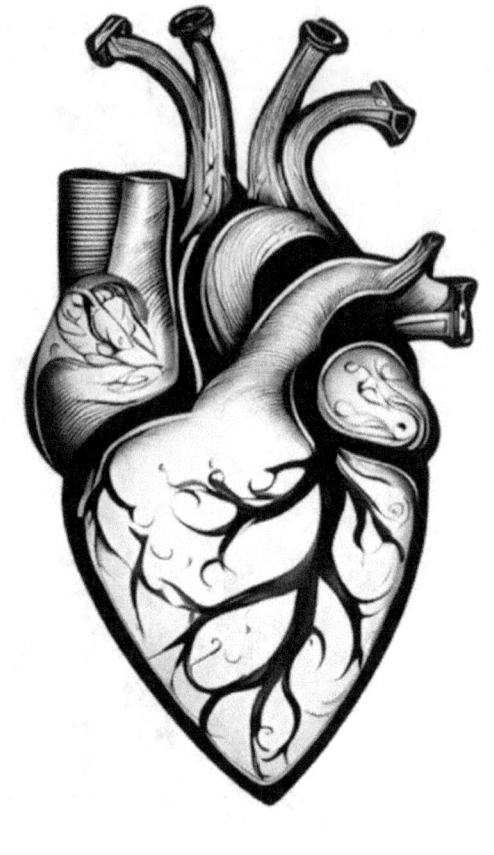
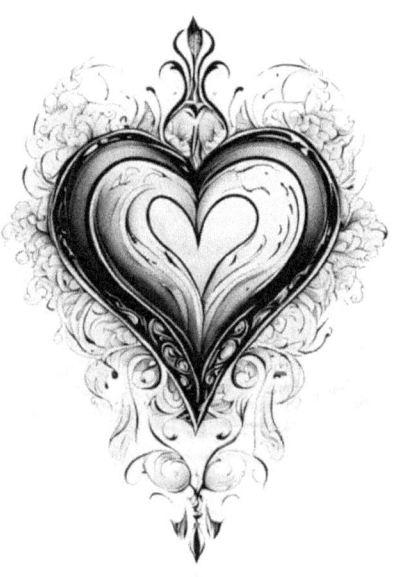
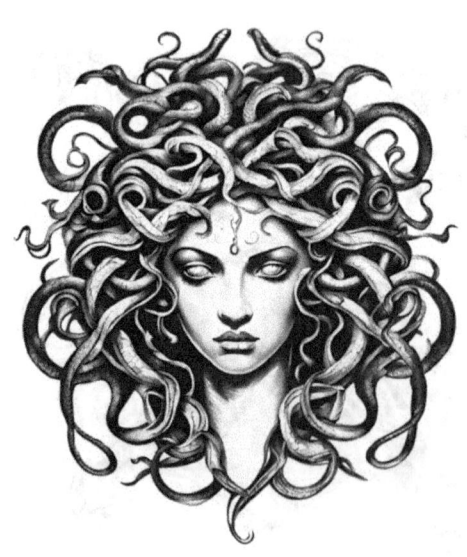

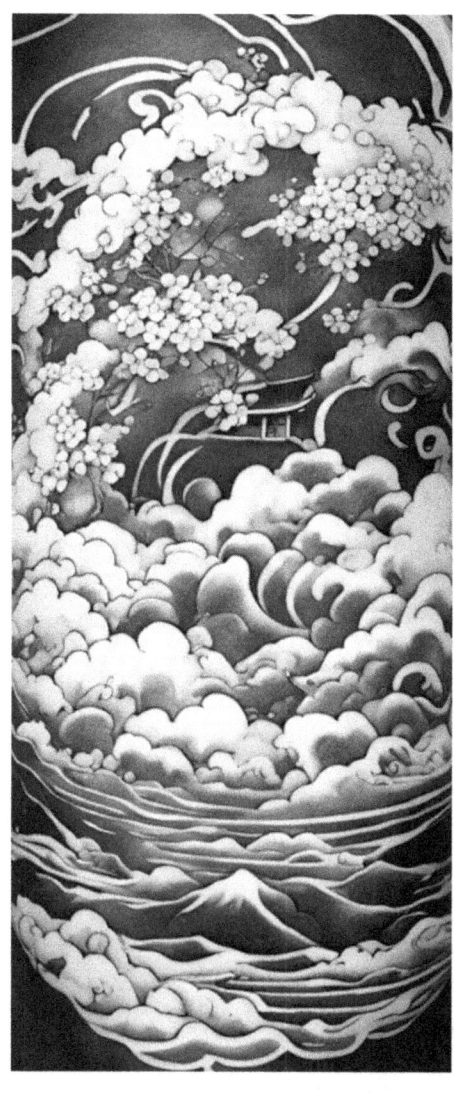
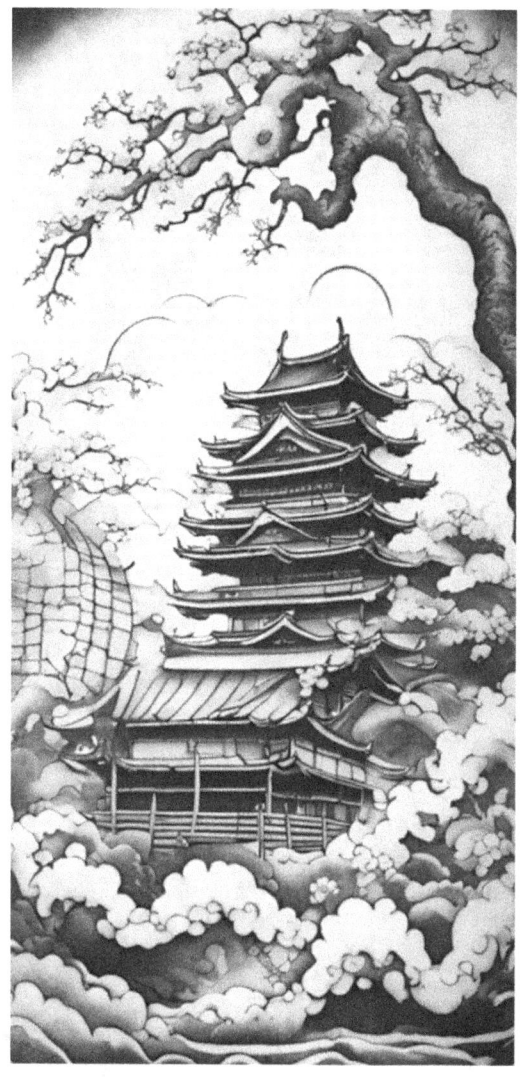
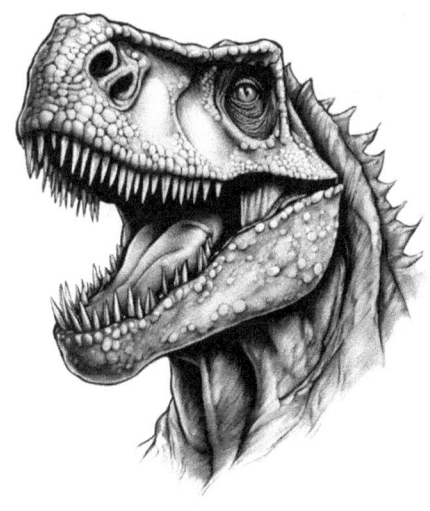
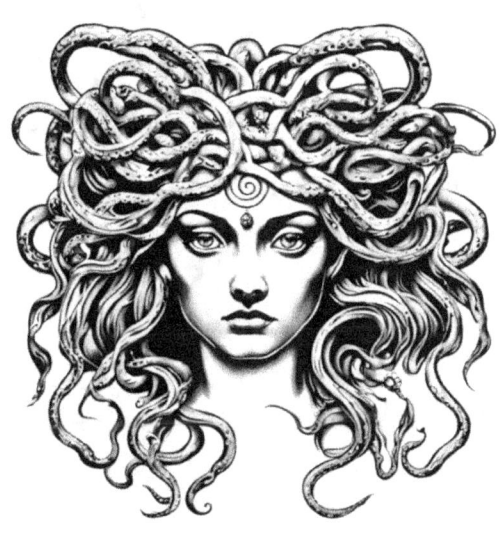

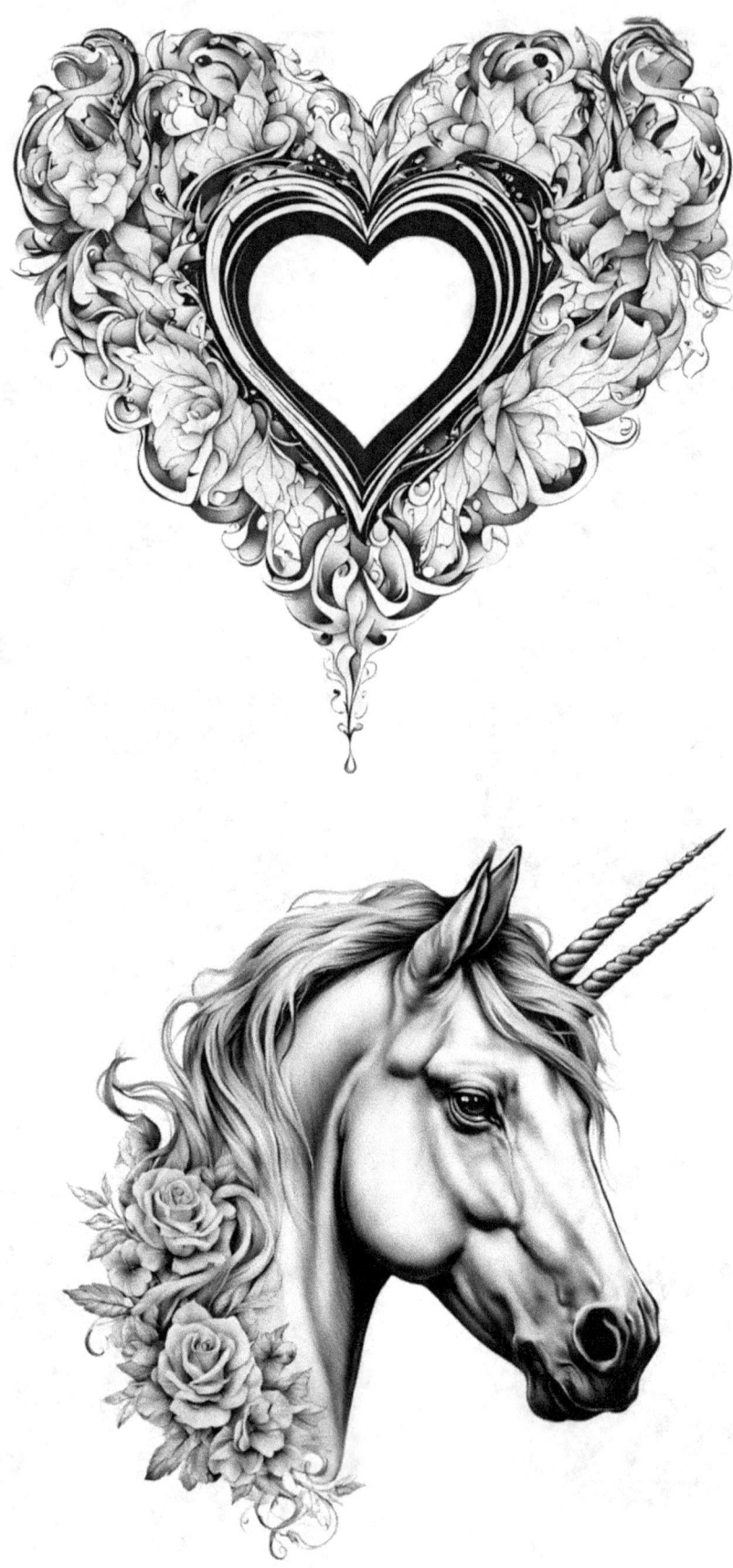

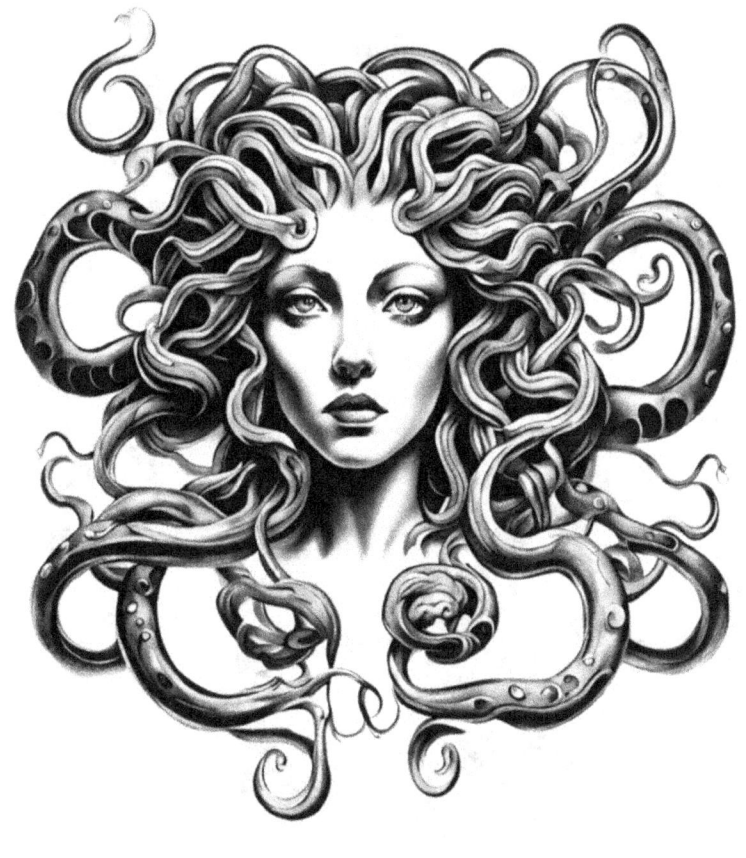
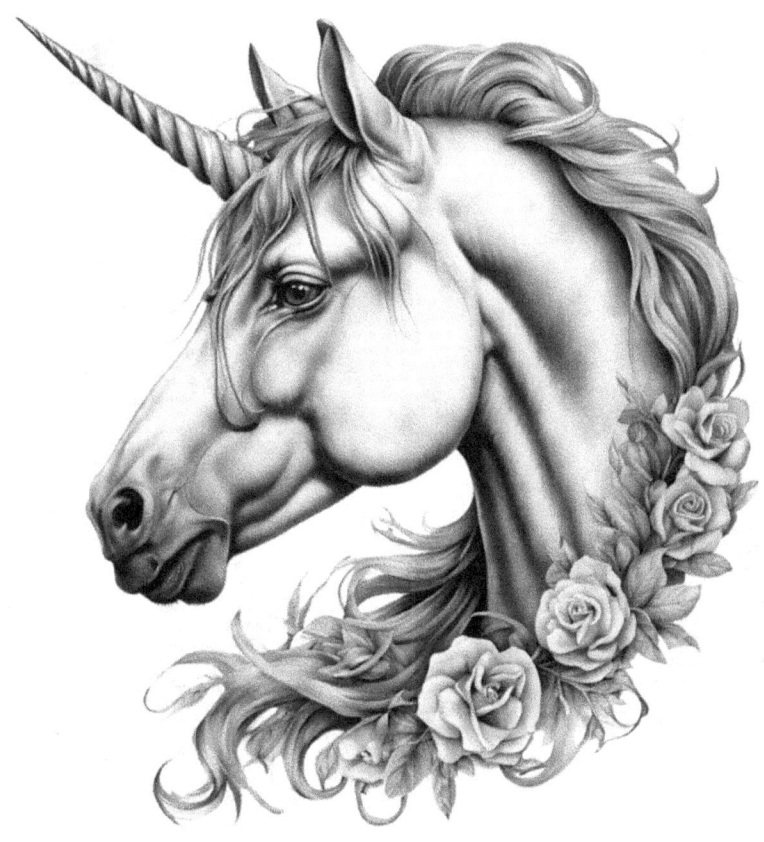

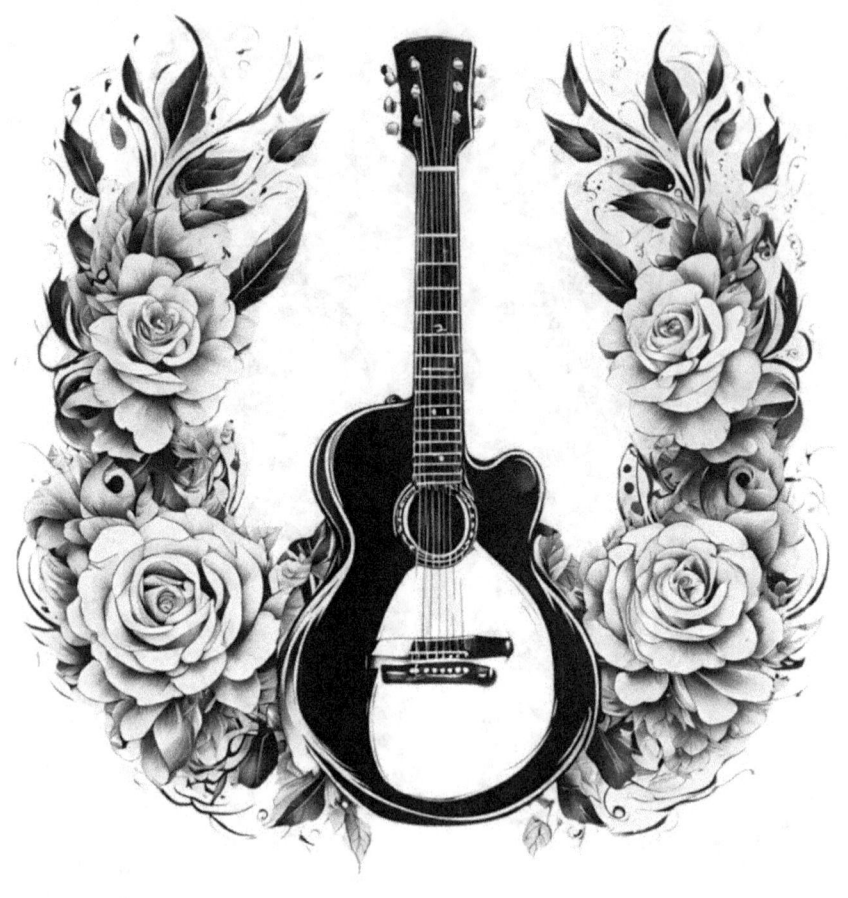
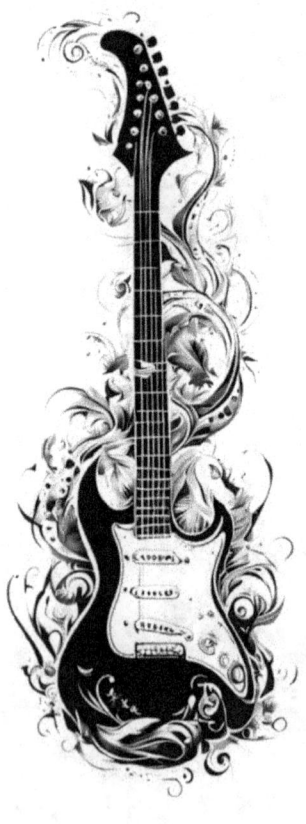
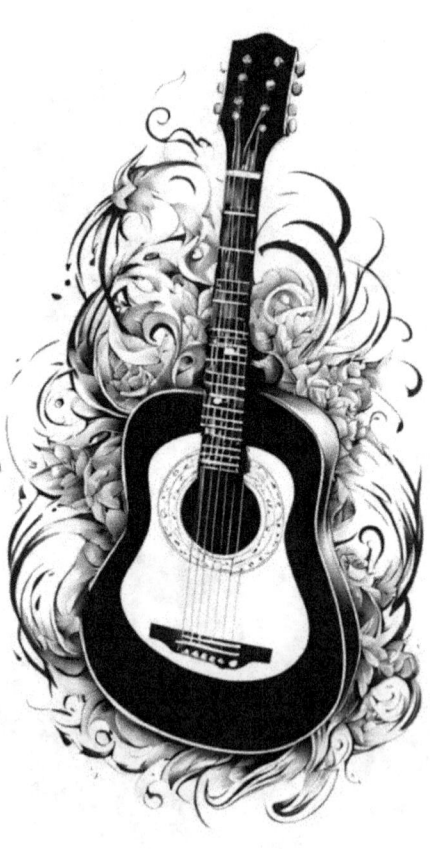

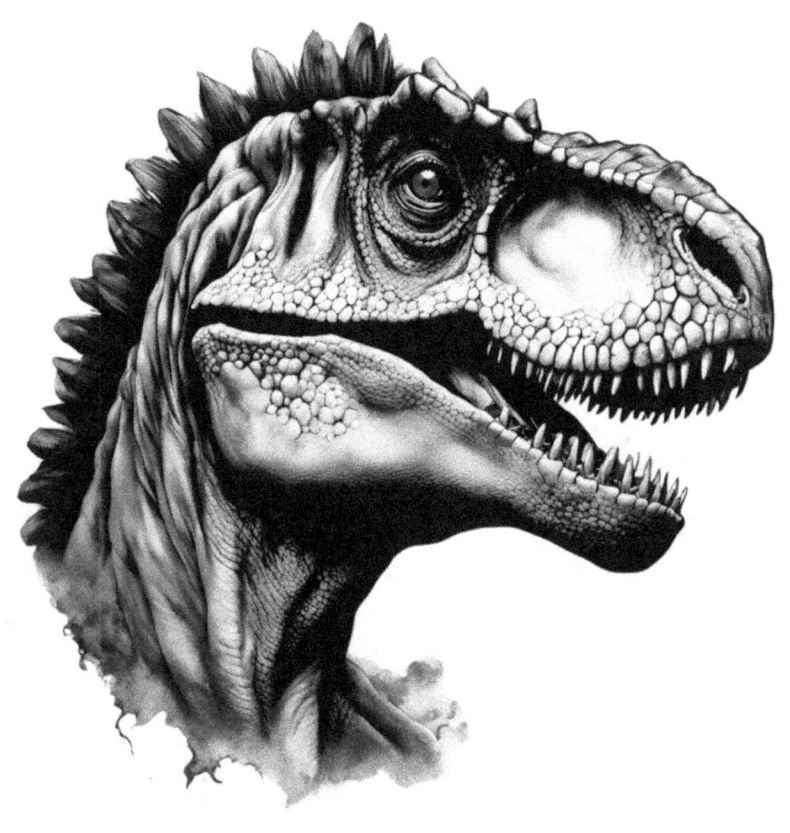
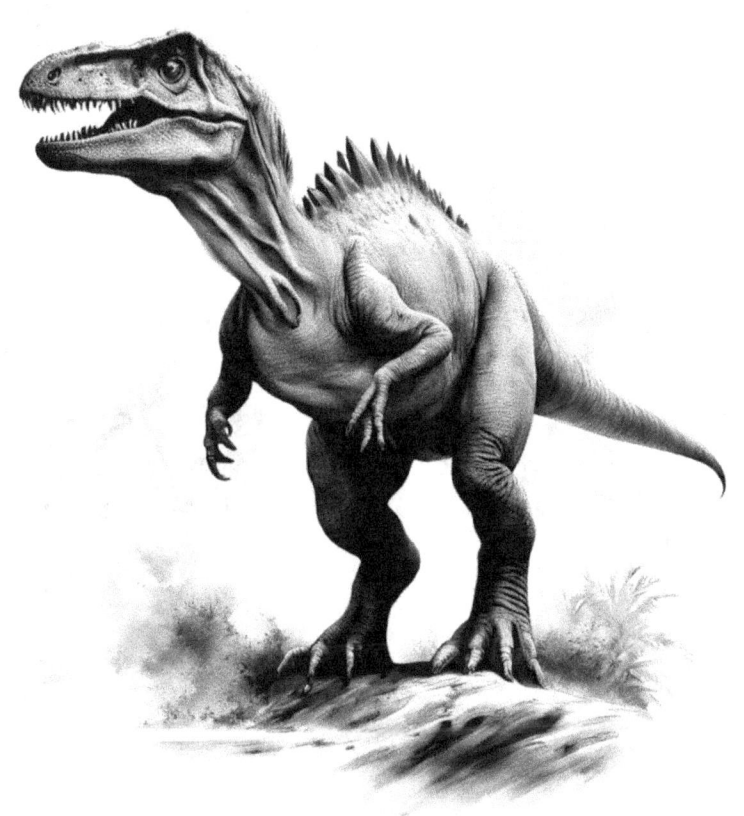

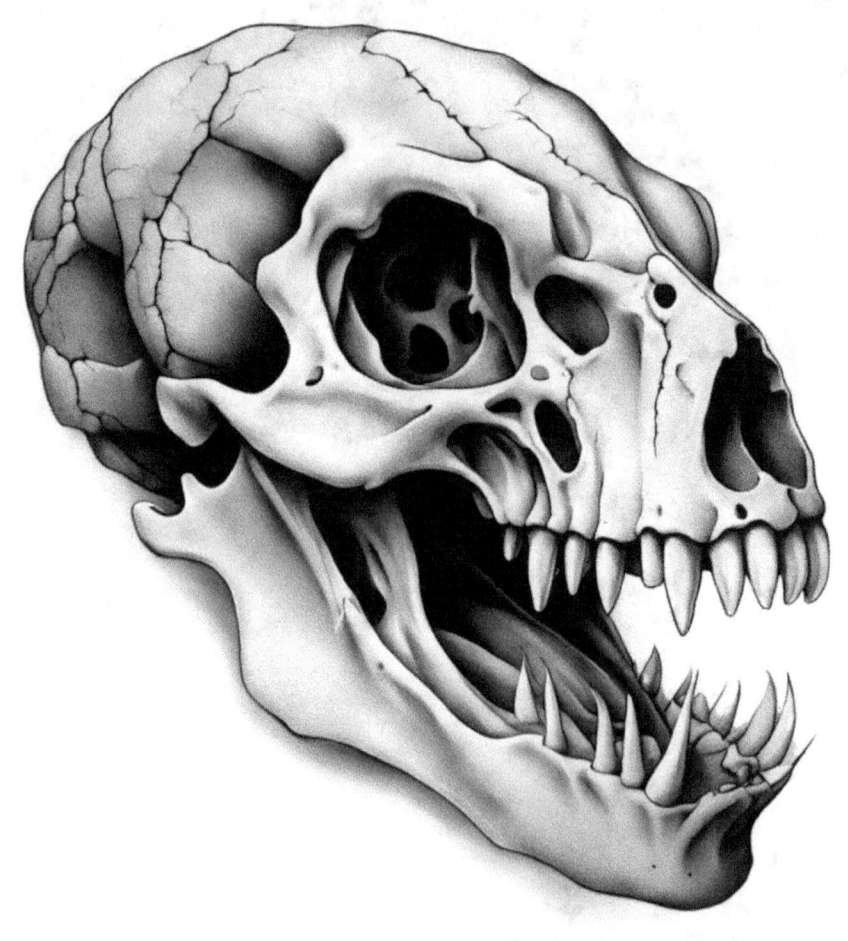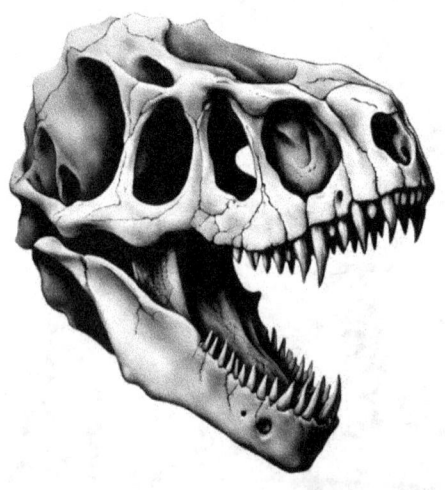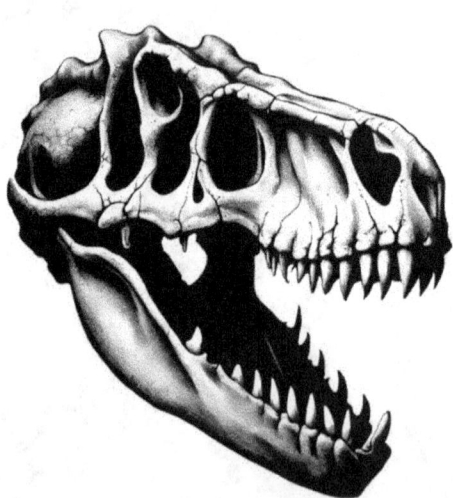

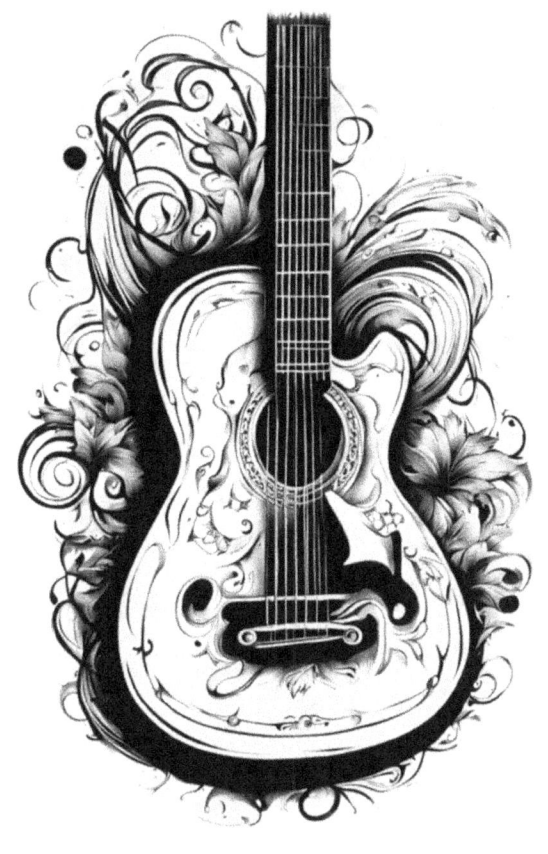
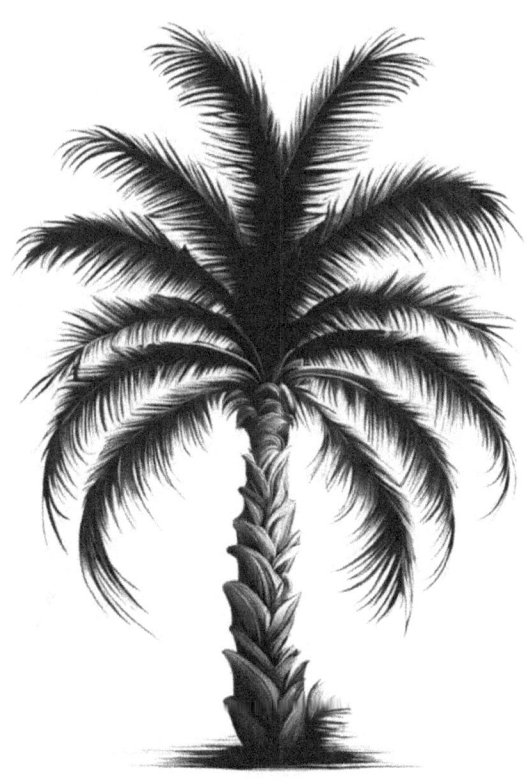

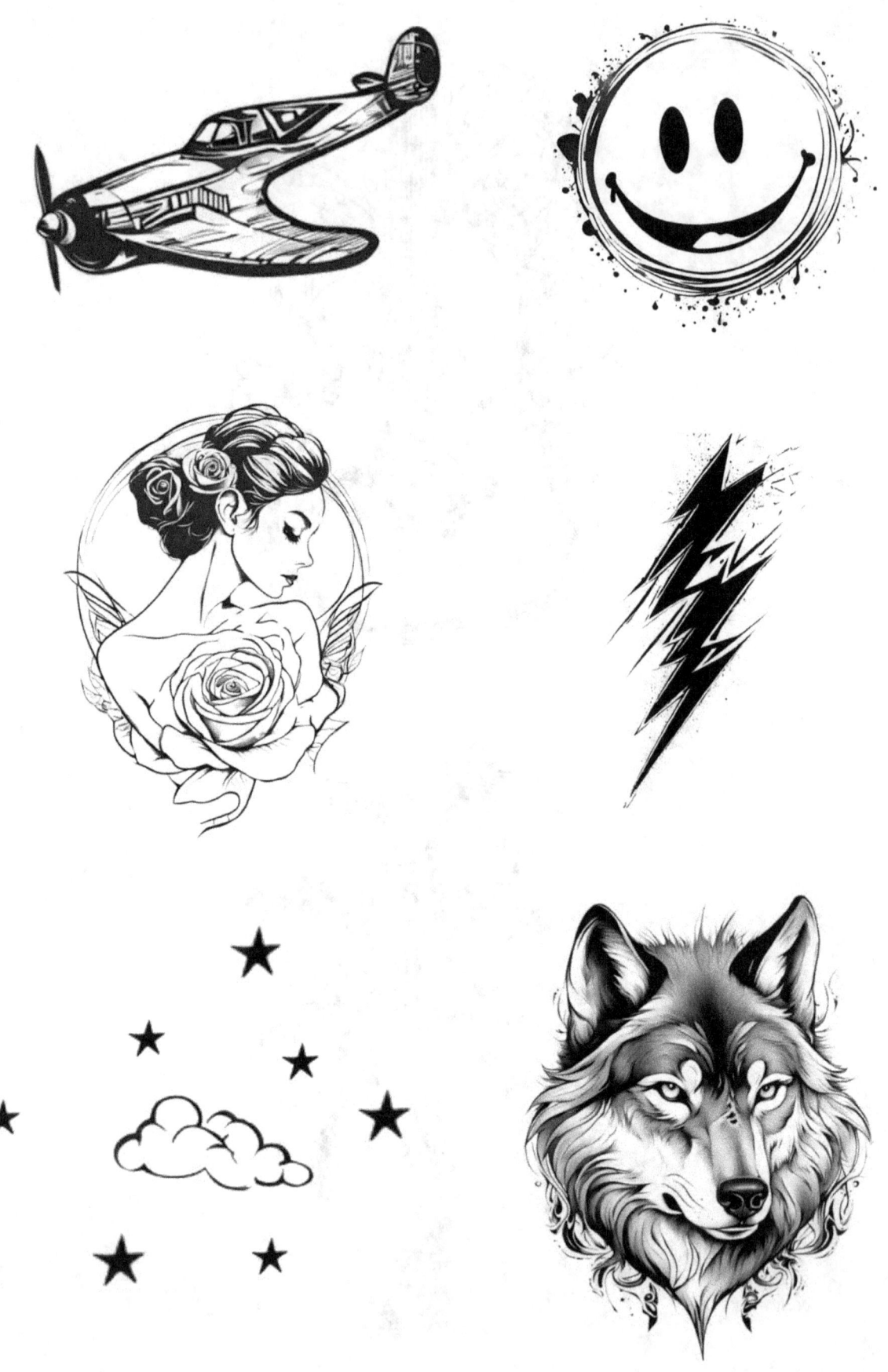

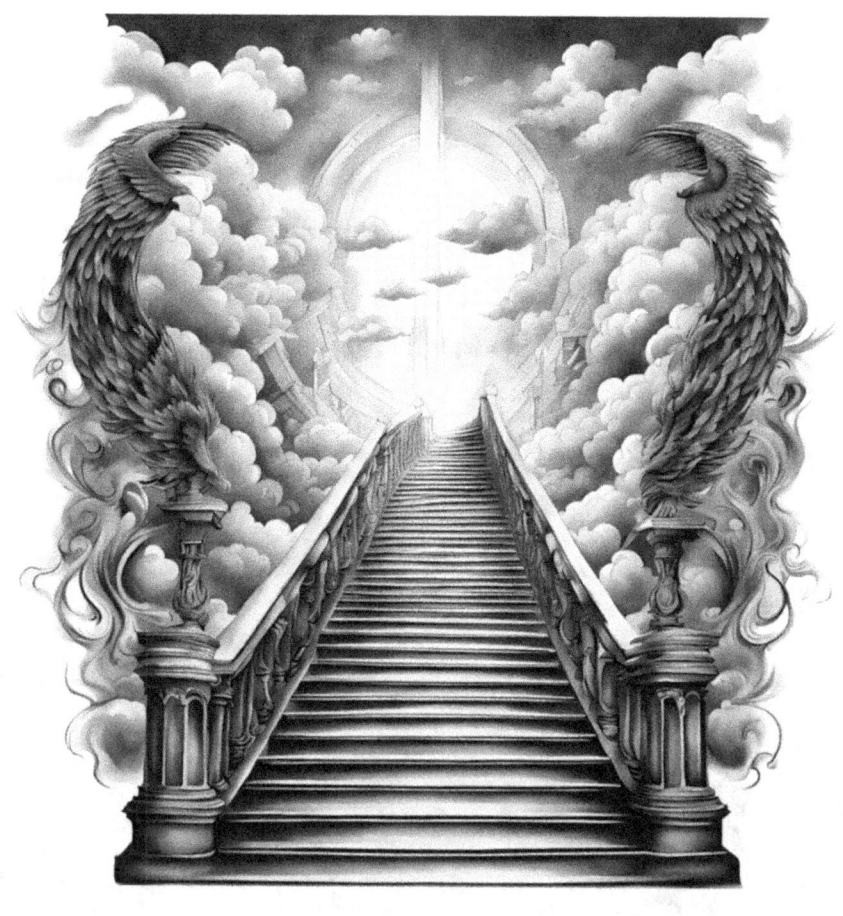
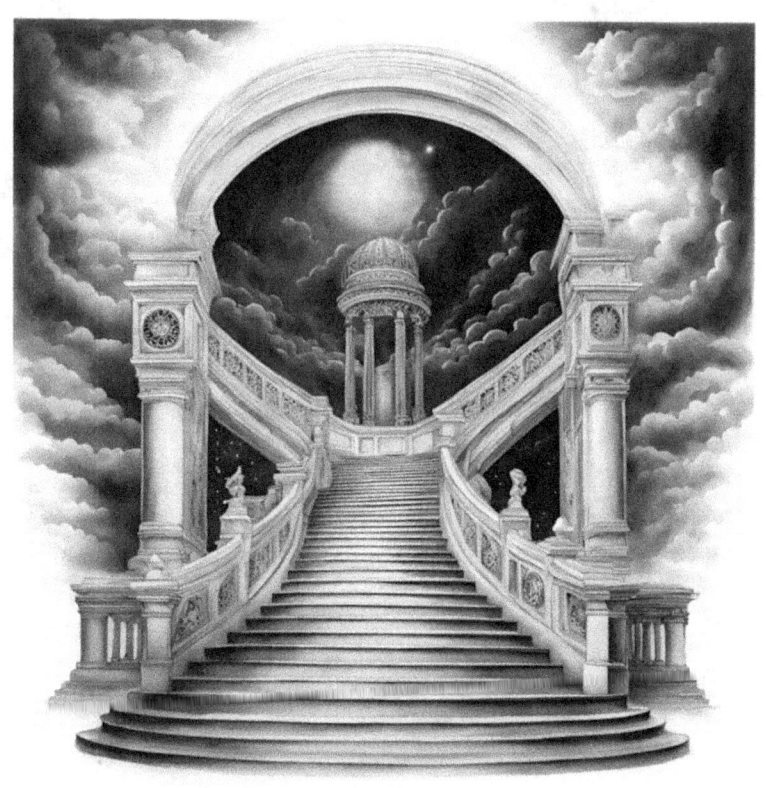

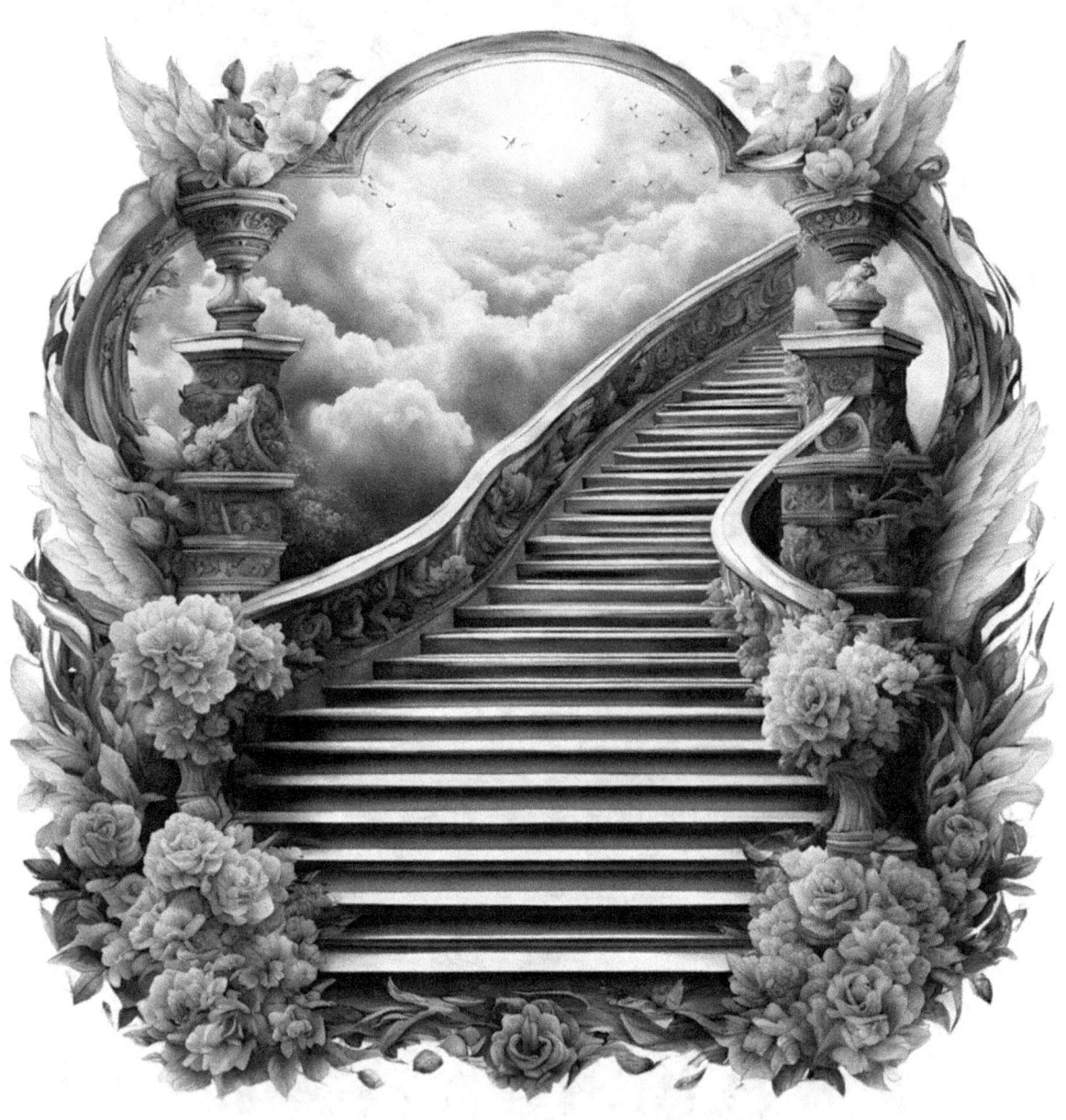

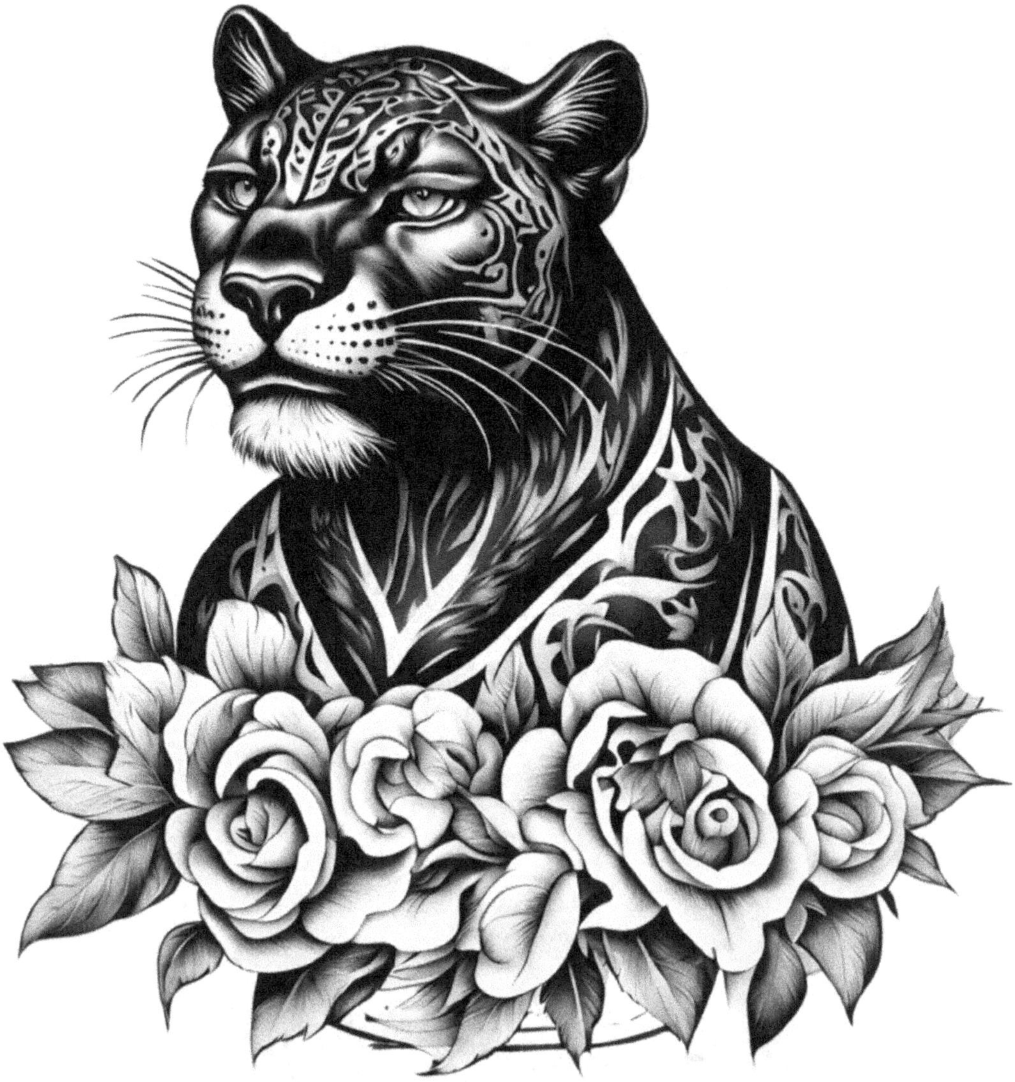

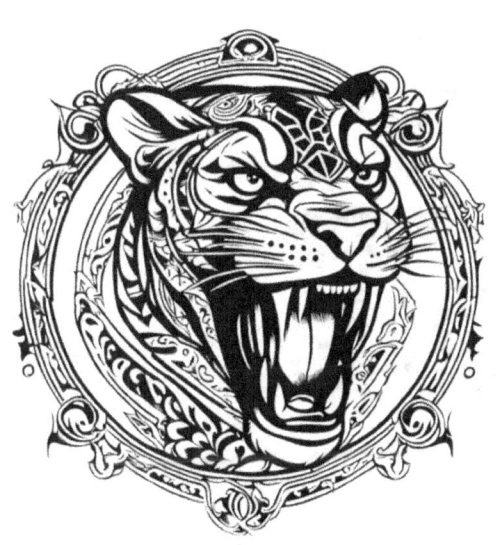
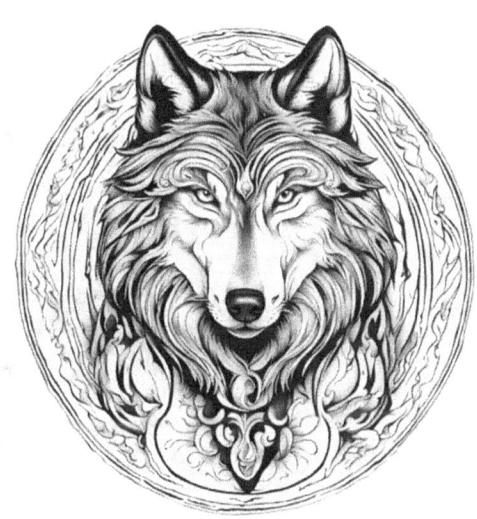

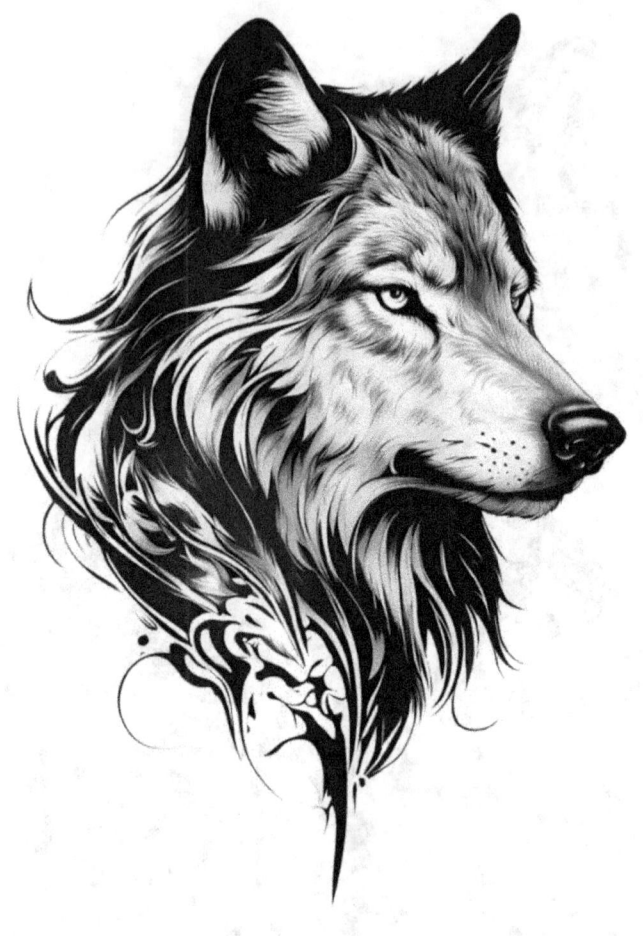
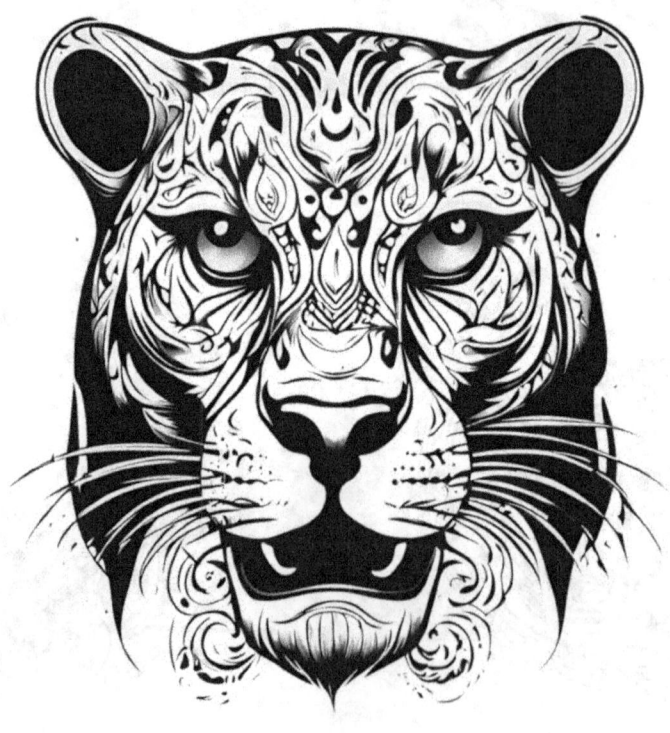

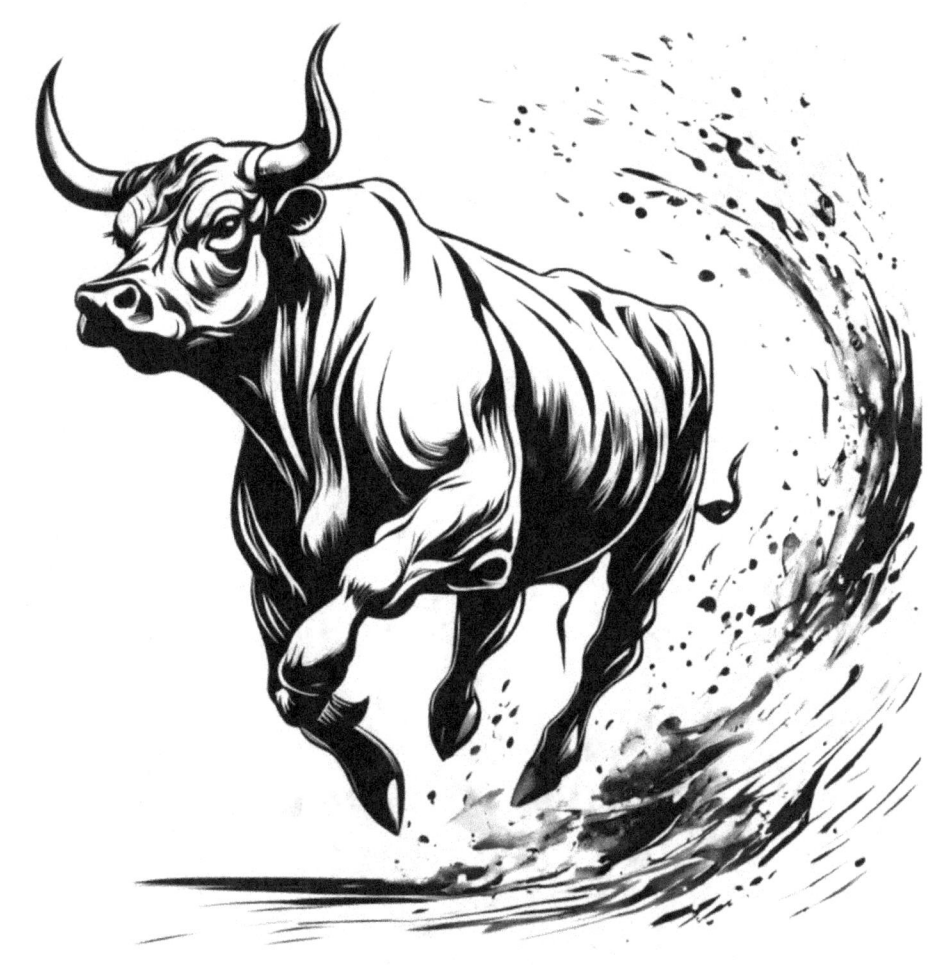
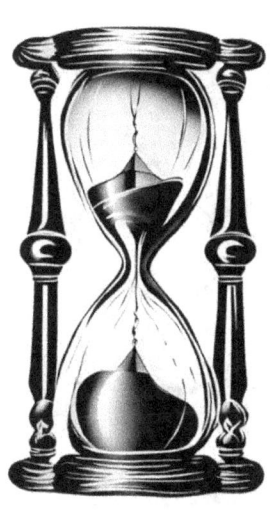
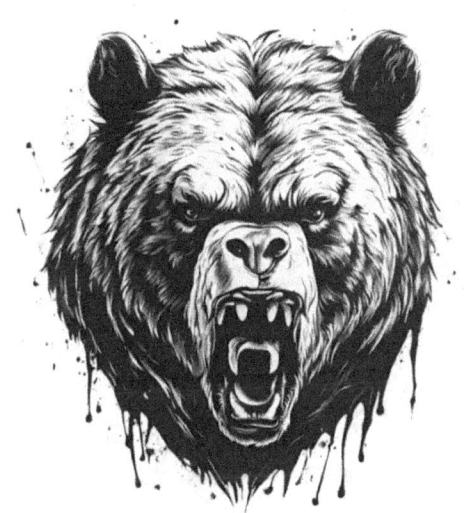

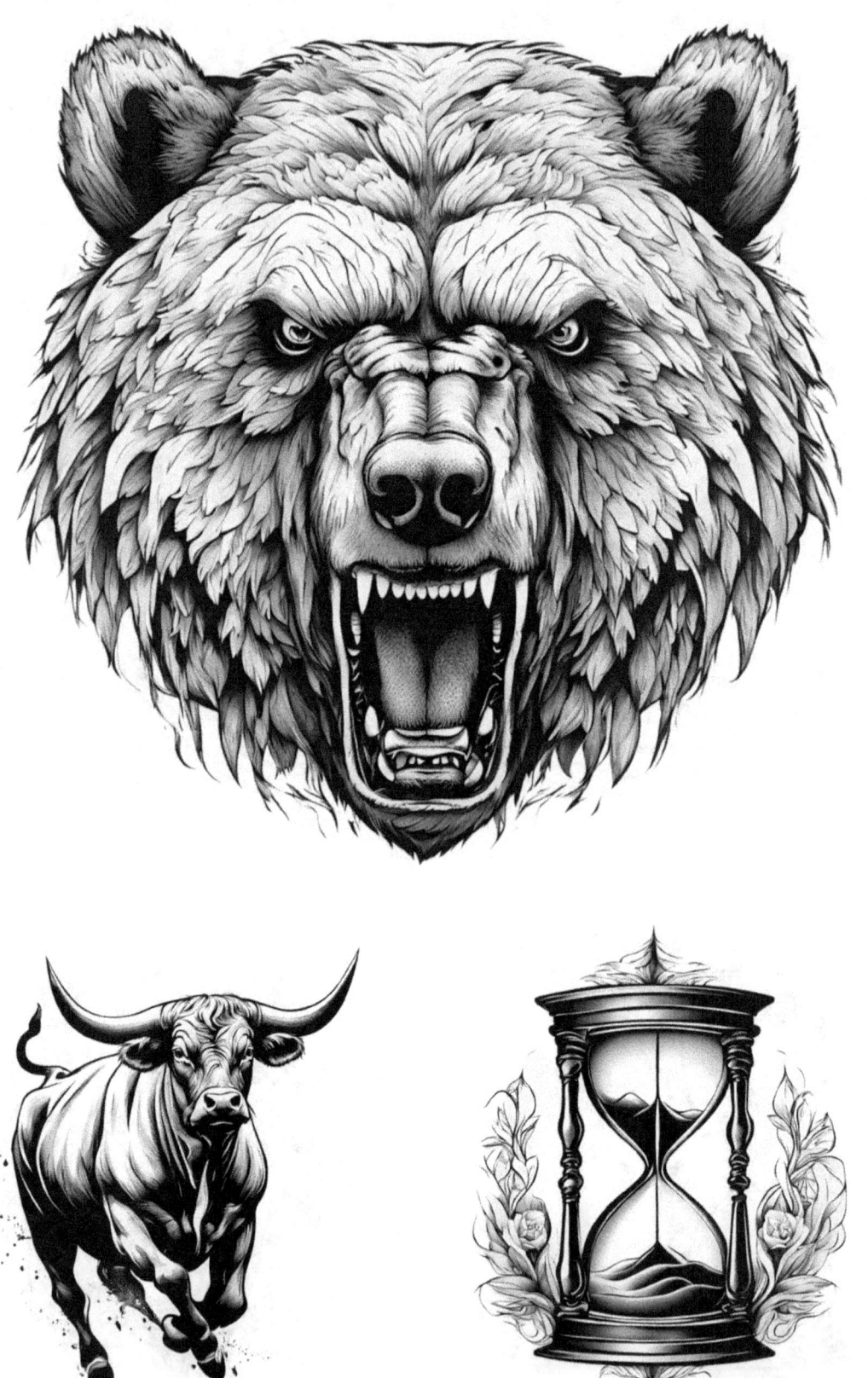

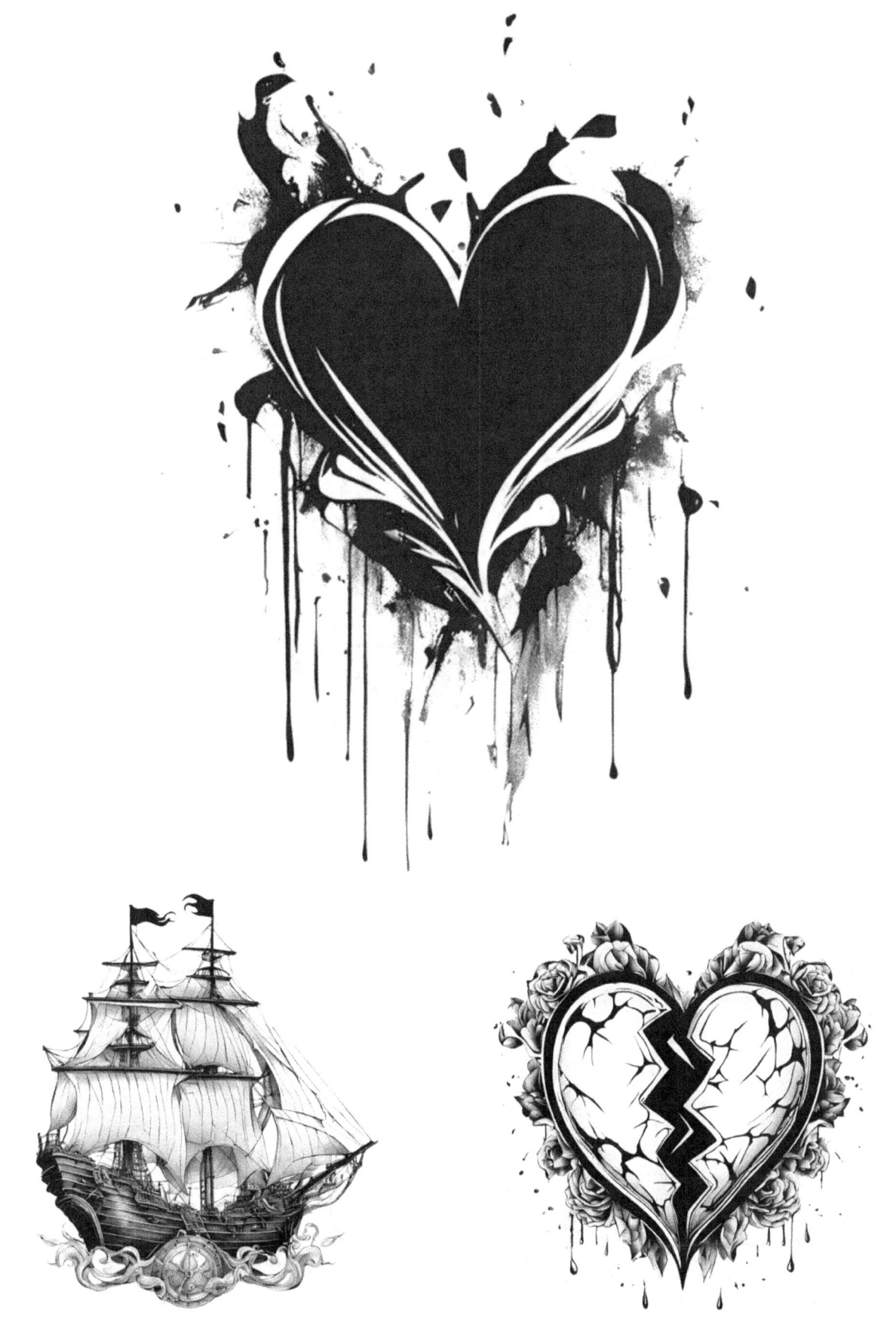

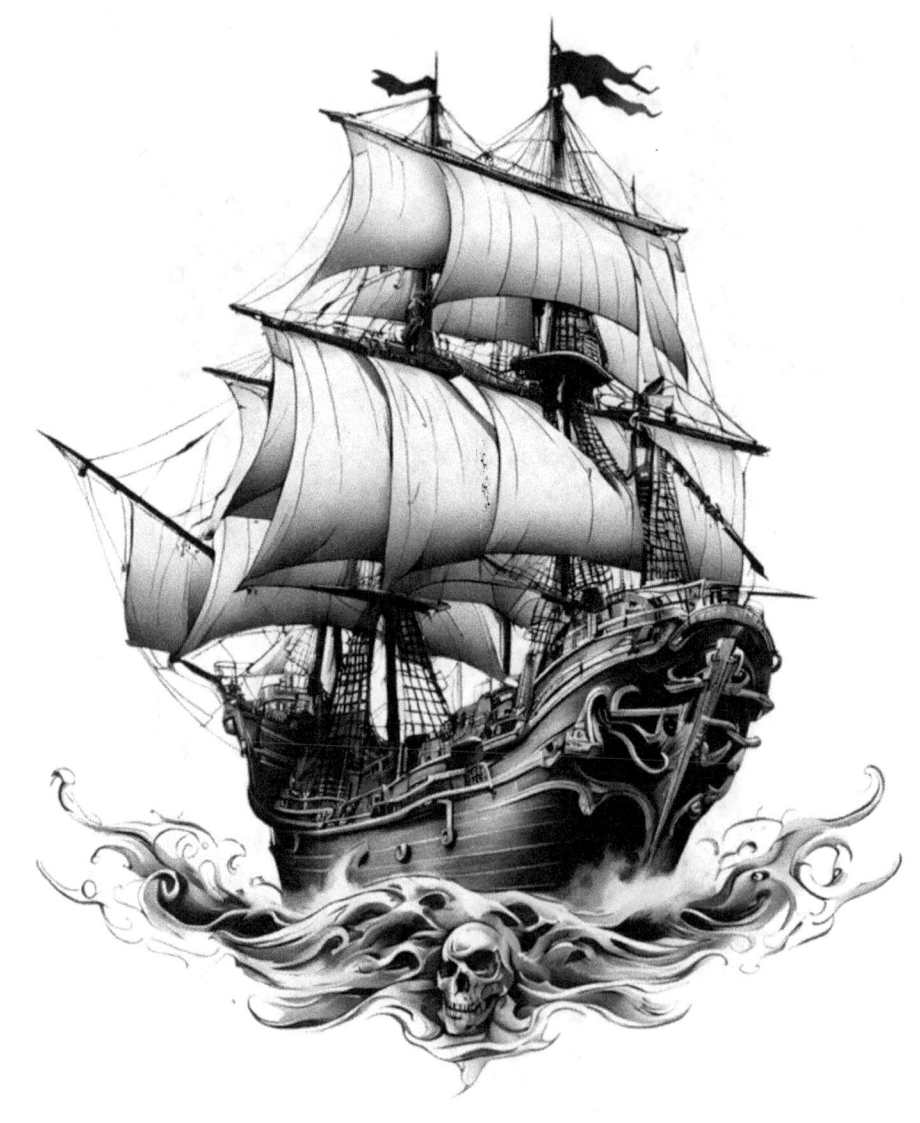
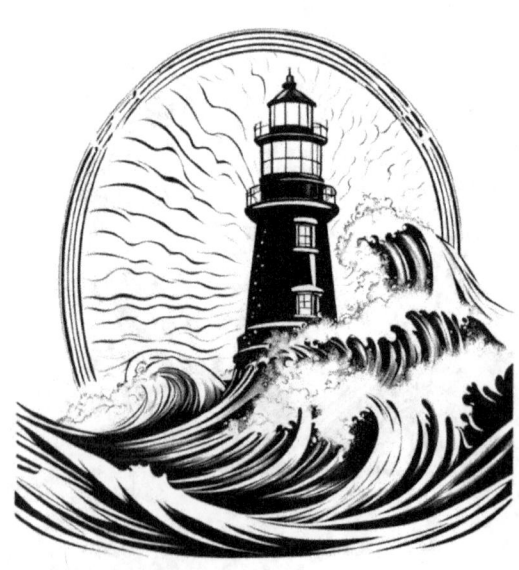
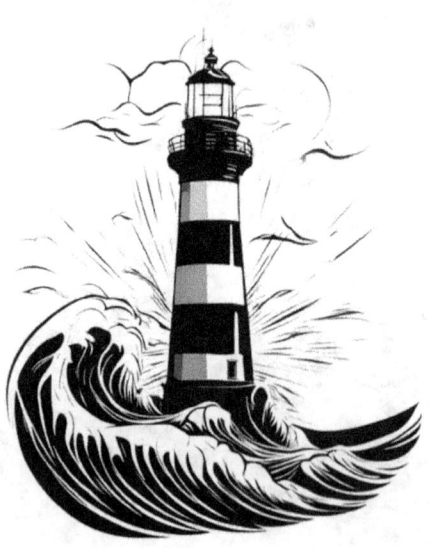

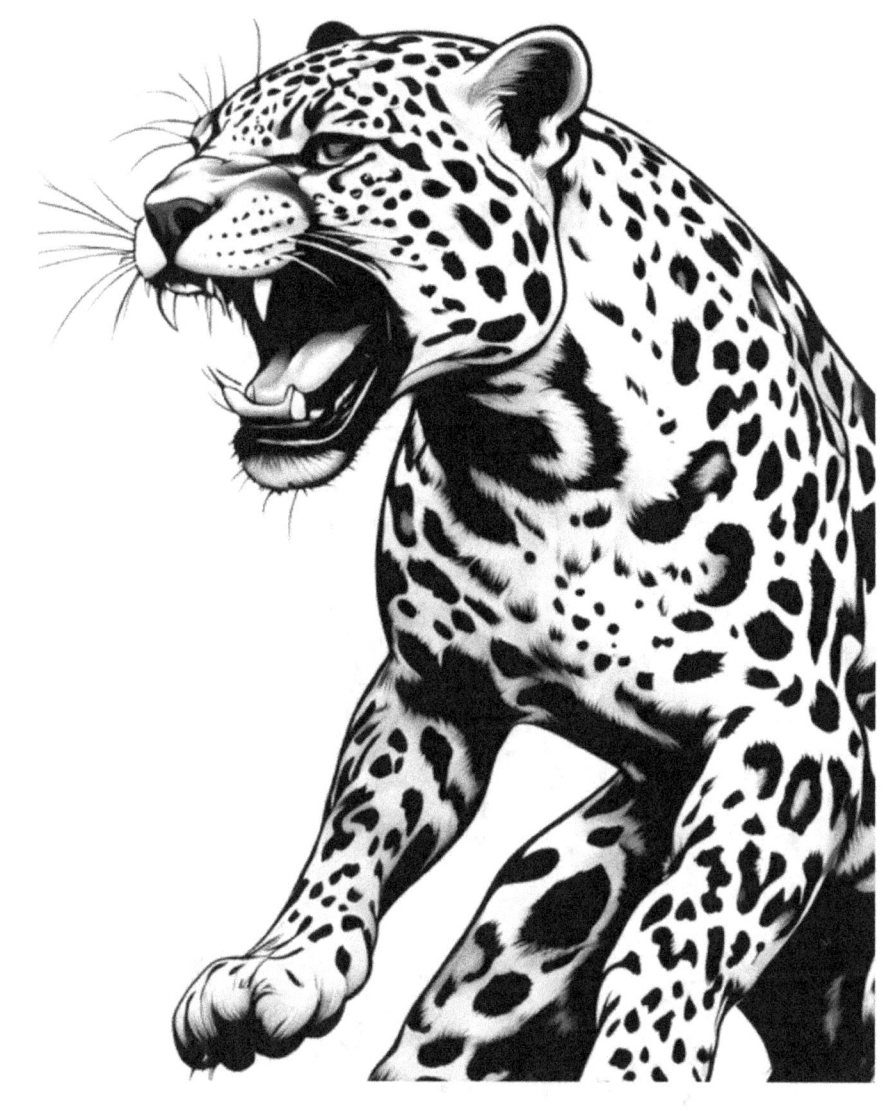
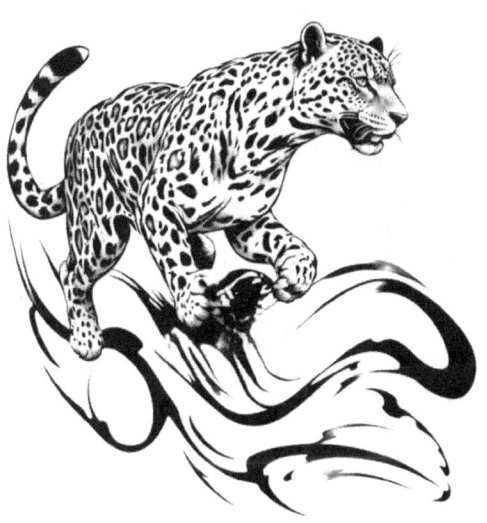
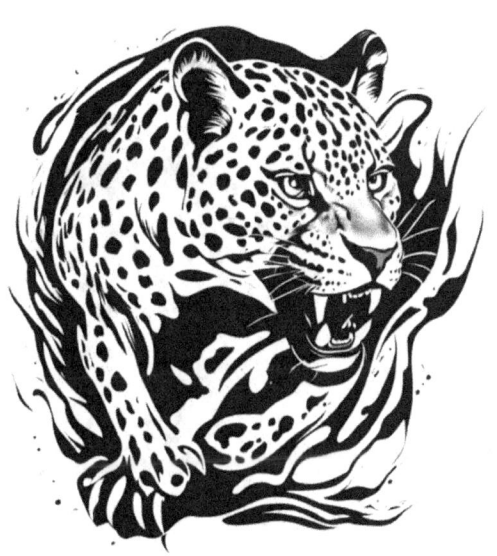

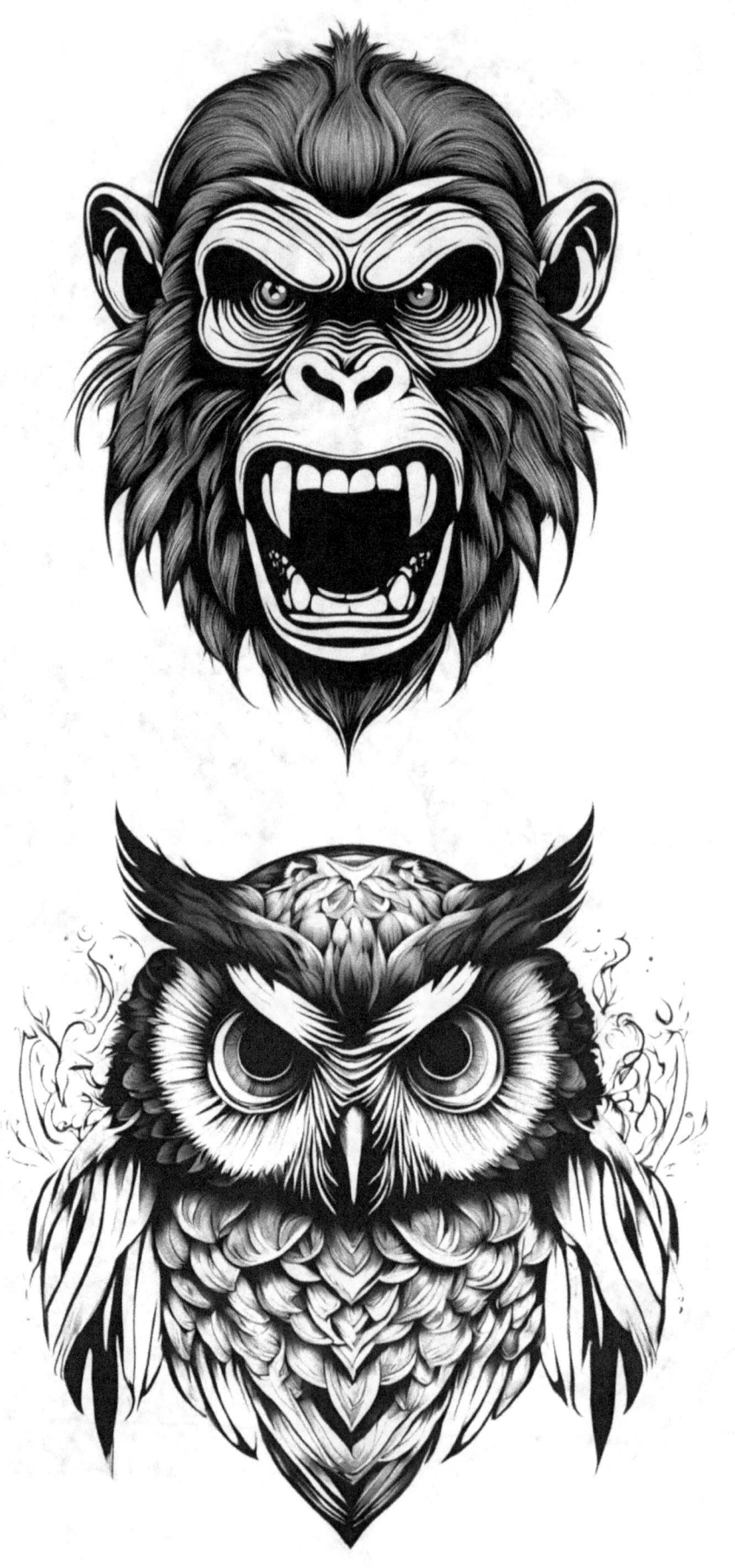

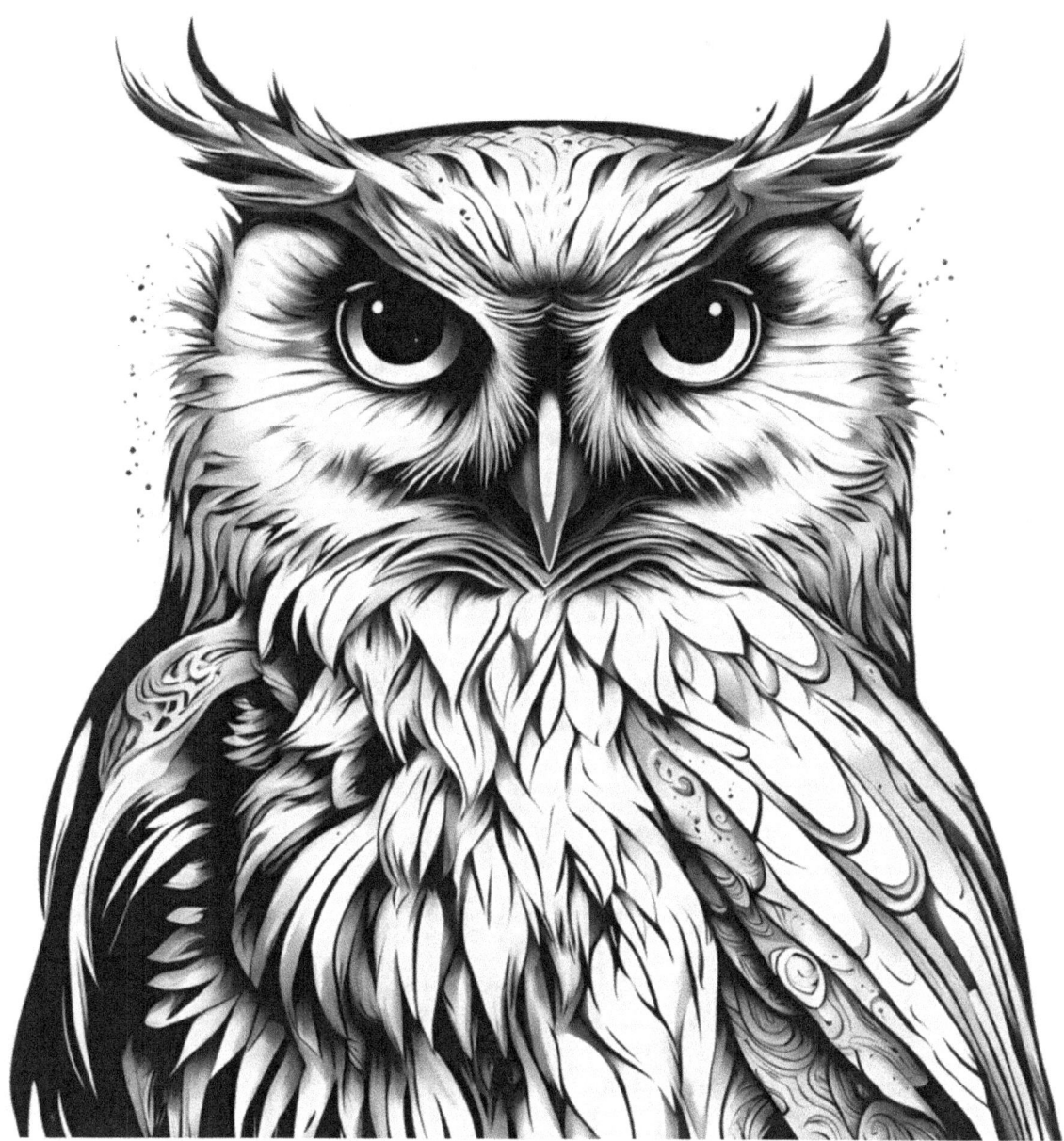

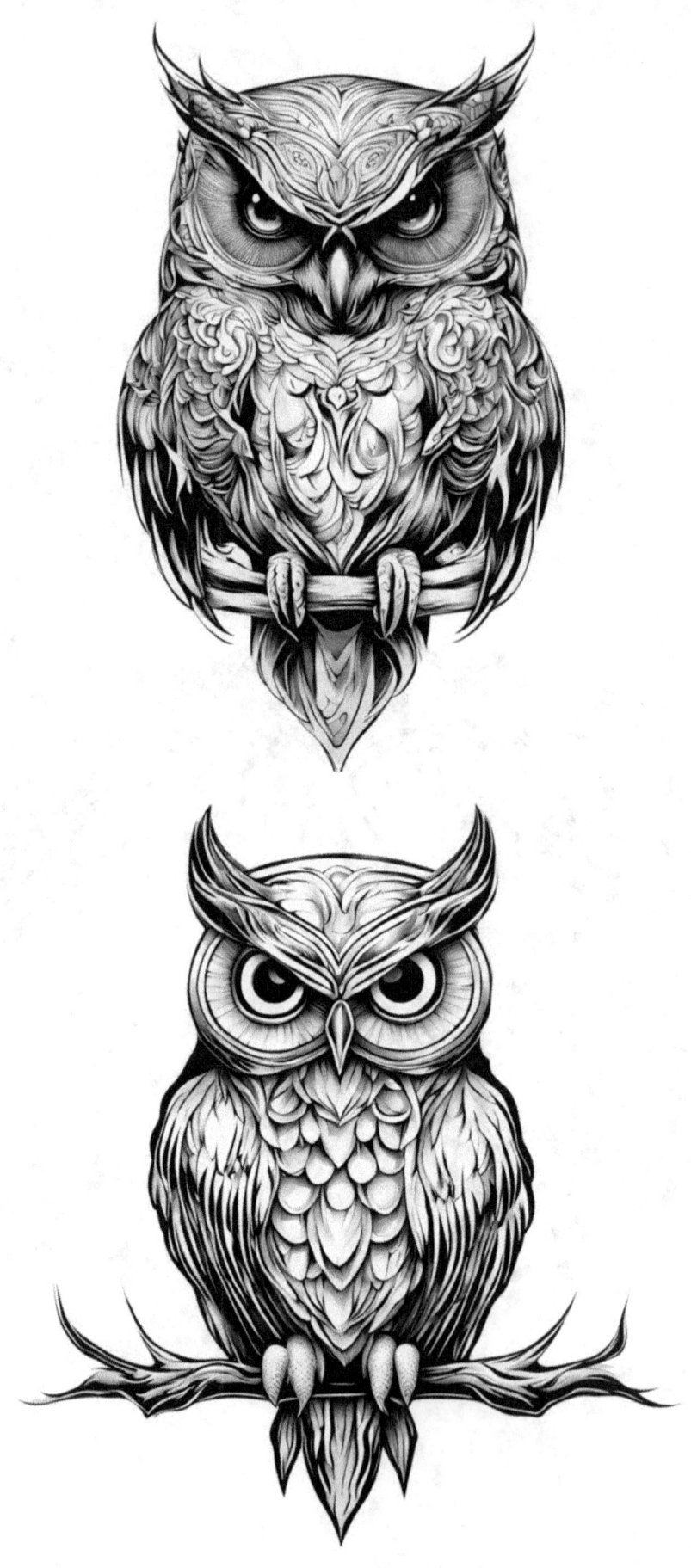

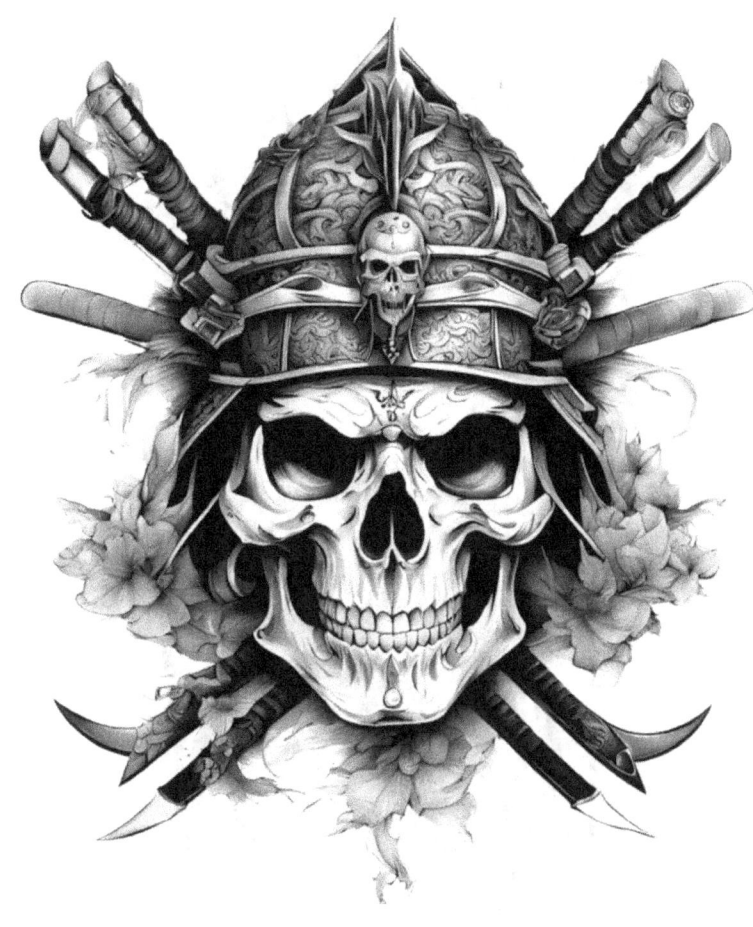
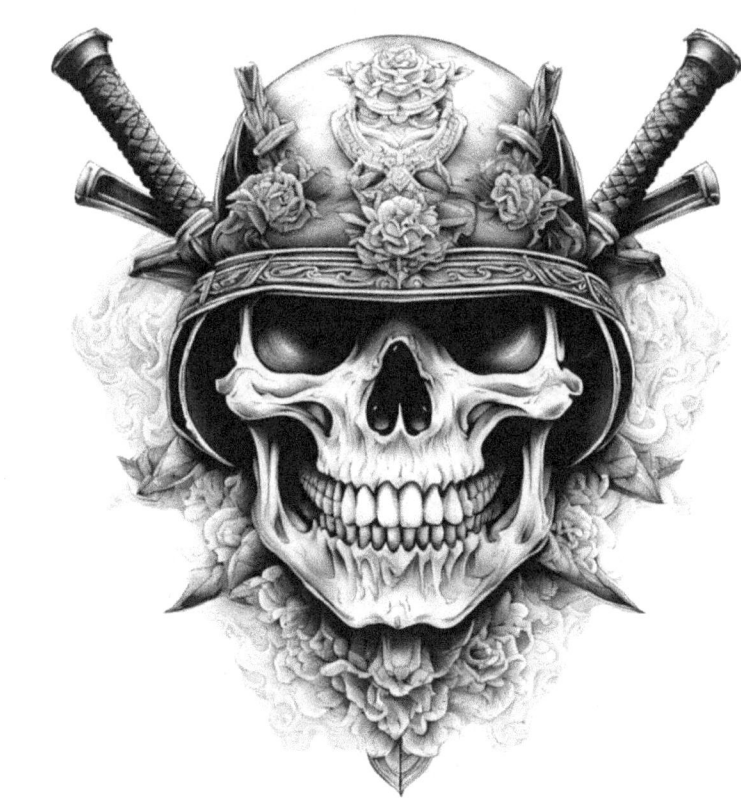

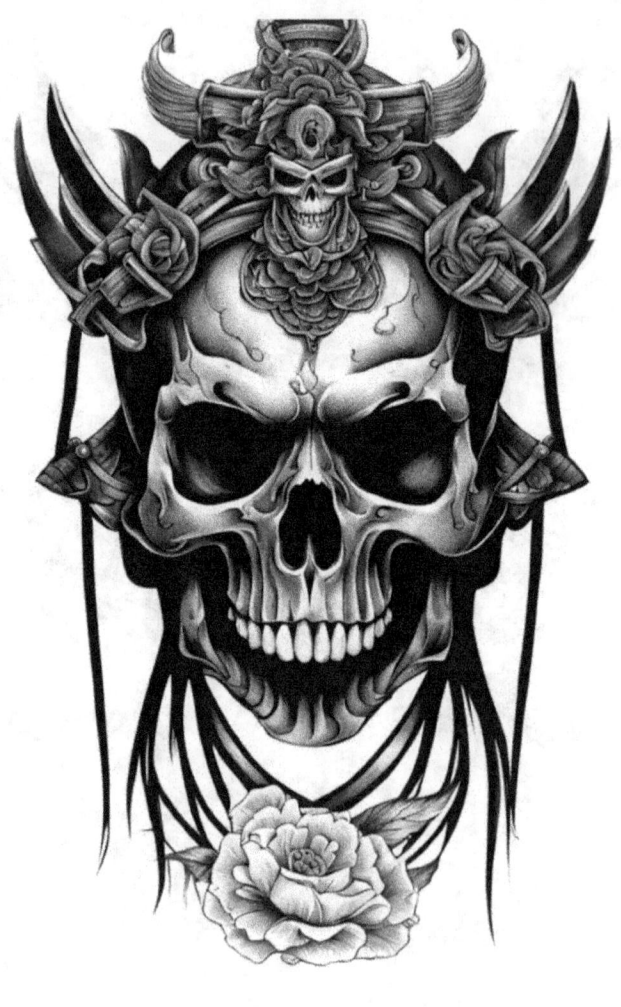
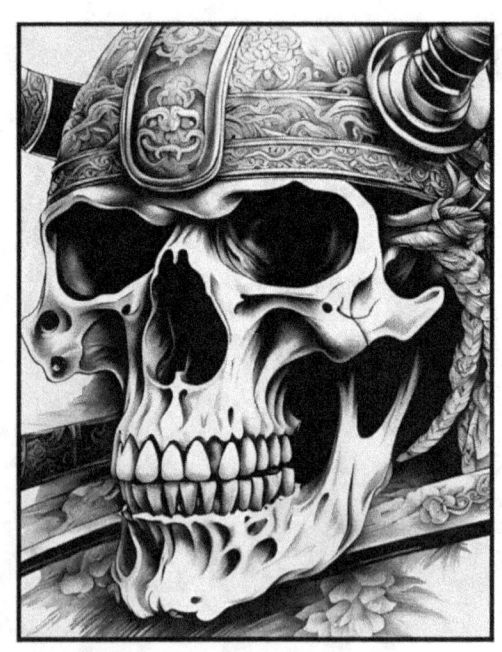

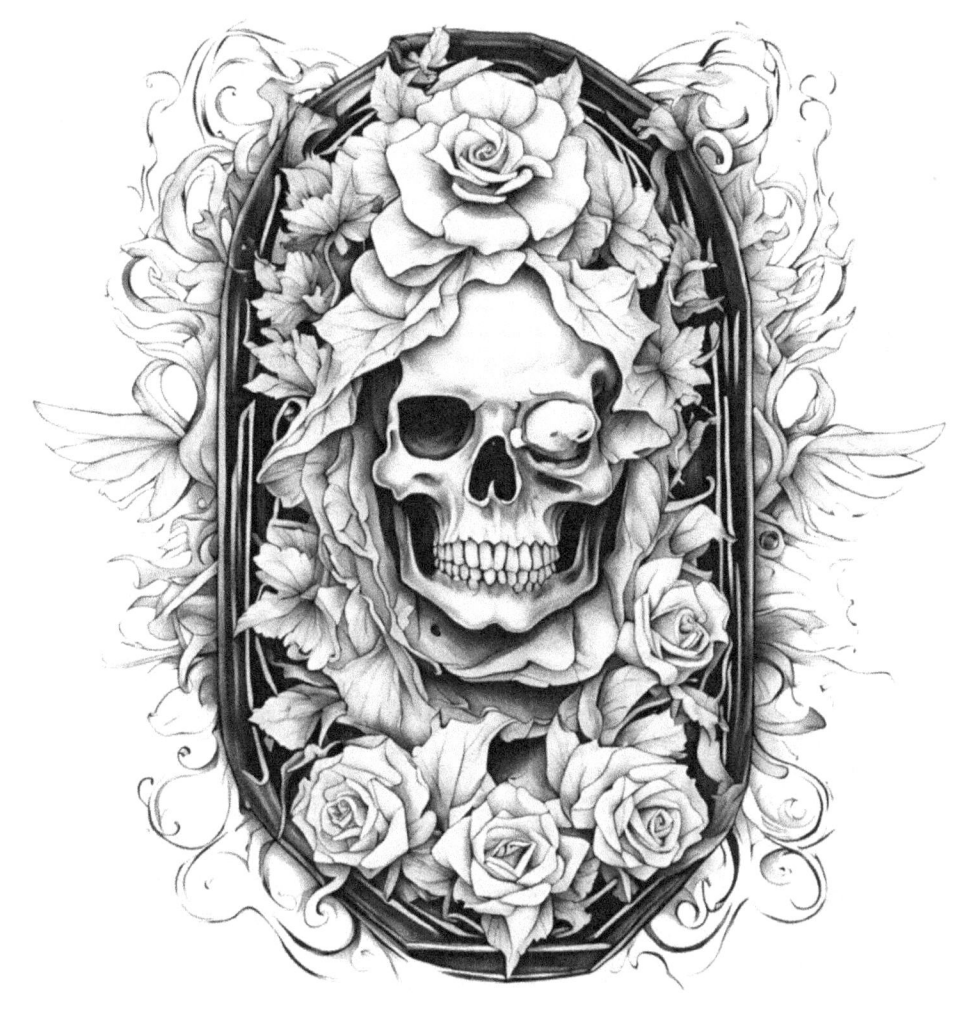
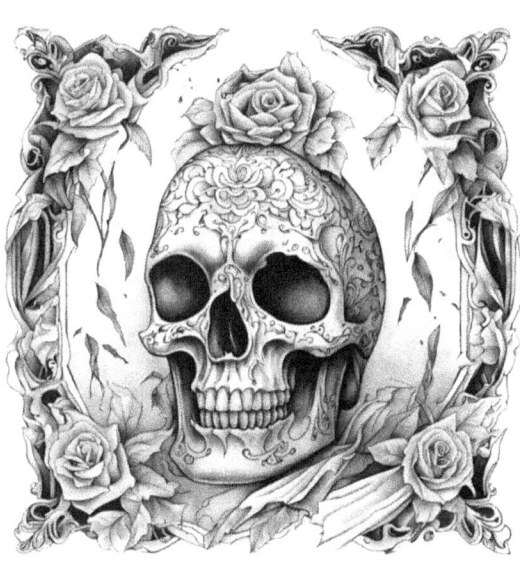
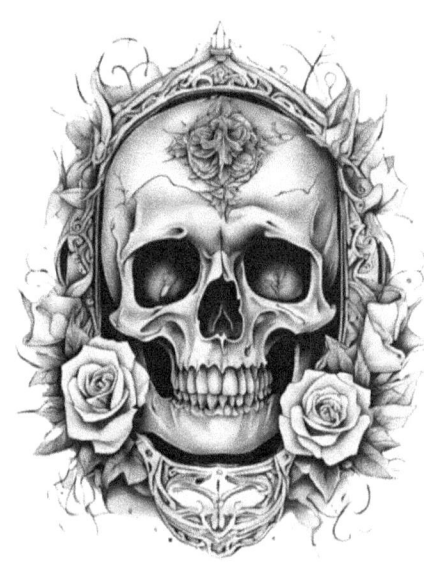

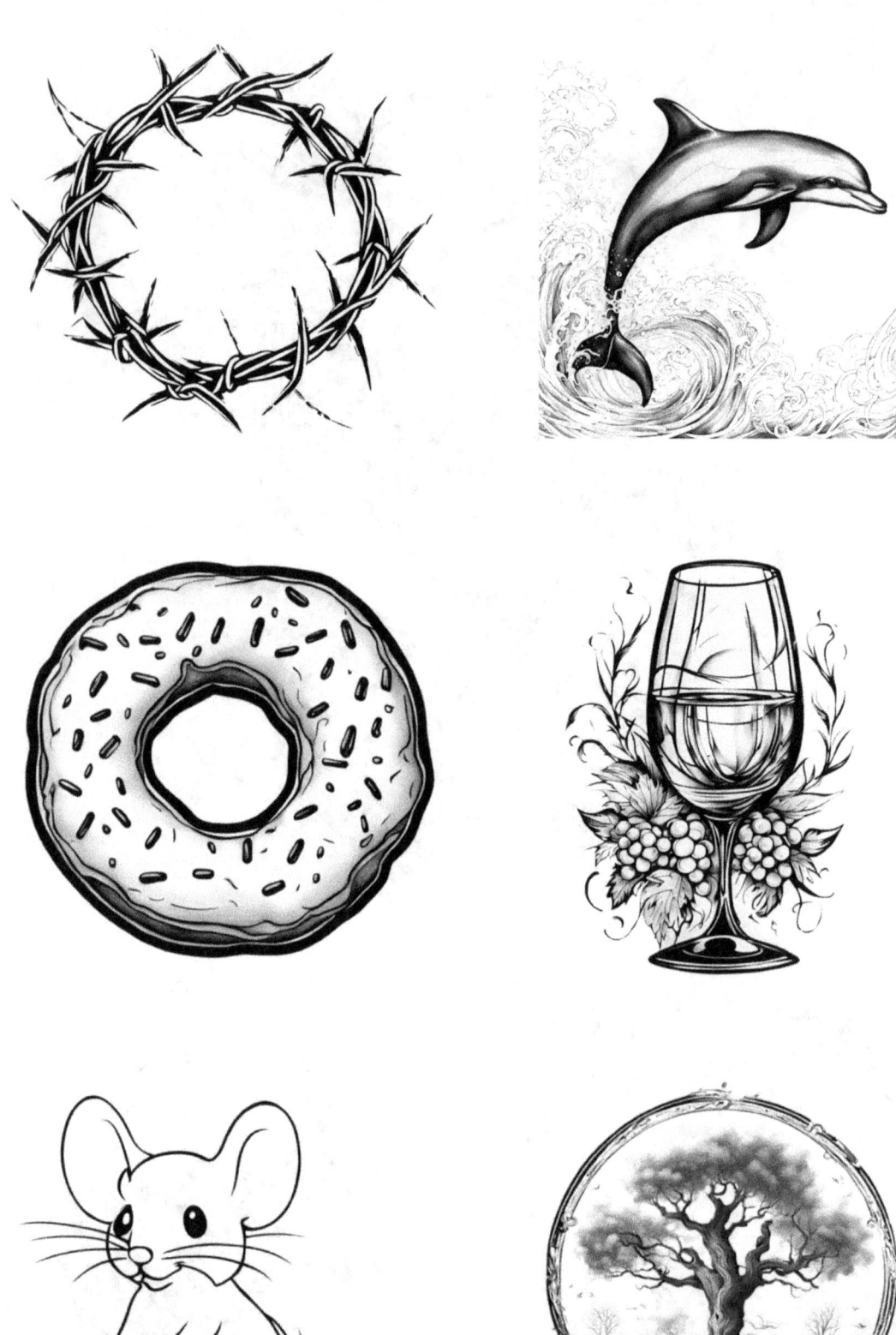

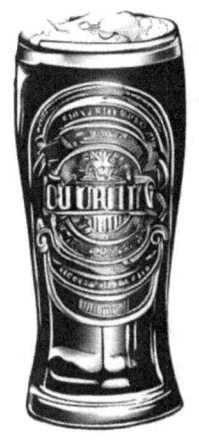
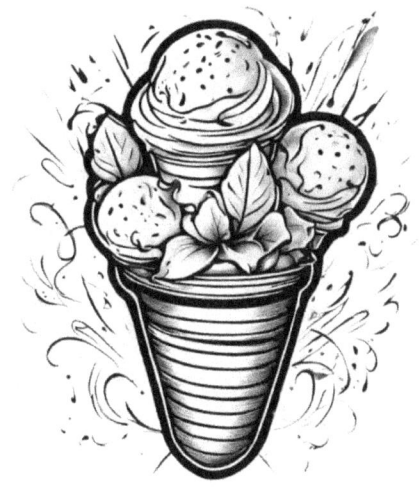
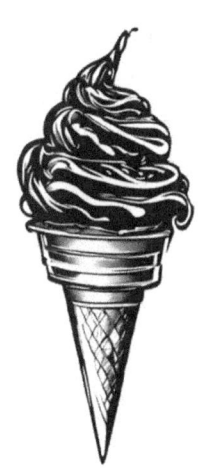
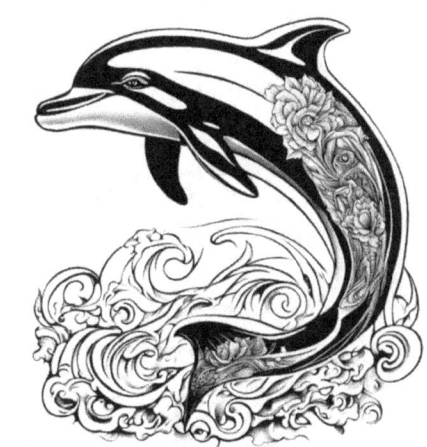
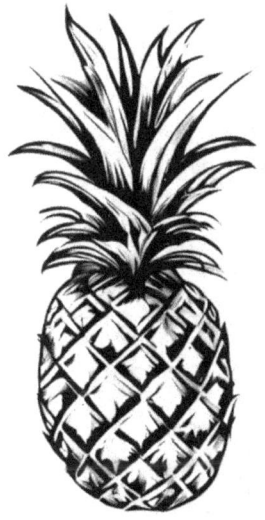
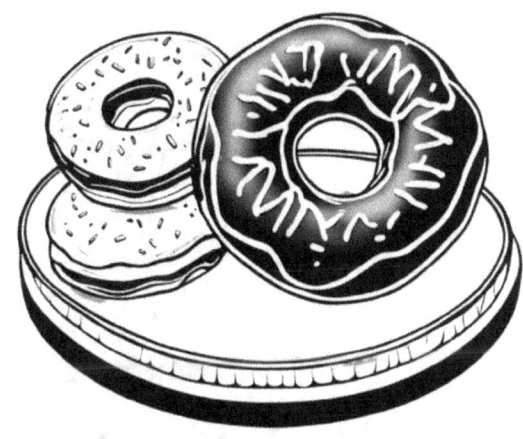

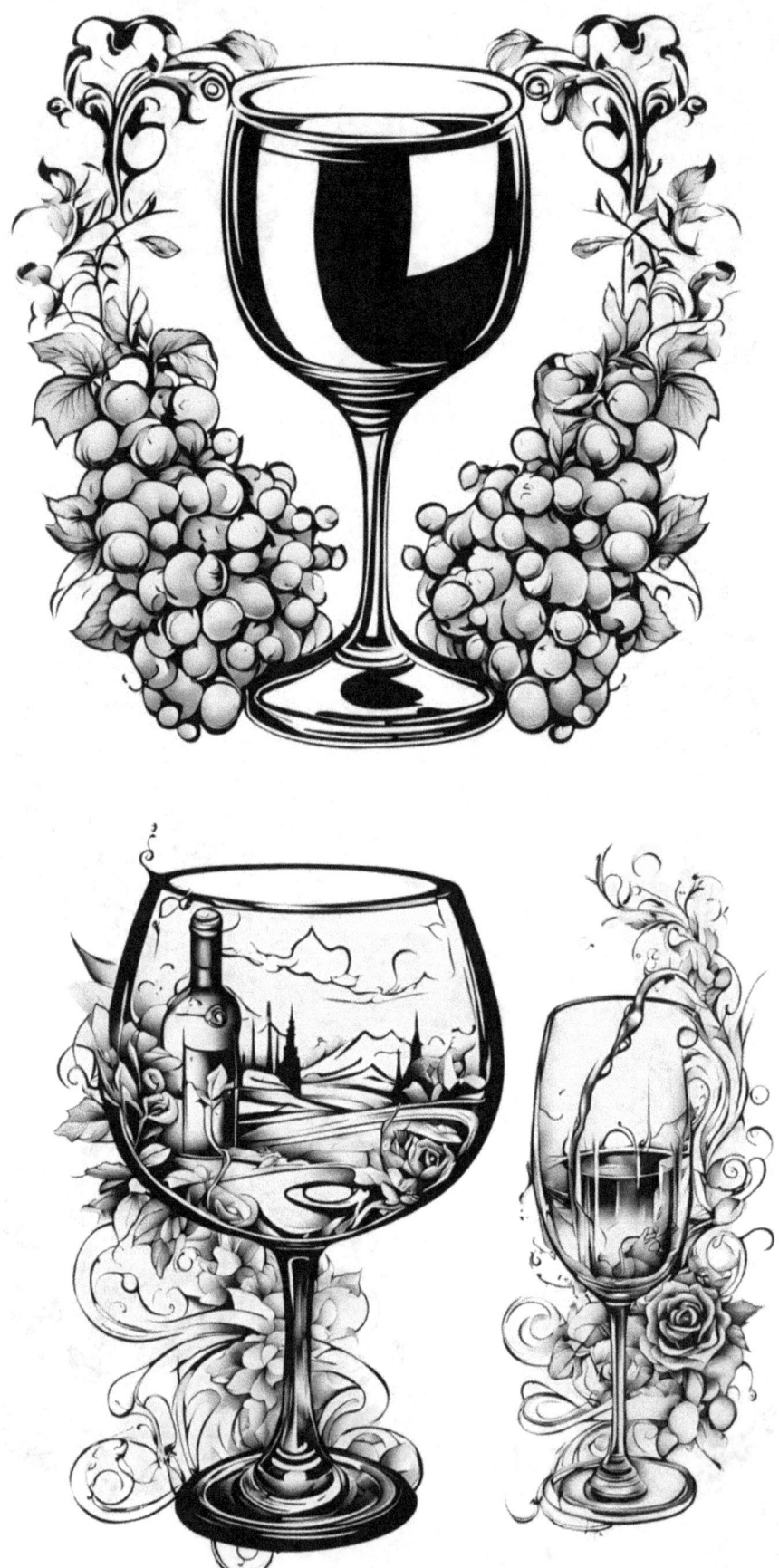

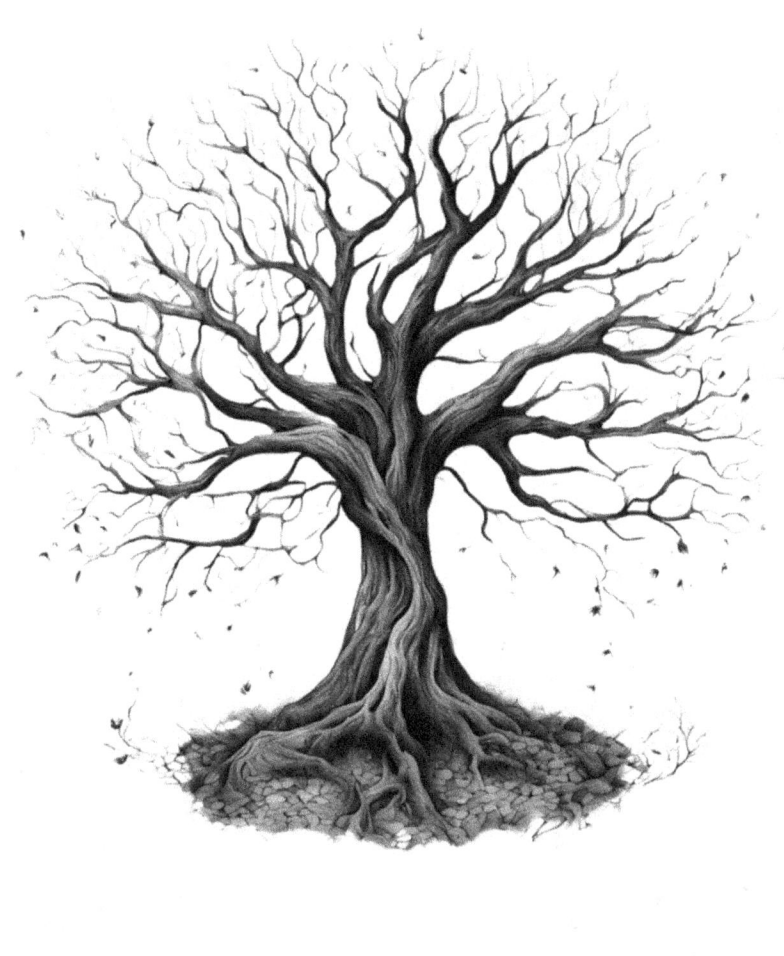
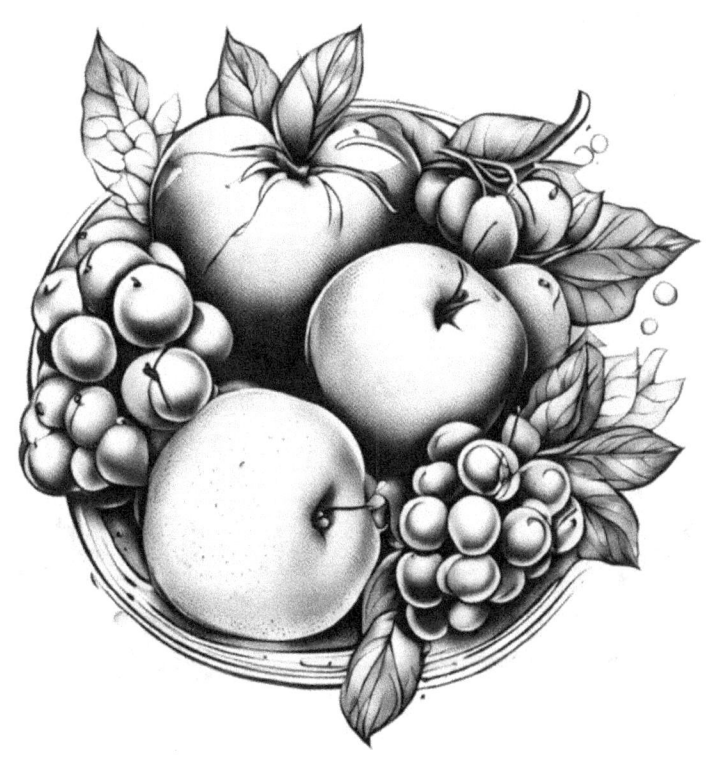

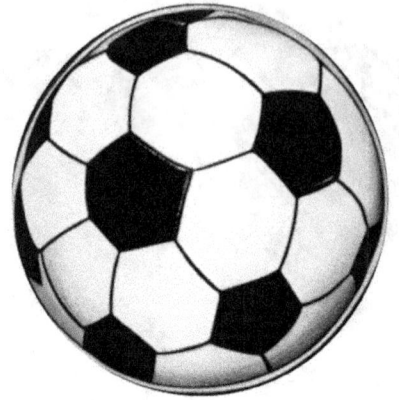
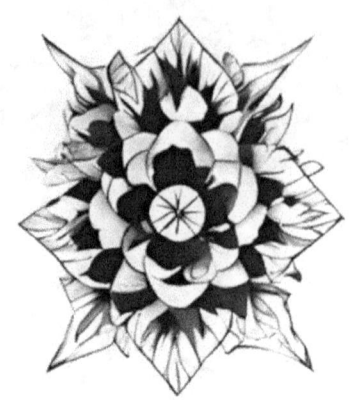
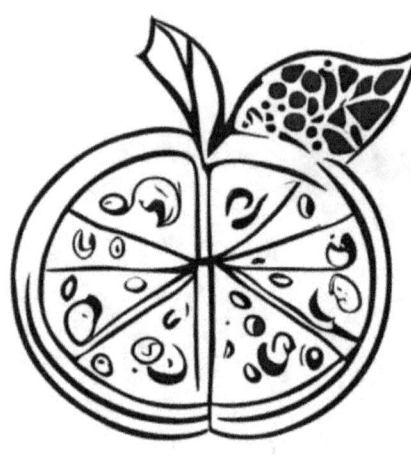
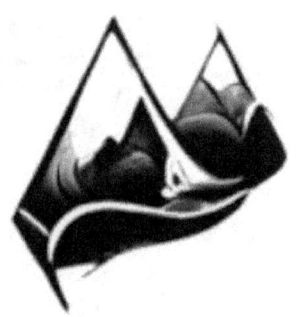
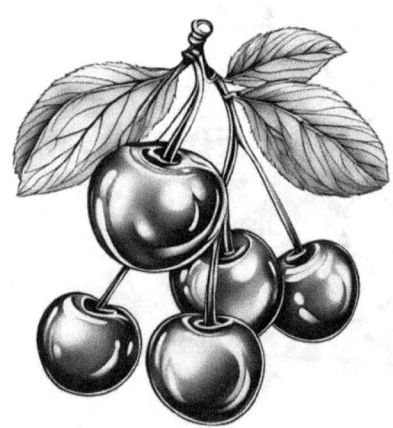

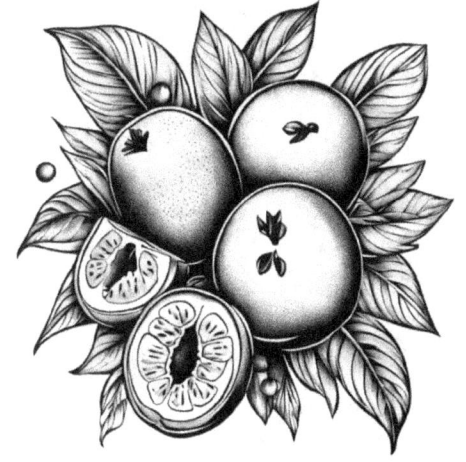

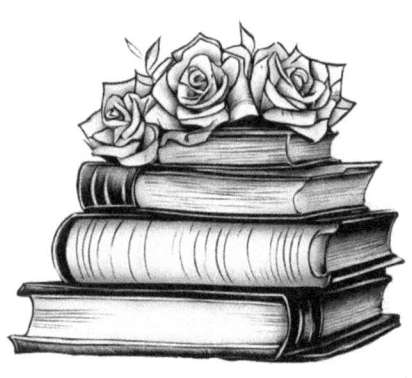
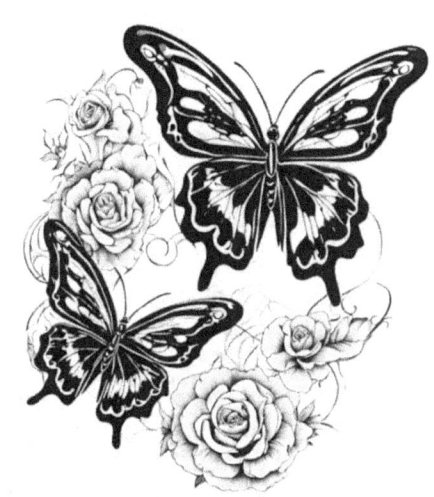
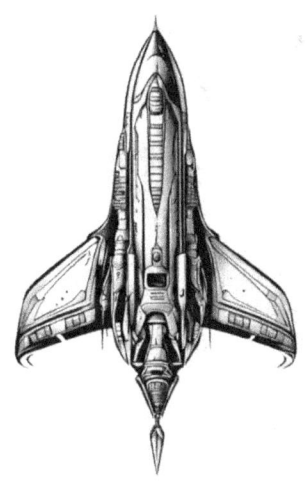
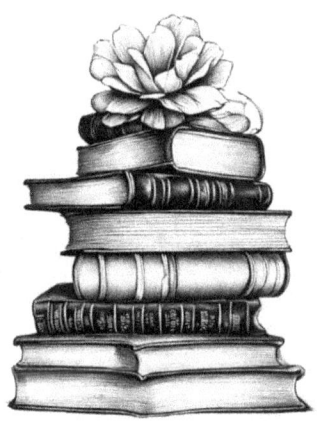

73

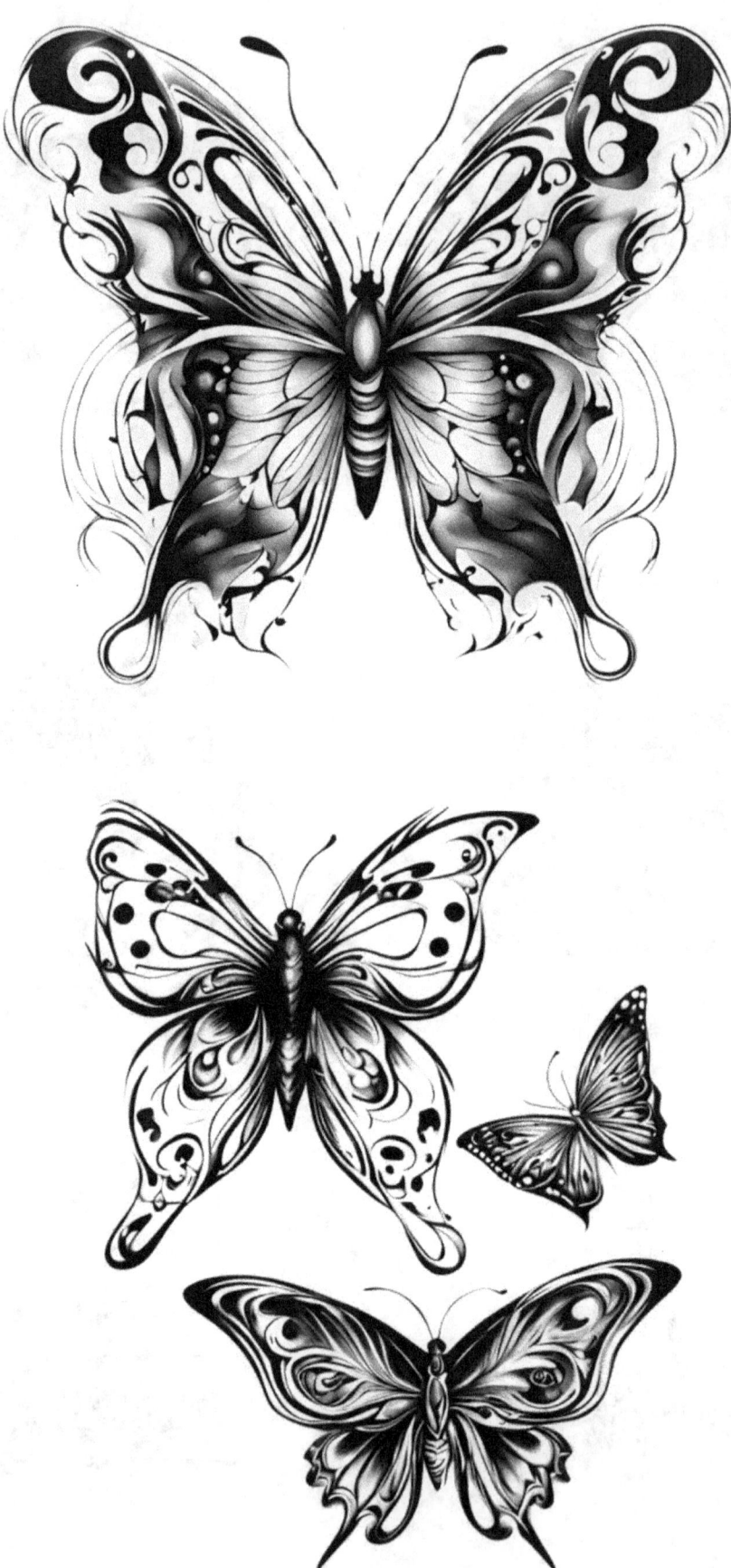

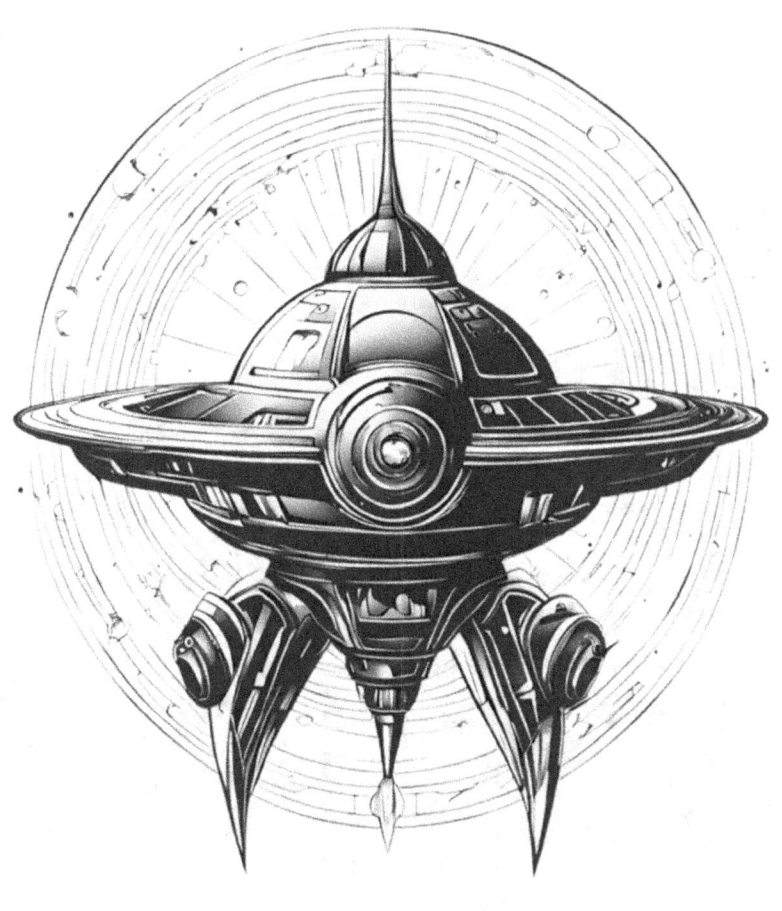
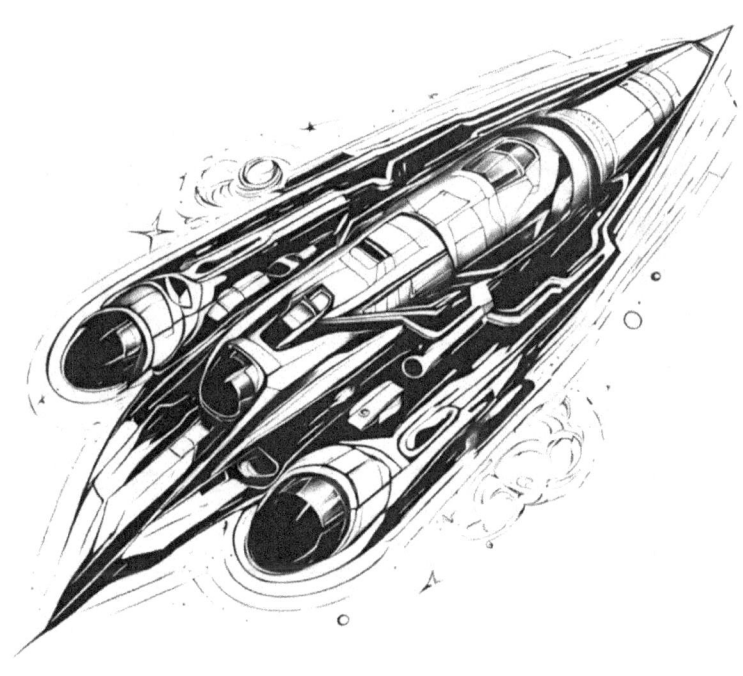

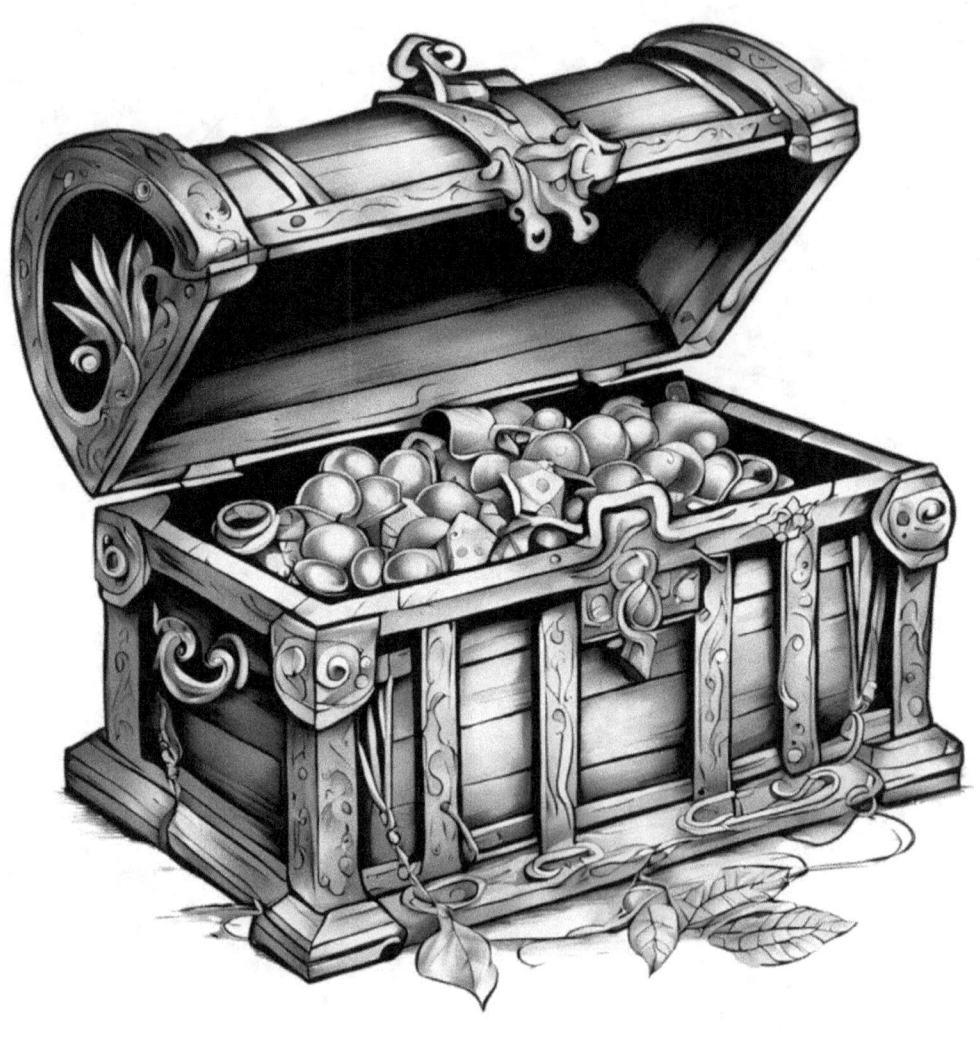
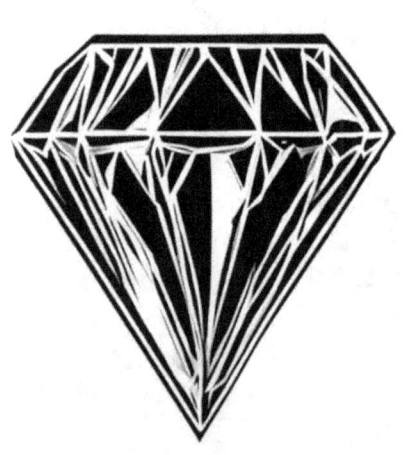
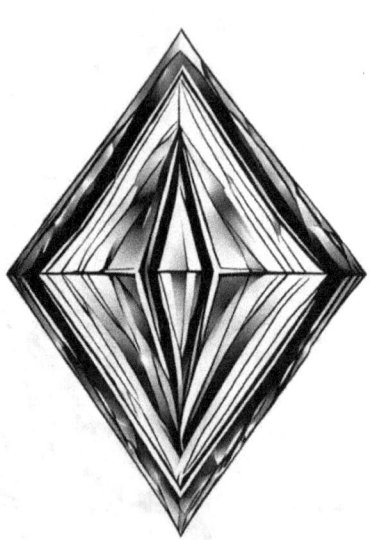

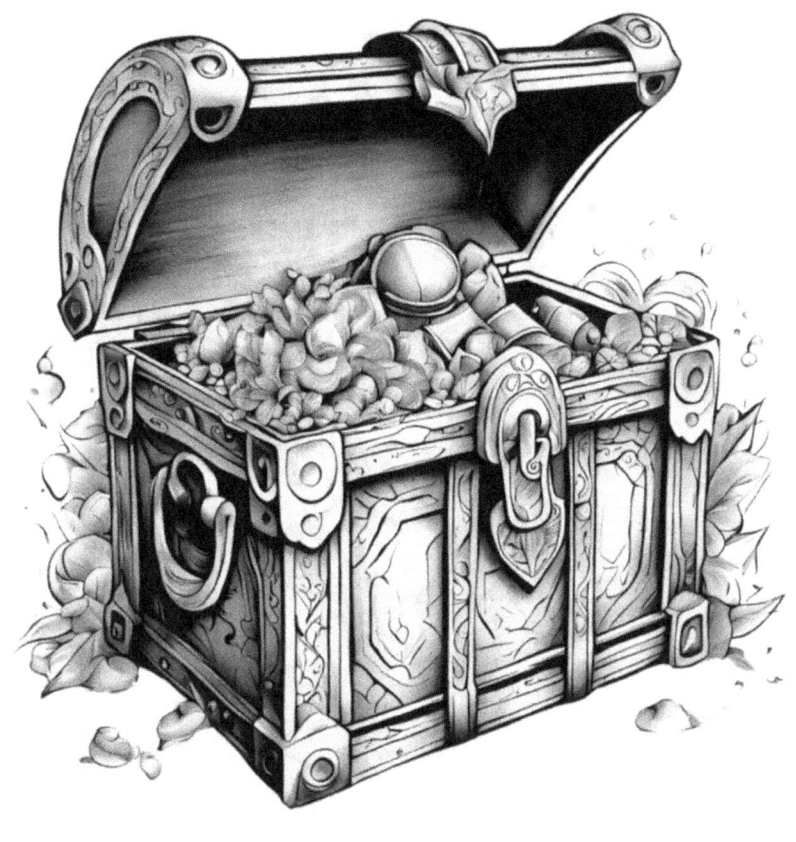
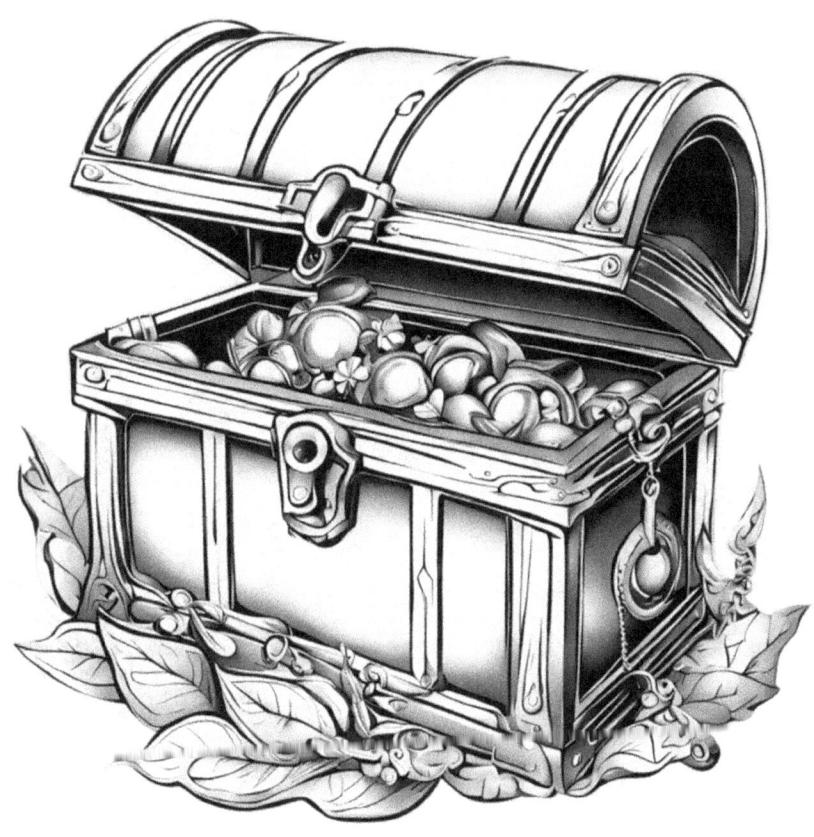

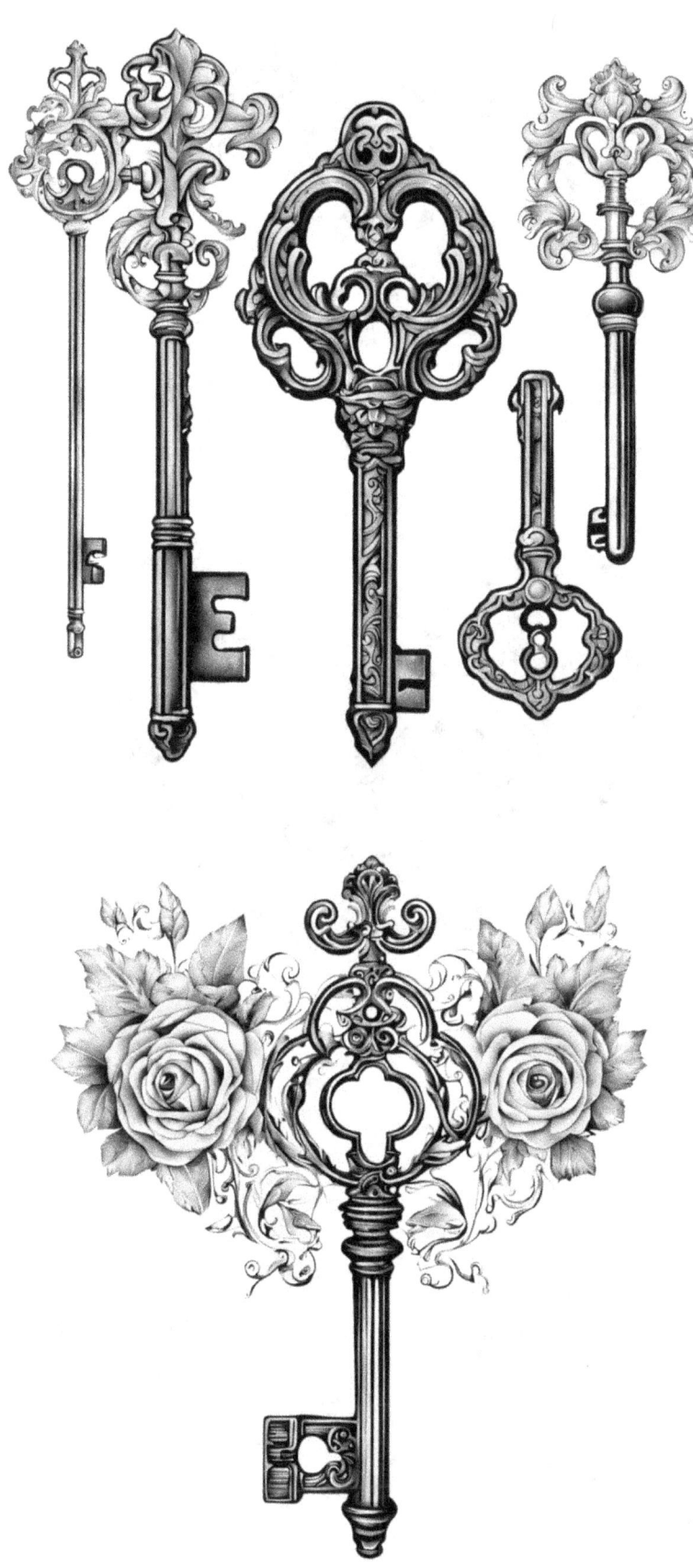

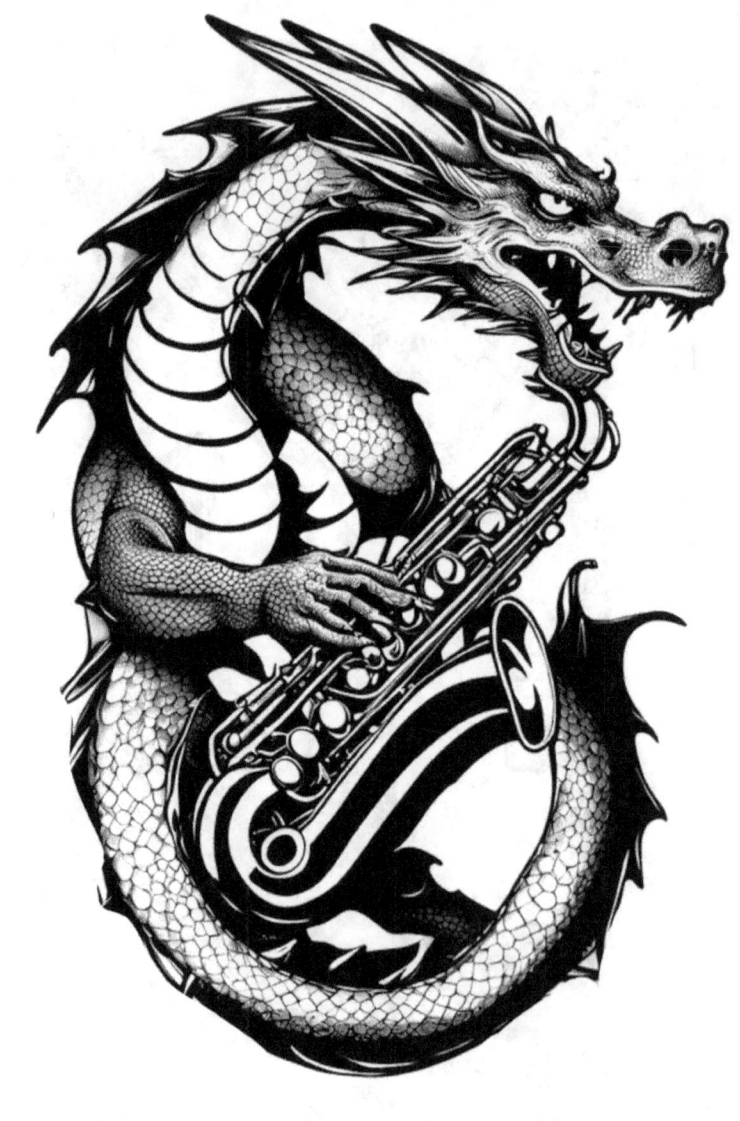
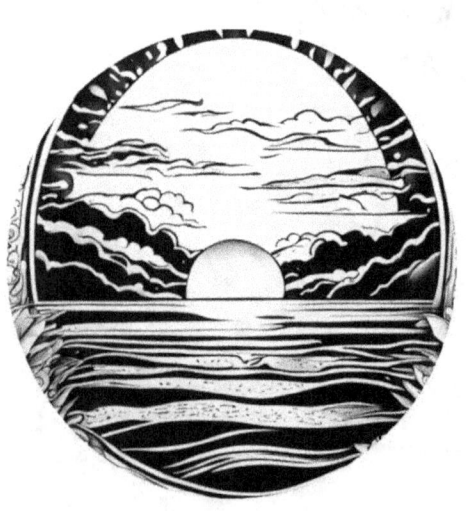
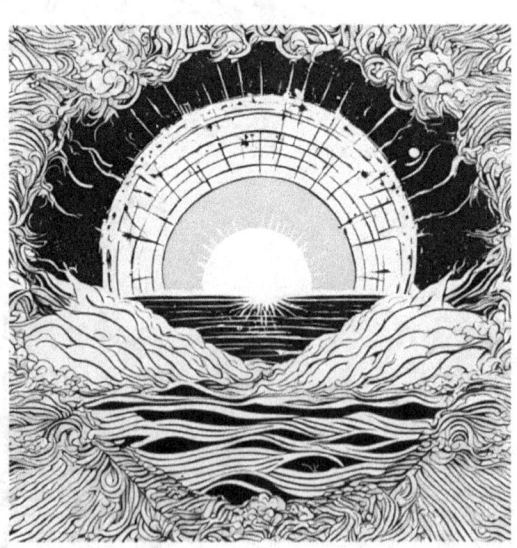

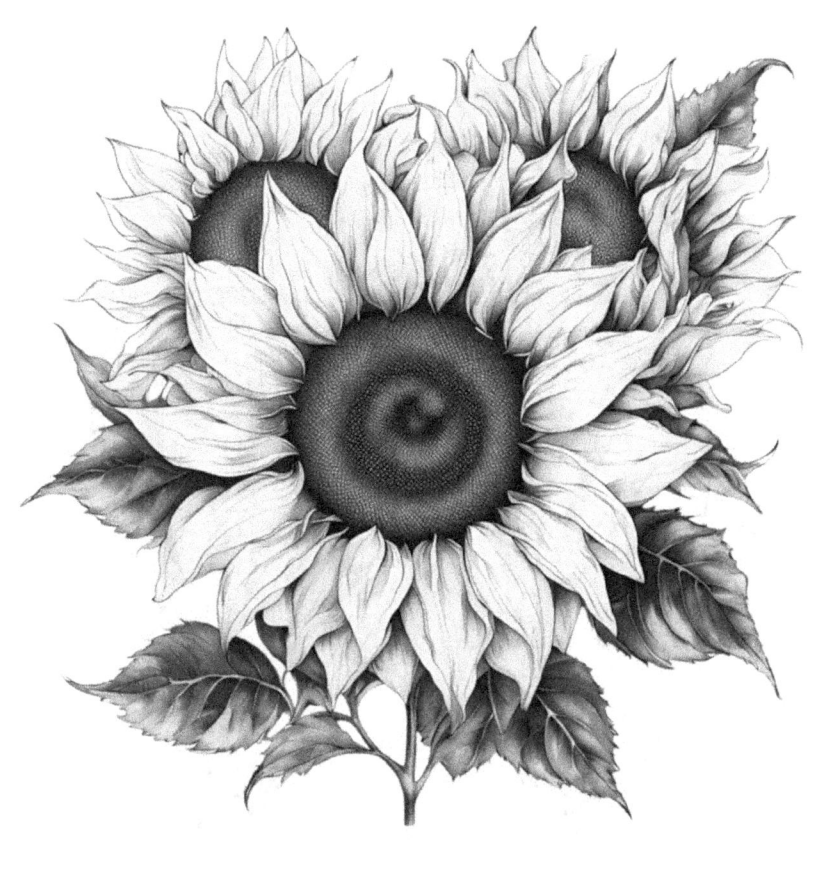
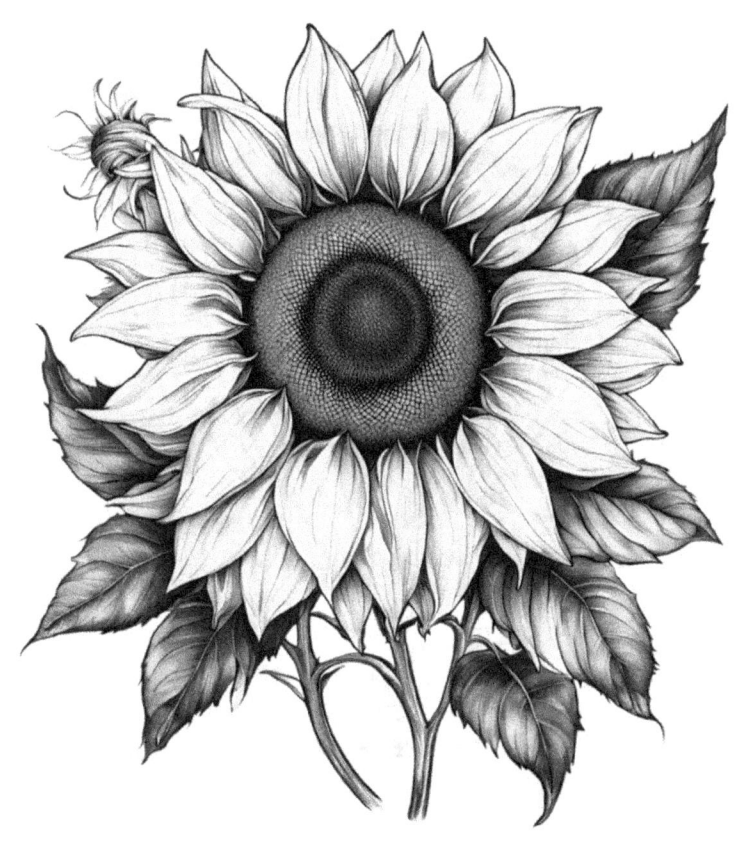

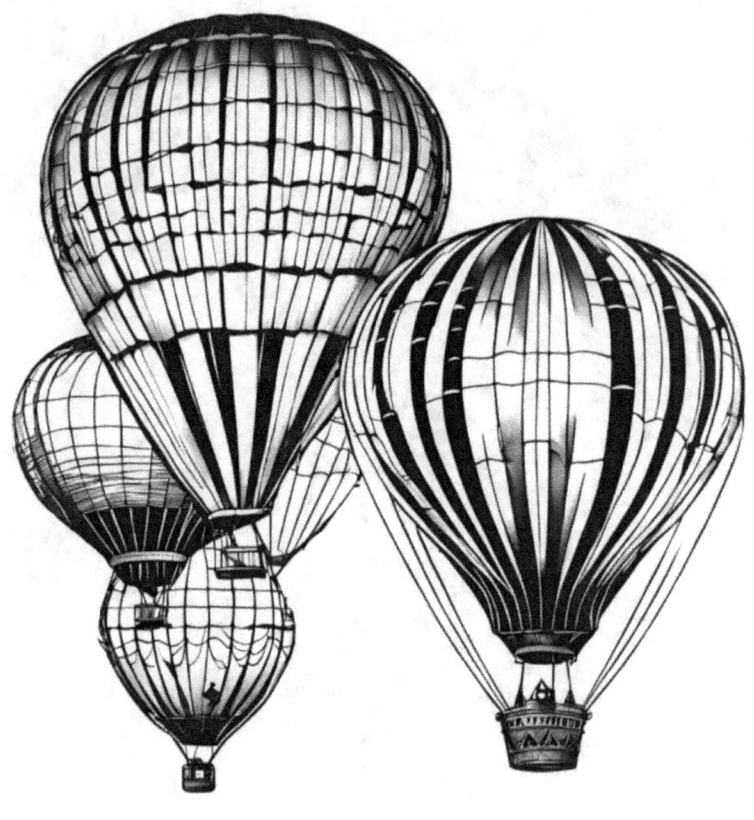
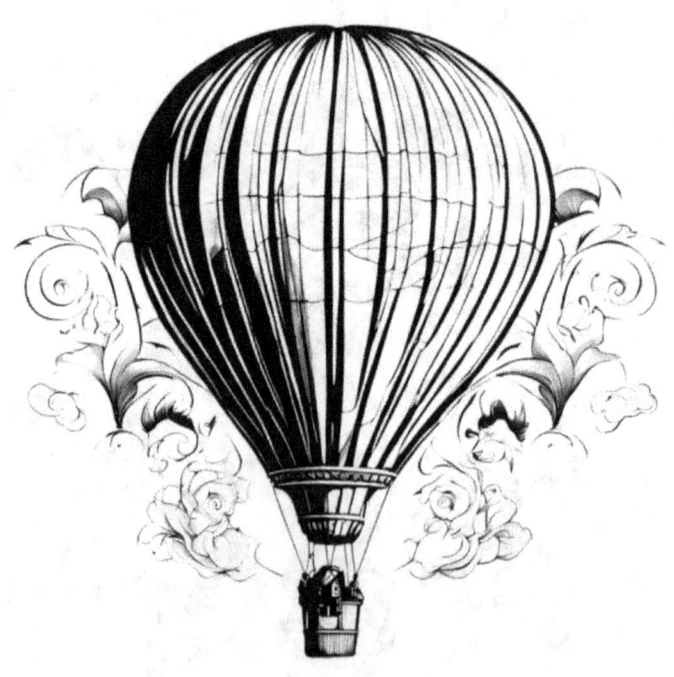

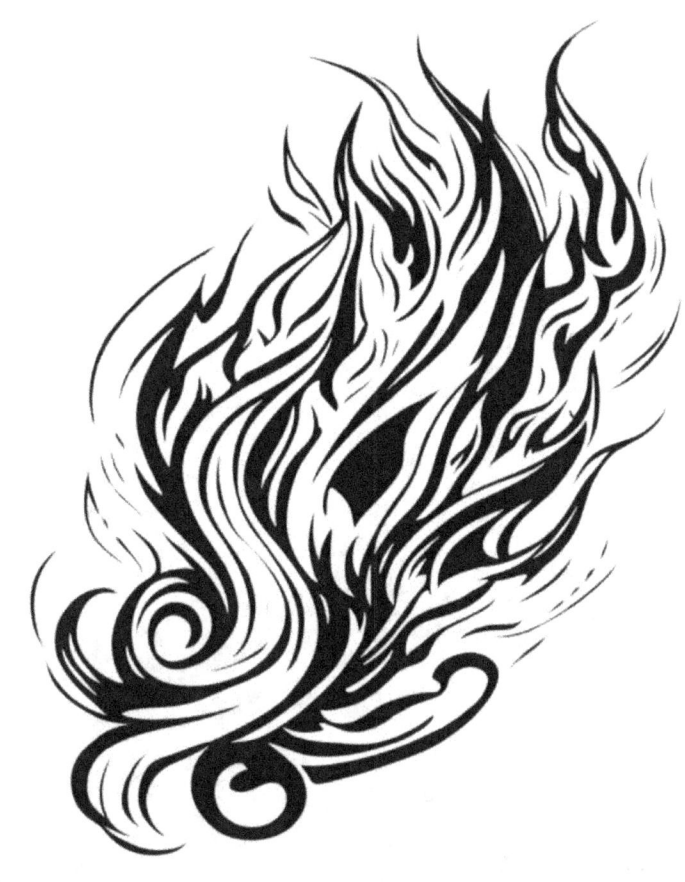
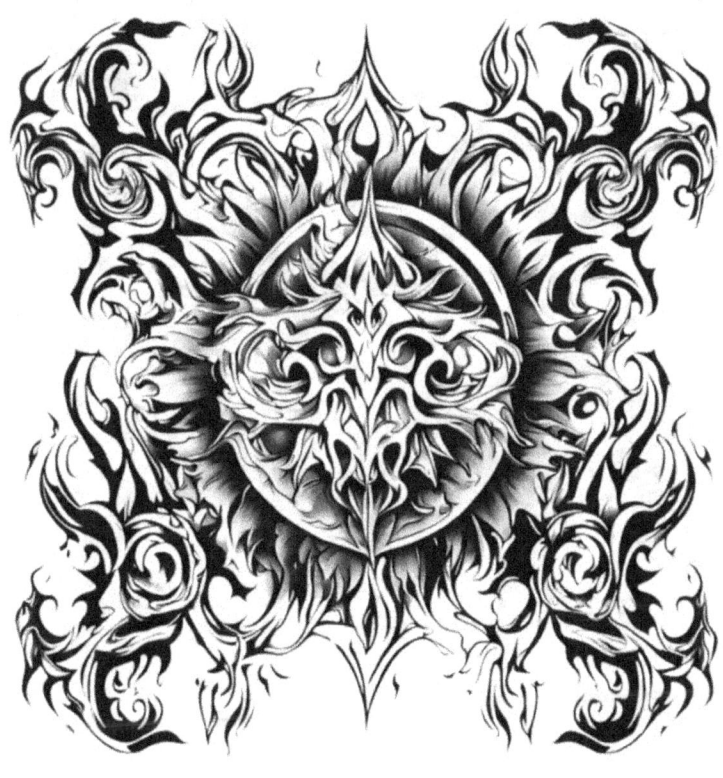

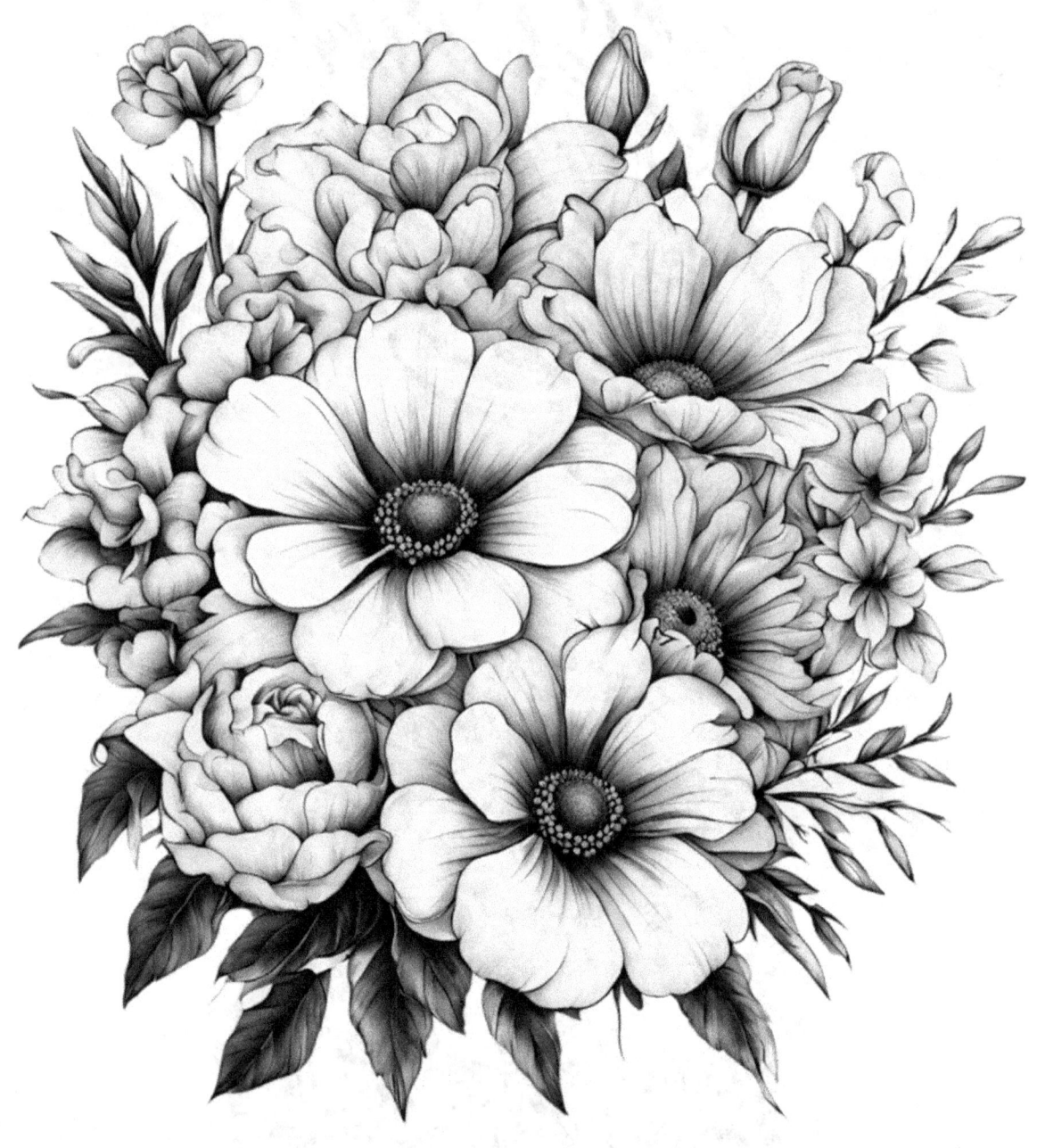

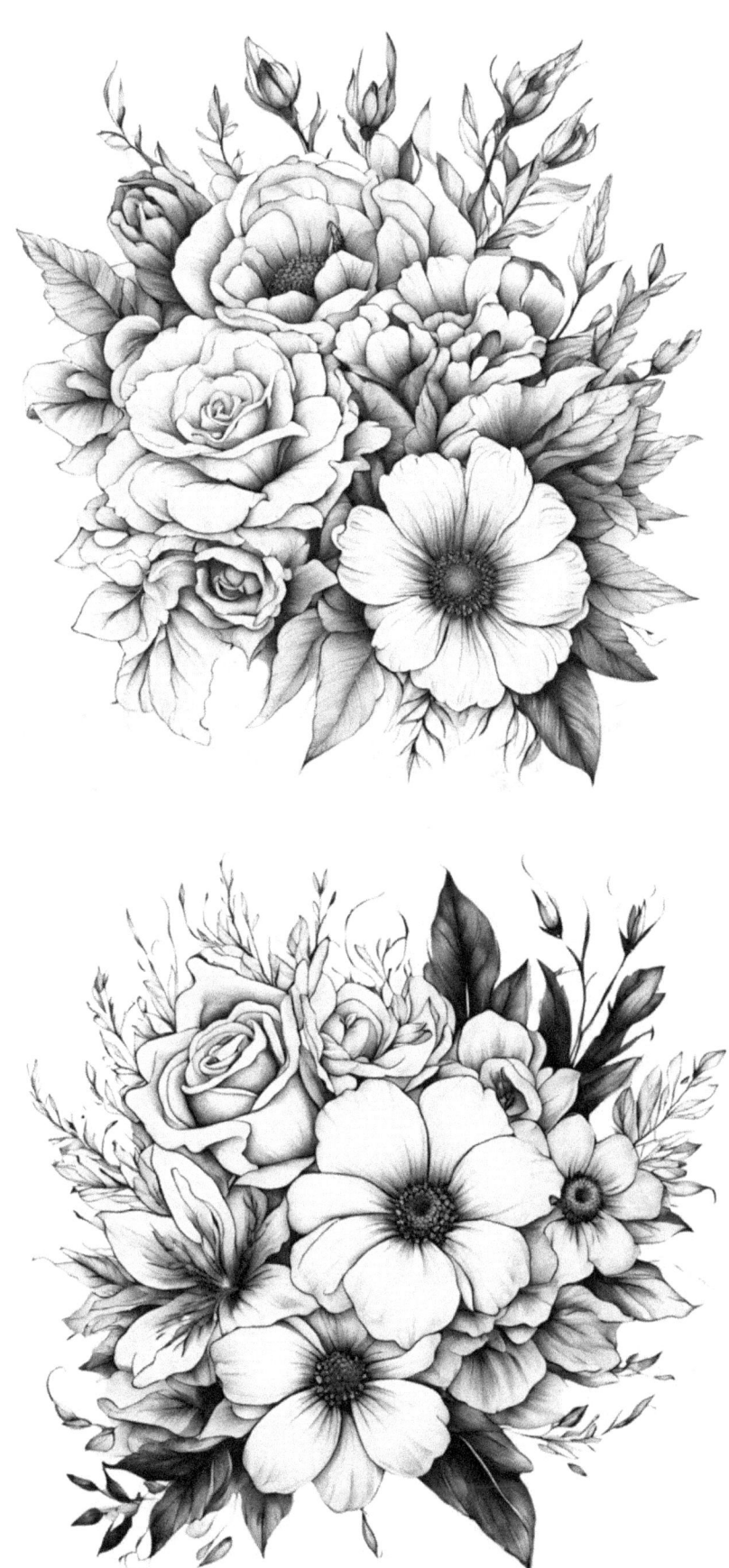

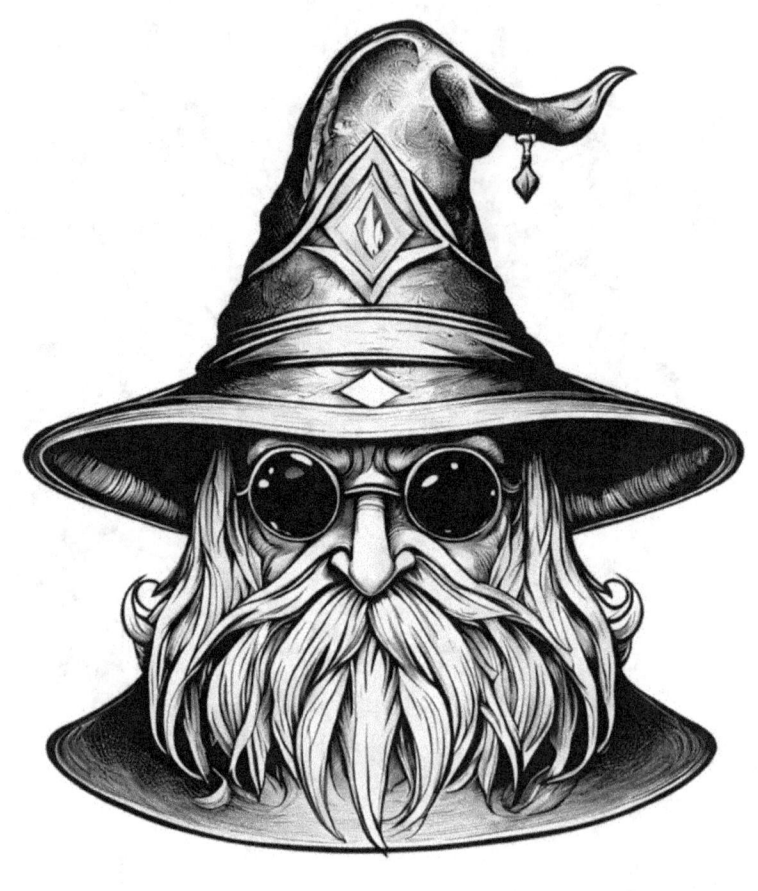
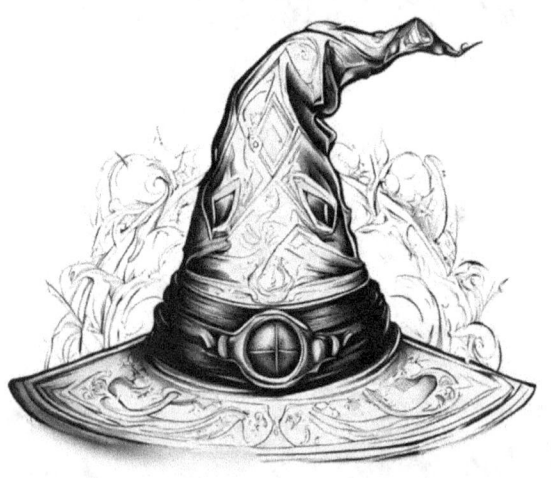
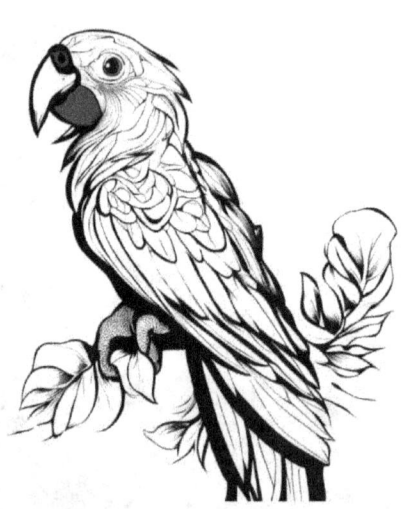

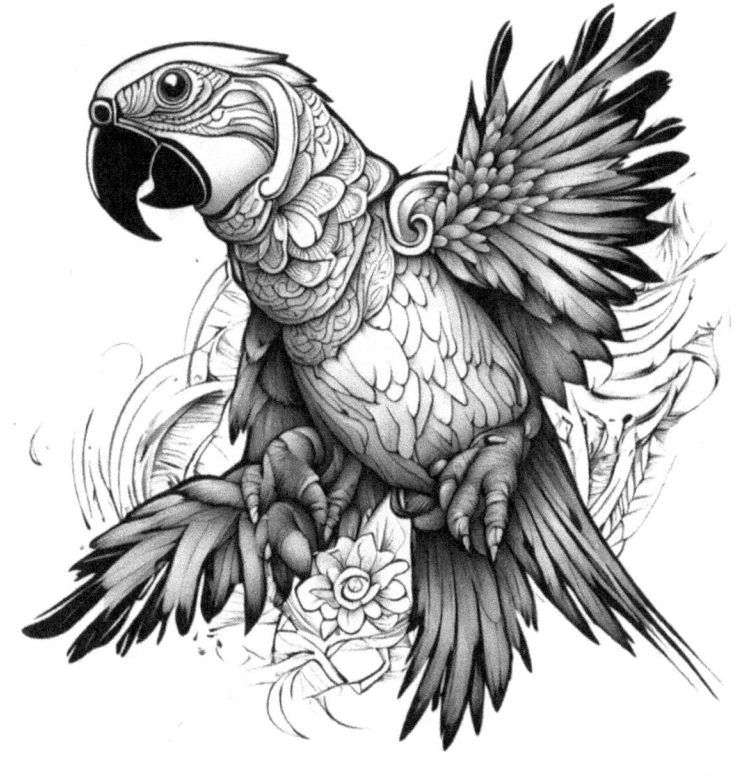
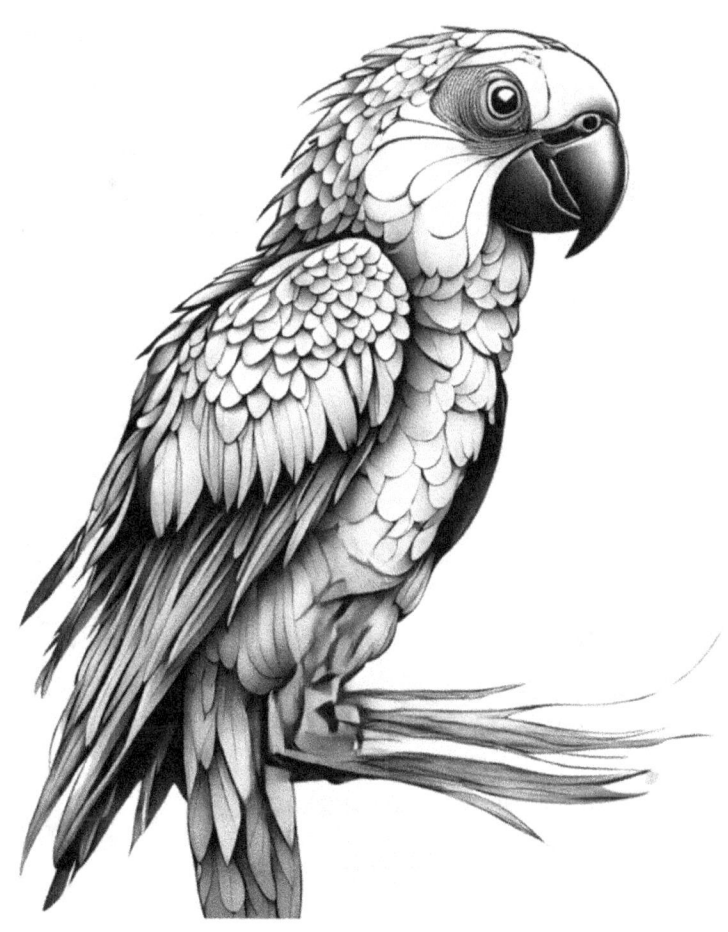

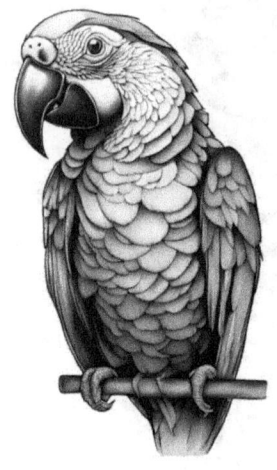
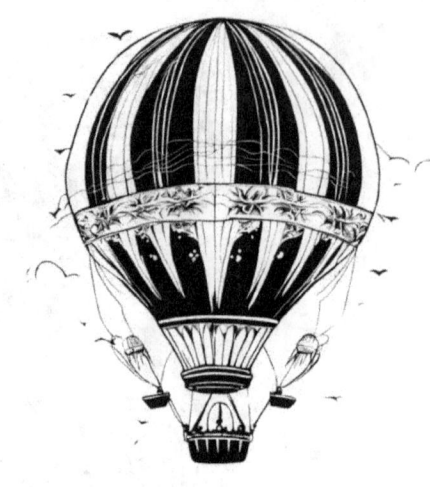
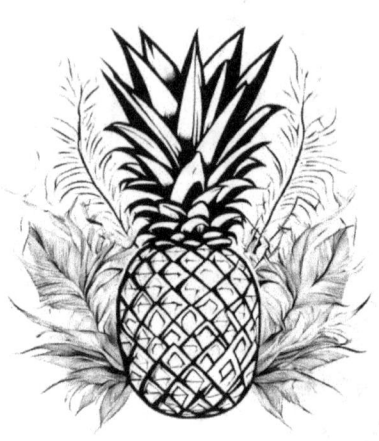
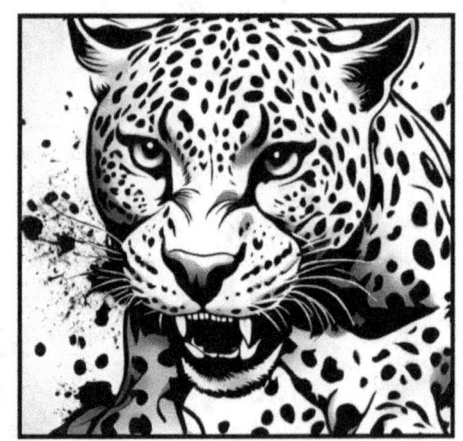

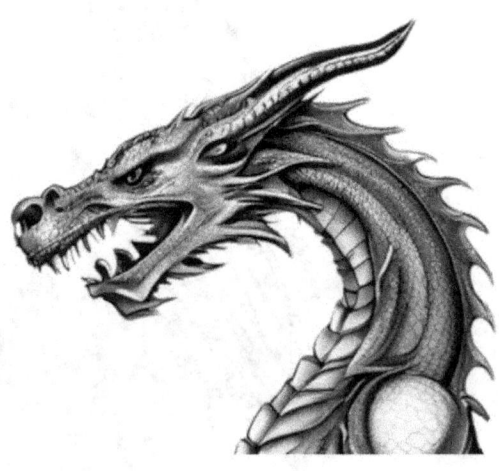

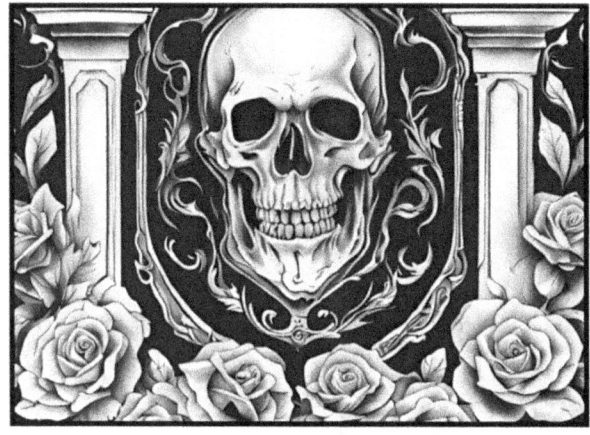
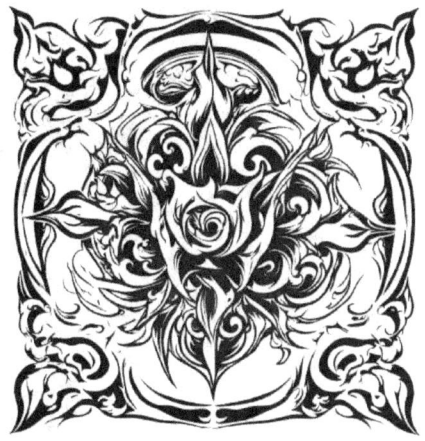
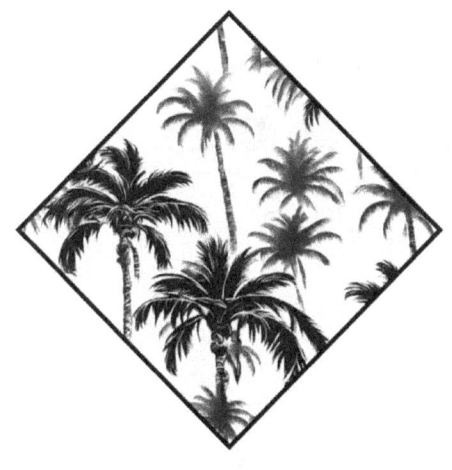
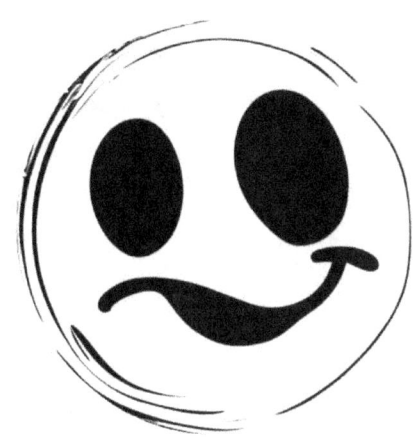
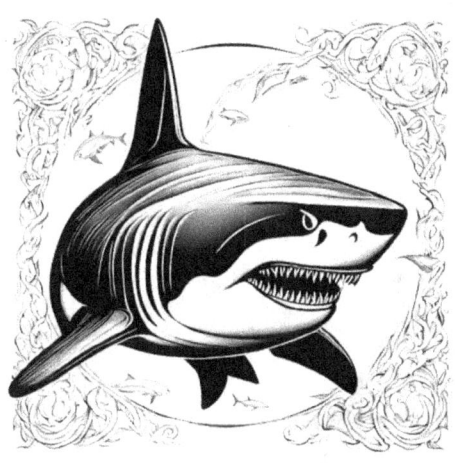
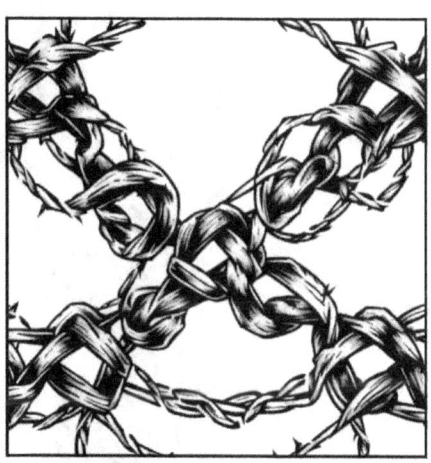

89

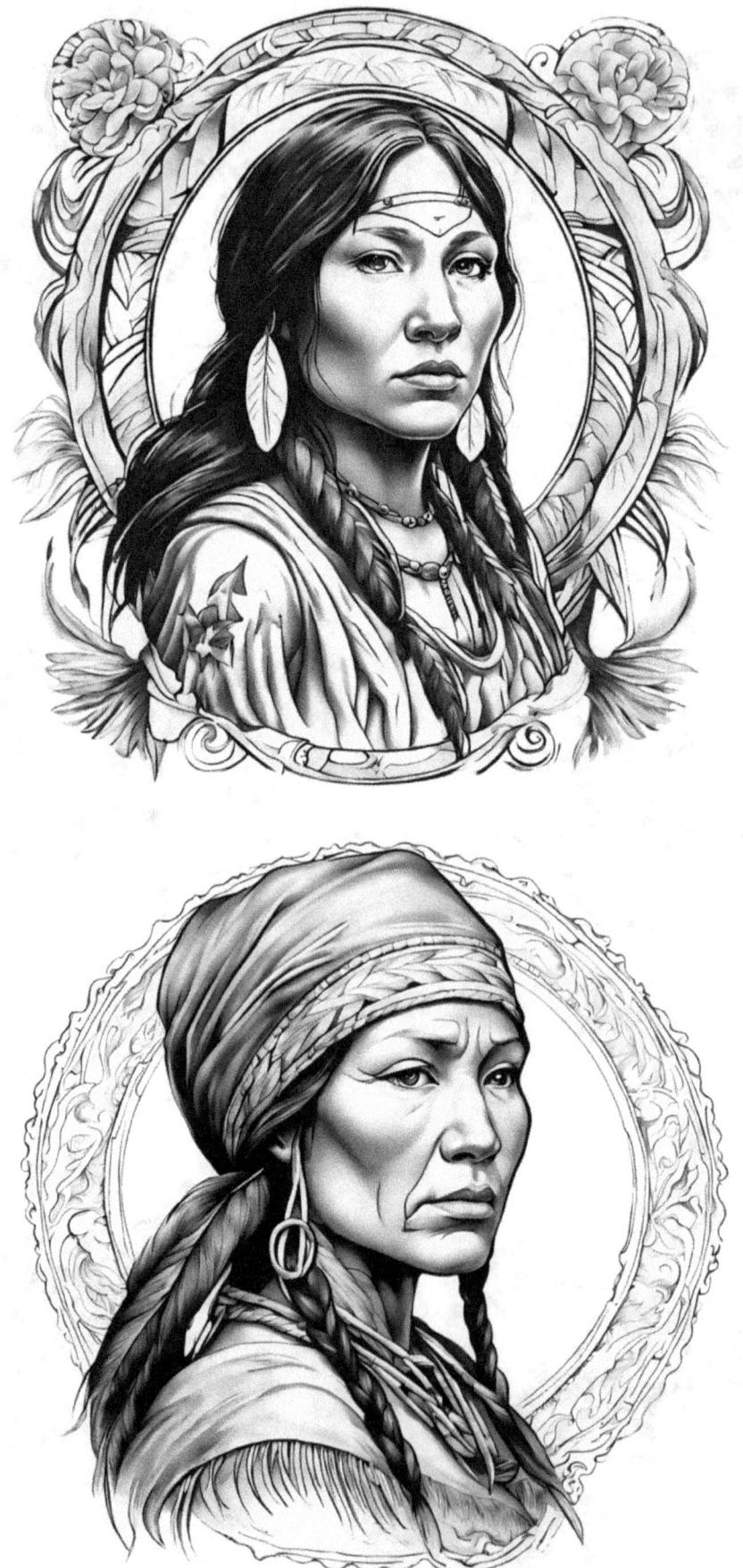

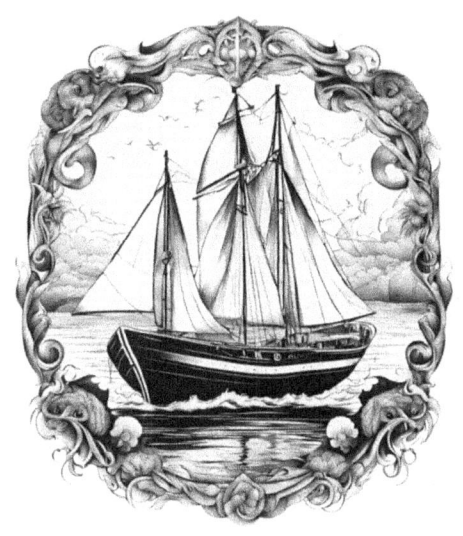
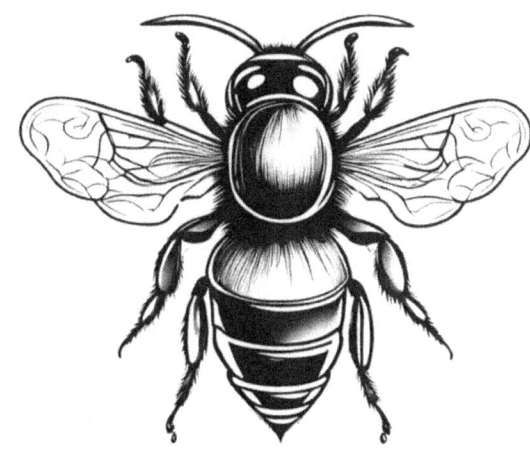
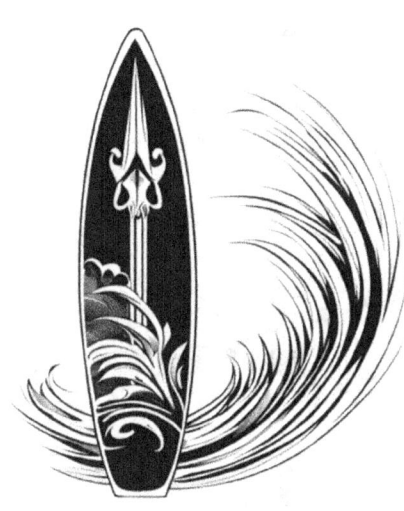
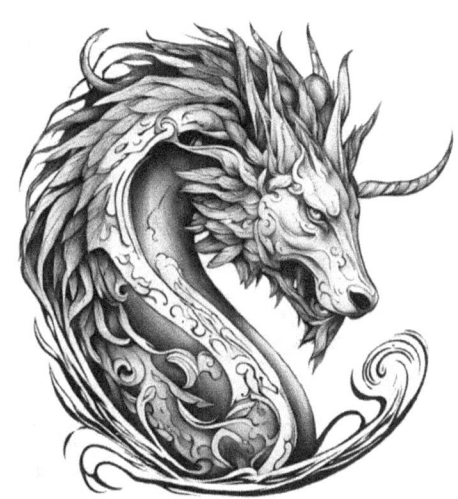
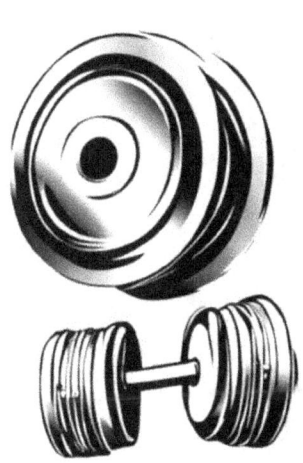
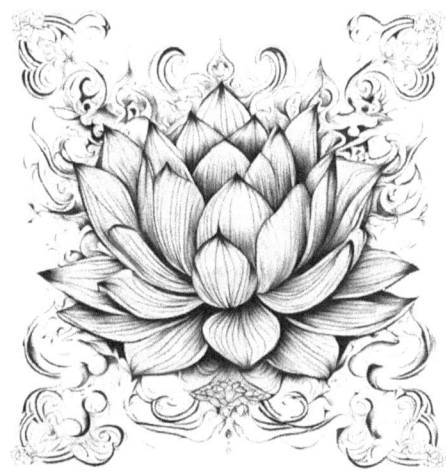

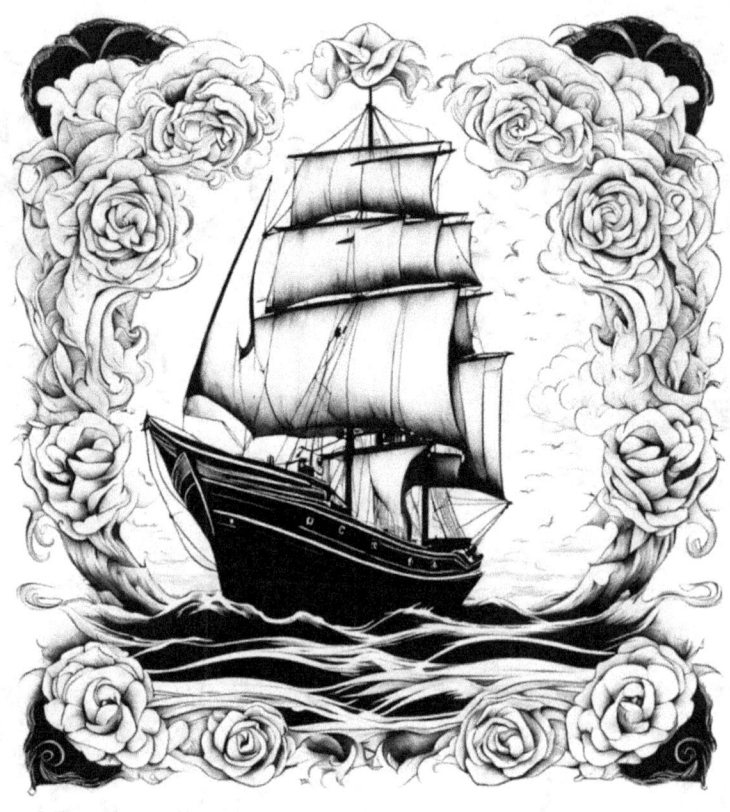
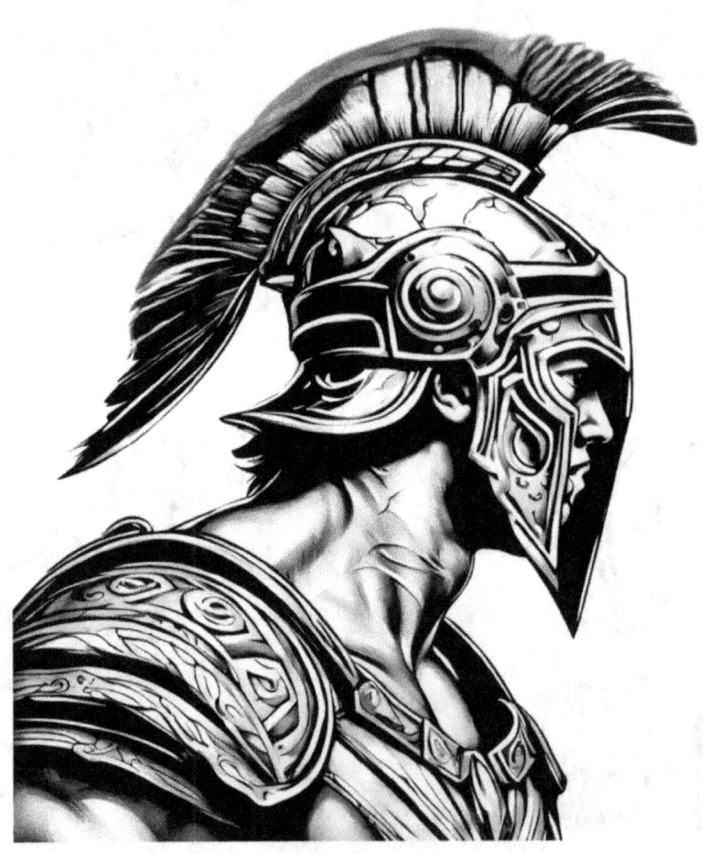

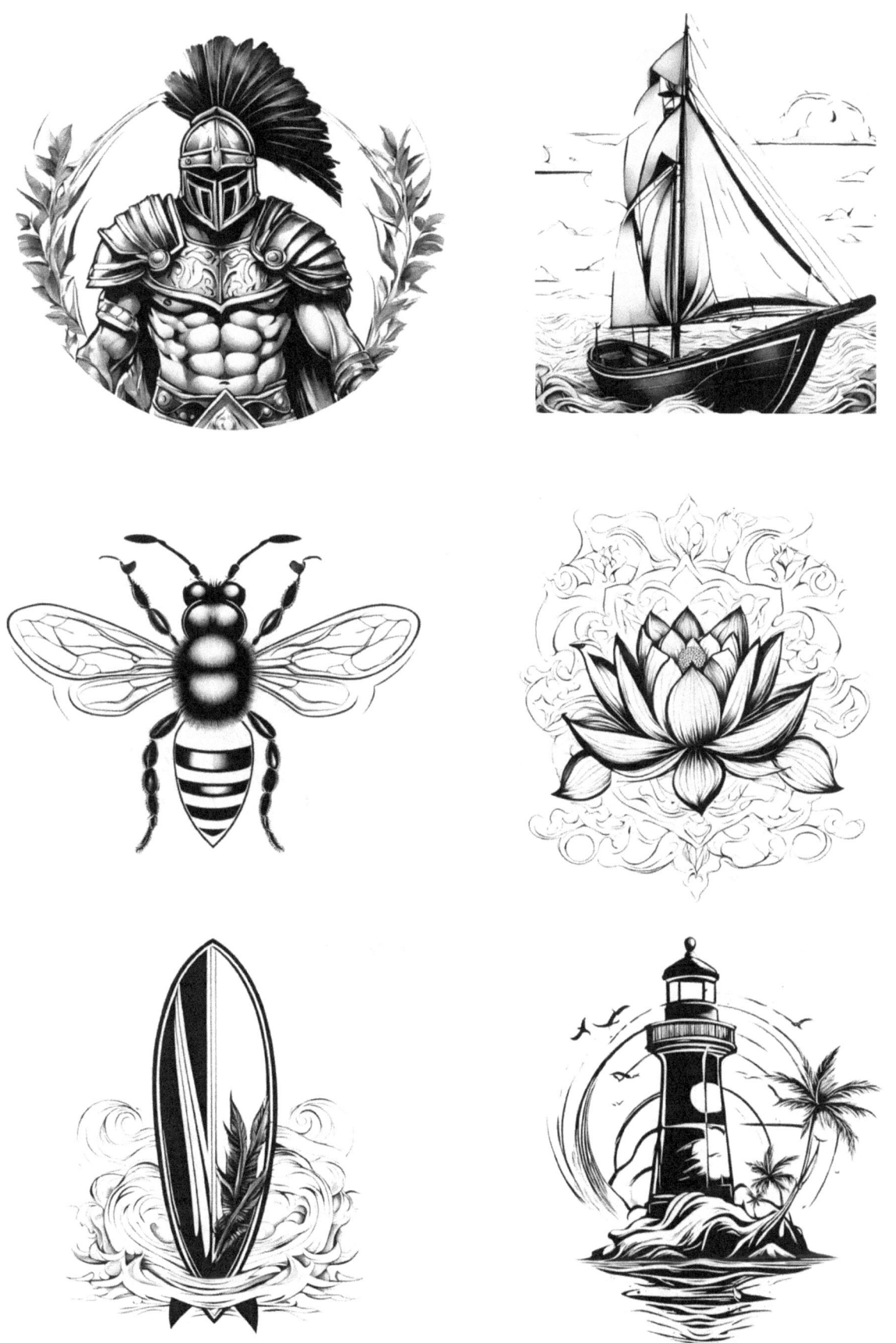

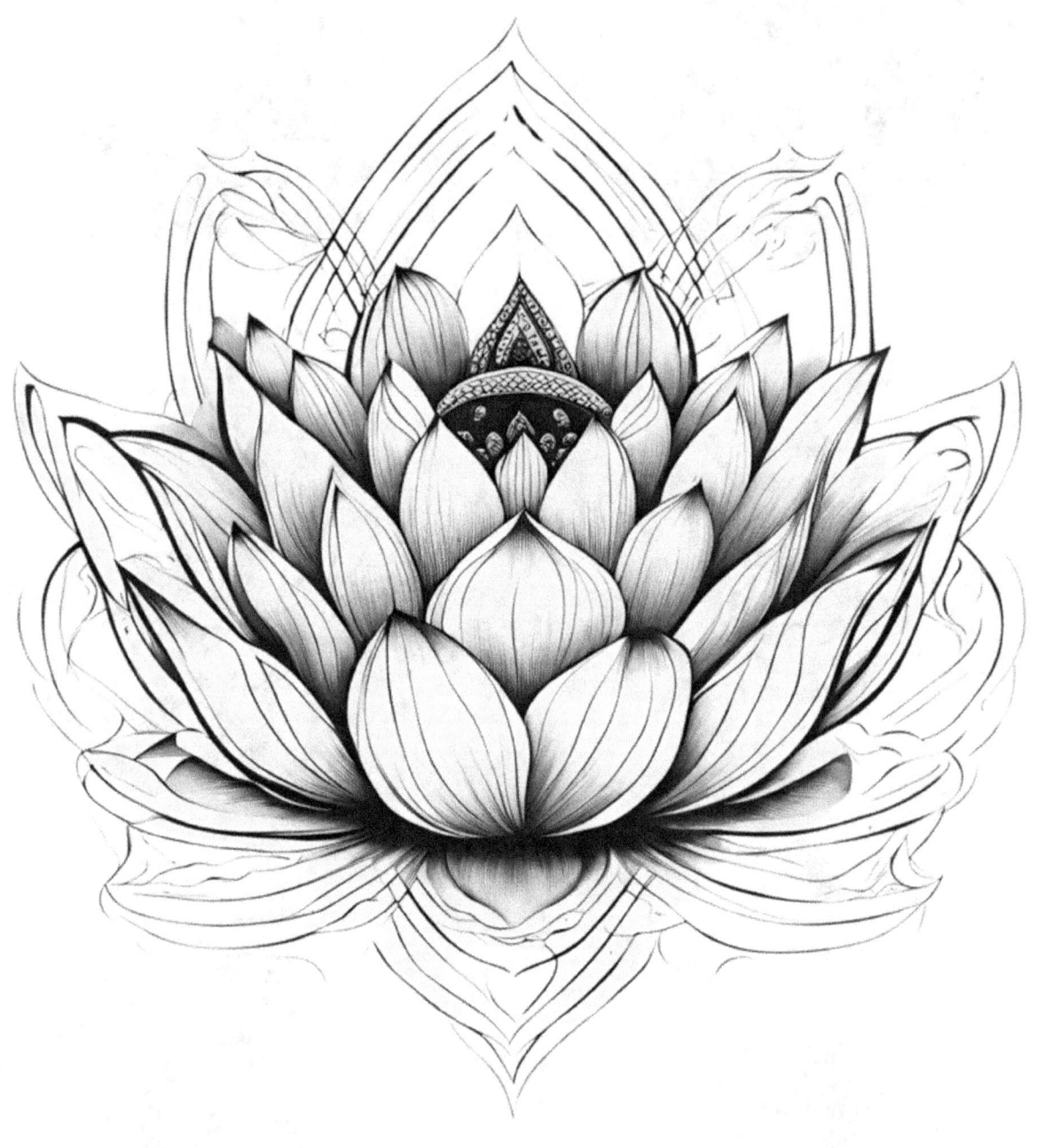

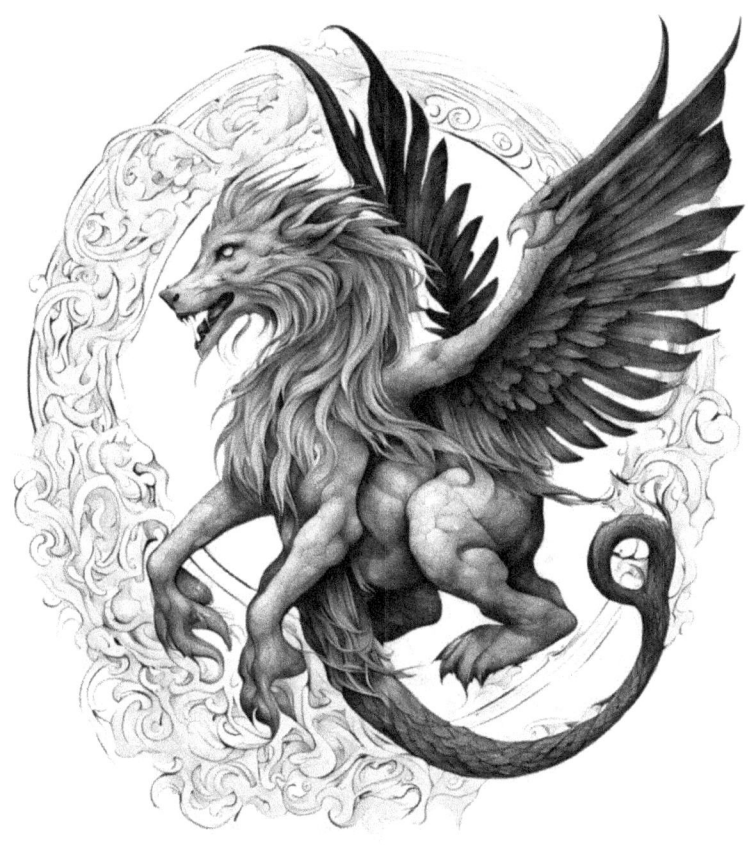
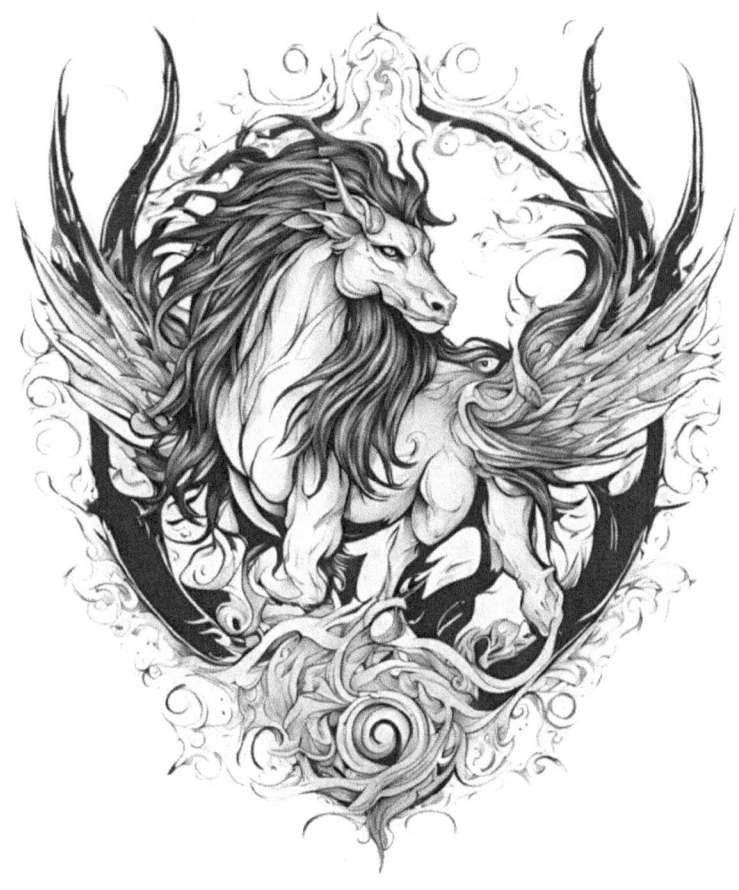

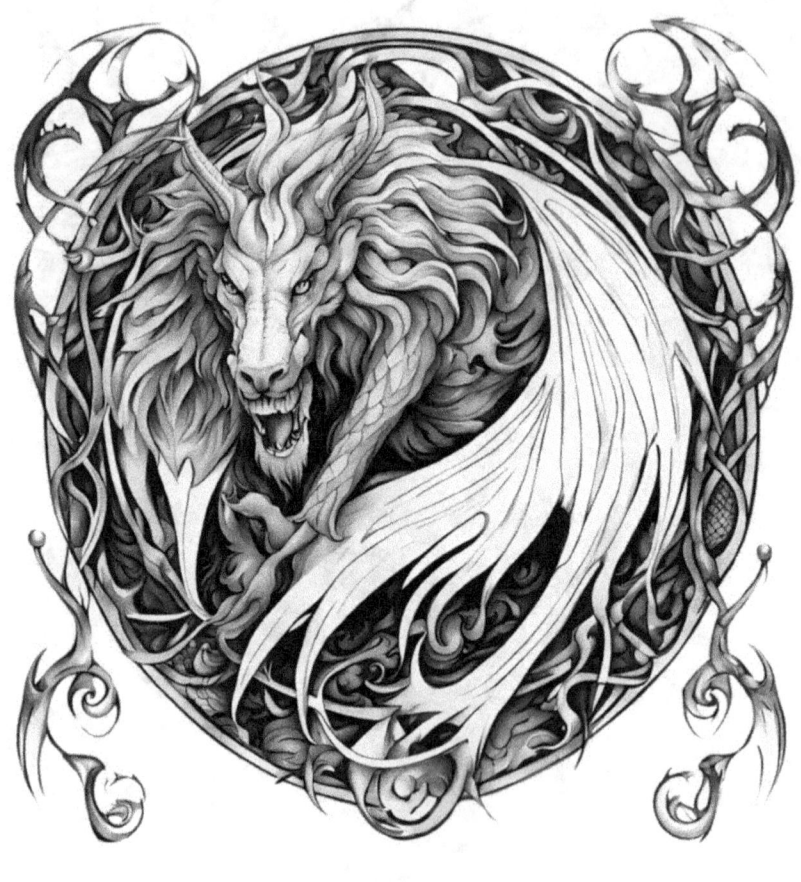
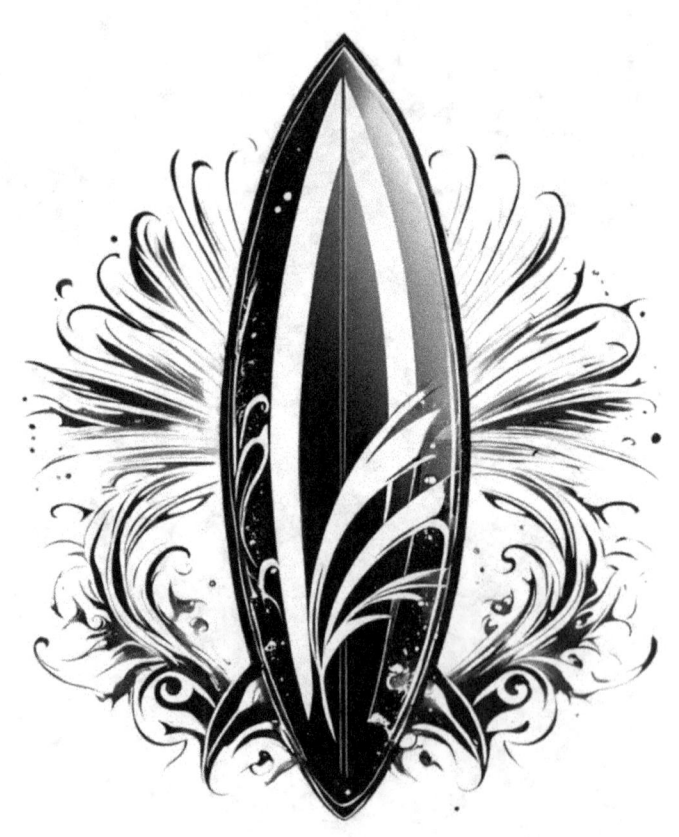

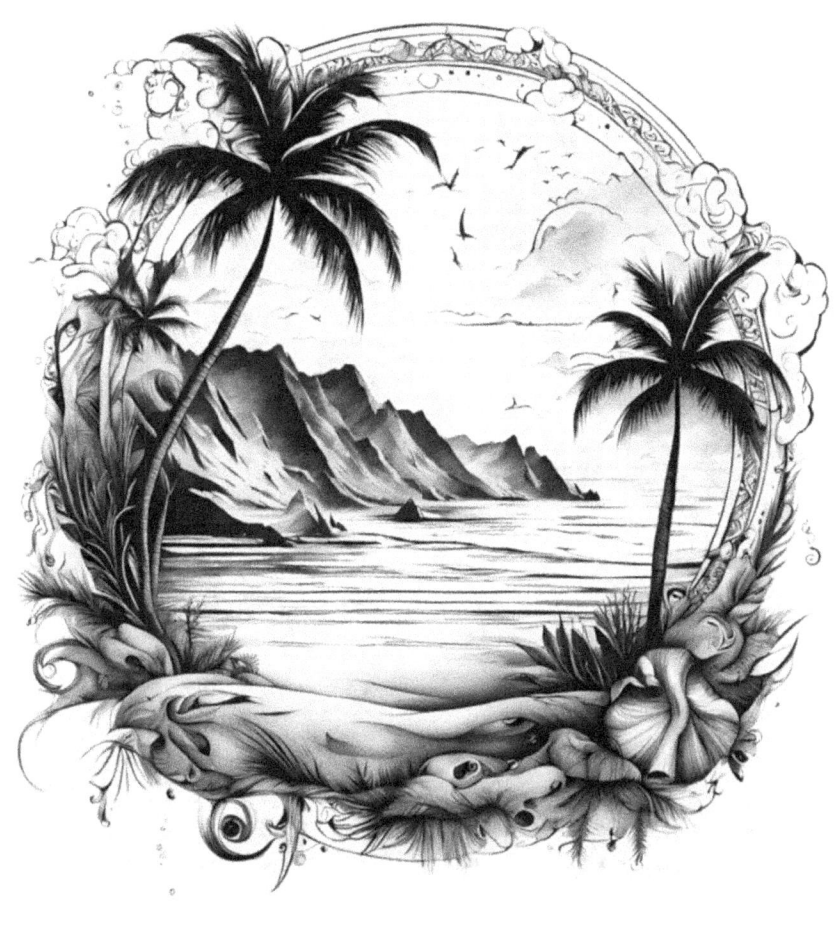
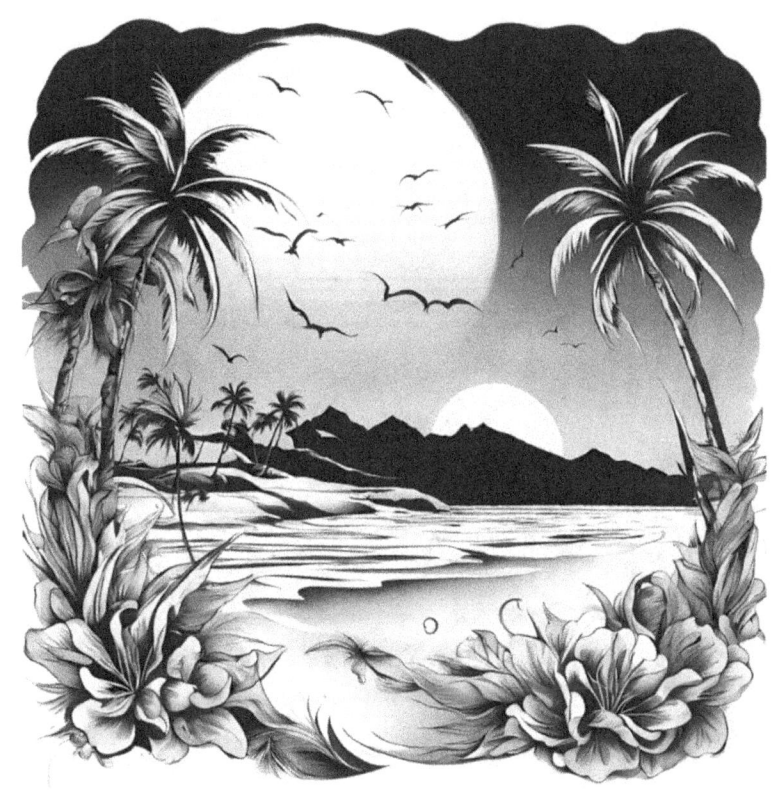

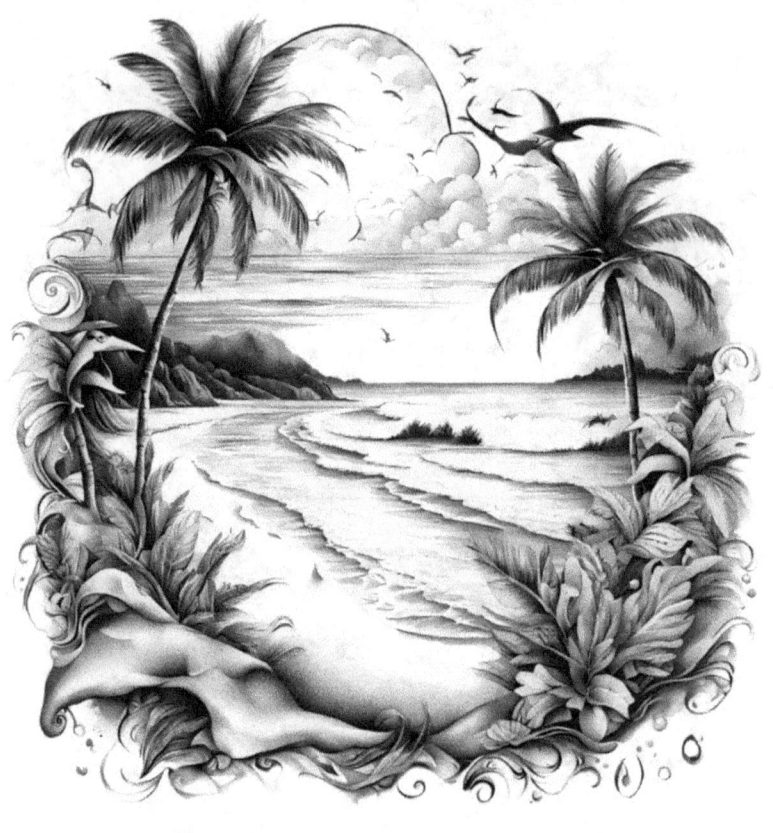
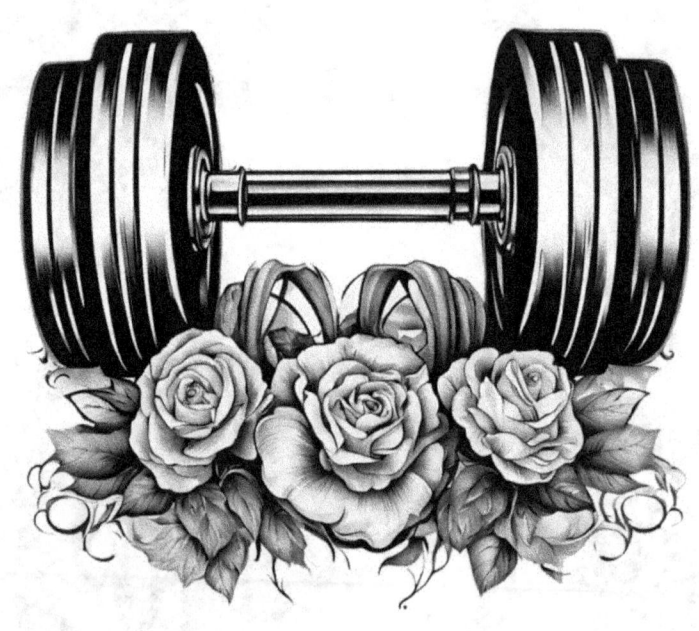

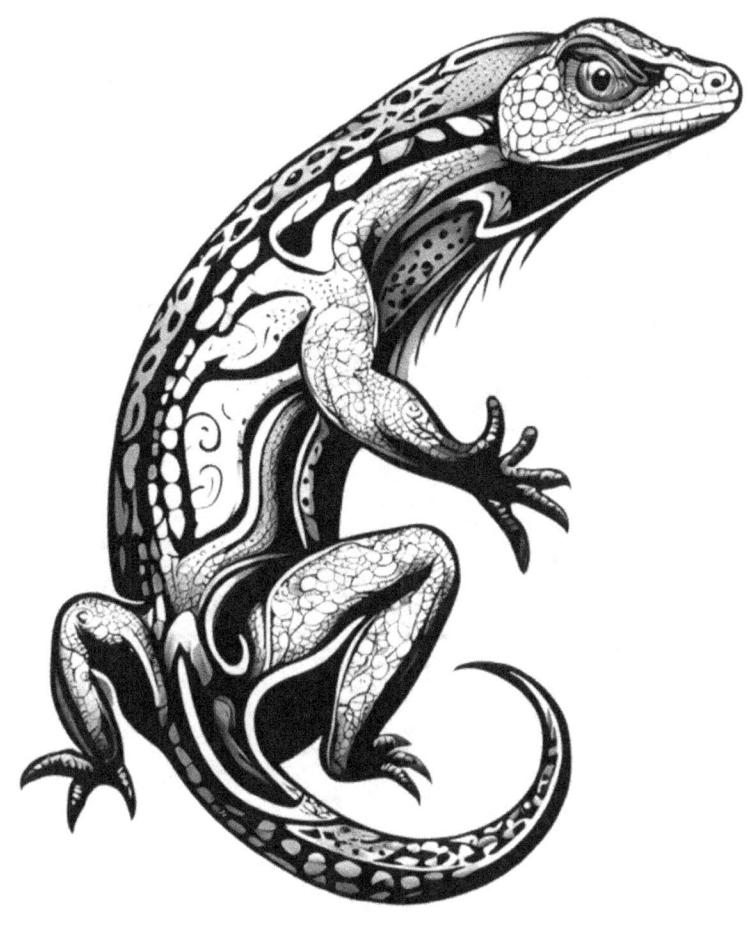
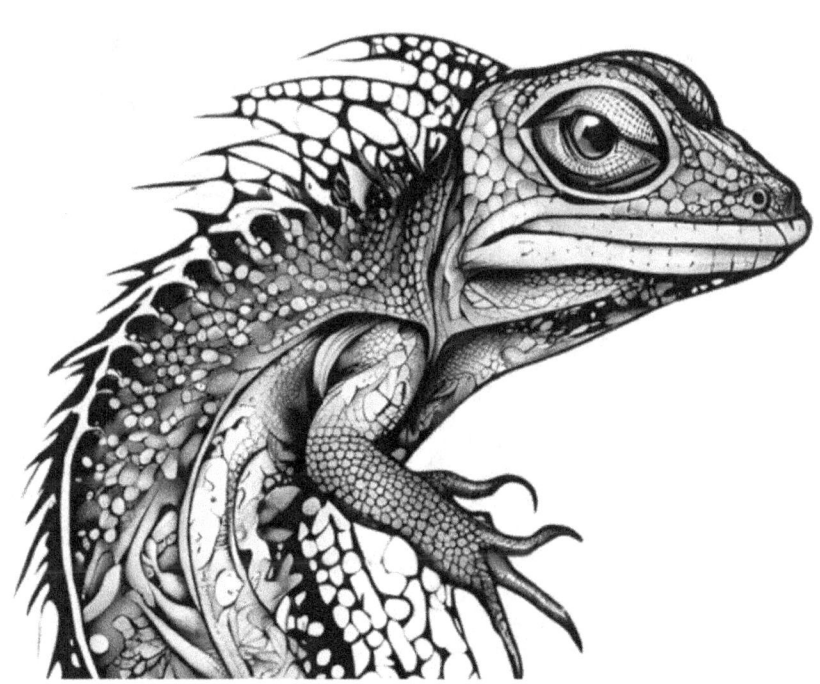

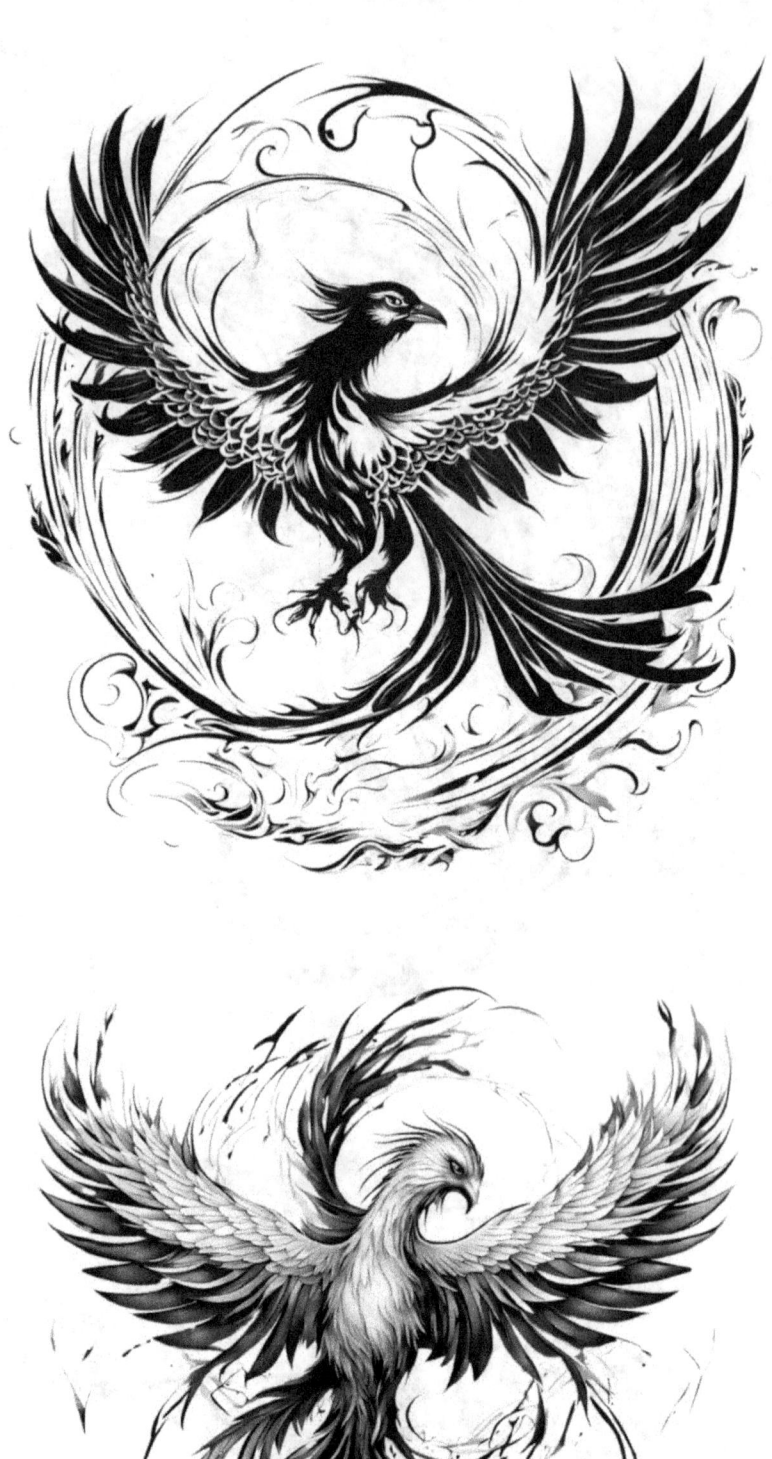

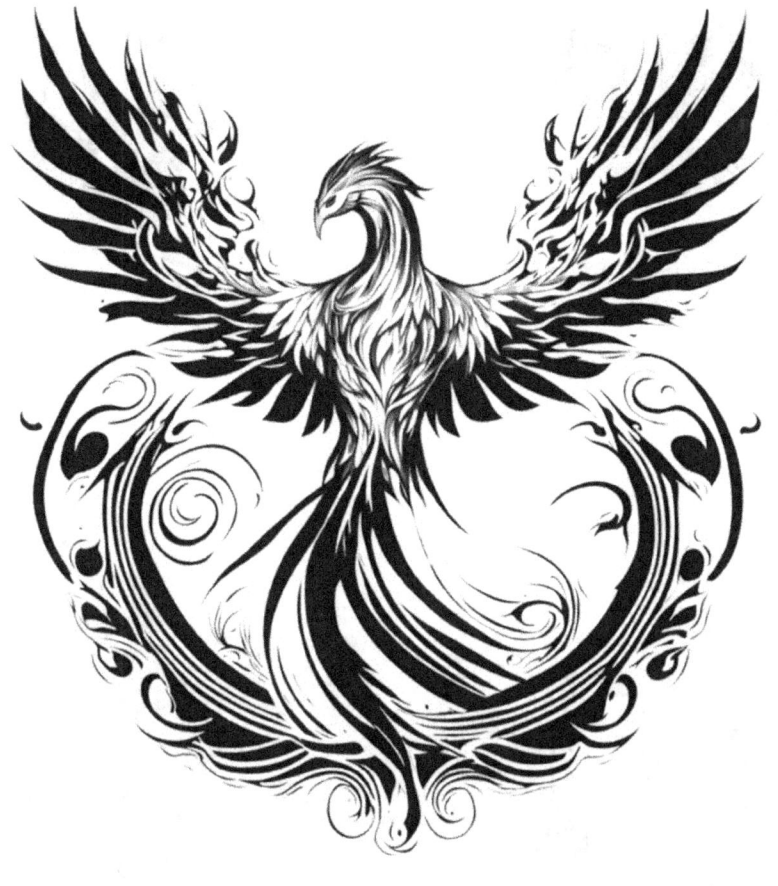
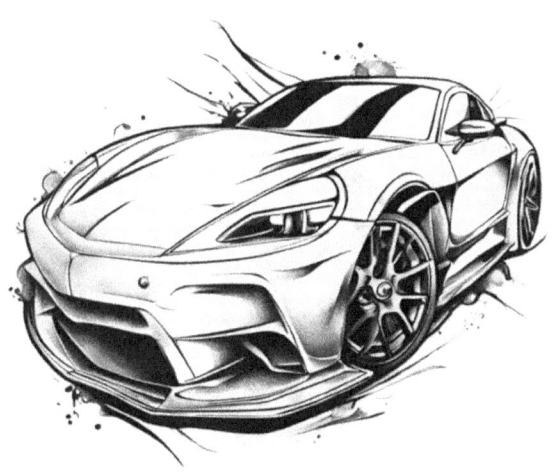
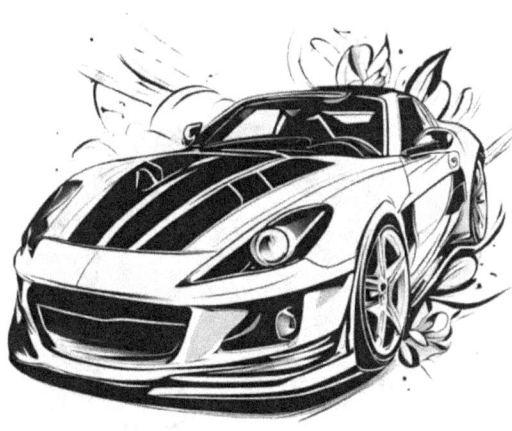

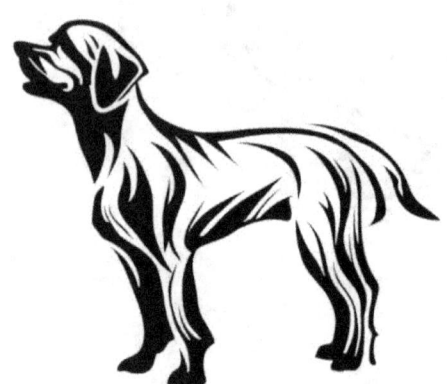
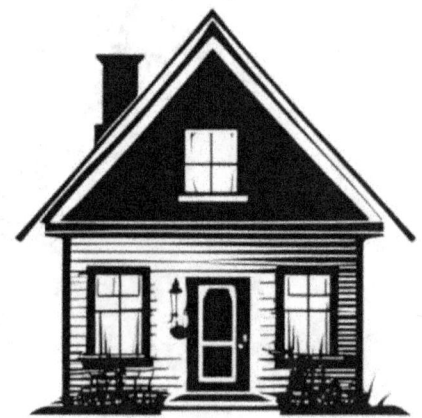
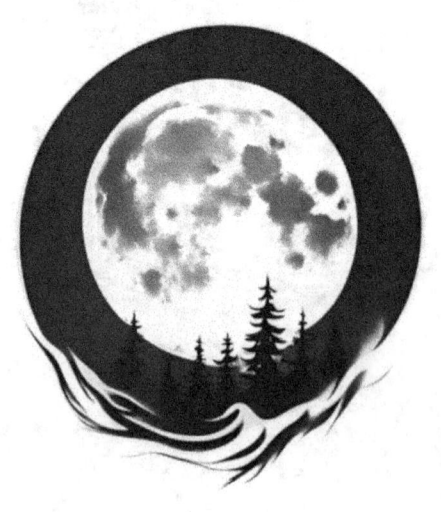
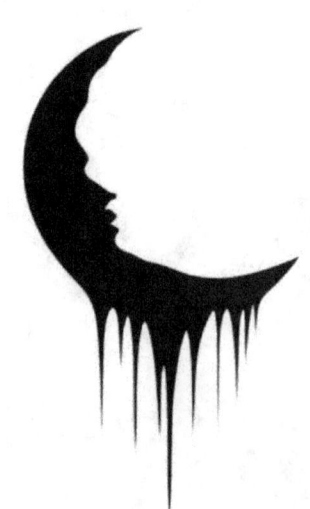

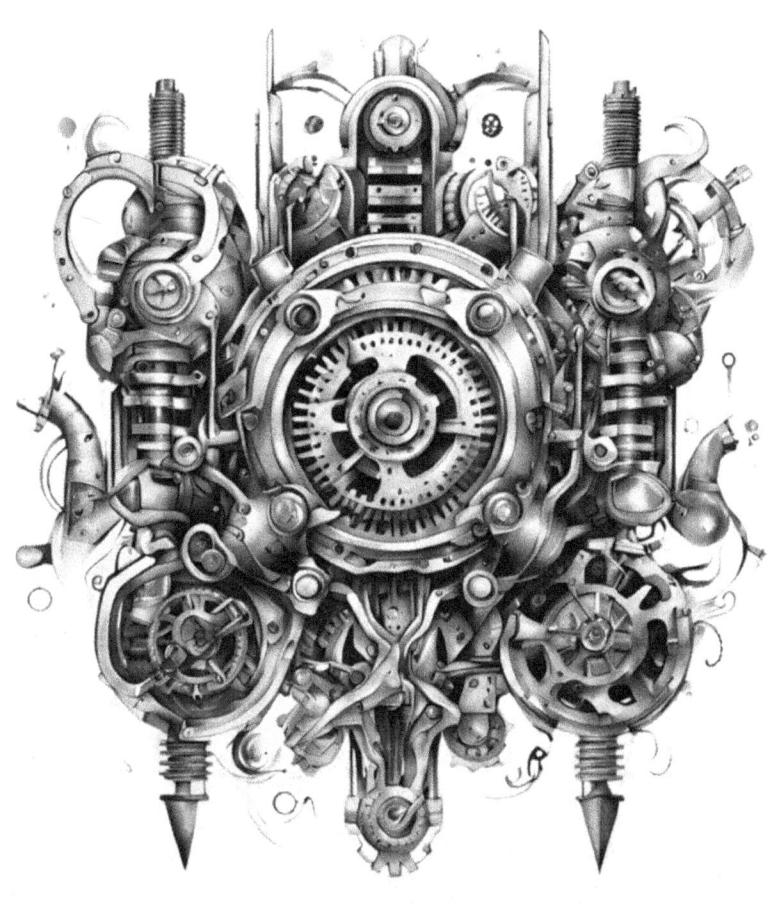
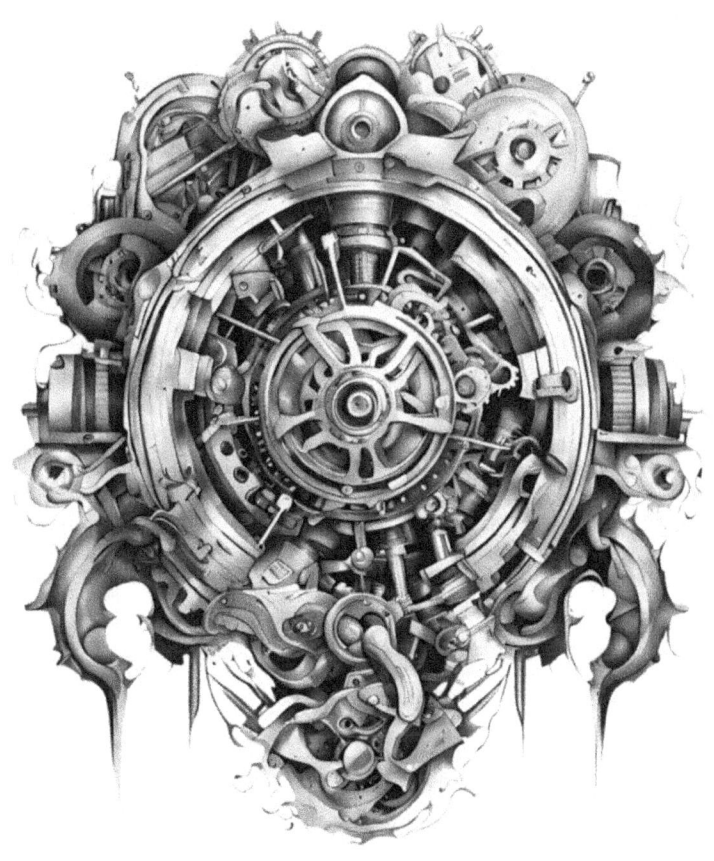

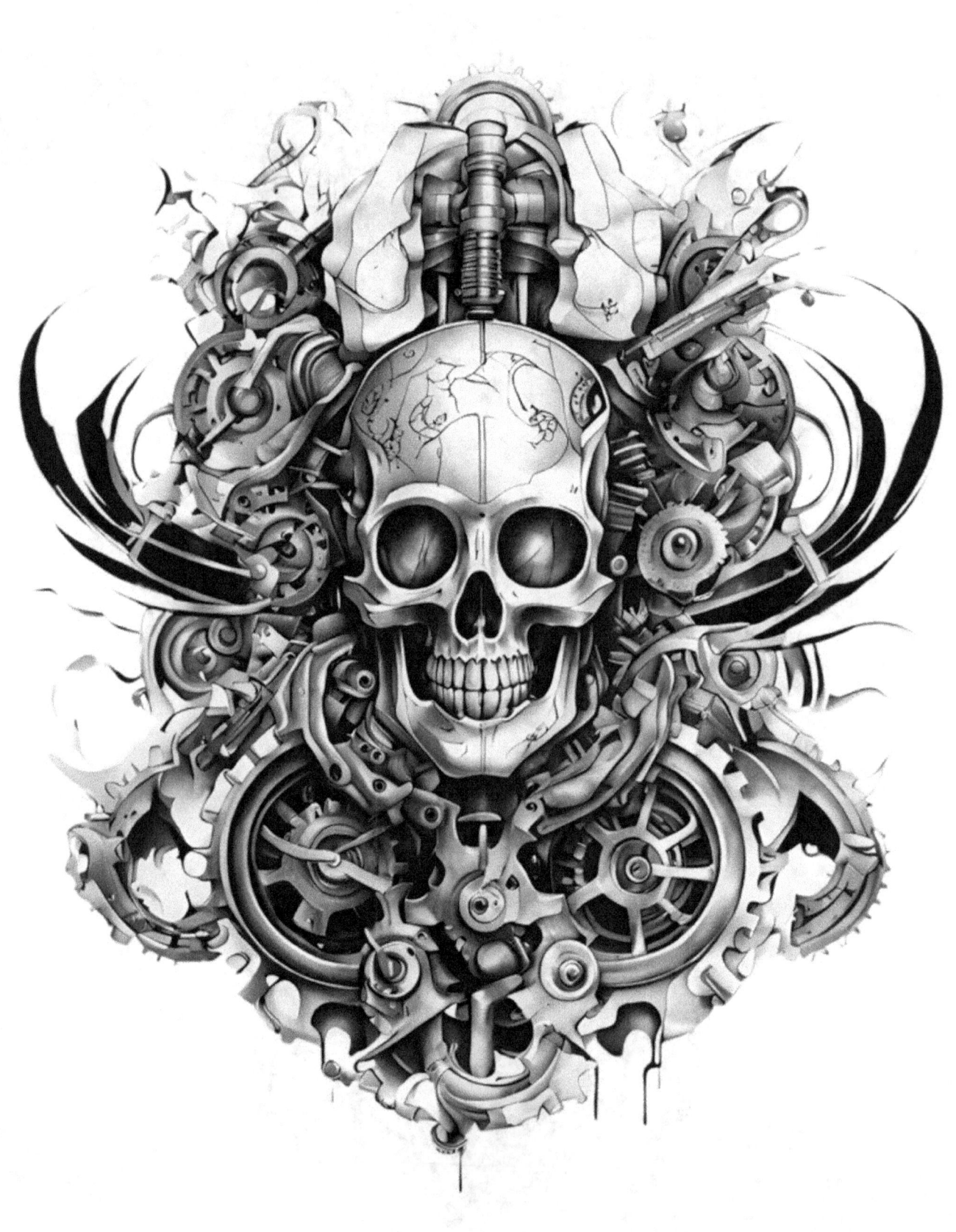

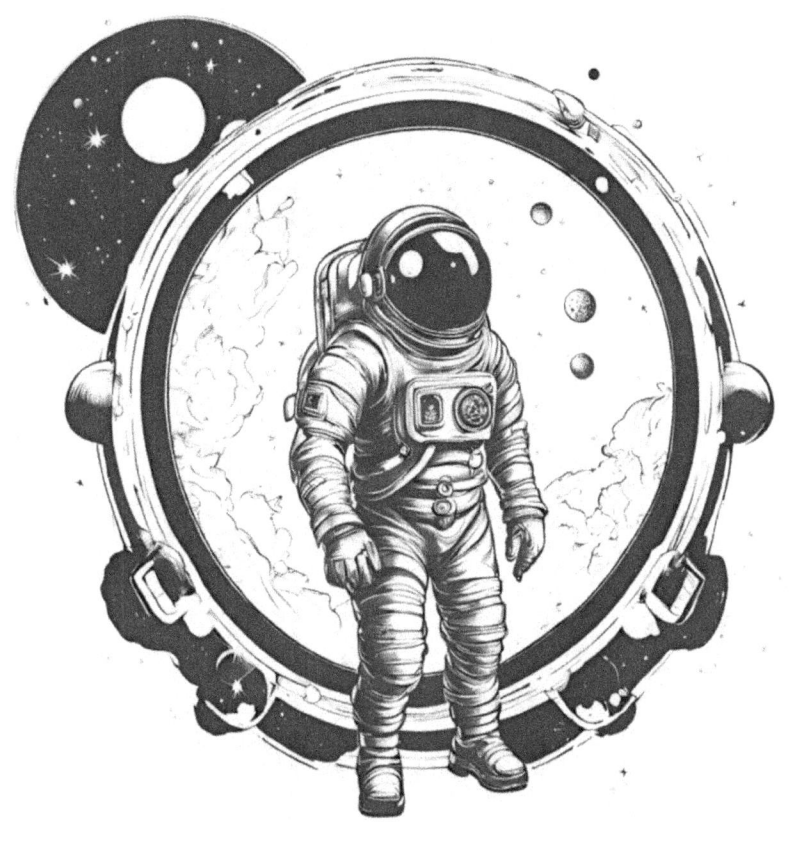
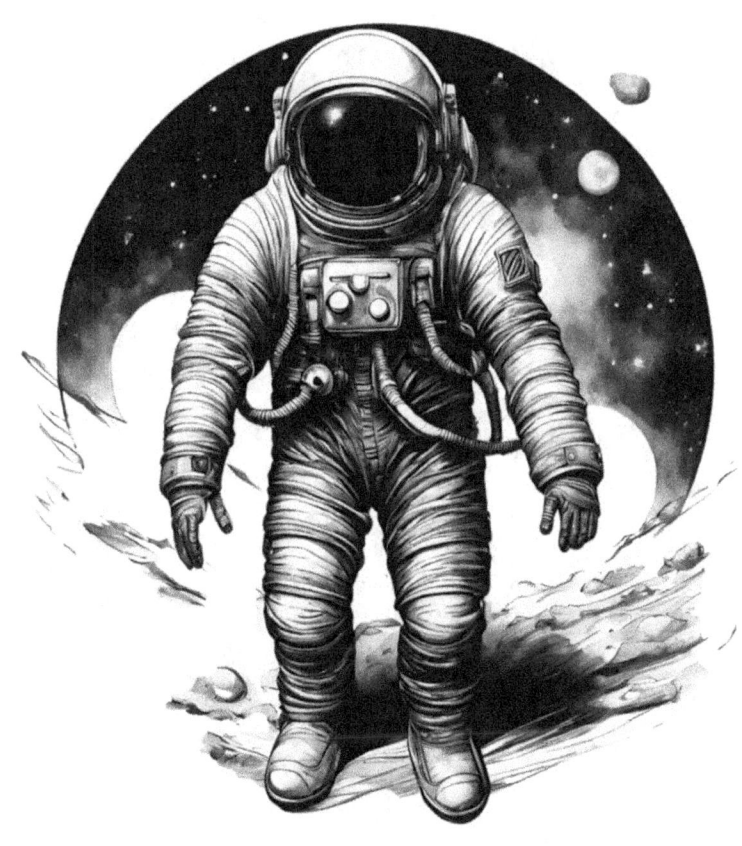

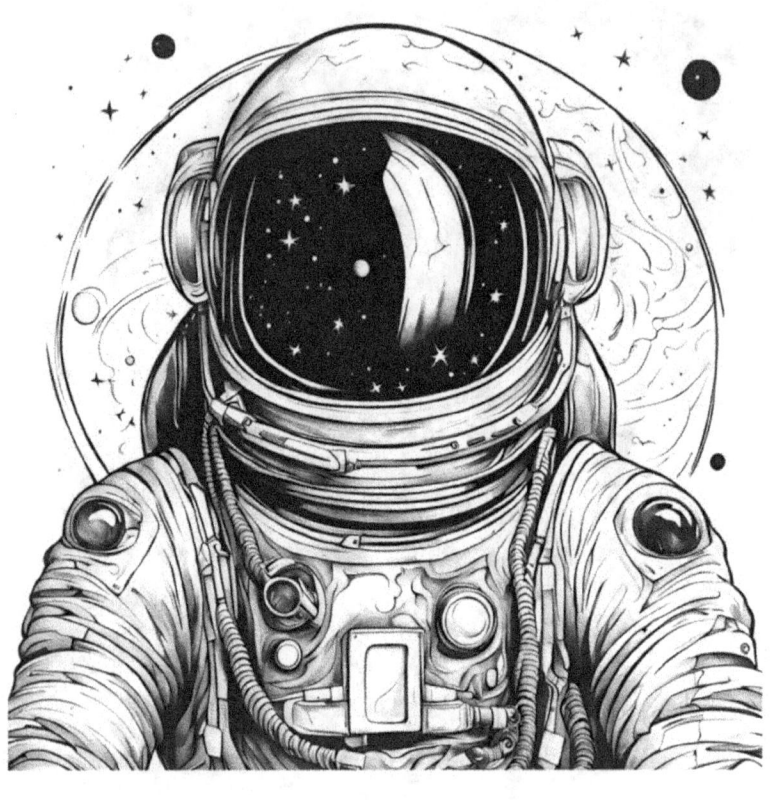
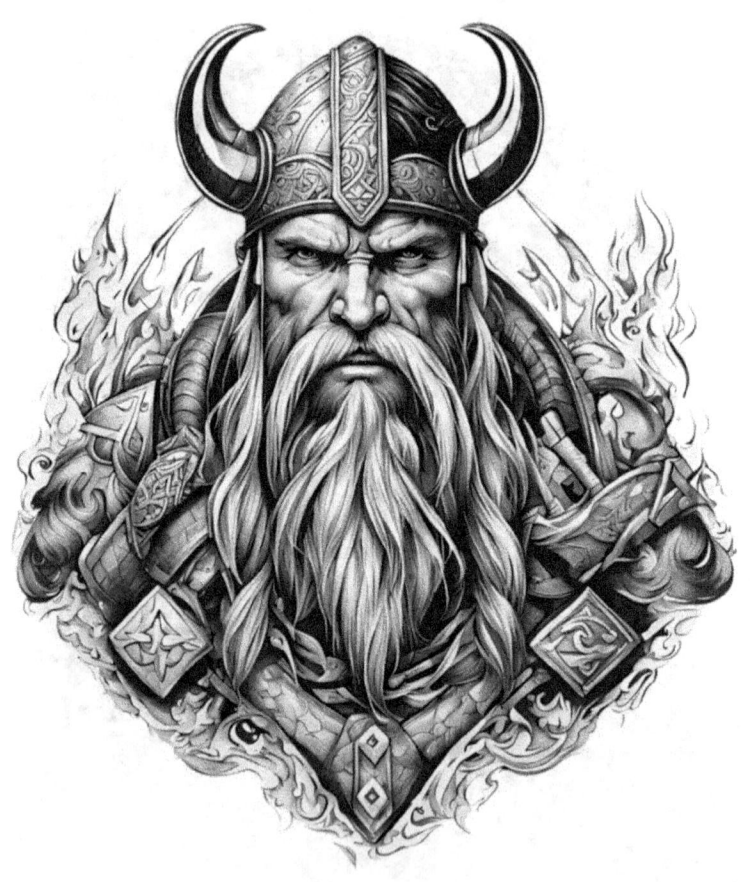

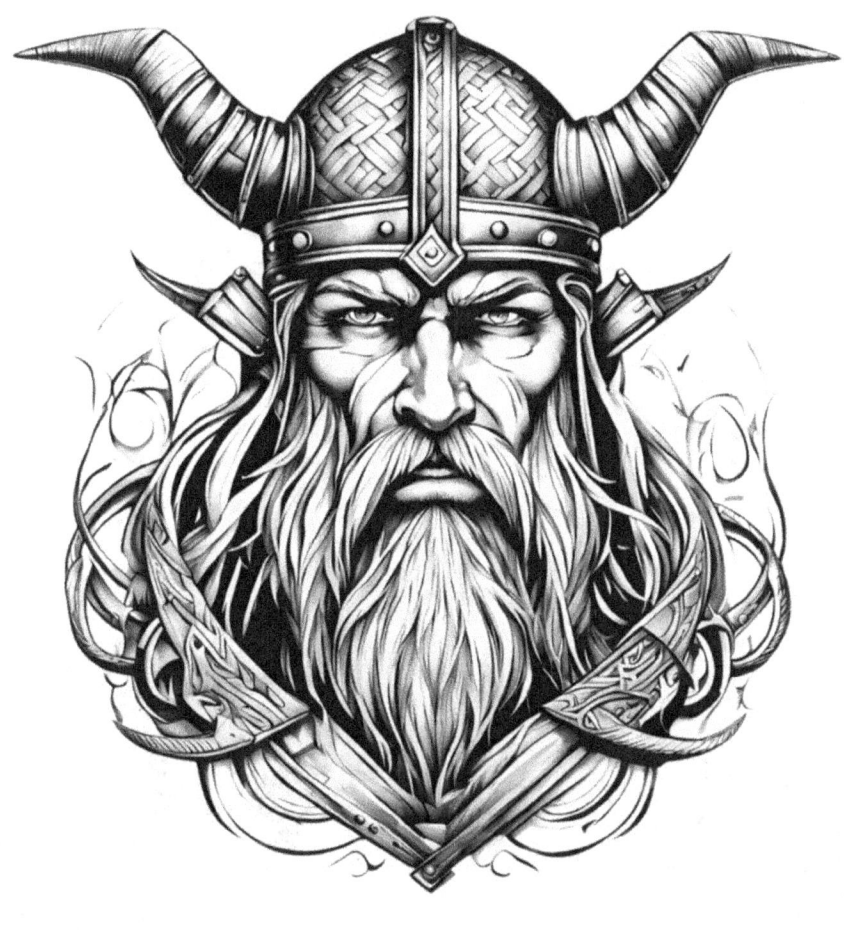
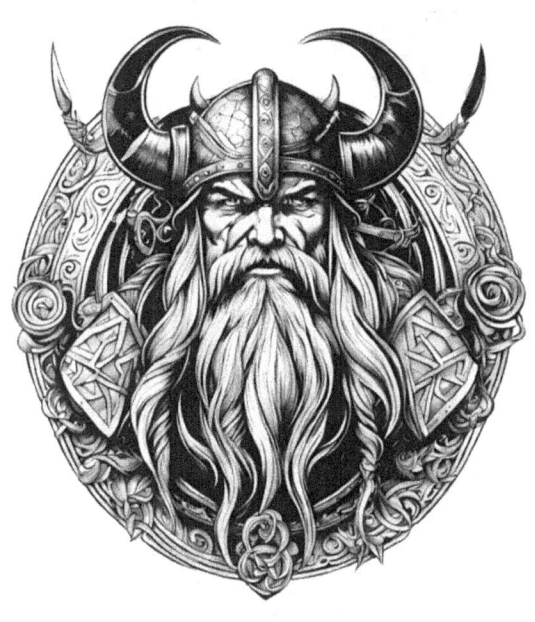
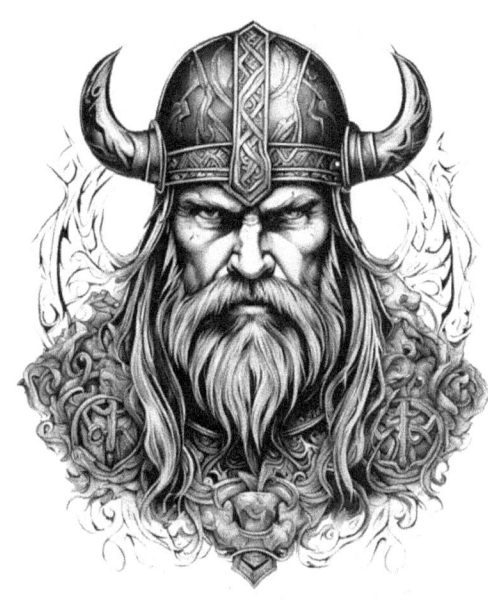

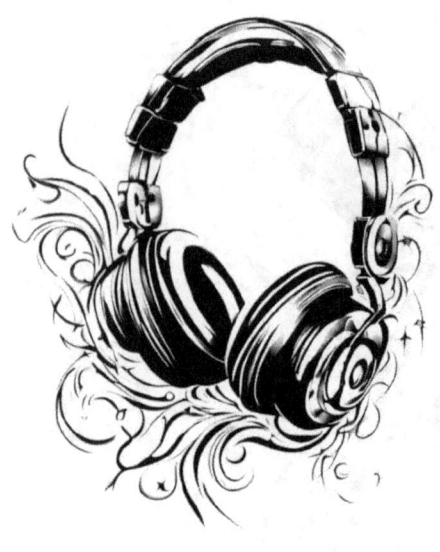
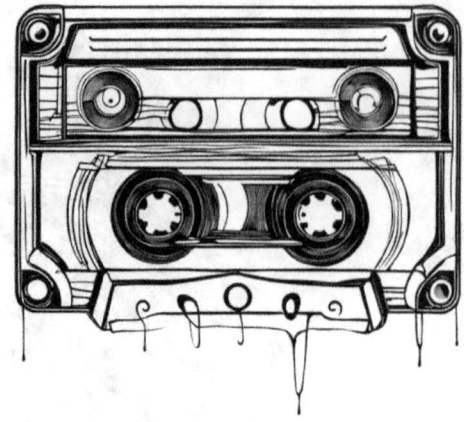
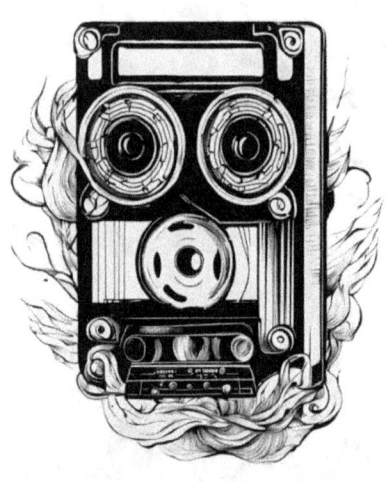
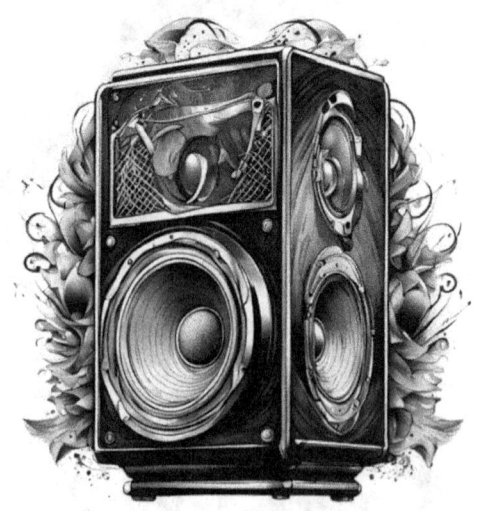
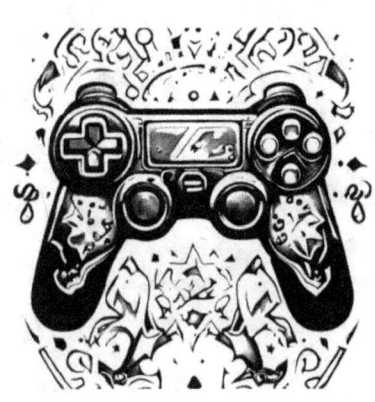
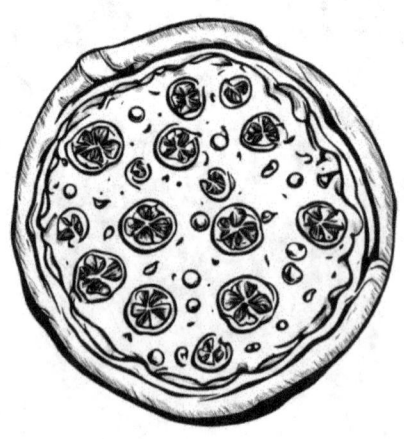

108

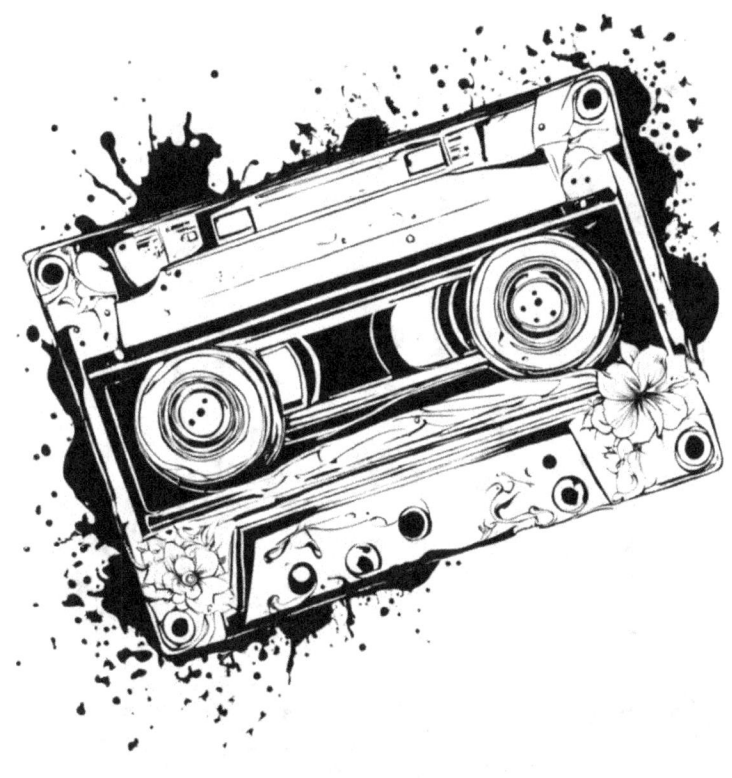
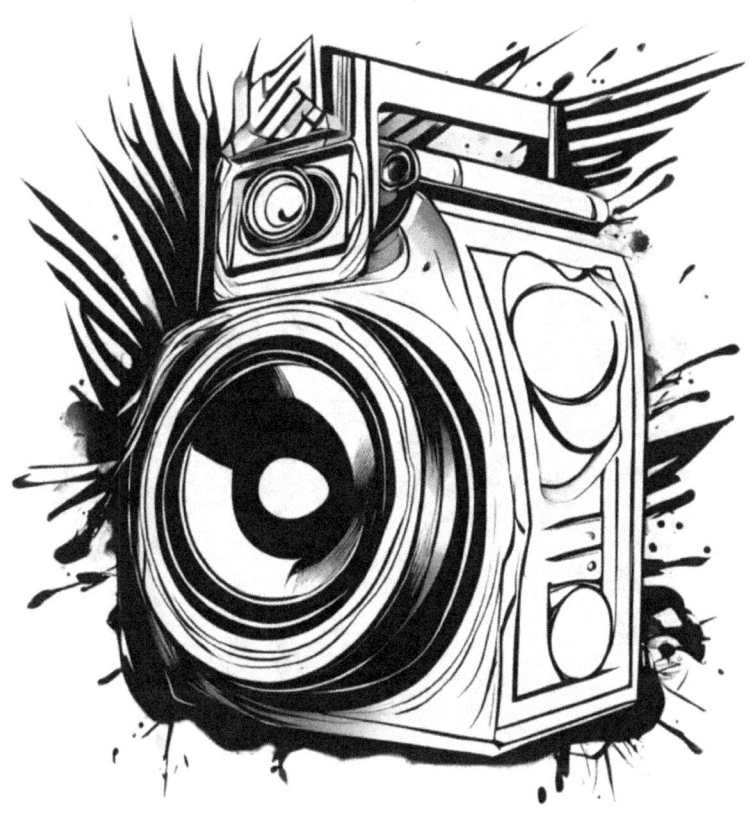

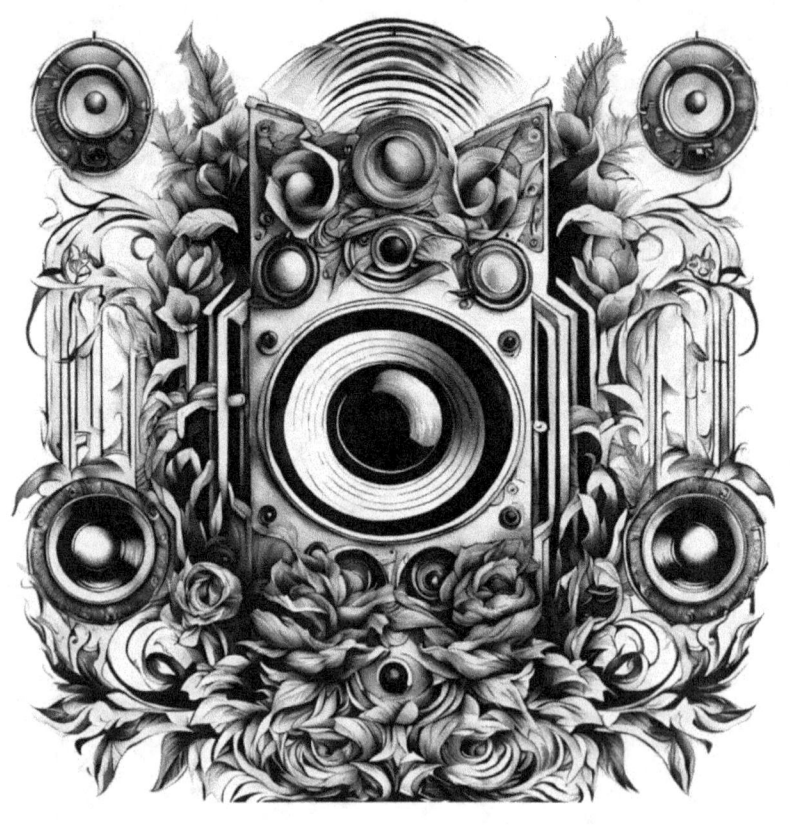
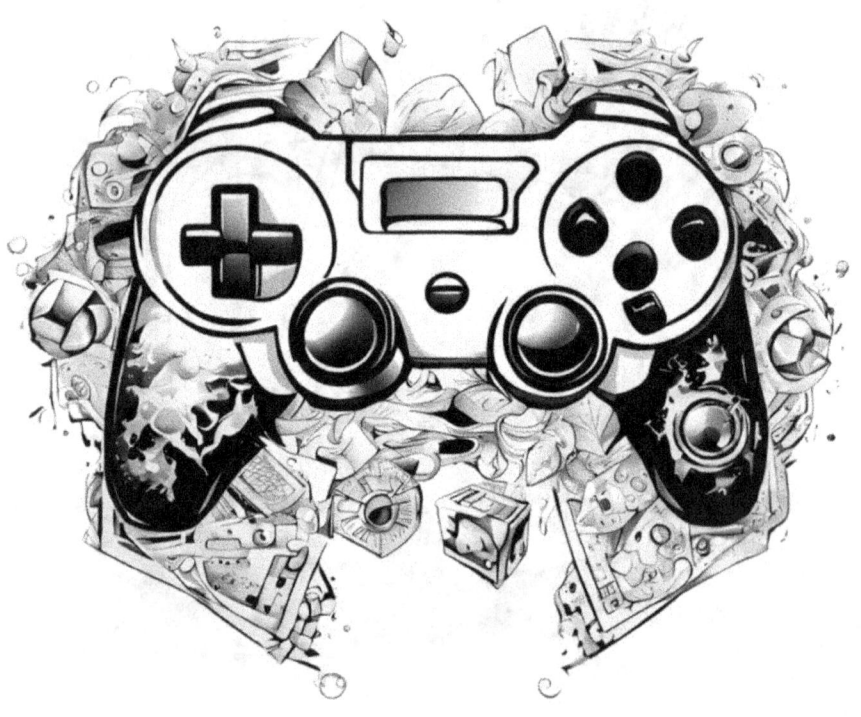

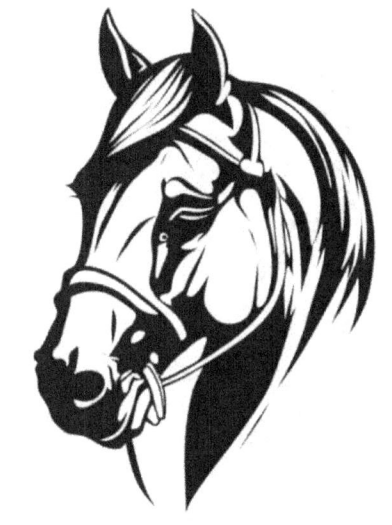
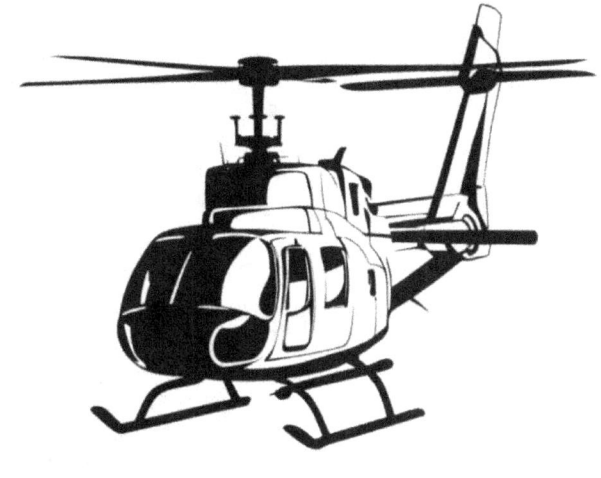
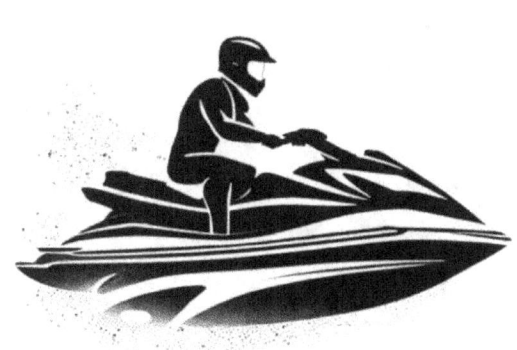
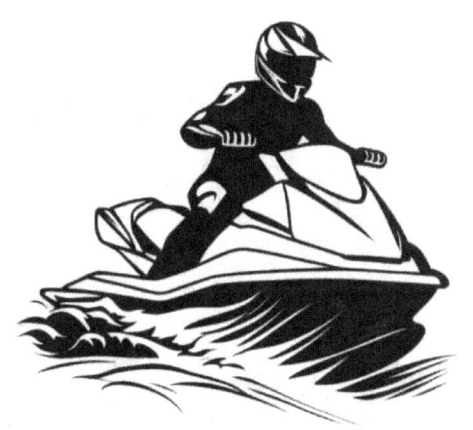
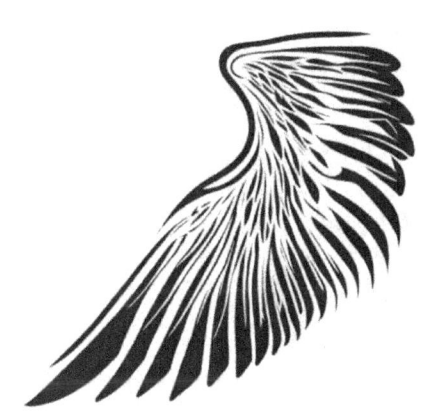
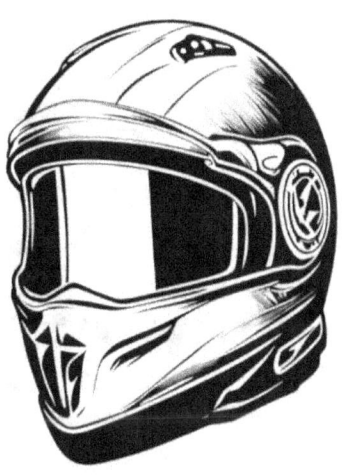

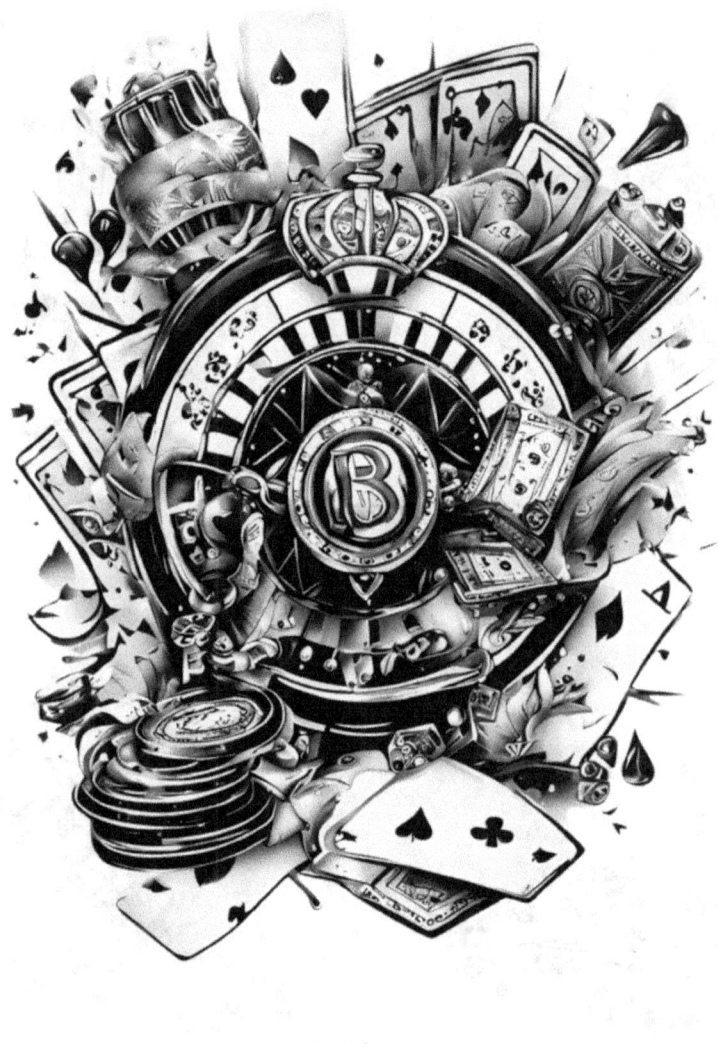
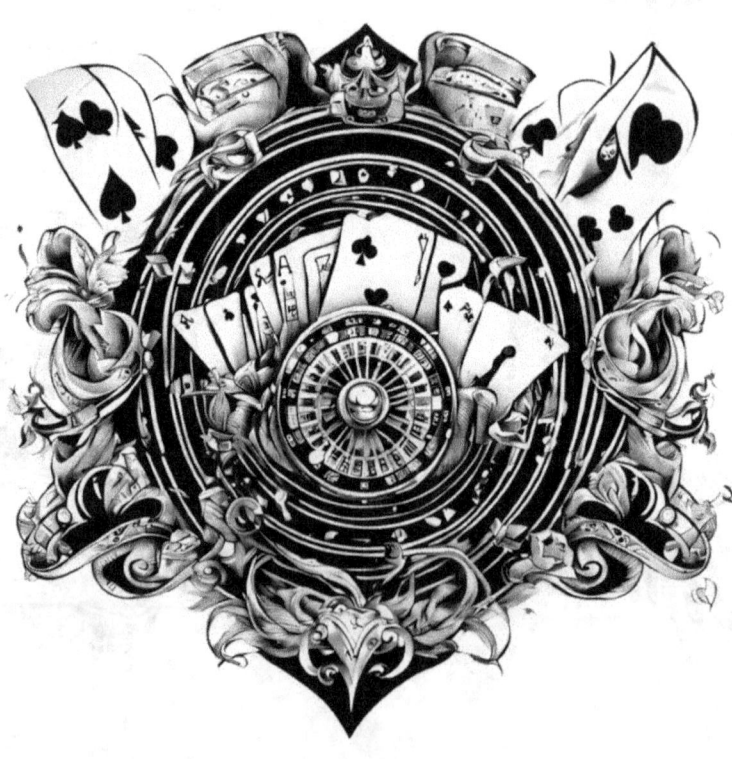

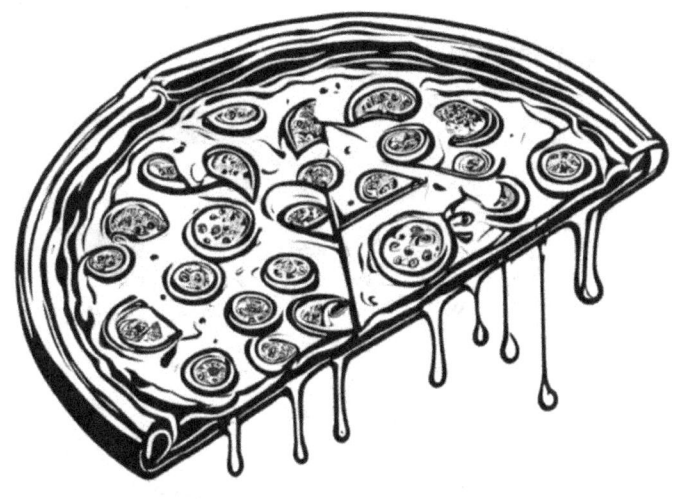

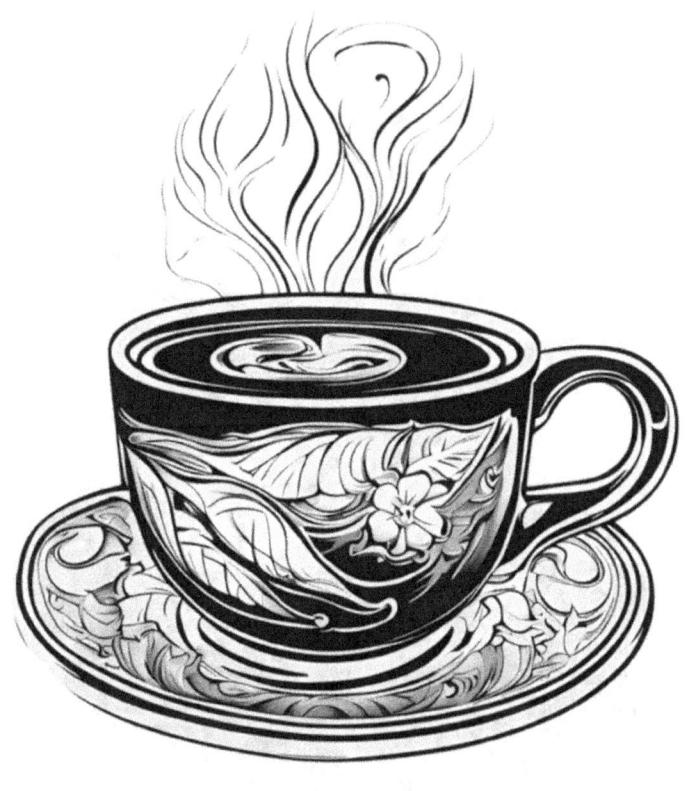

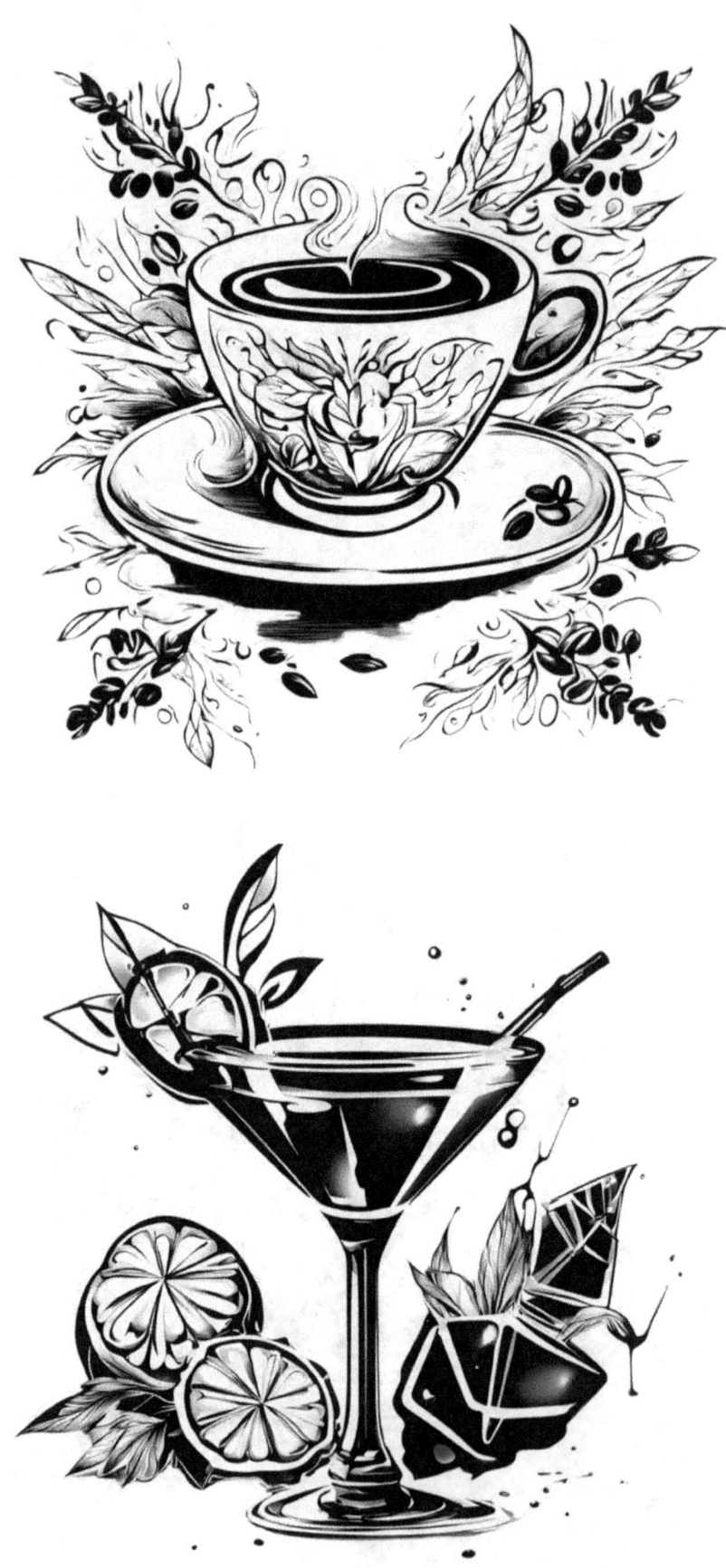

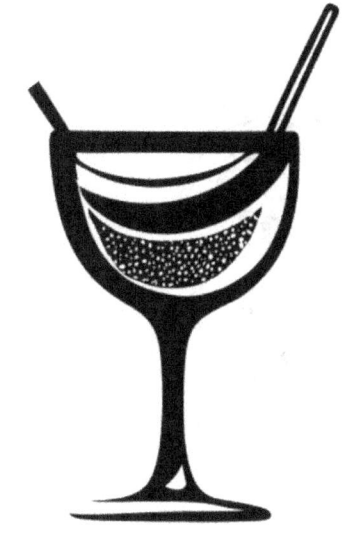
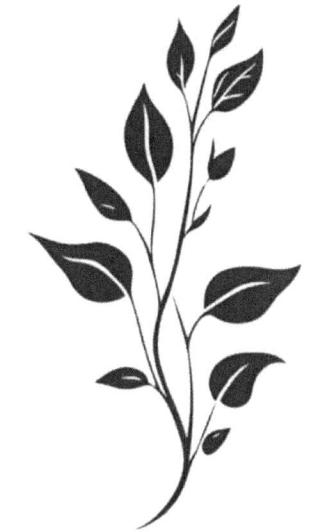
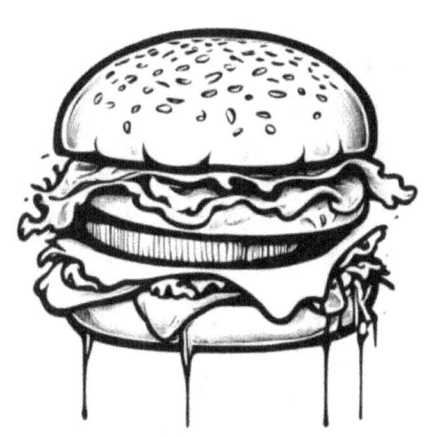

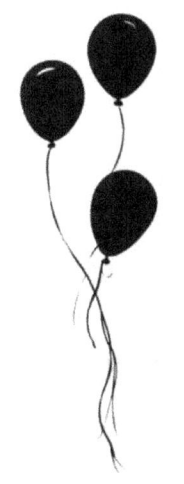

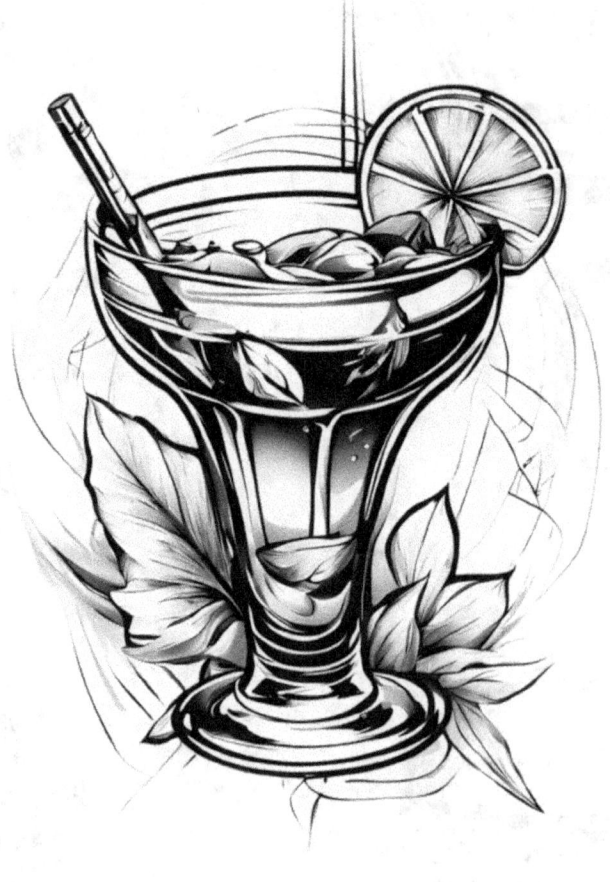
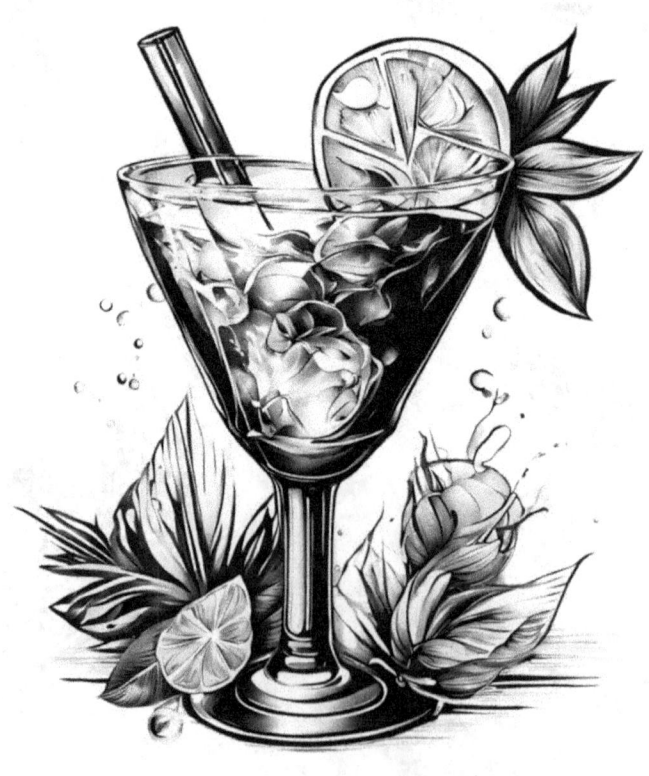

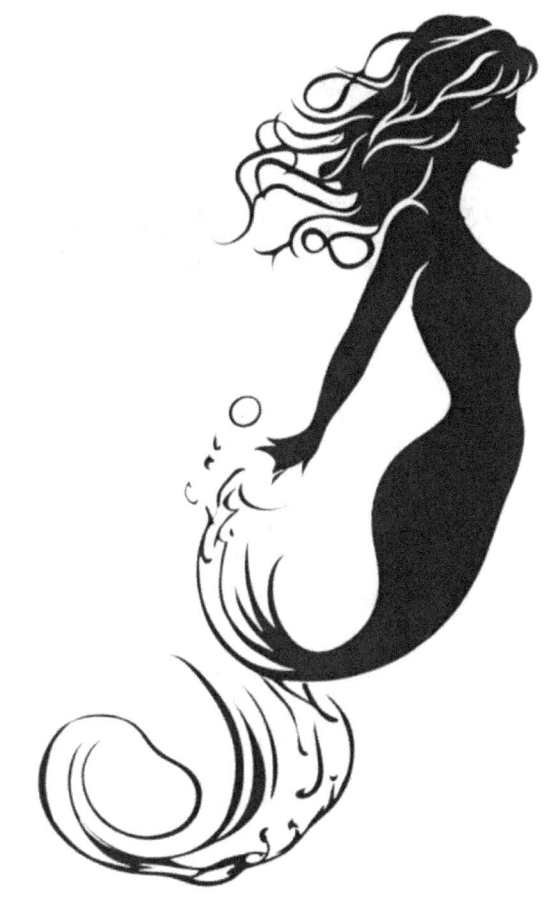
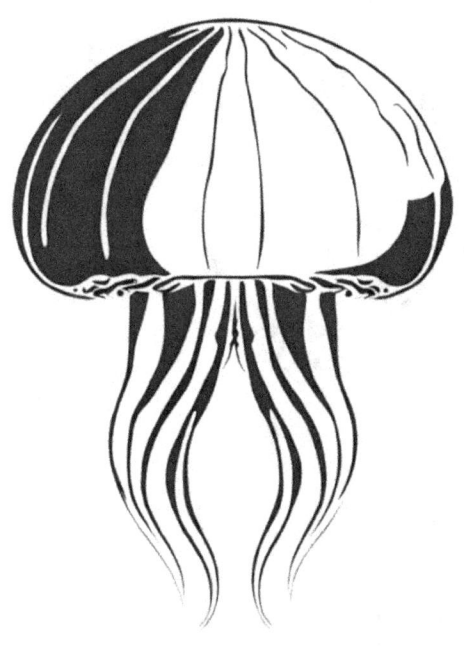
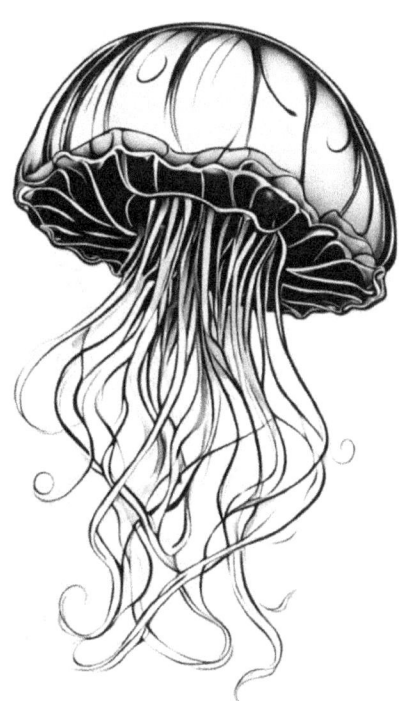

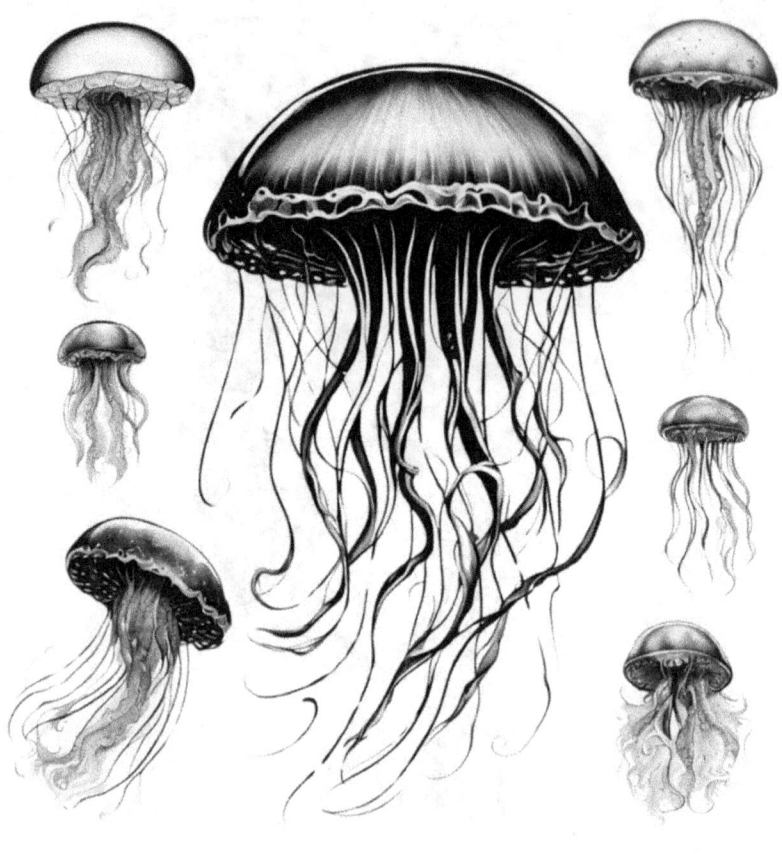
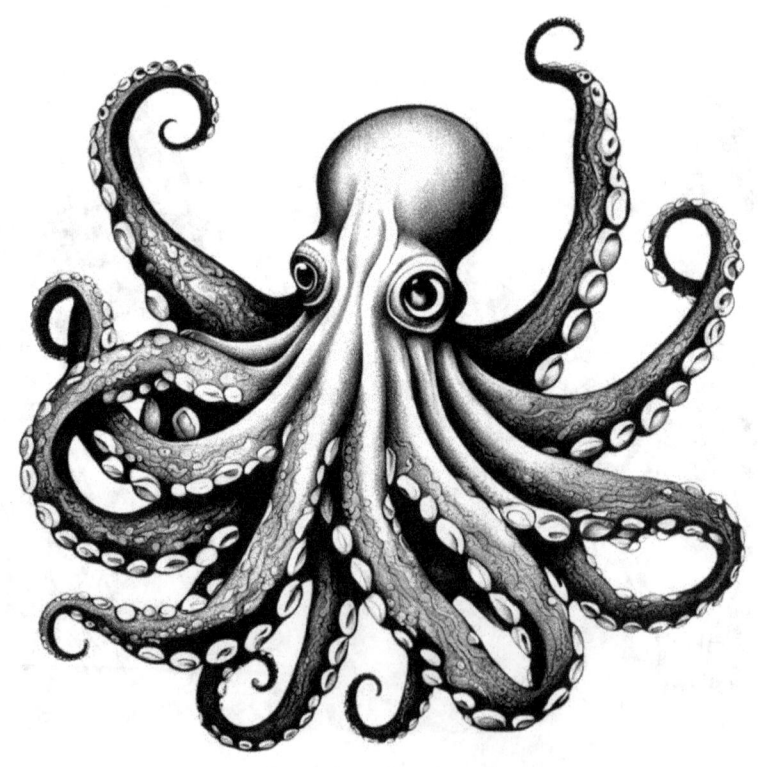

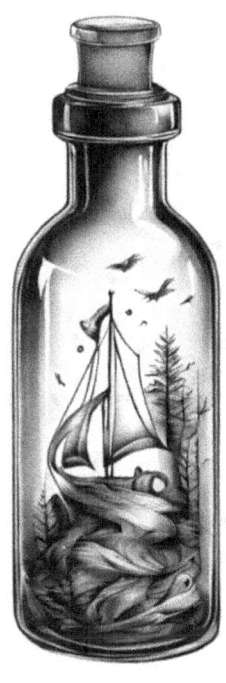
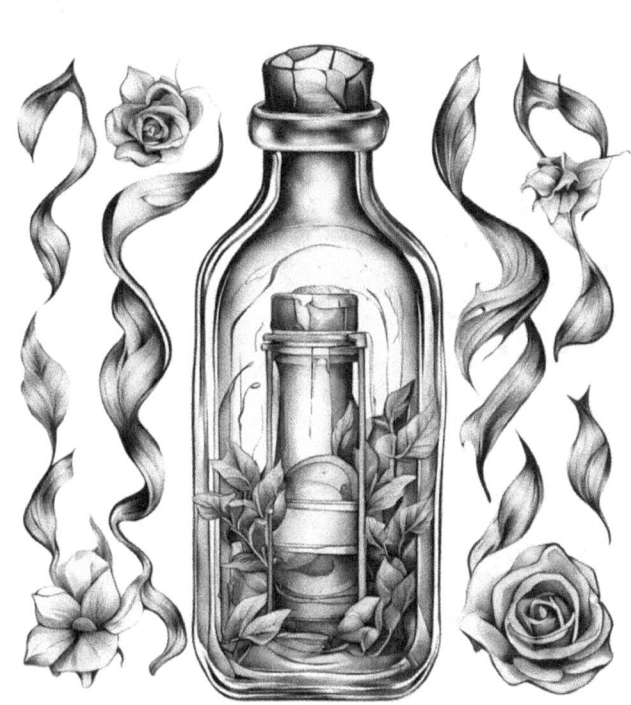

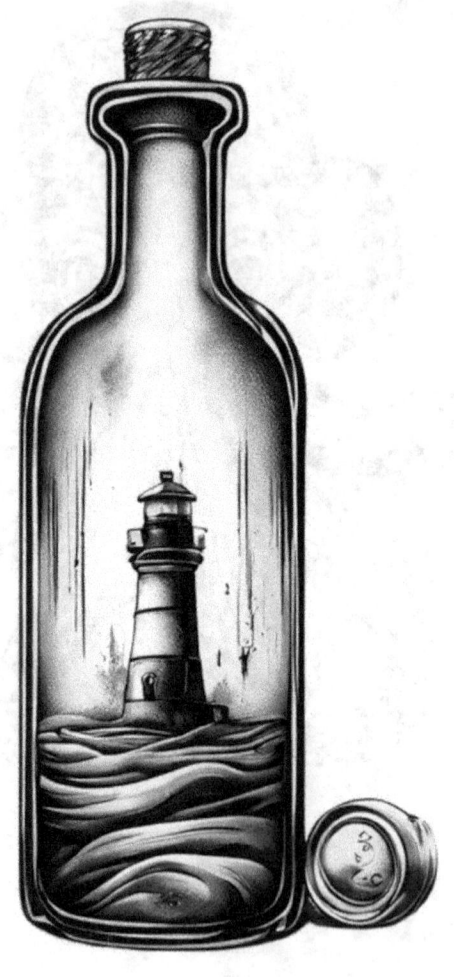
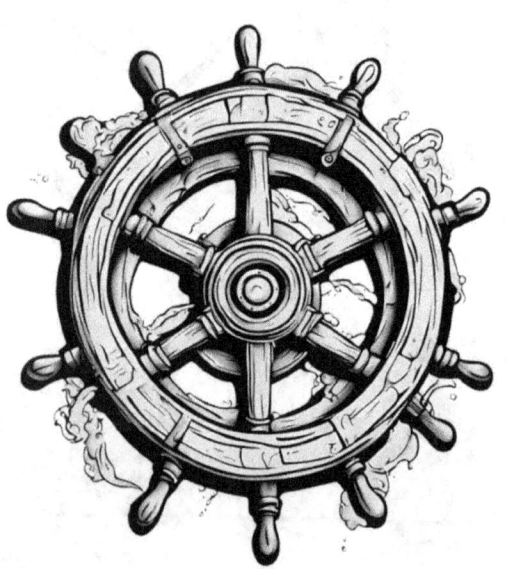
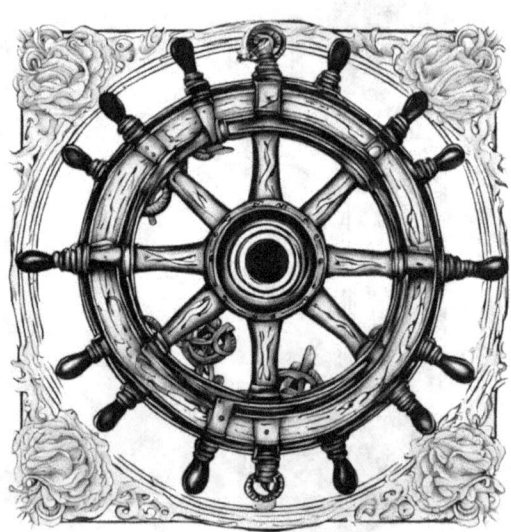

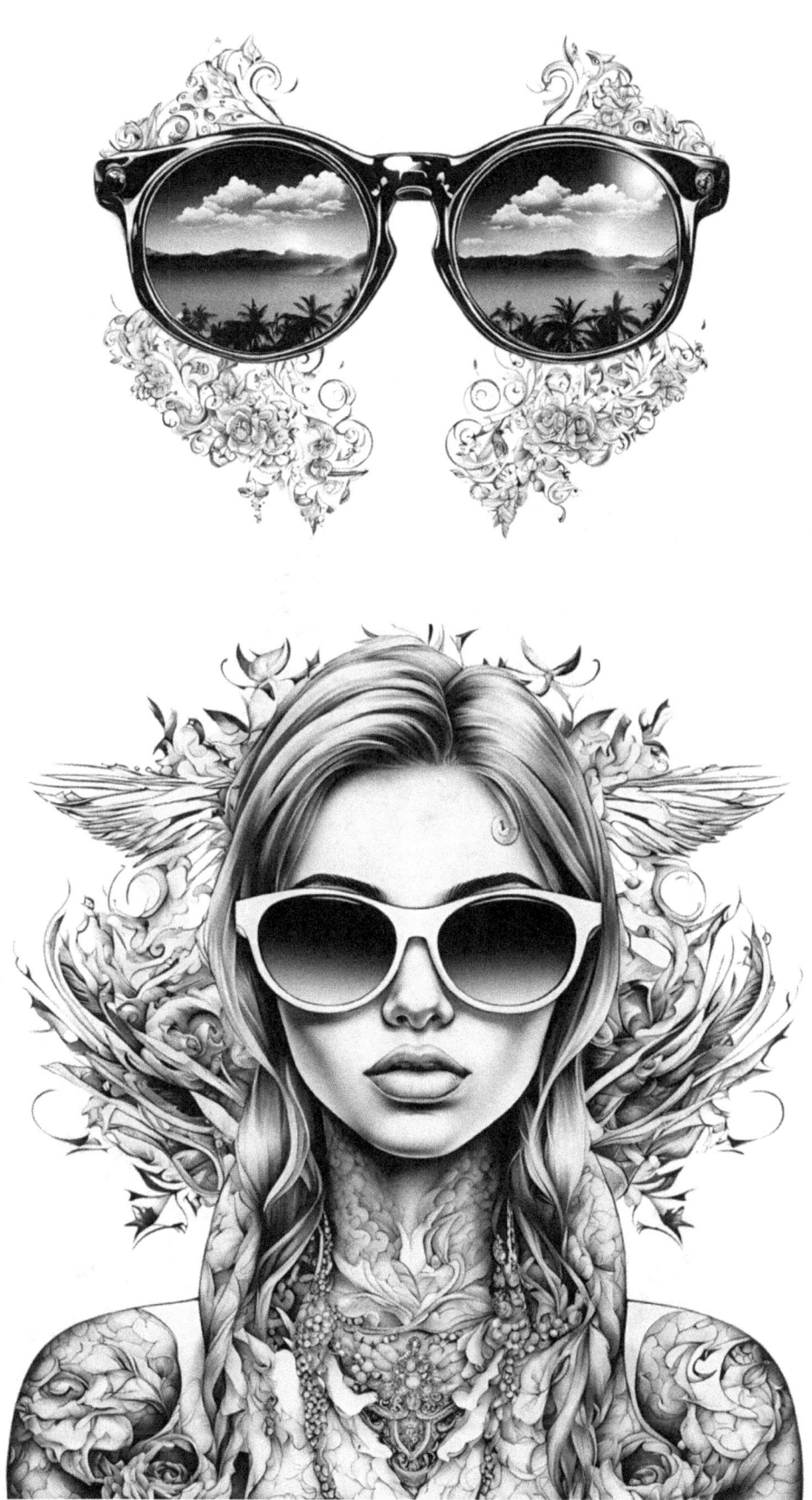

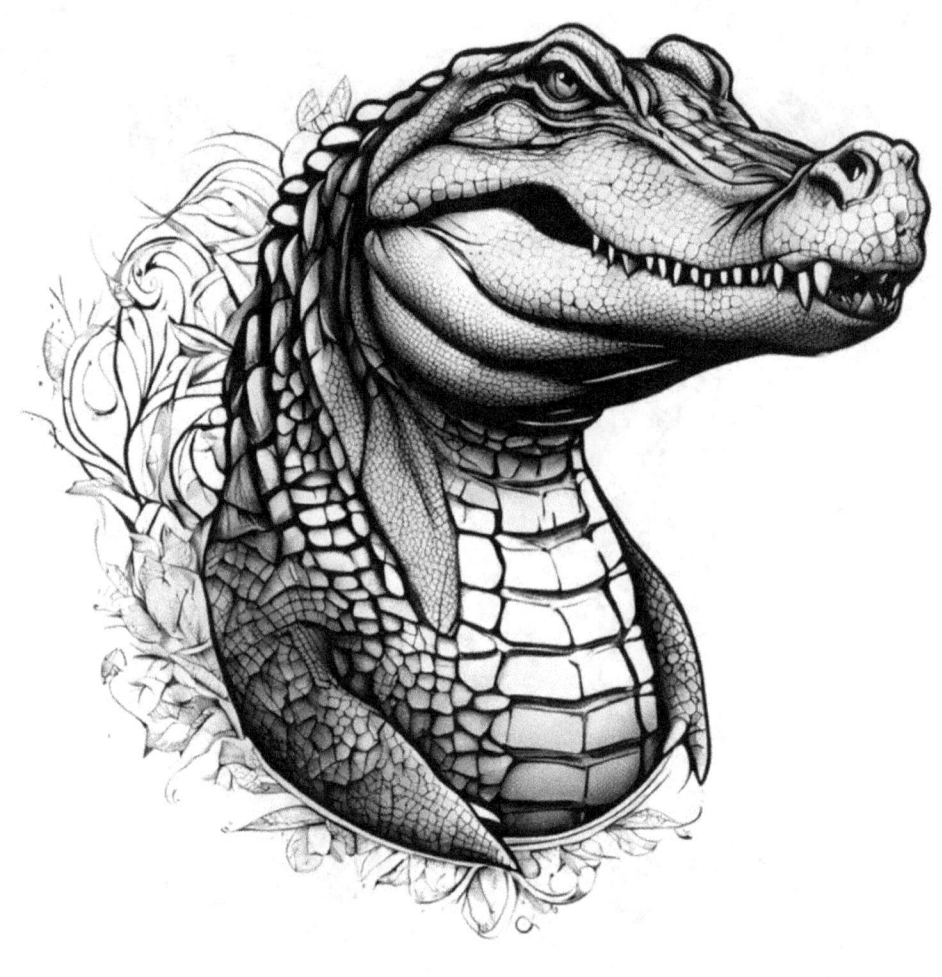
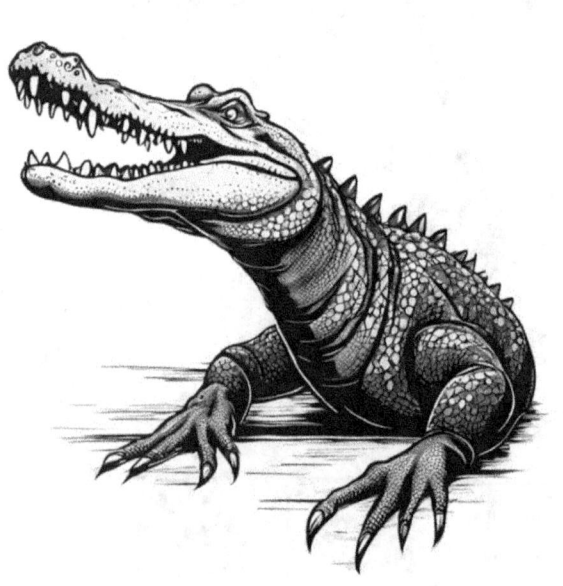
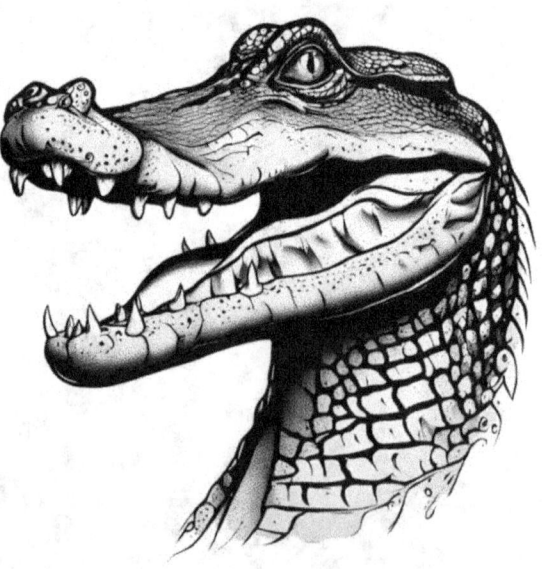

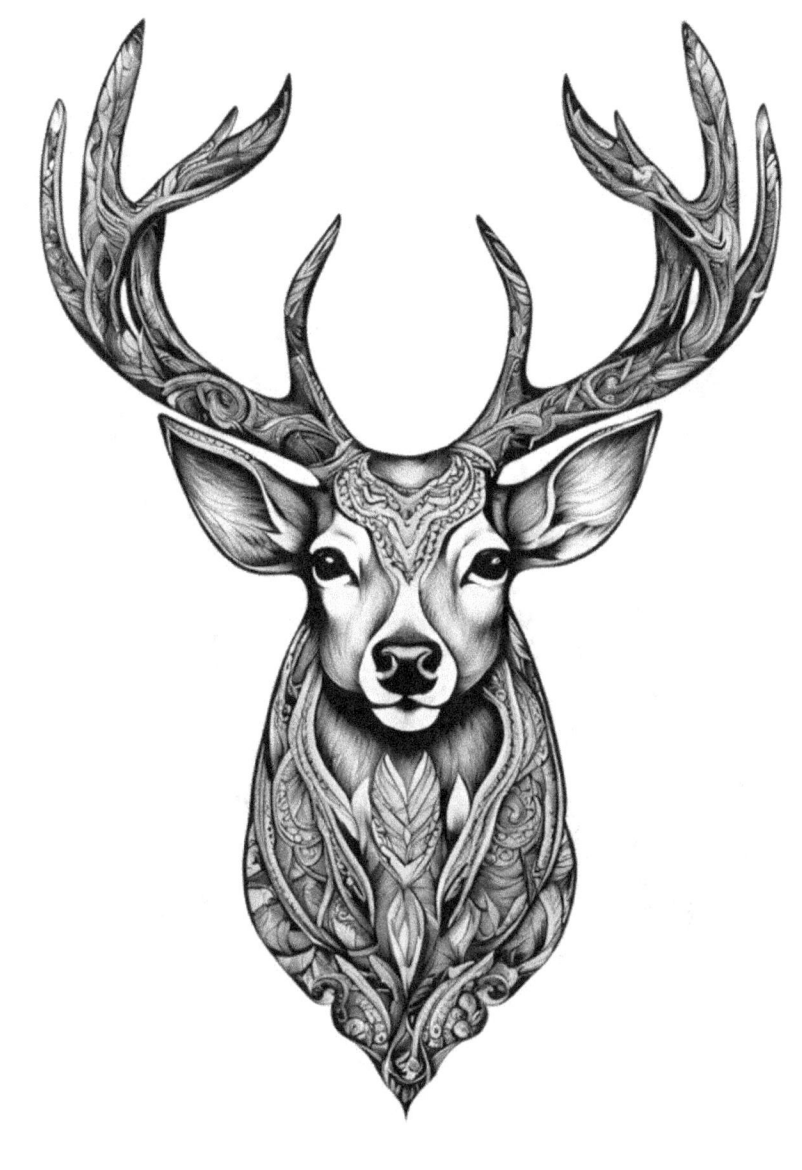
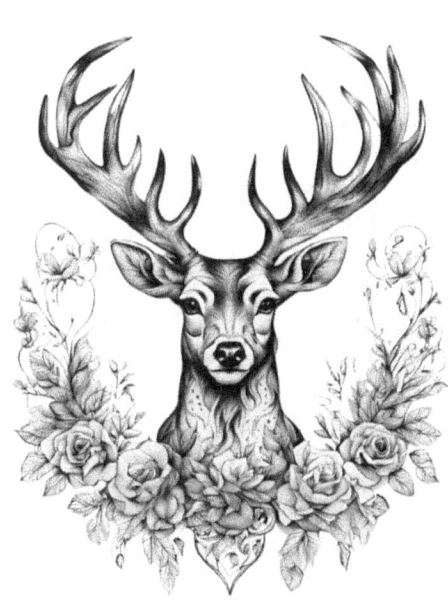
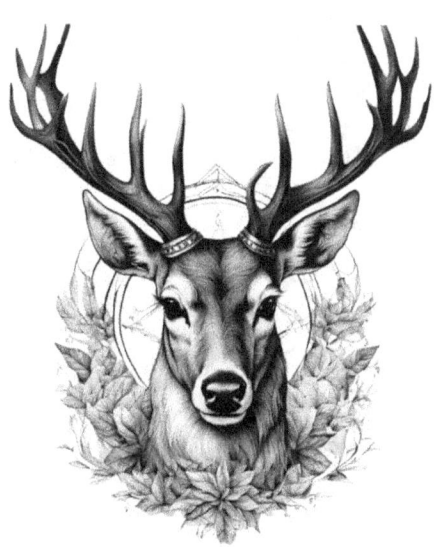

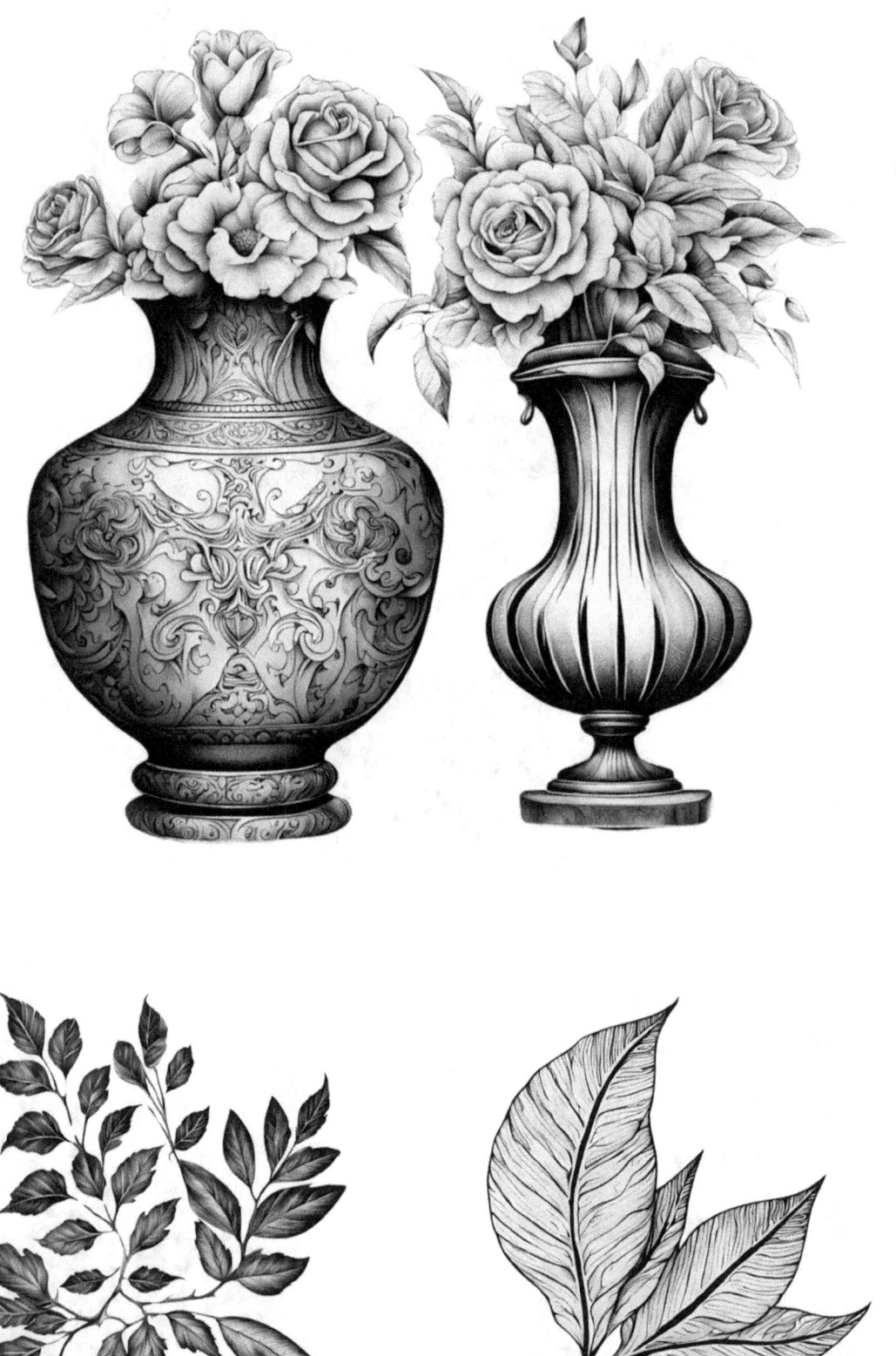

124

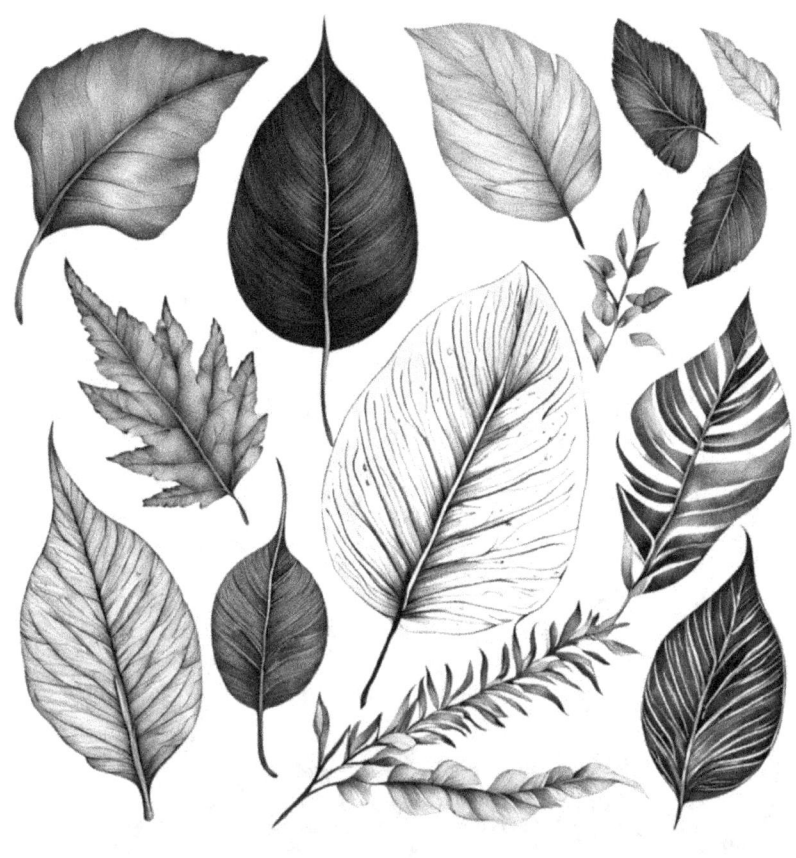
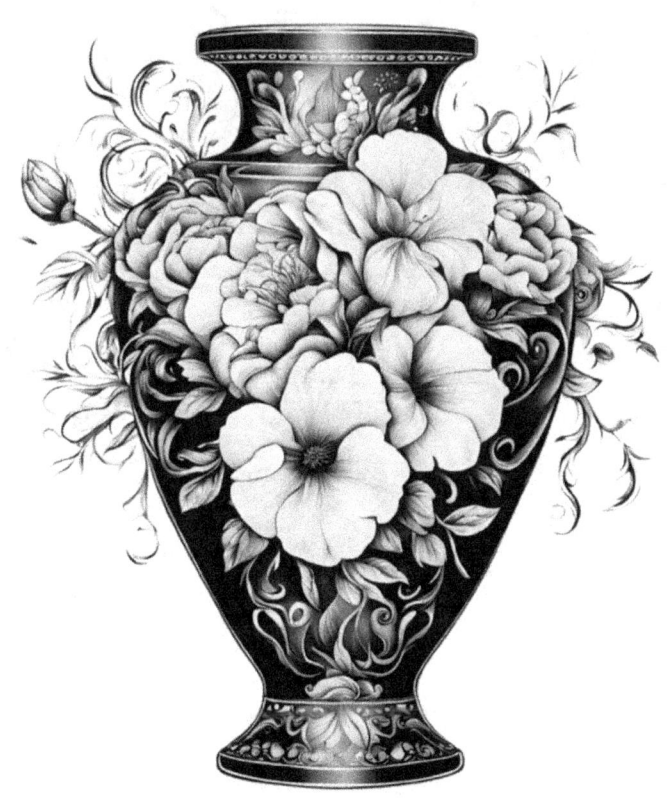

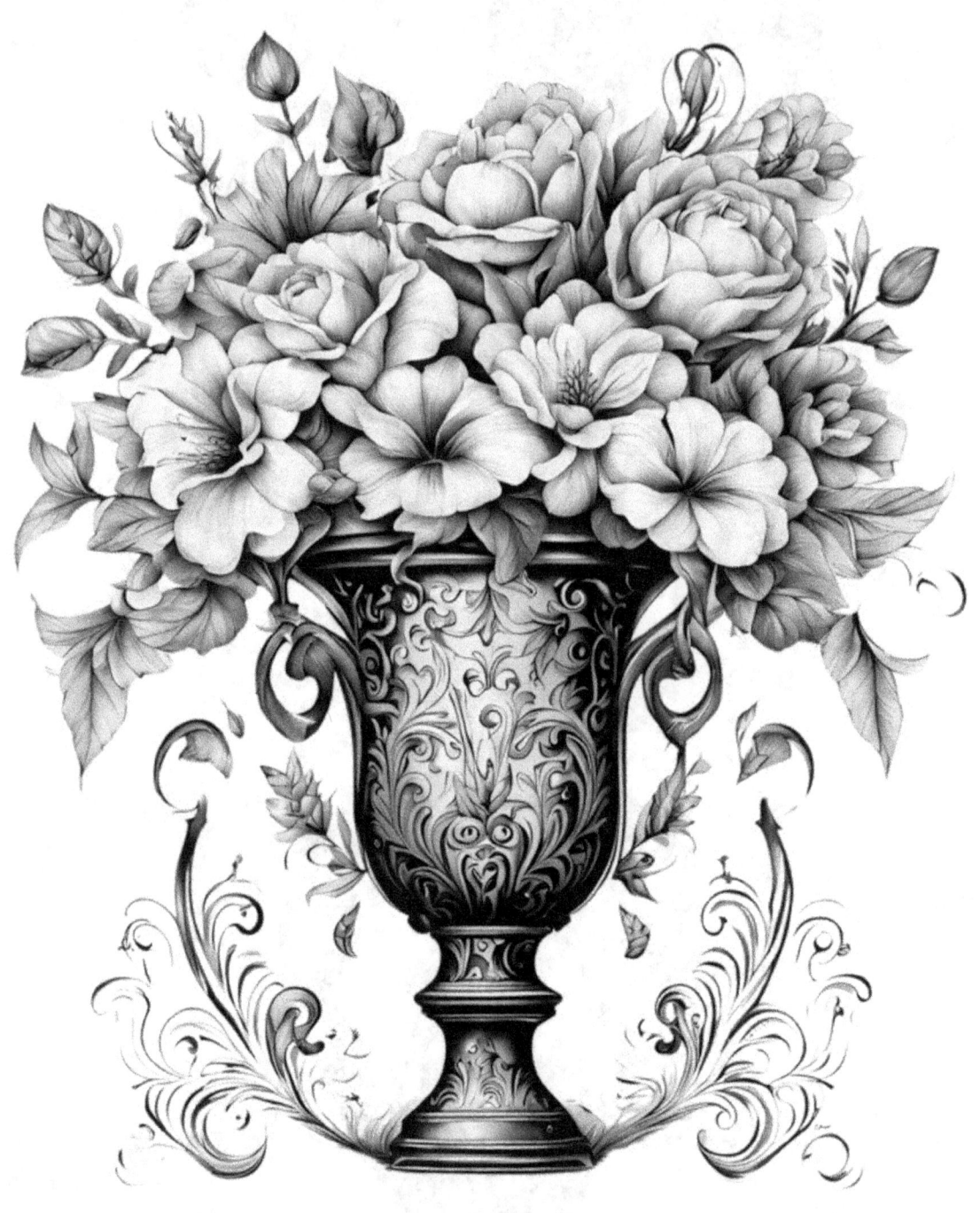

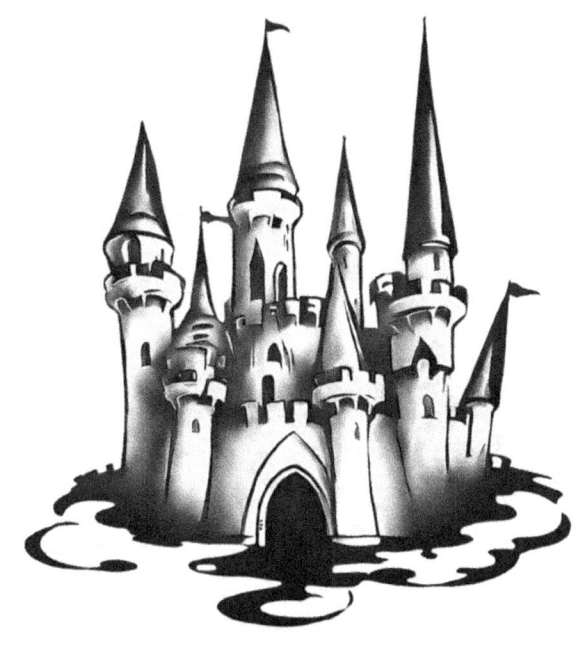
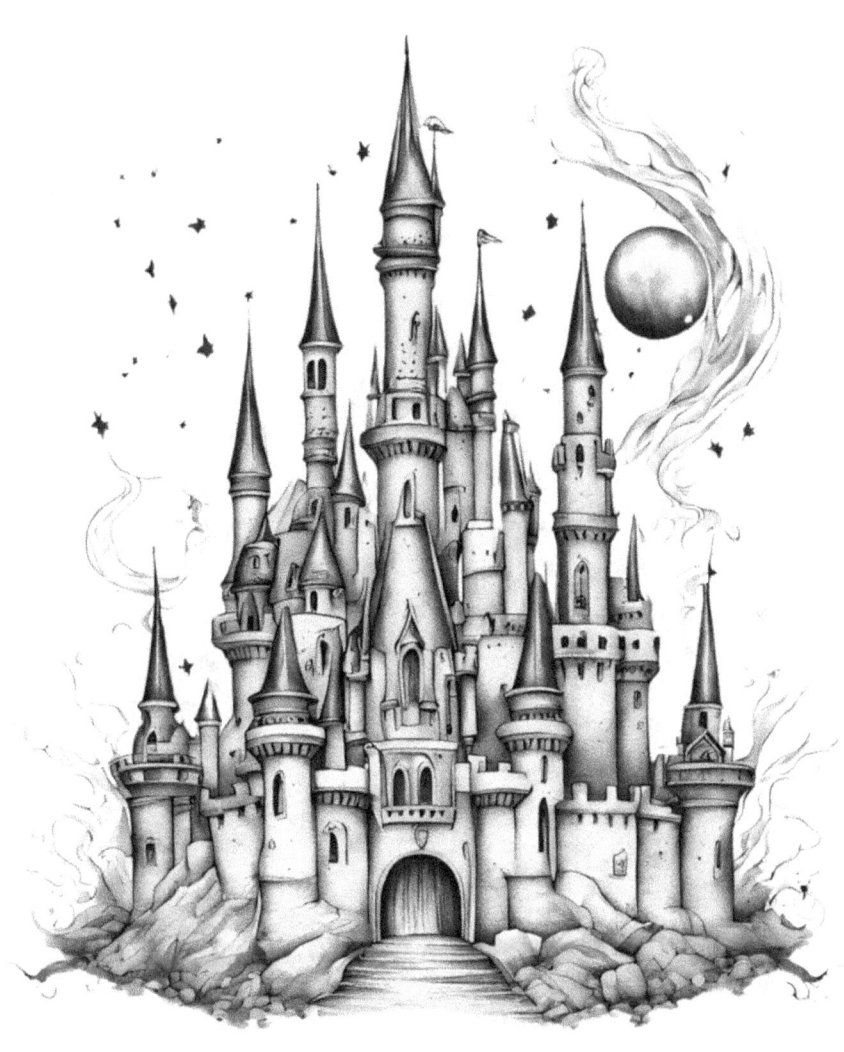

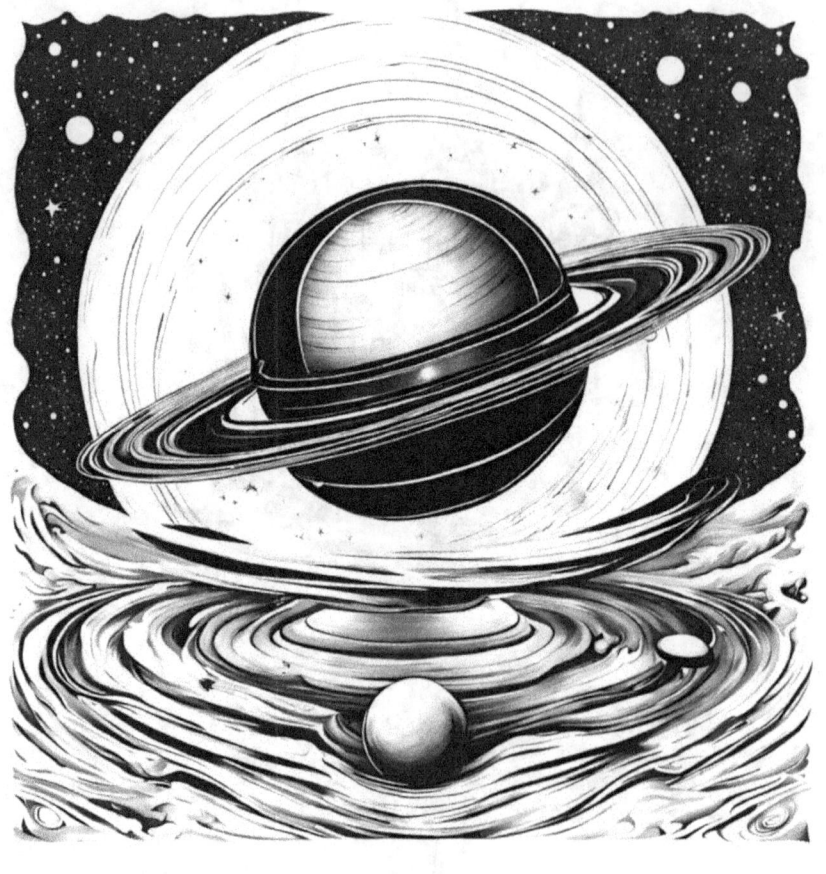
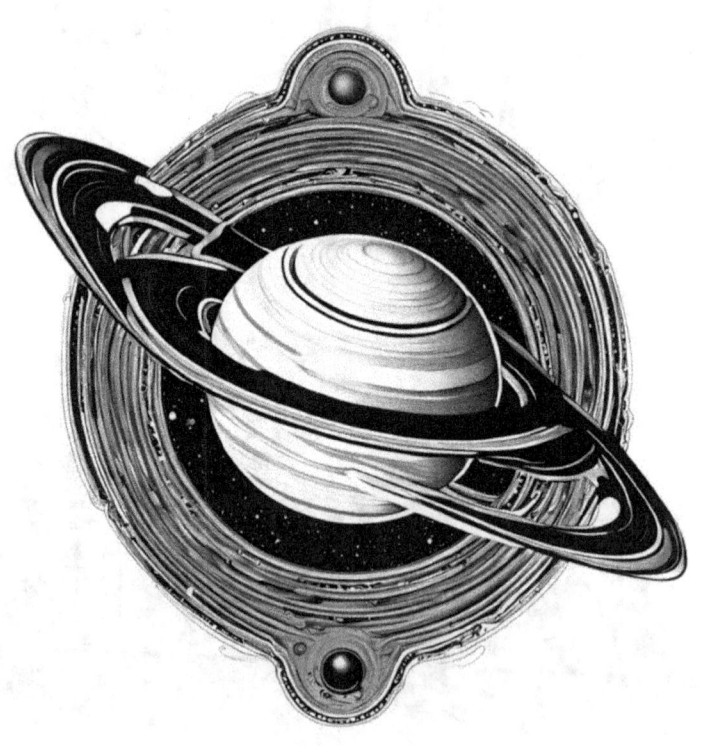

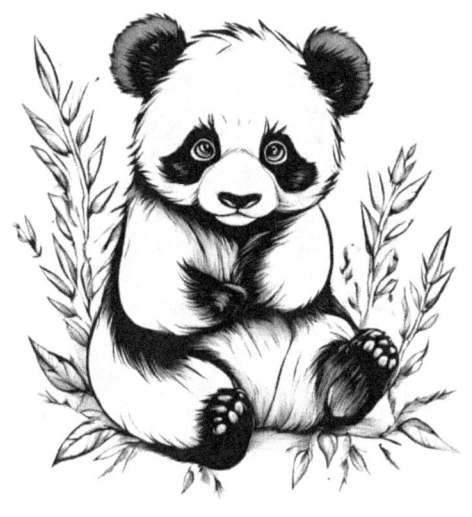
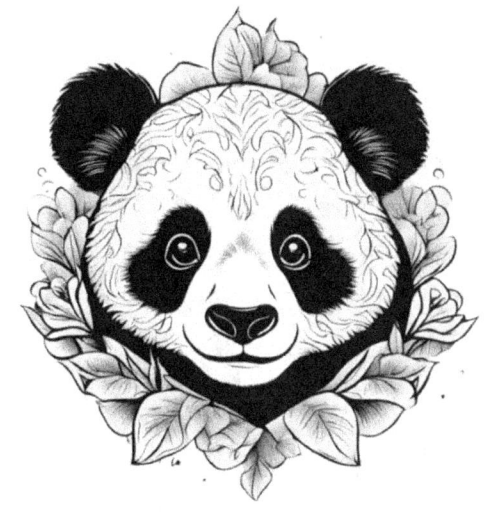
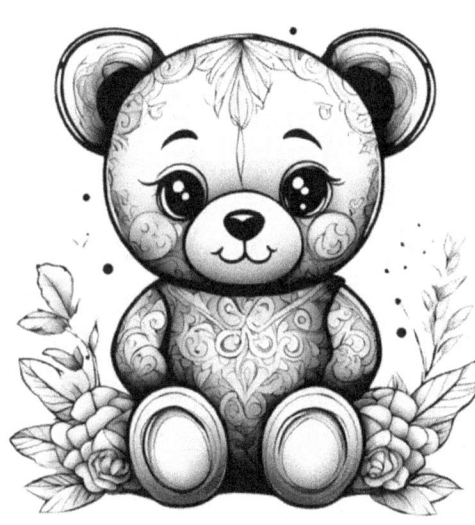
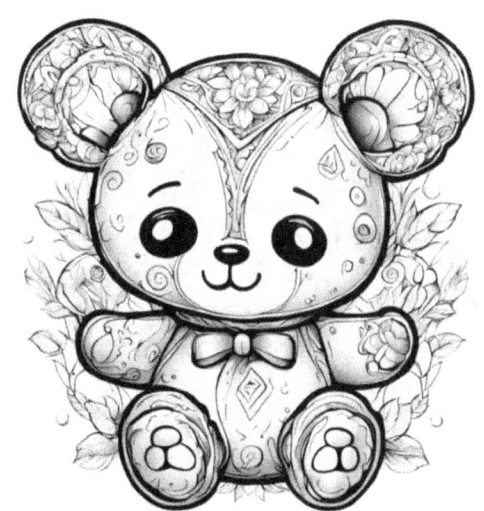
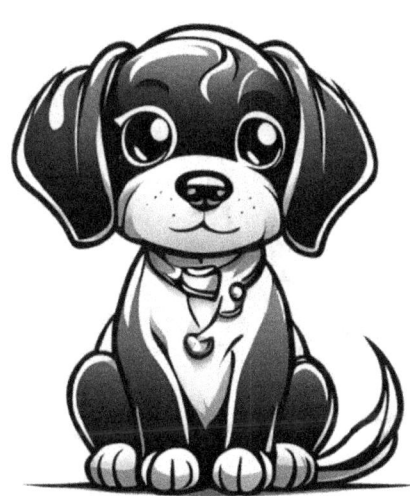
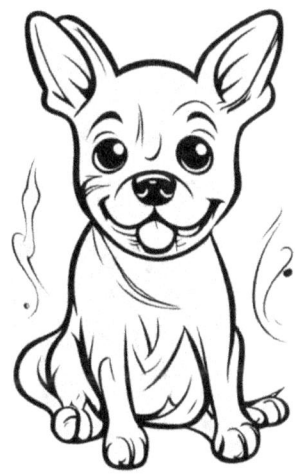

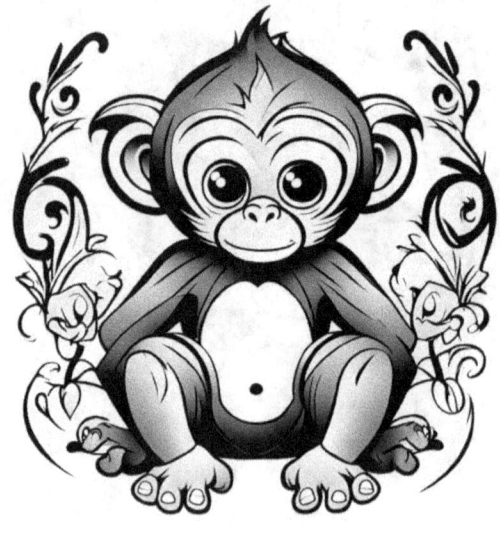
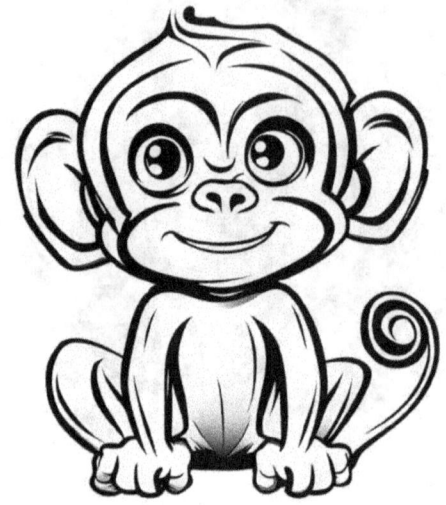
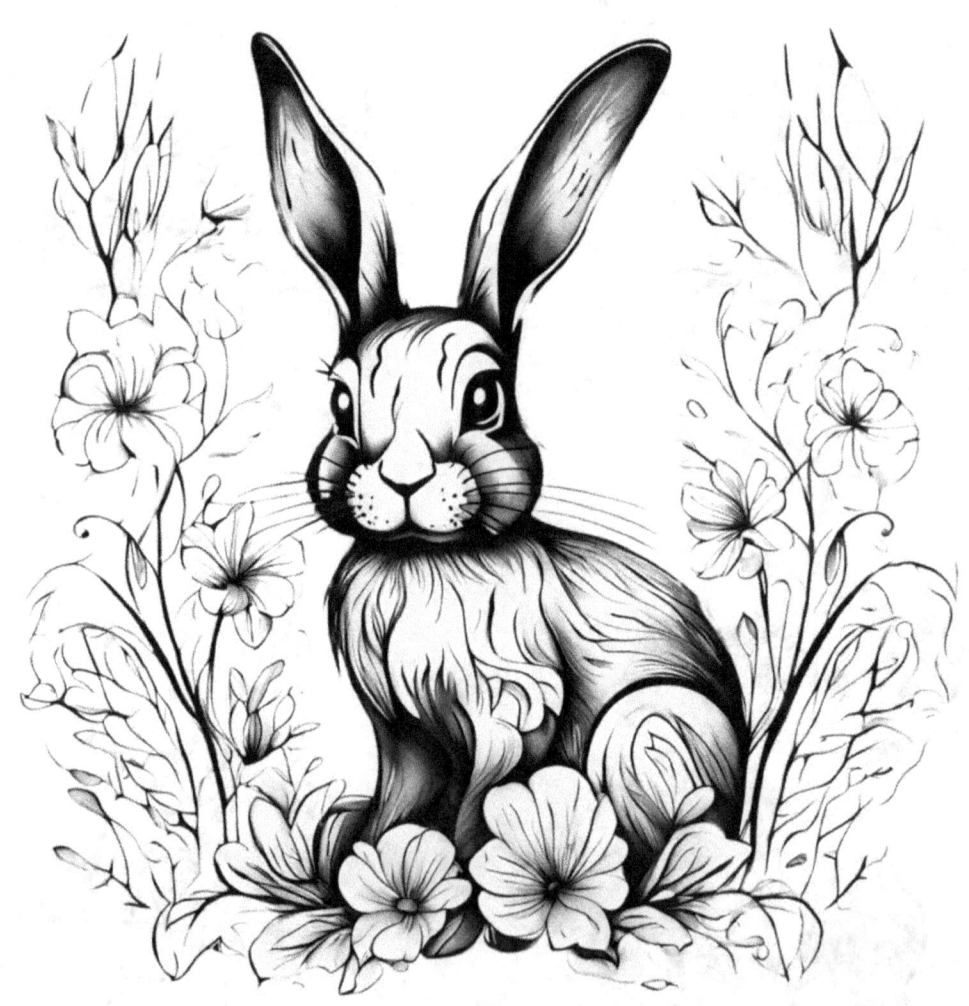

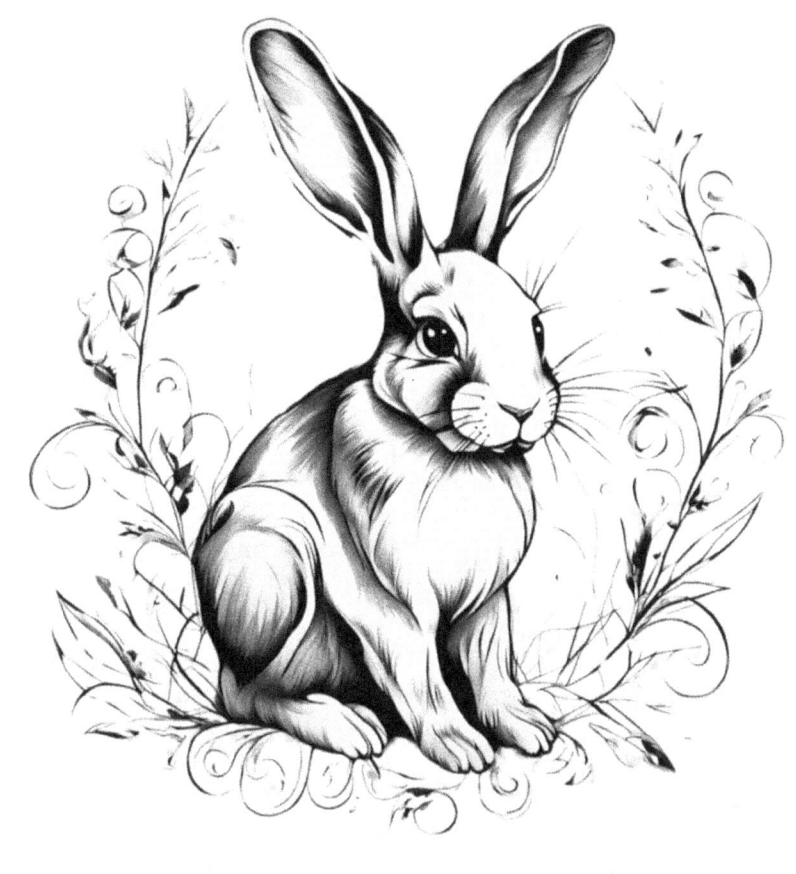
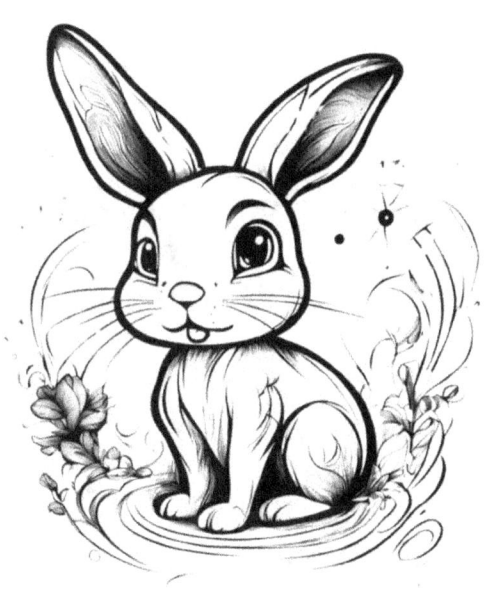
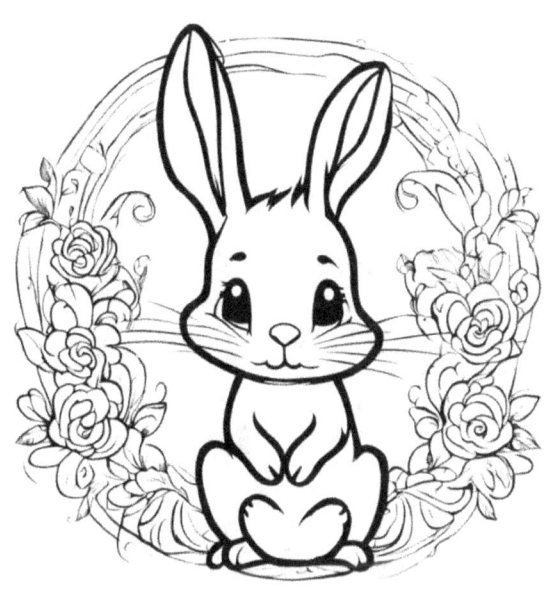

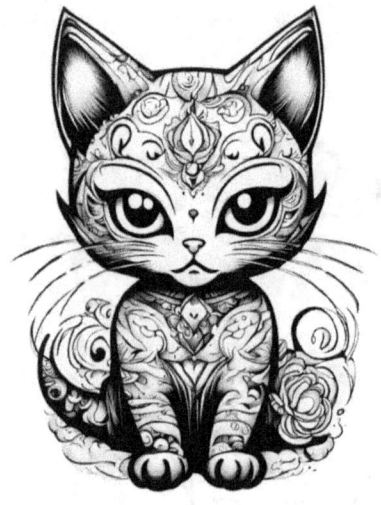
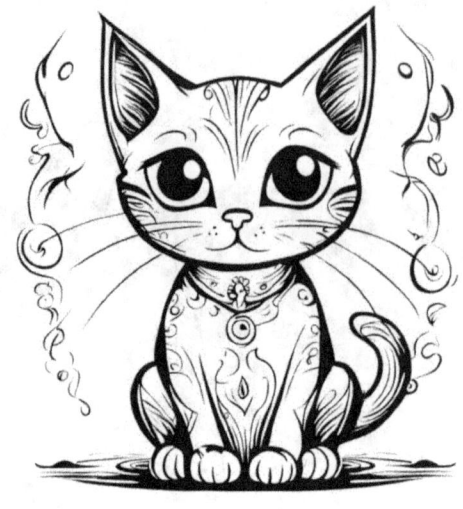
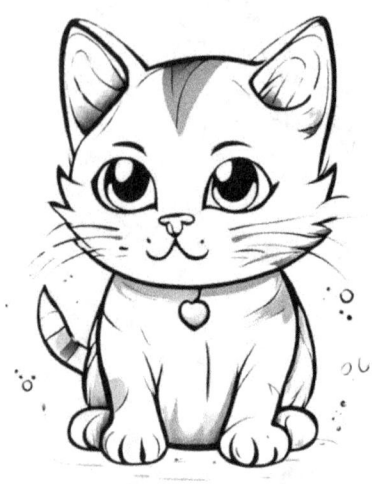
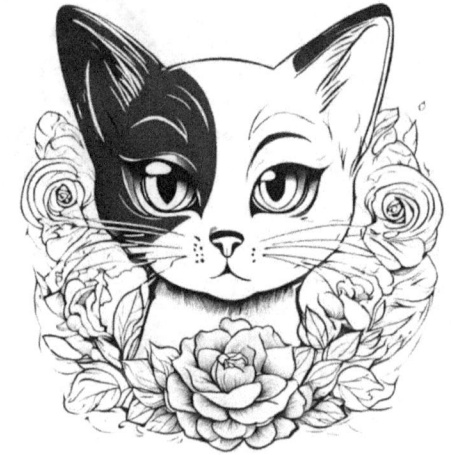
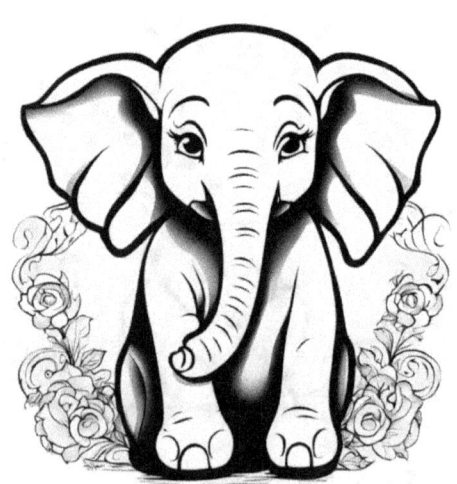
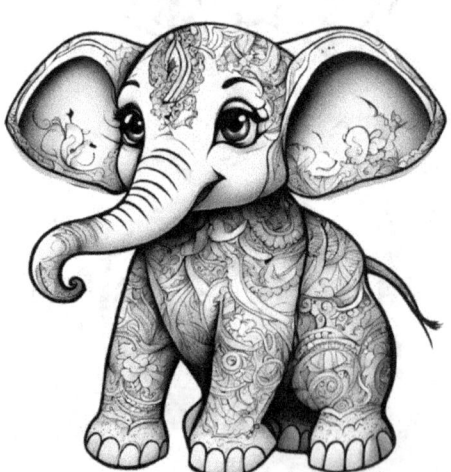

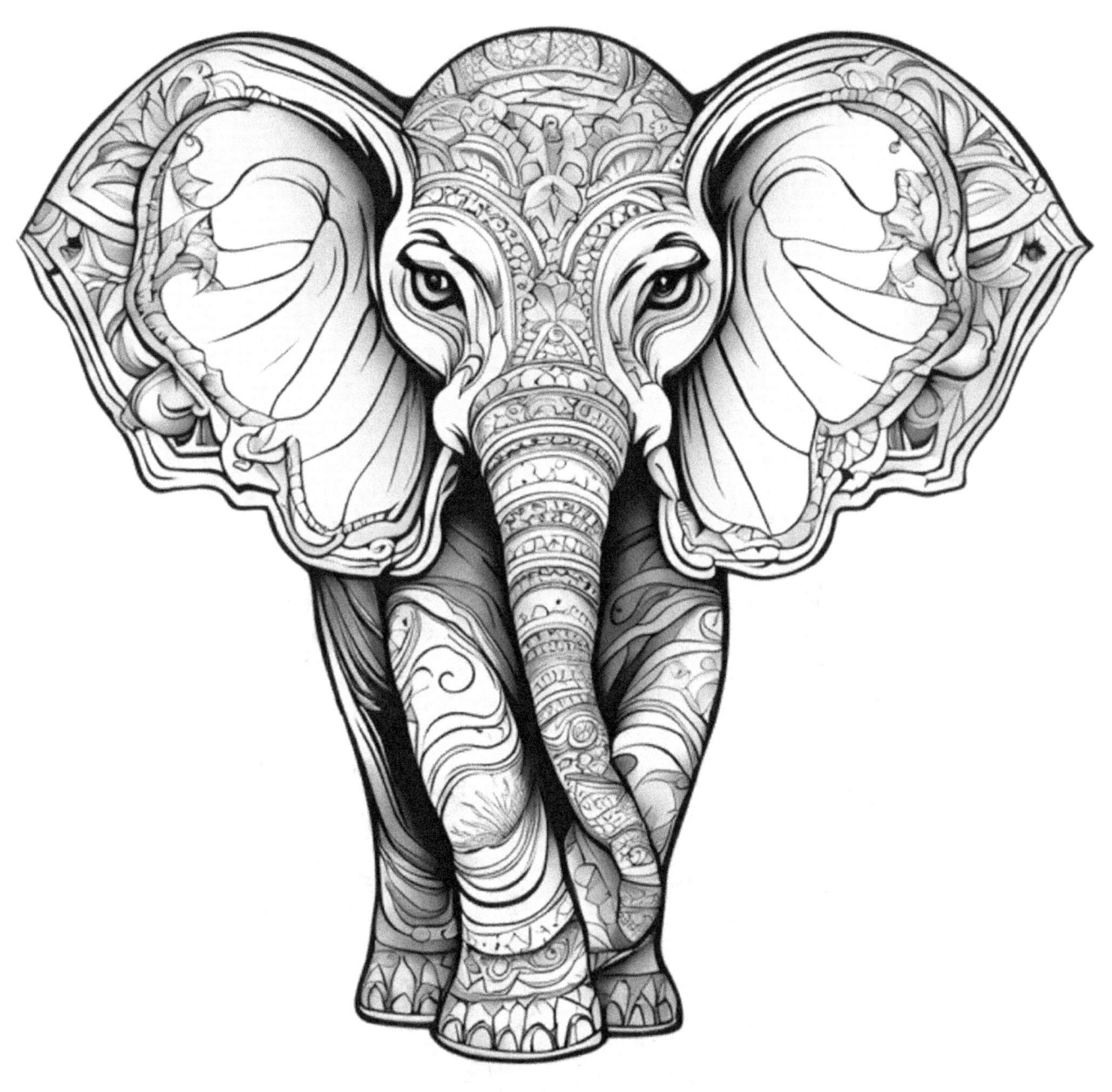

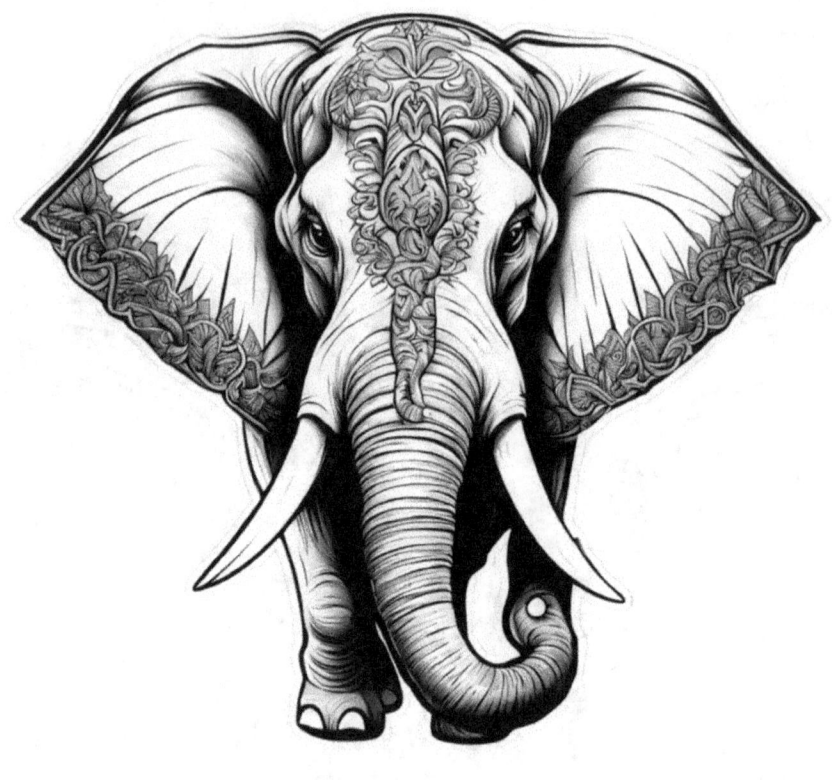
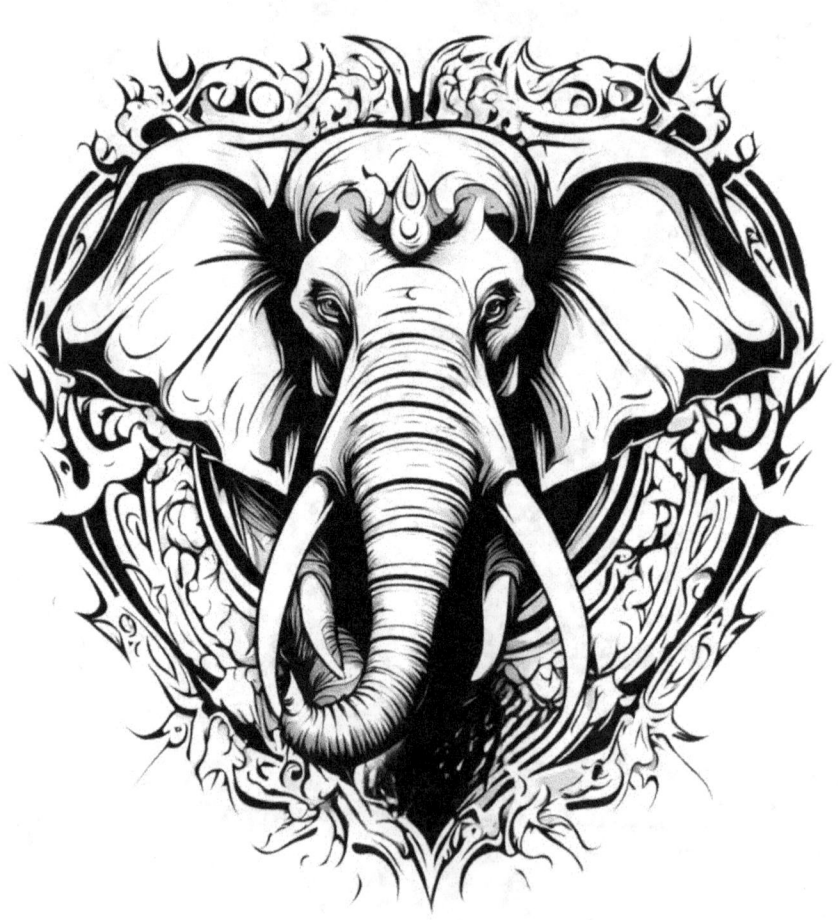

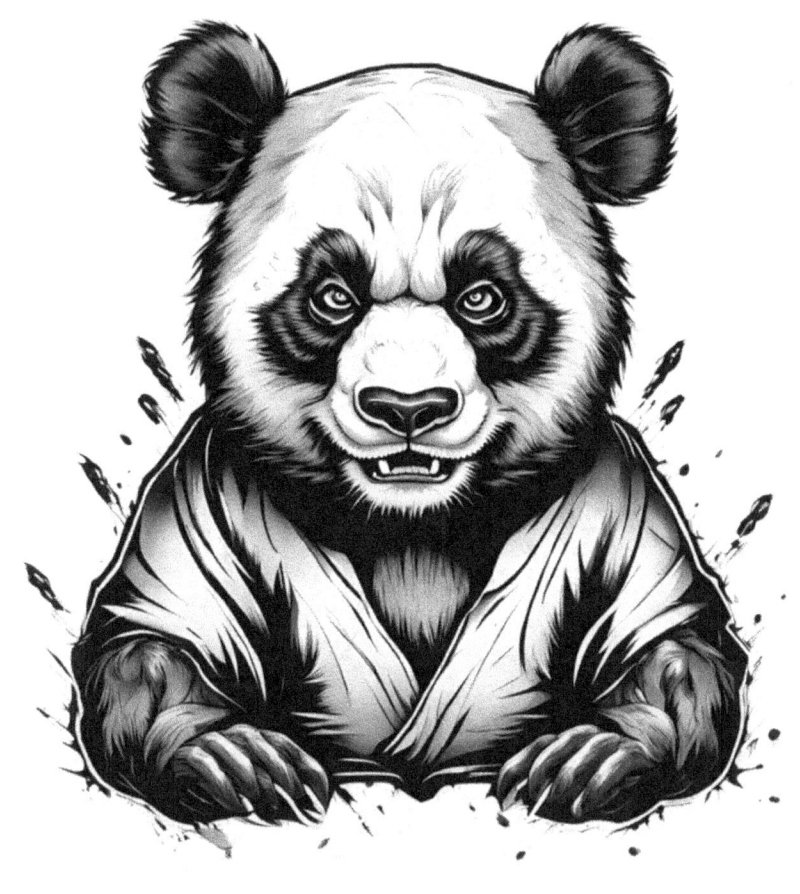
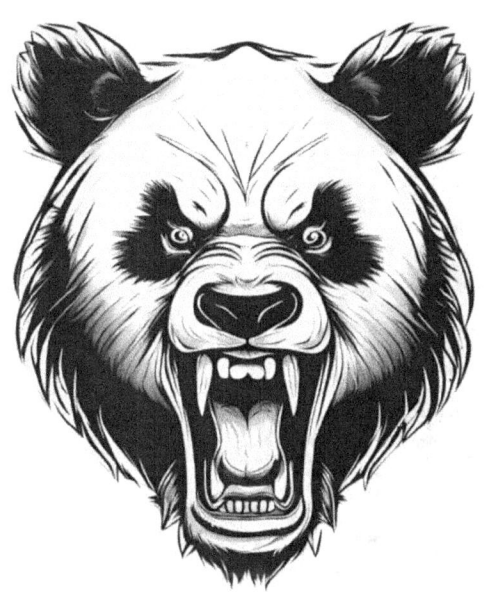
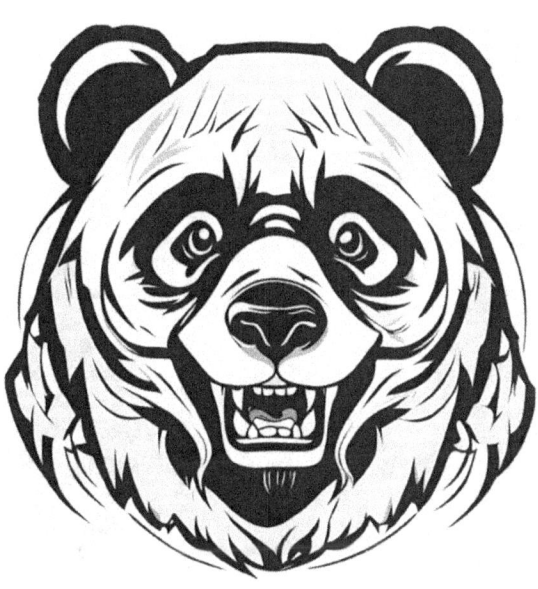

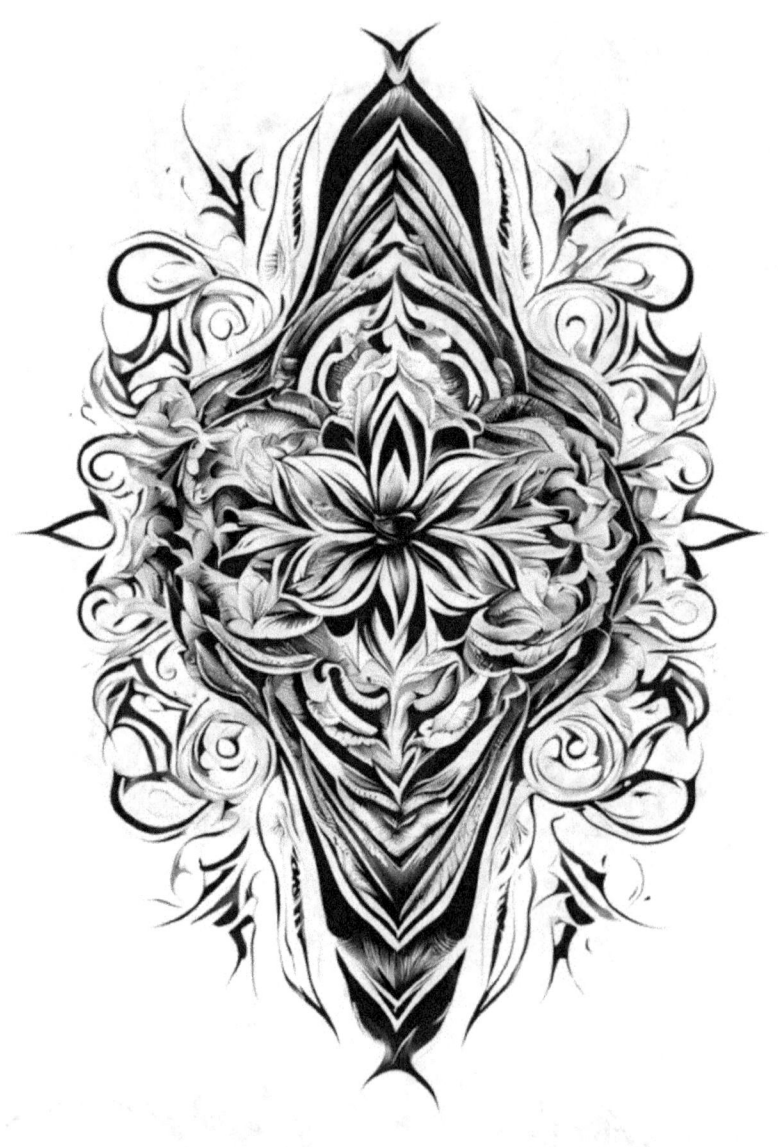
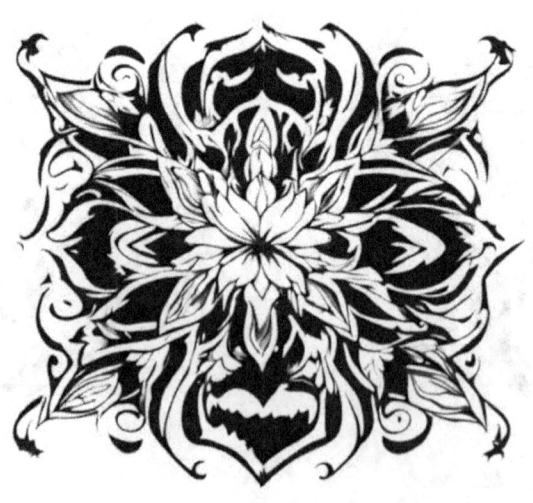

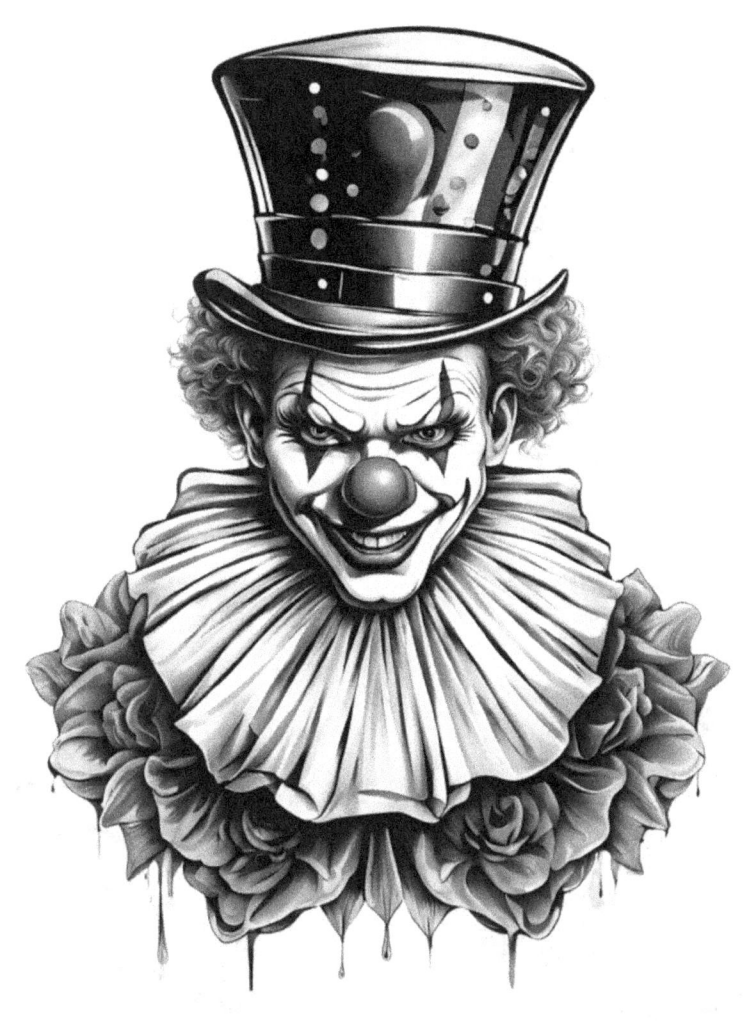
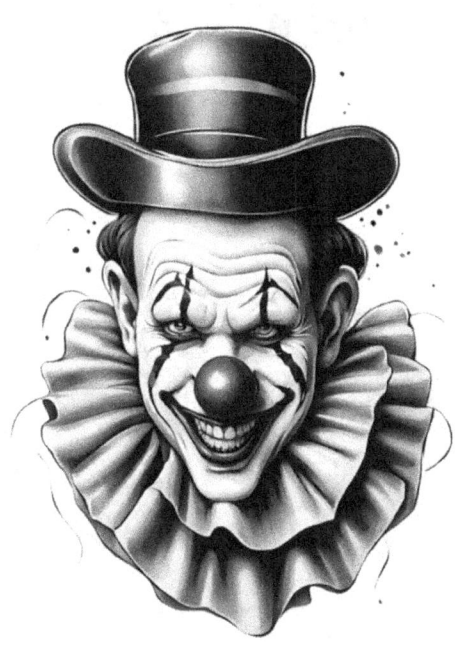
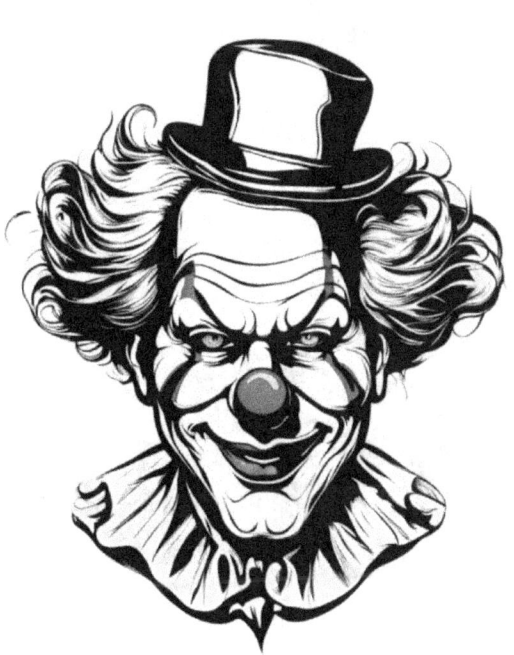

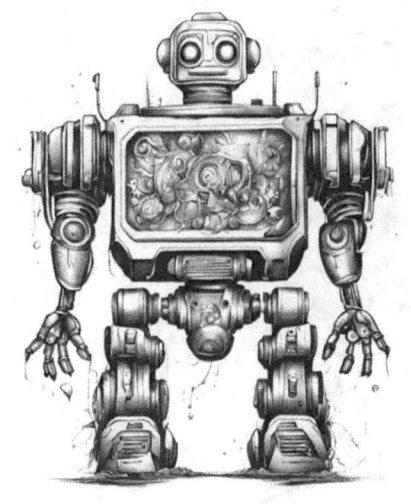
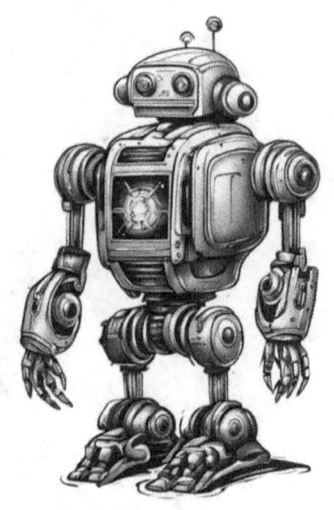
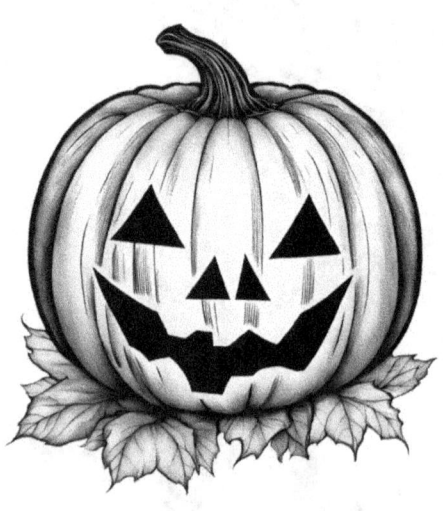
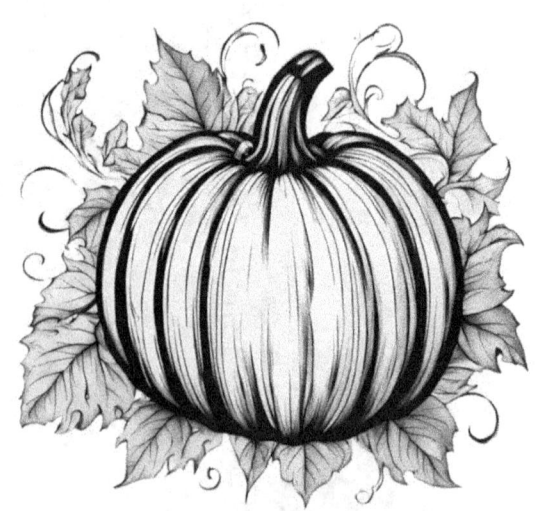
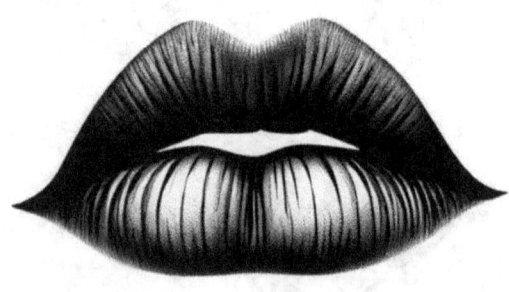
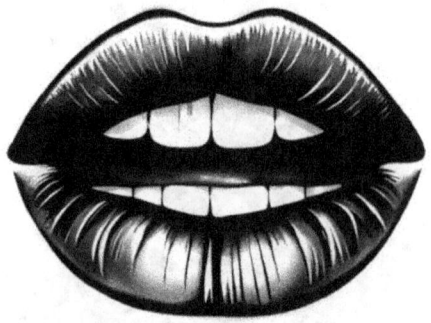

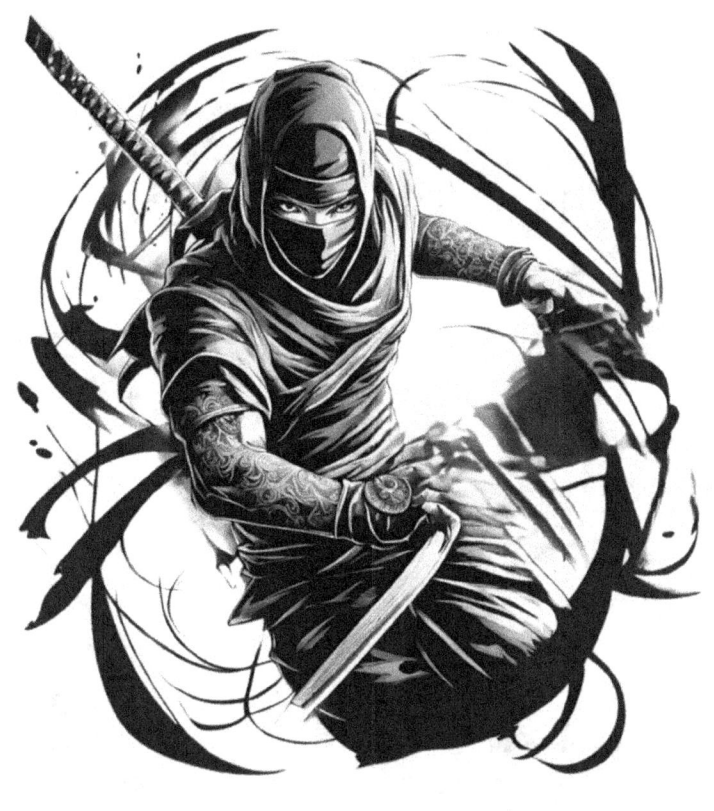
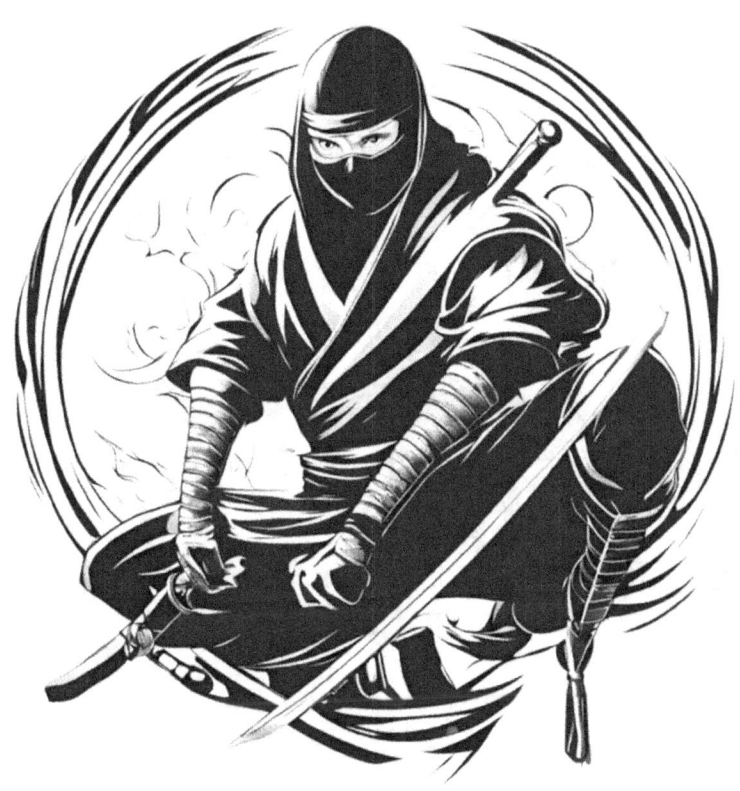

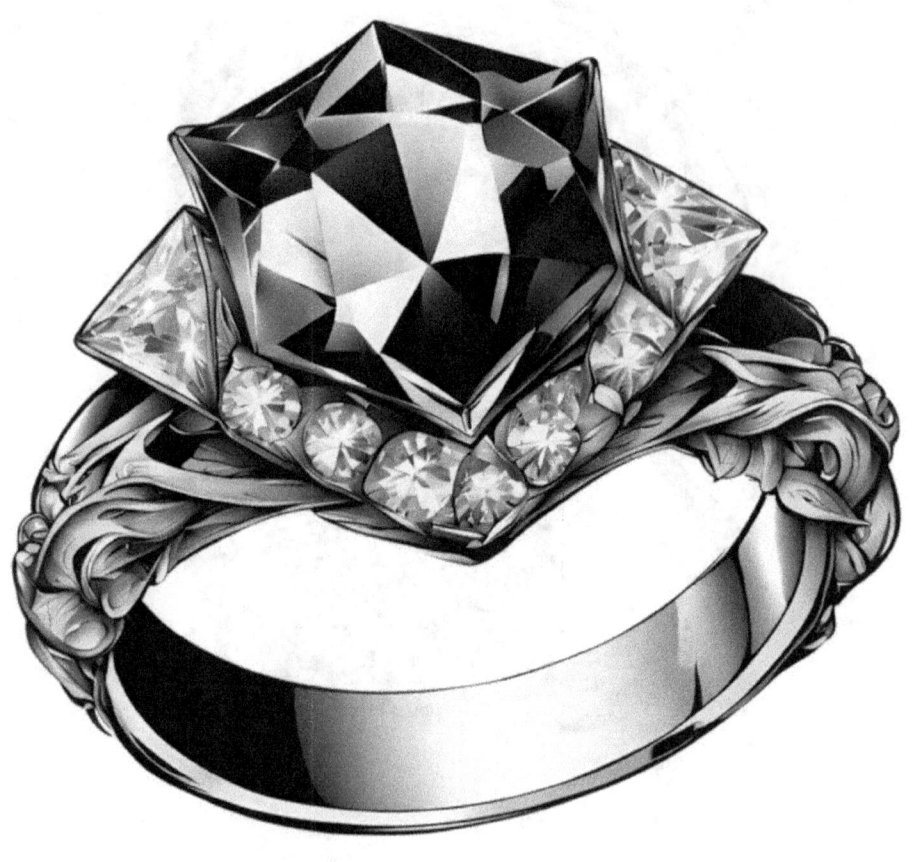
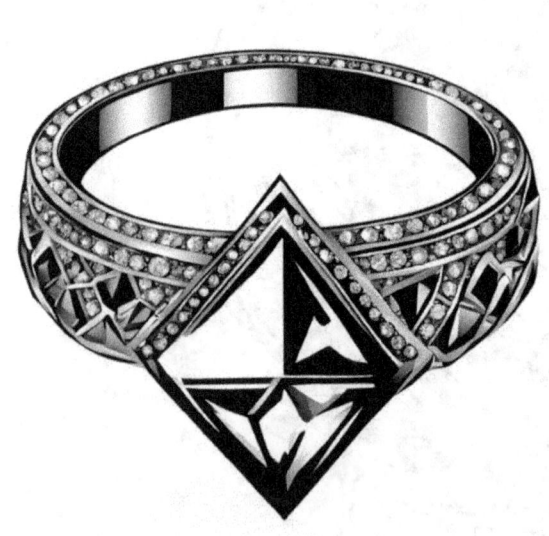
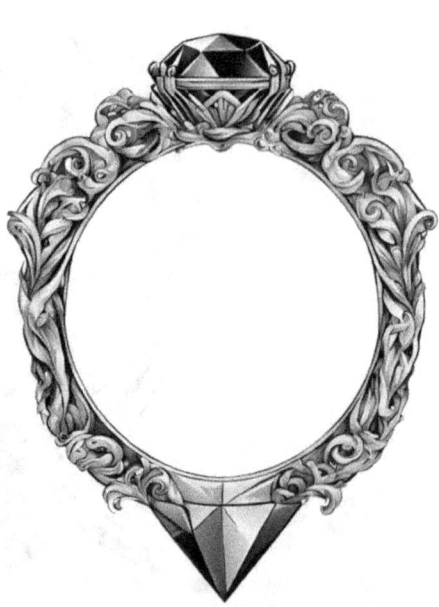

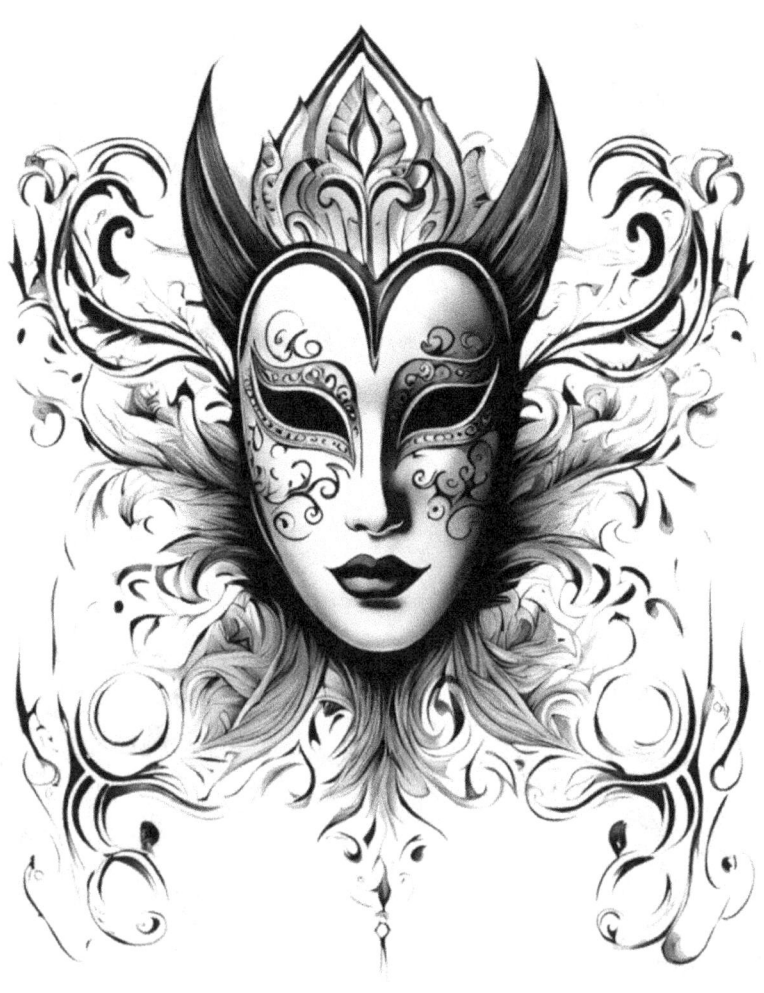
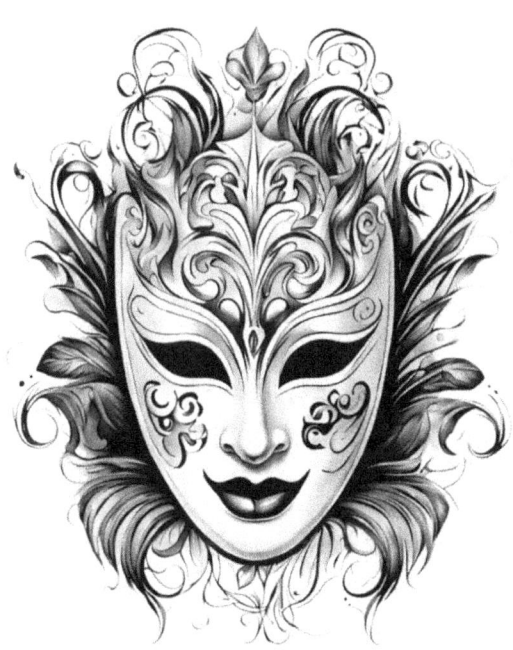
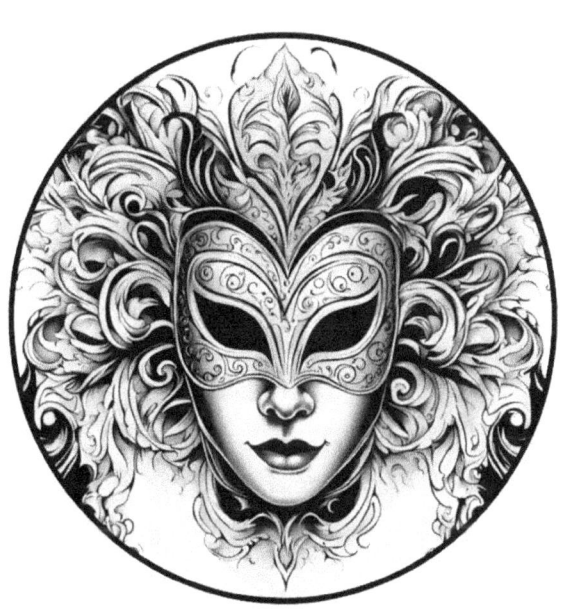

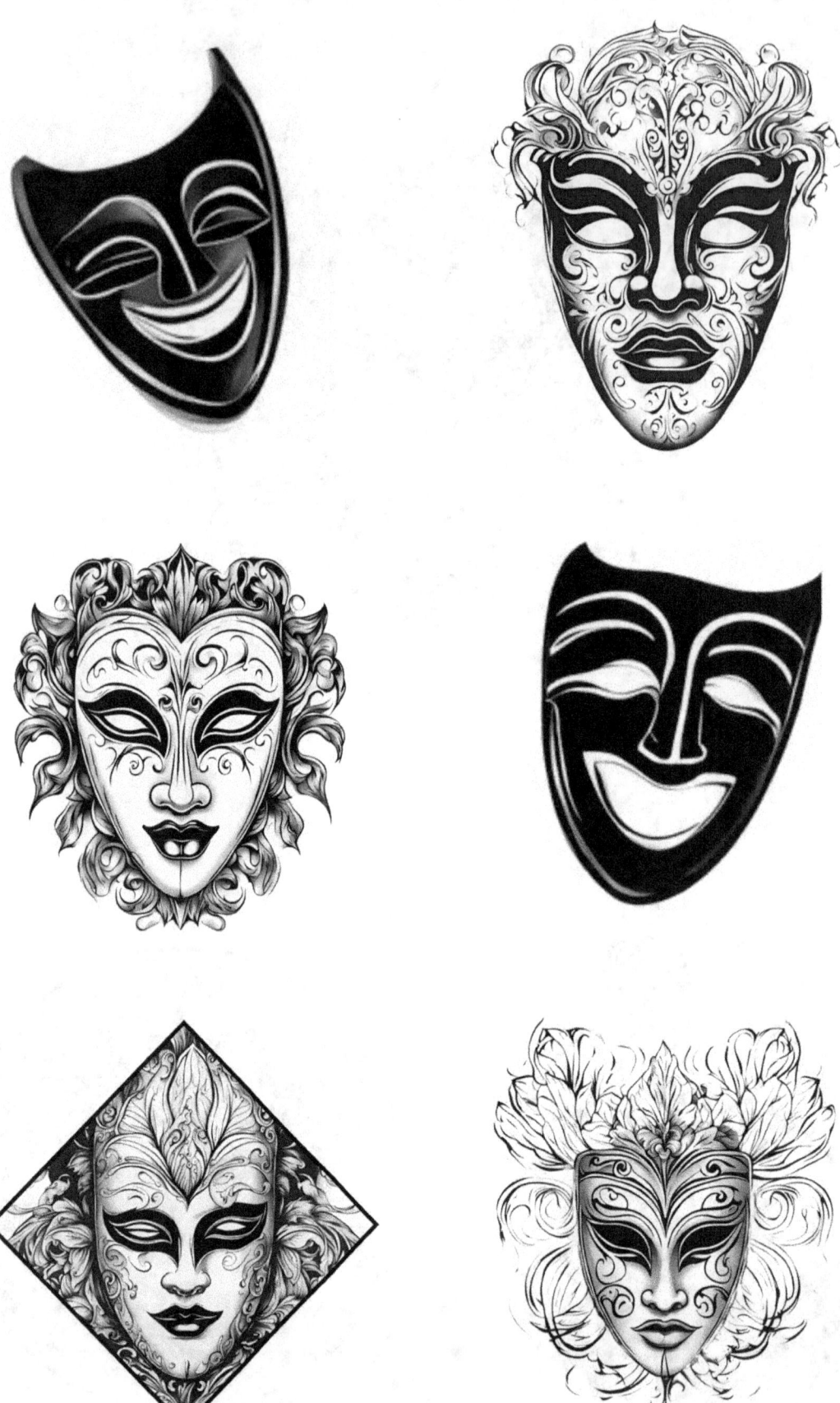

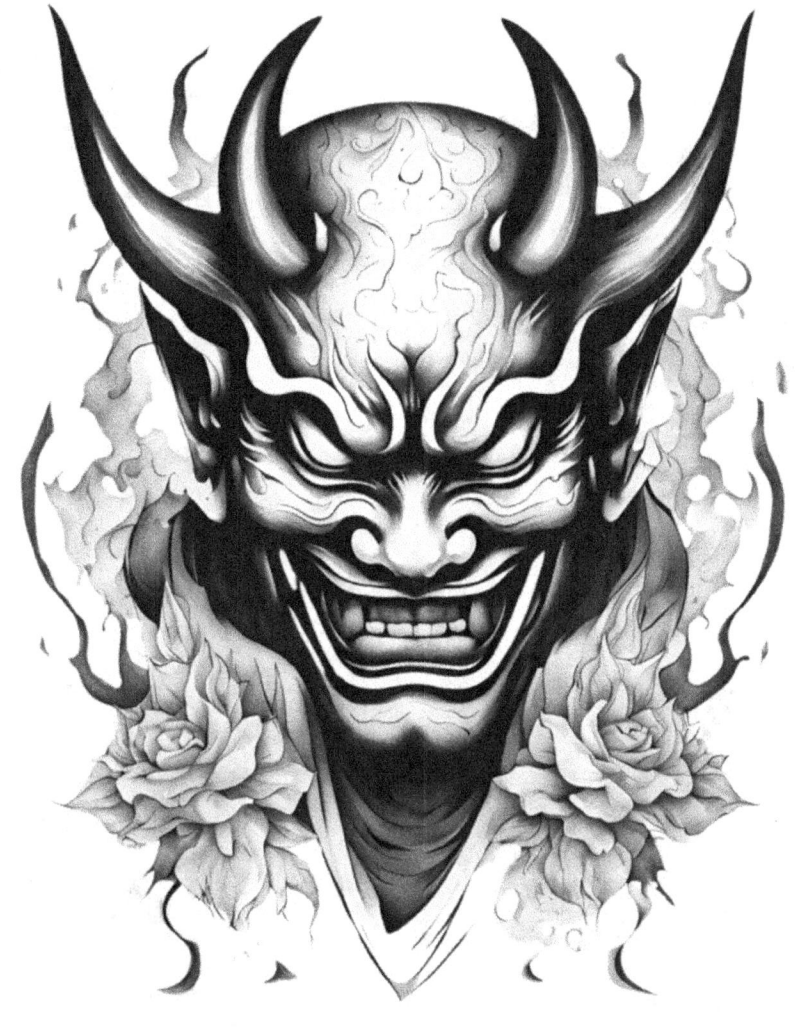
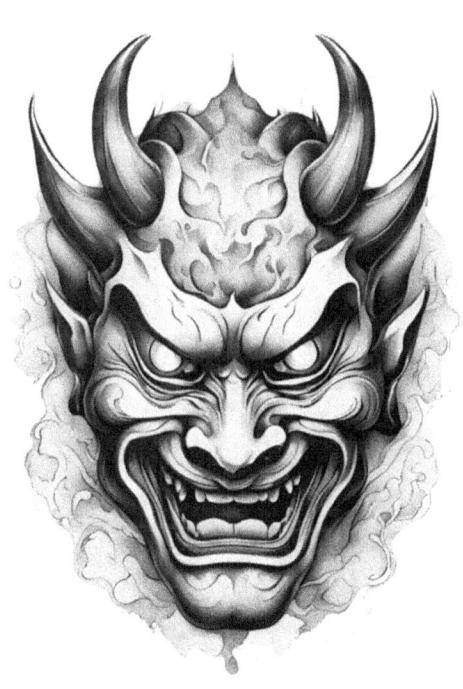
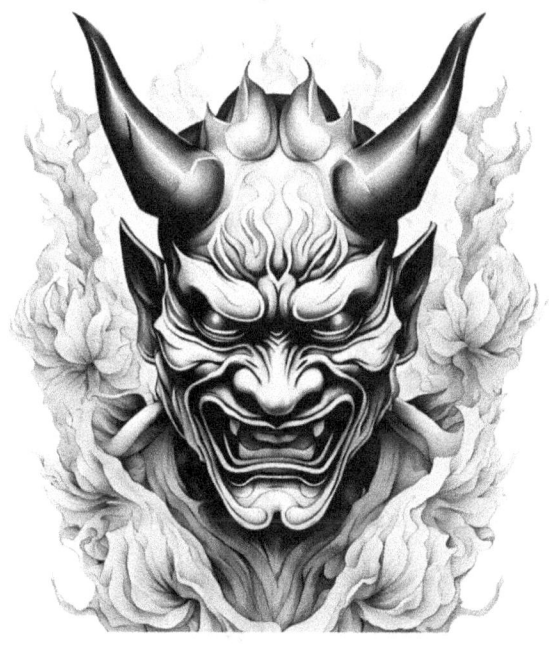

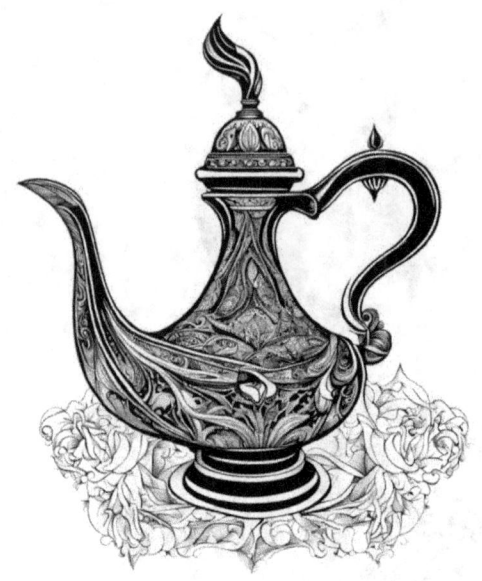
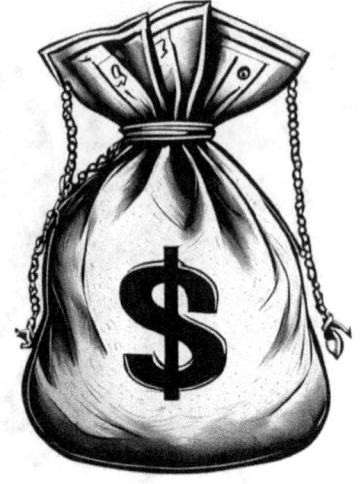
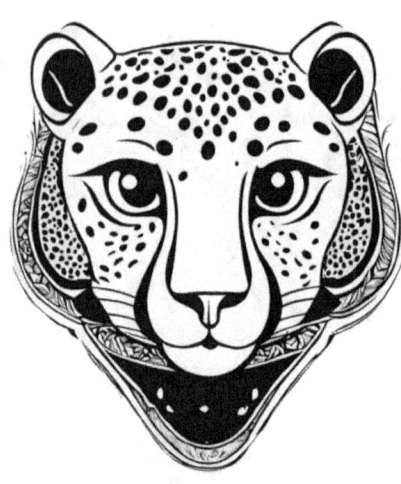
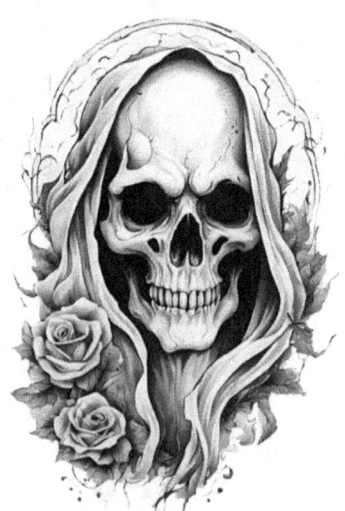
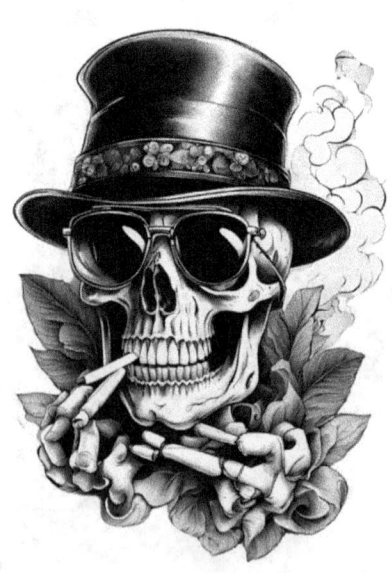
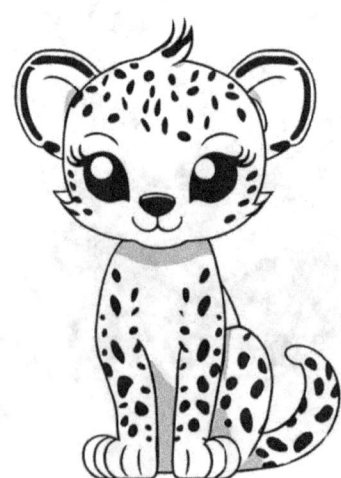

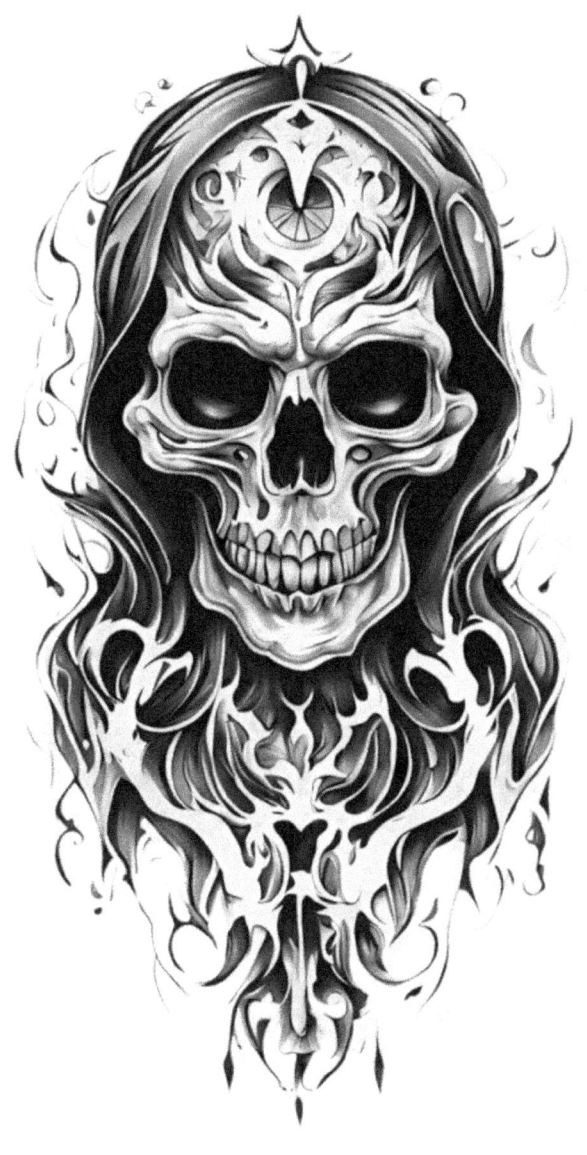
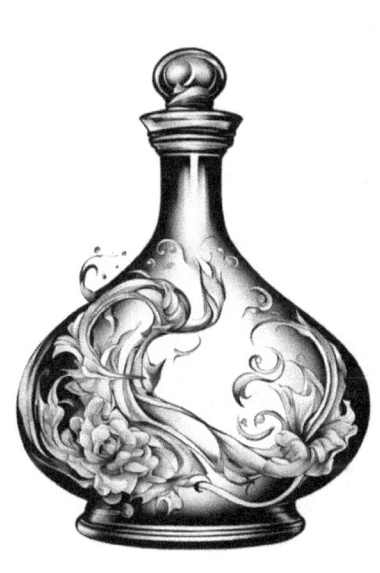
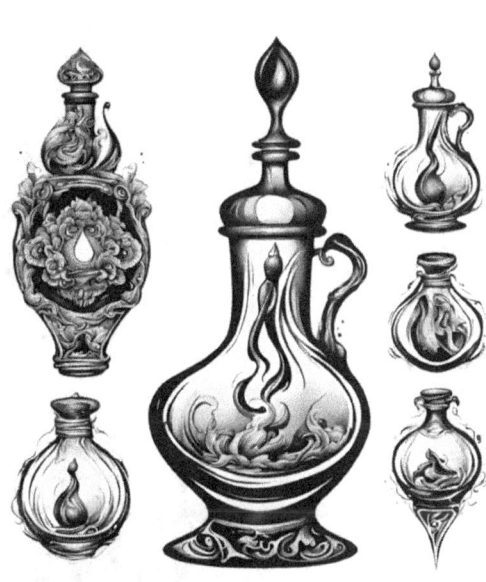

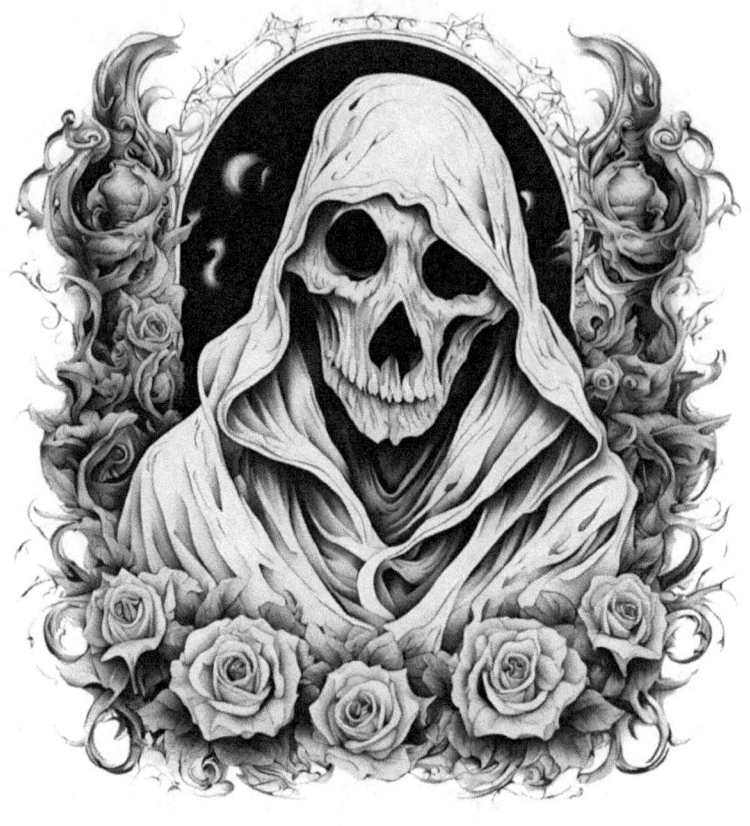
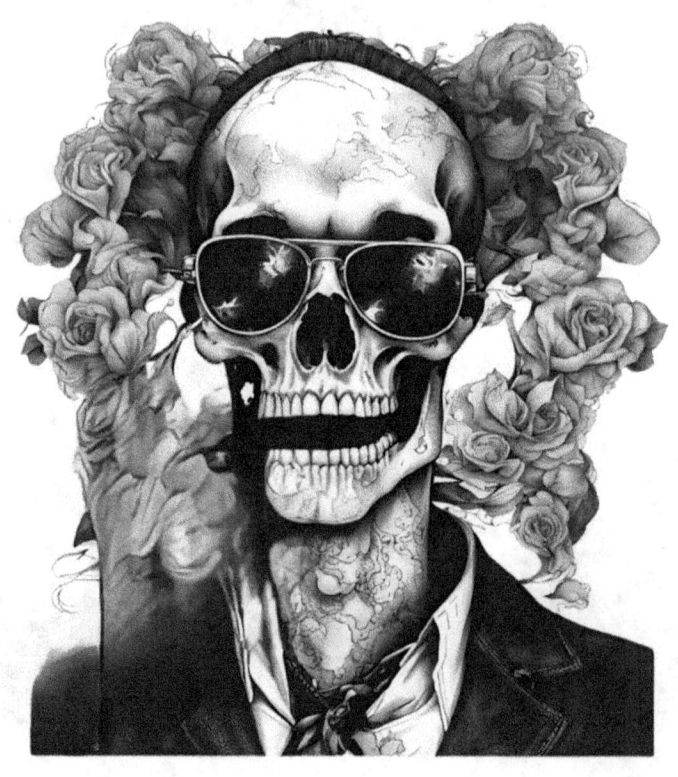

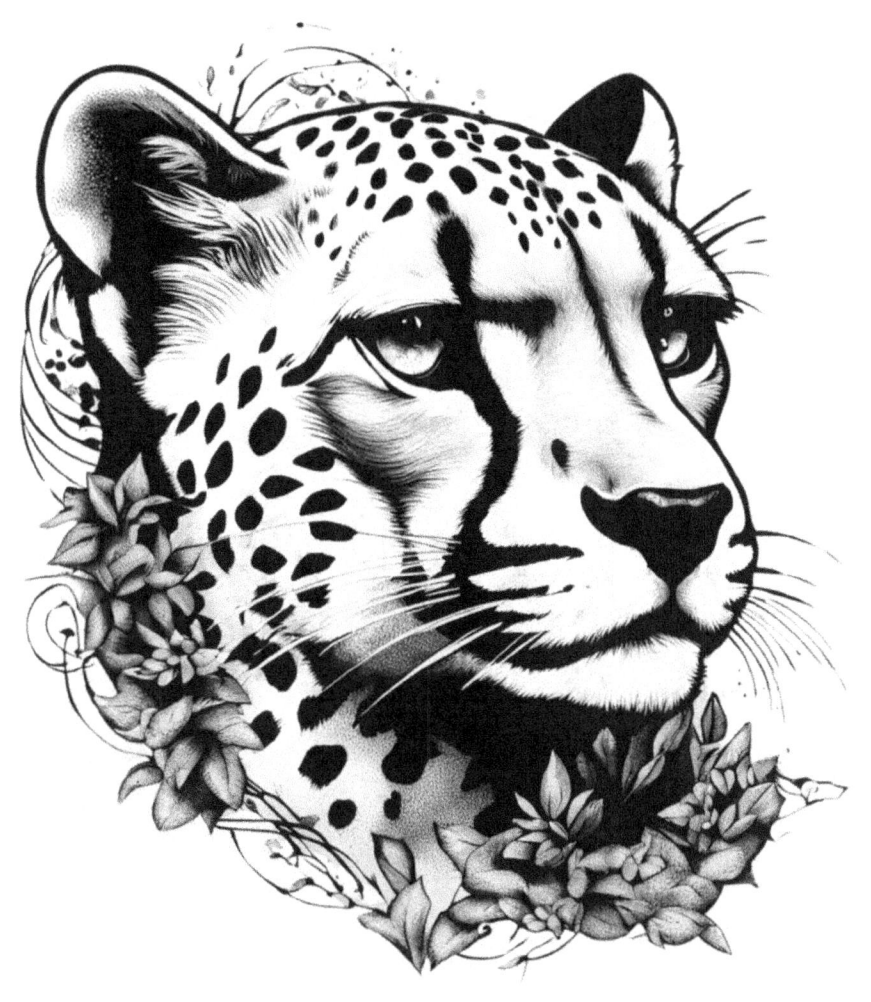
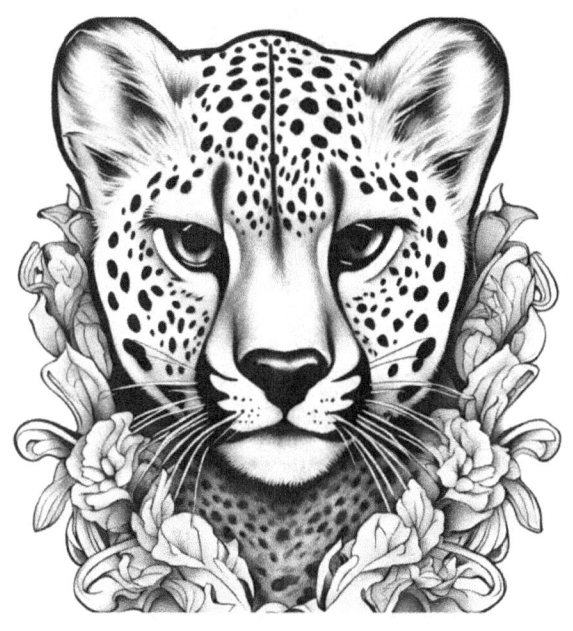
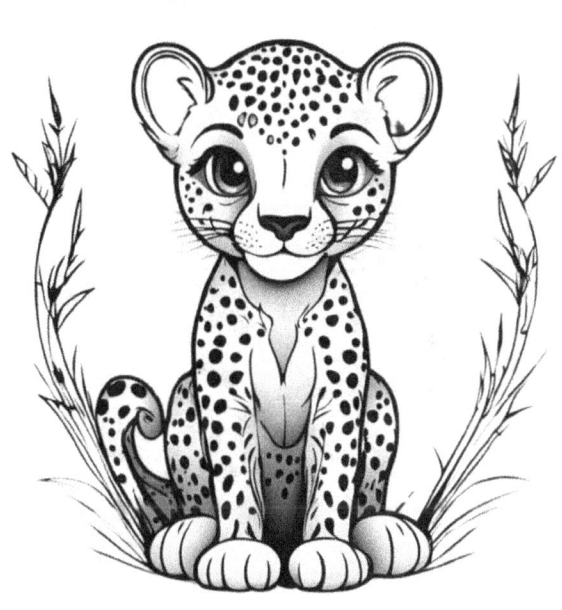

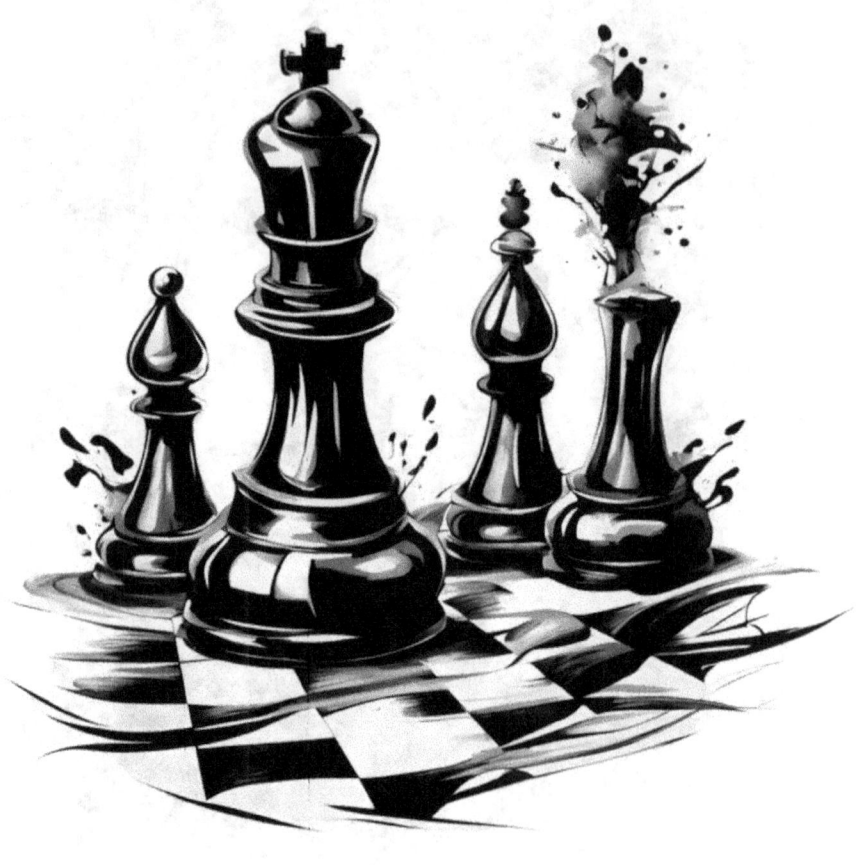
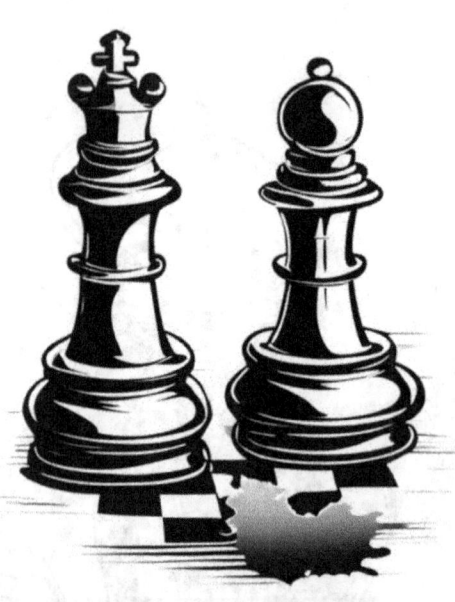
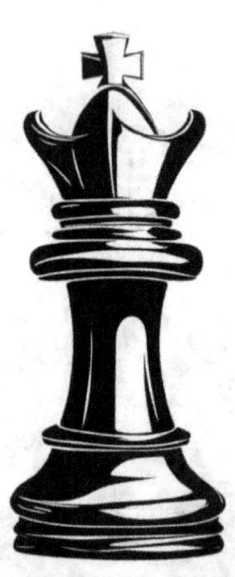

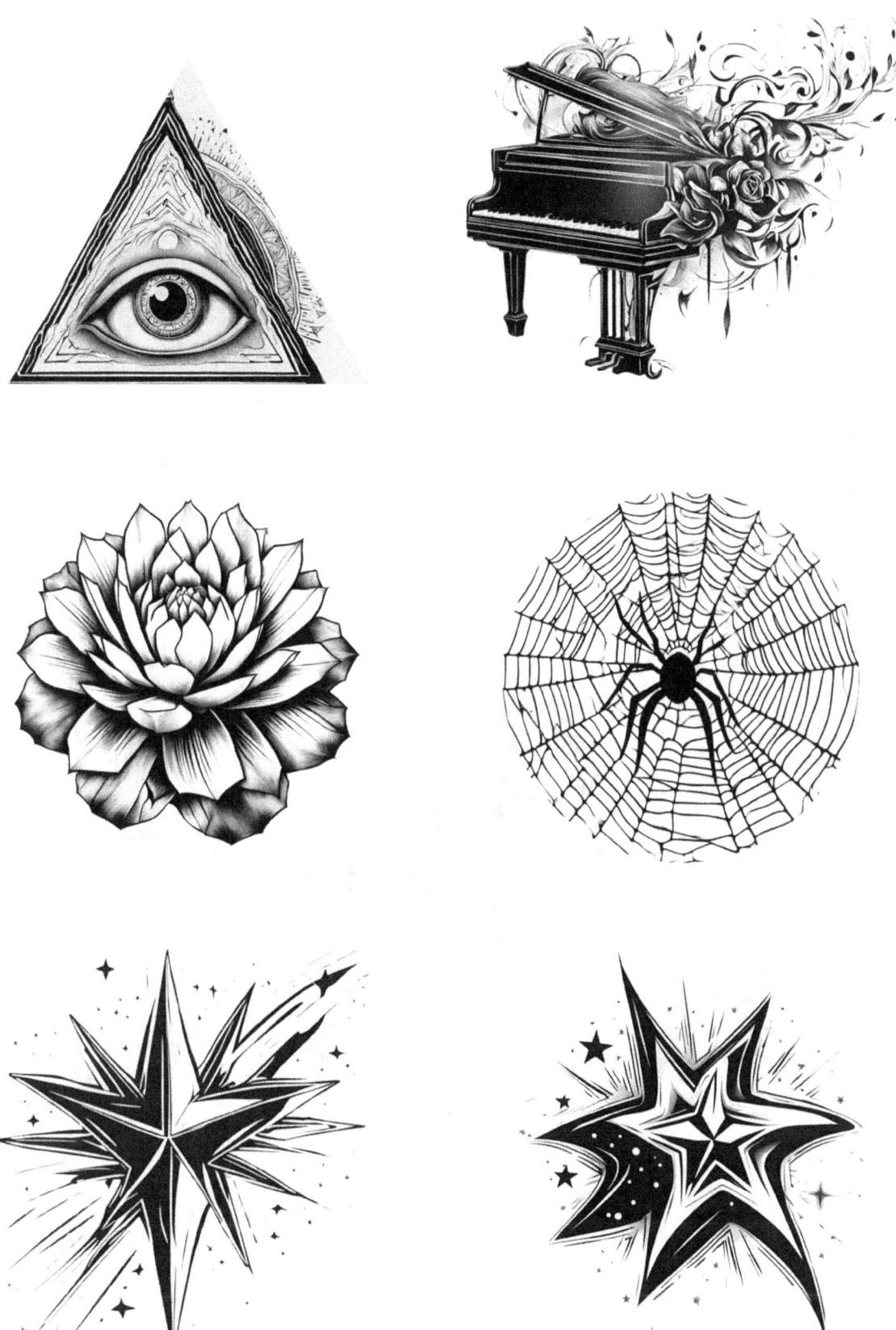

149

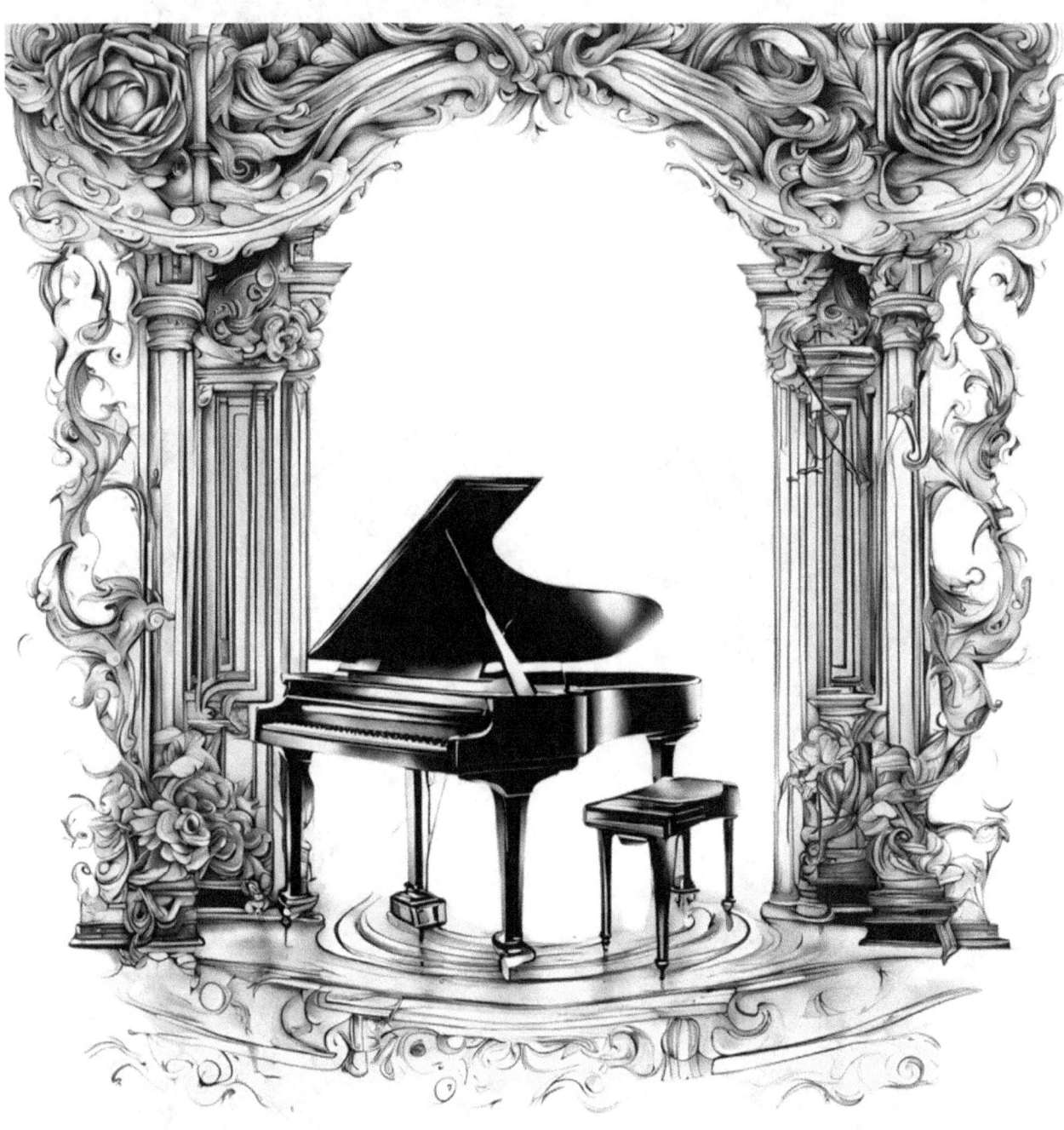

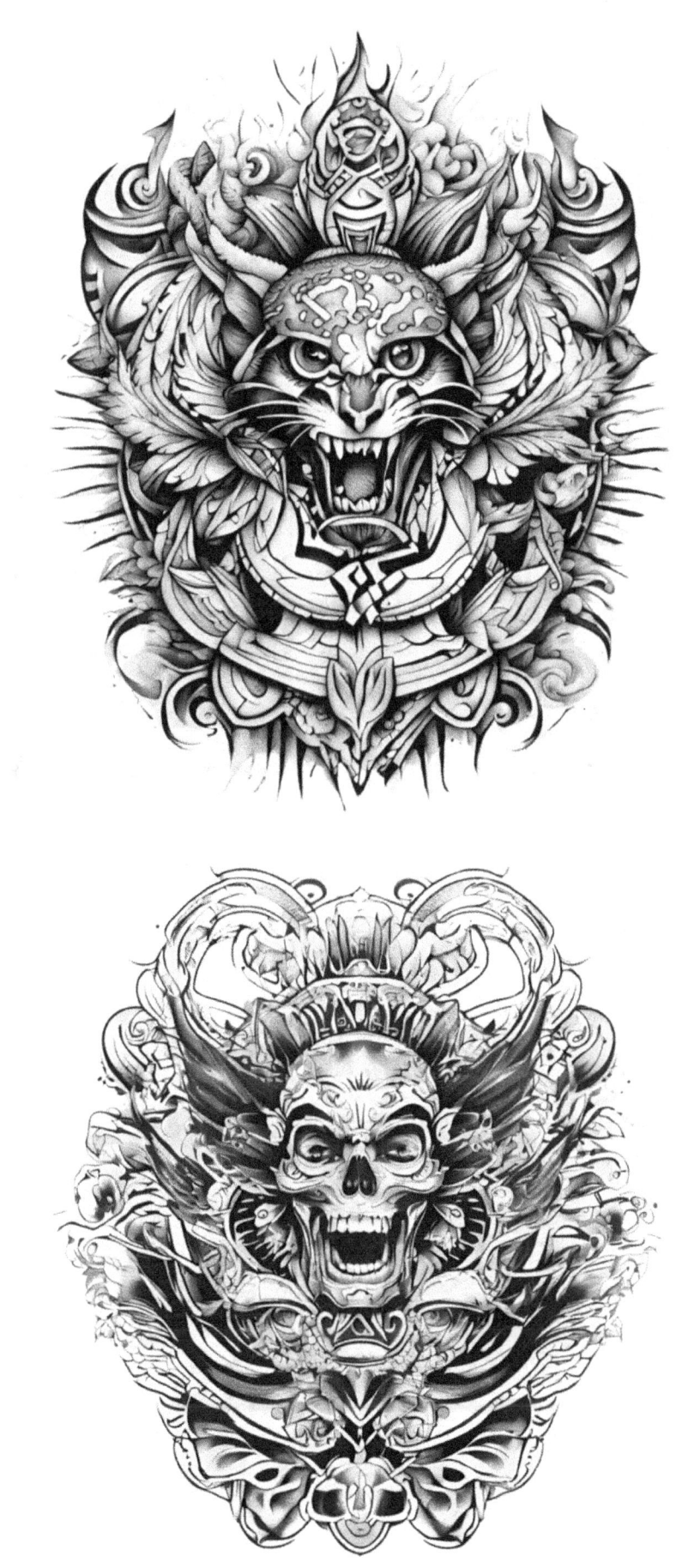

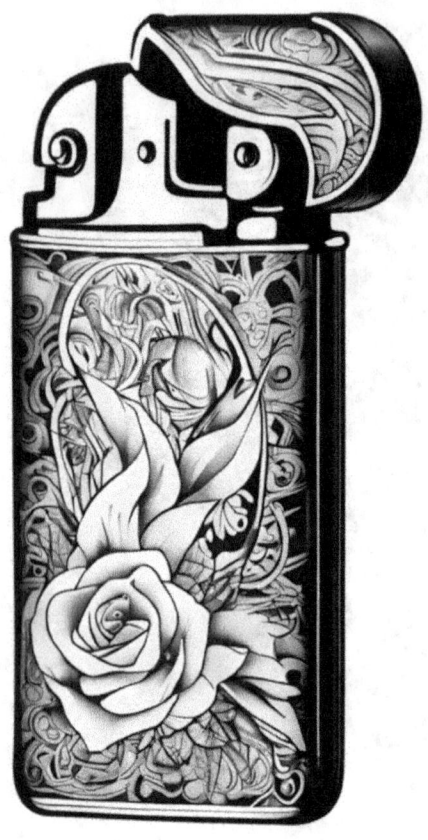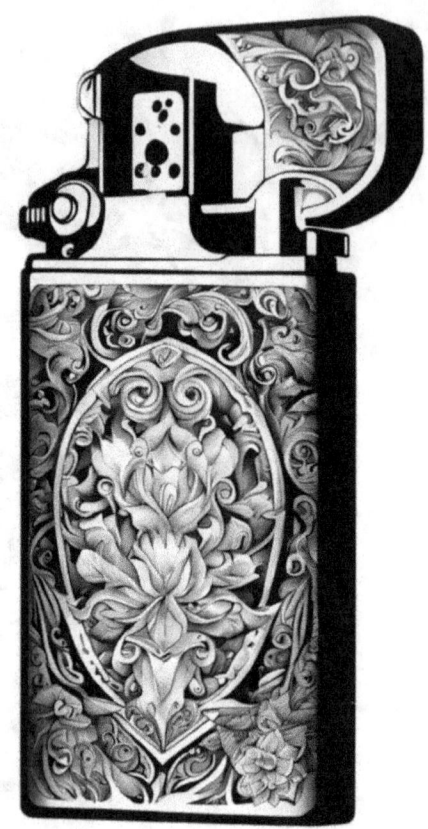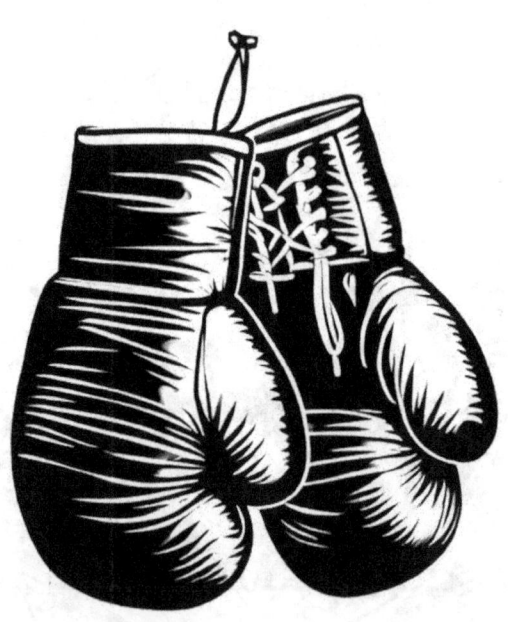

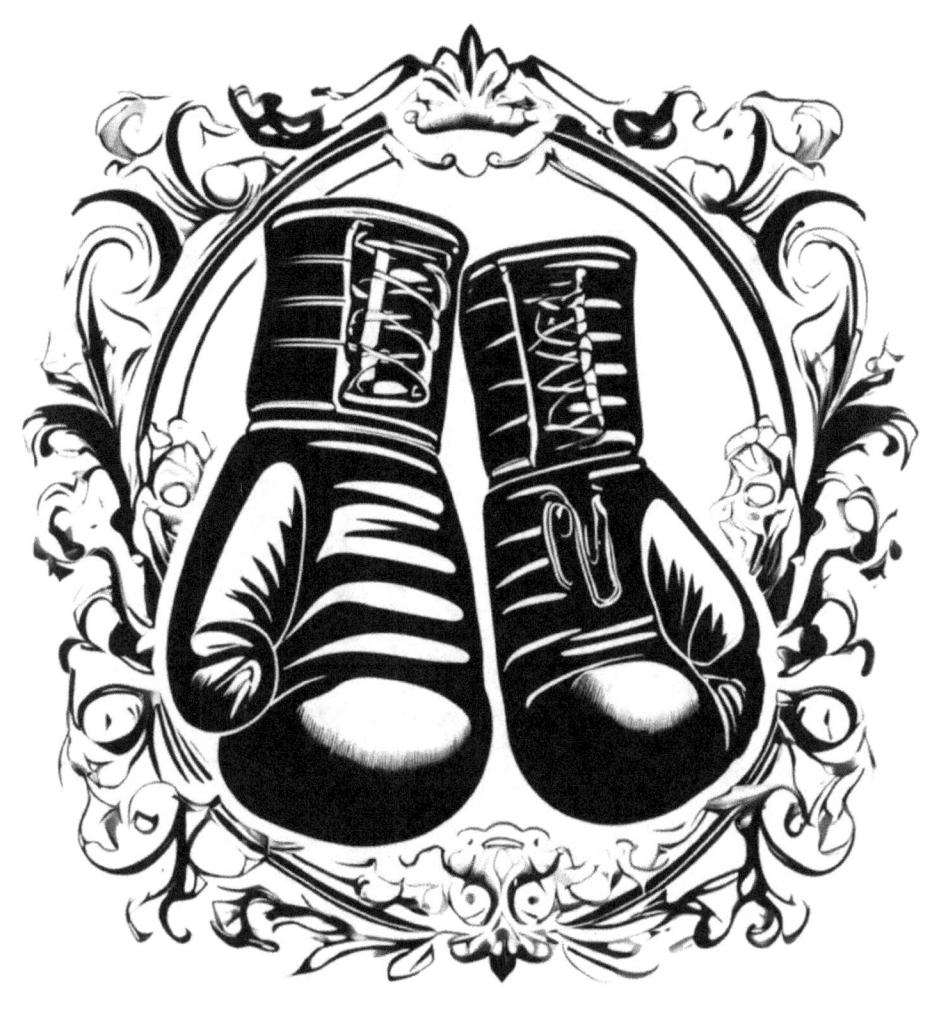
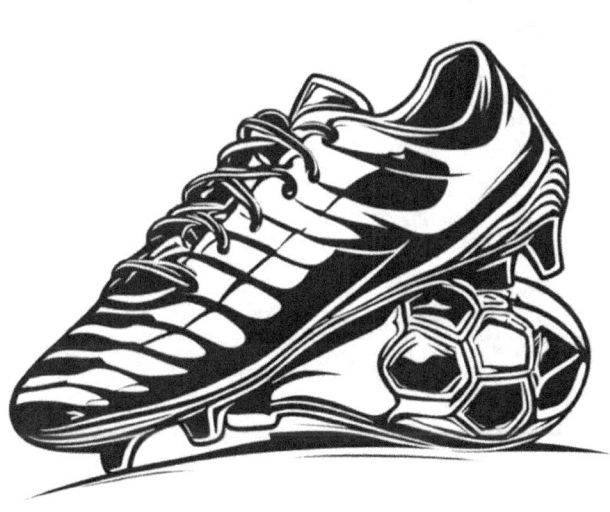
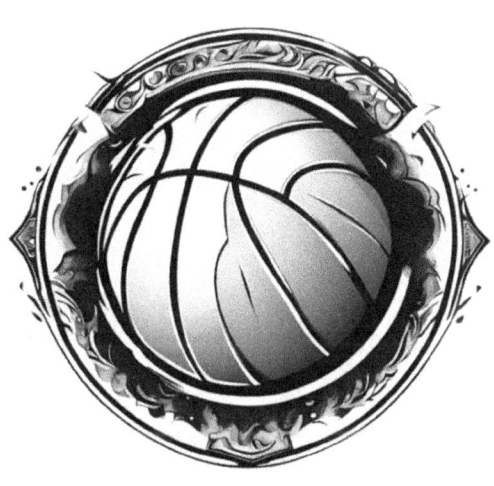

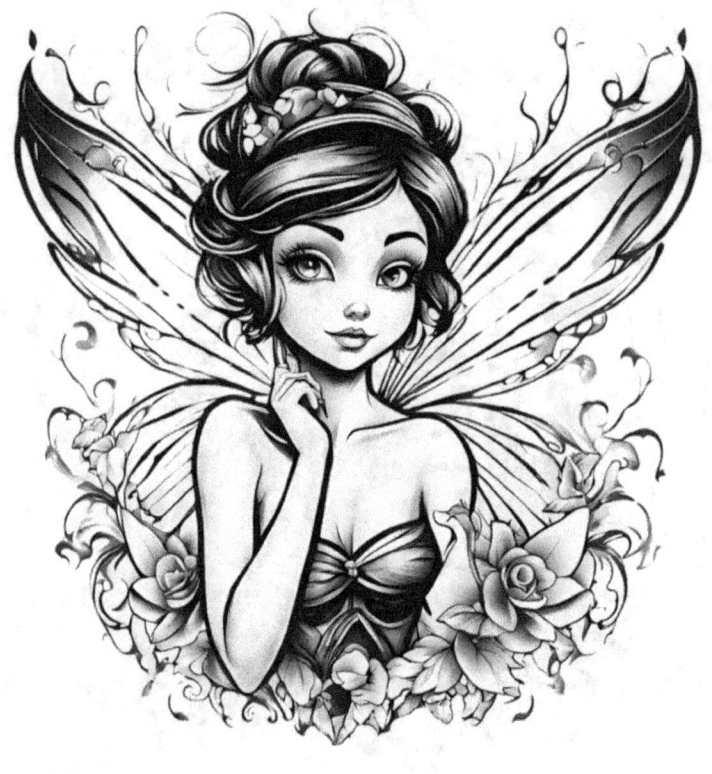
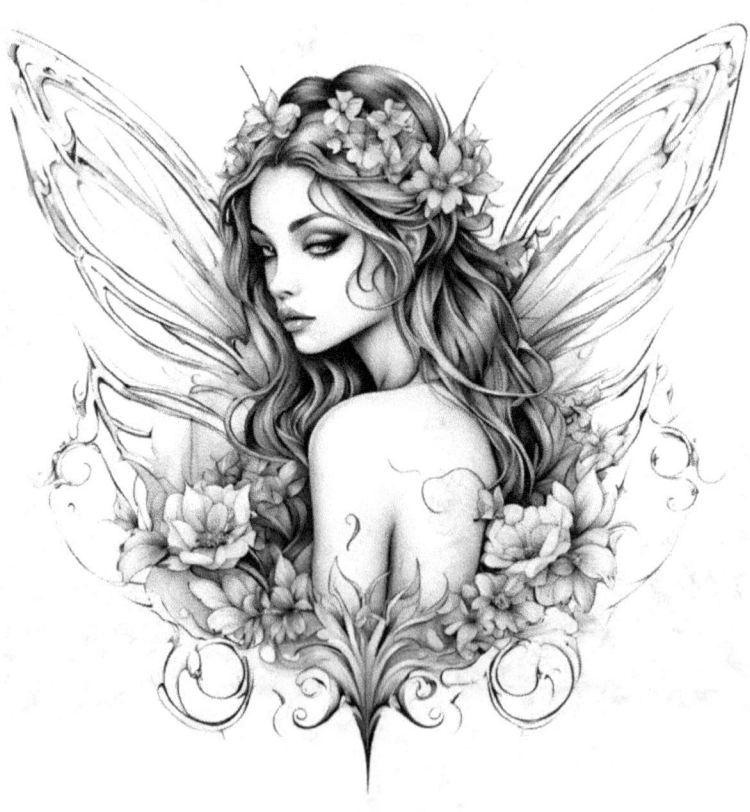

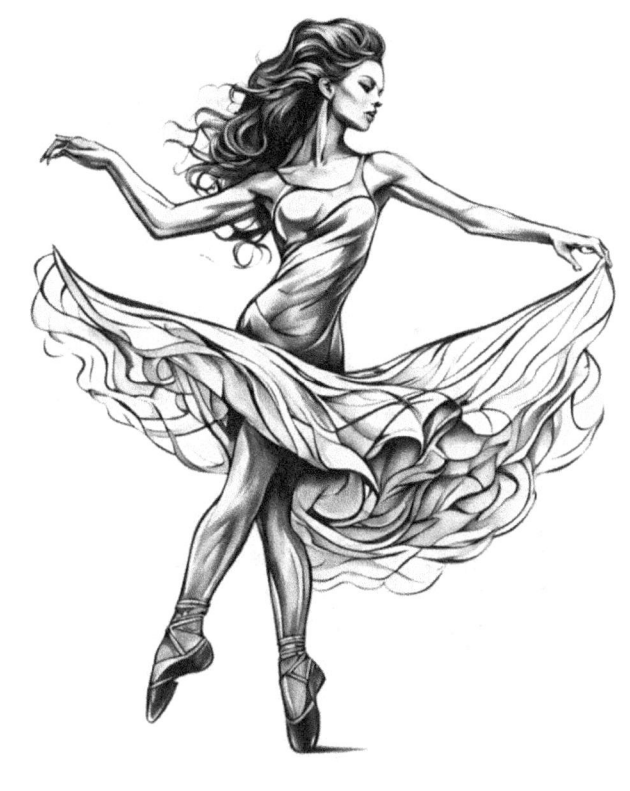
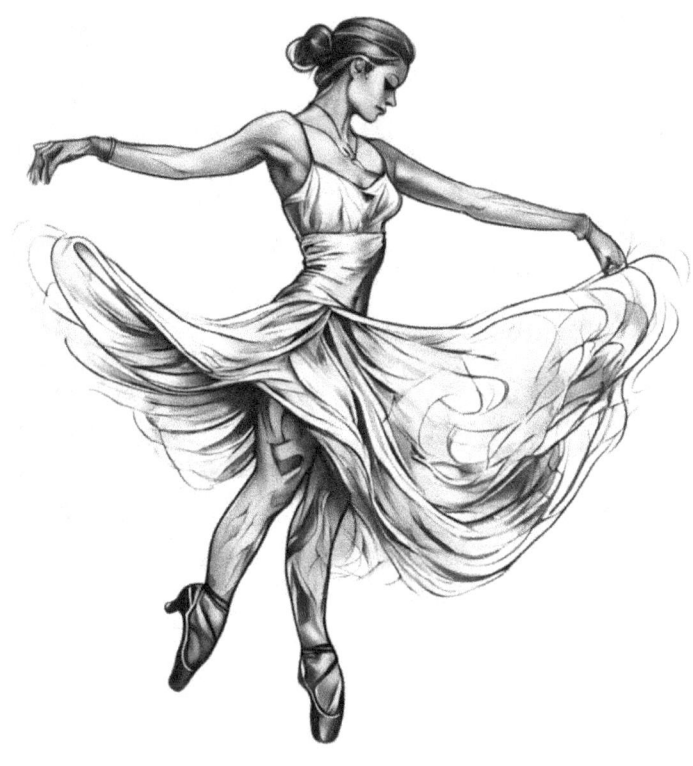

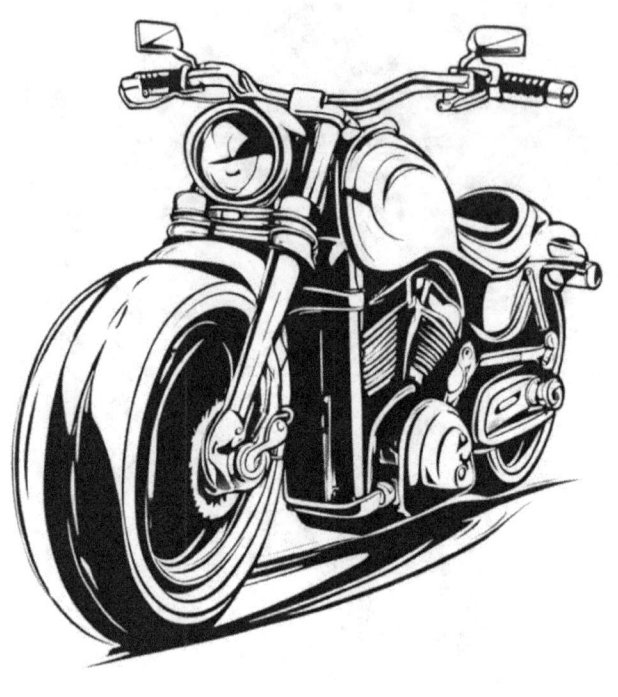
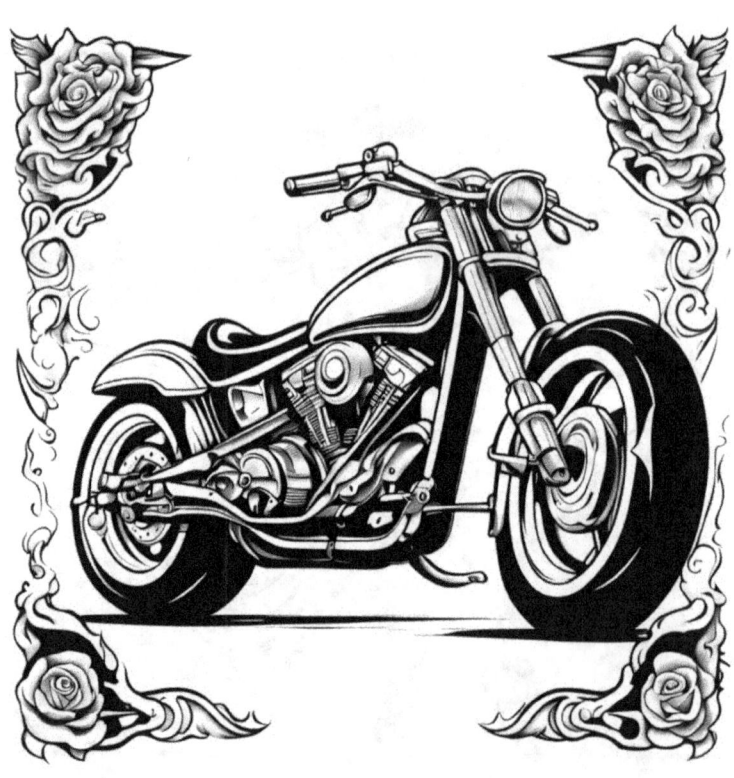

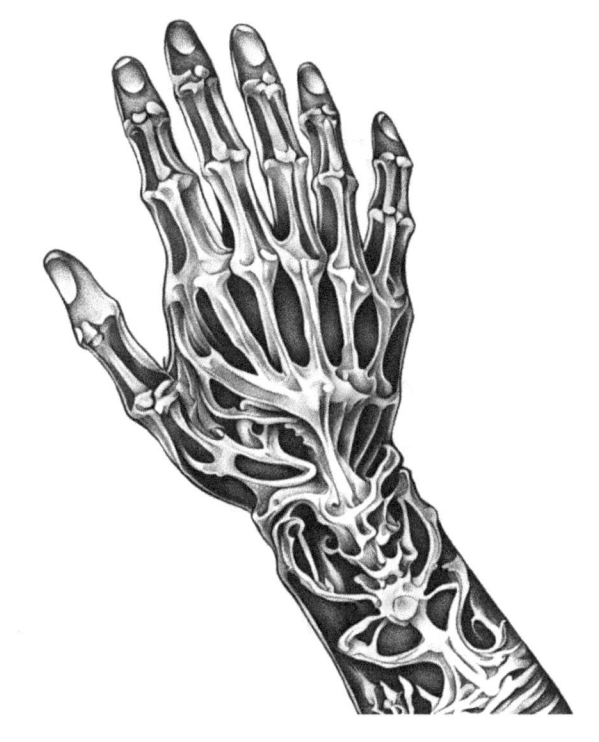
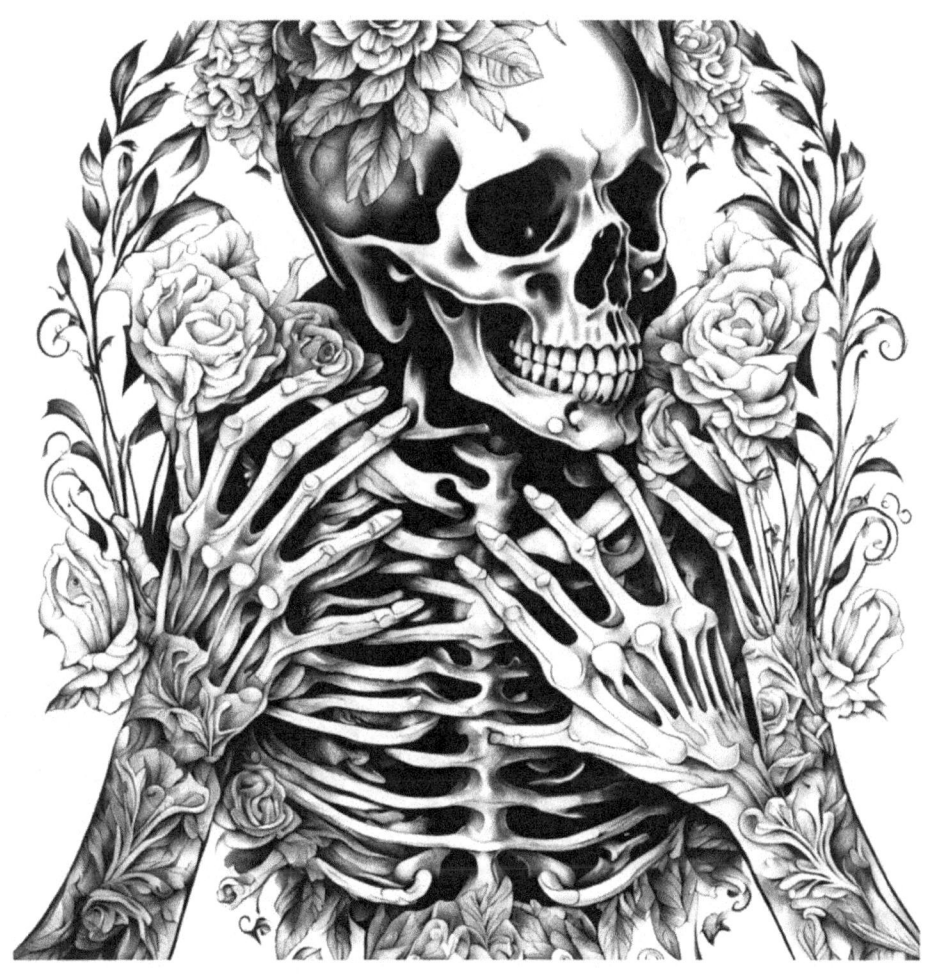

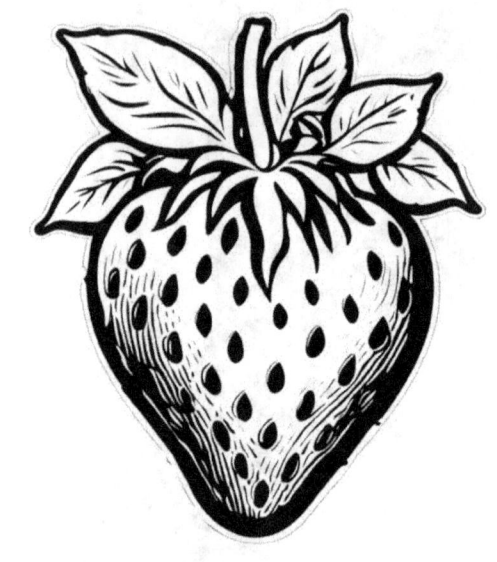
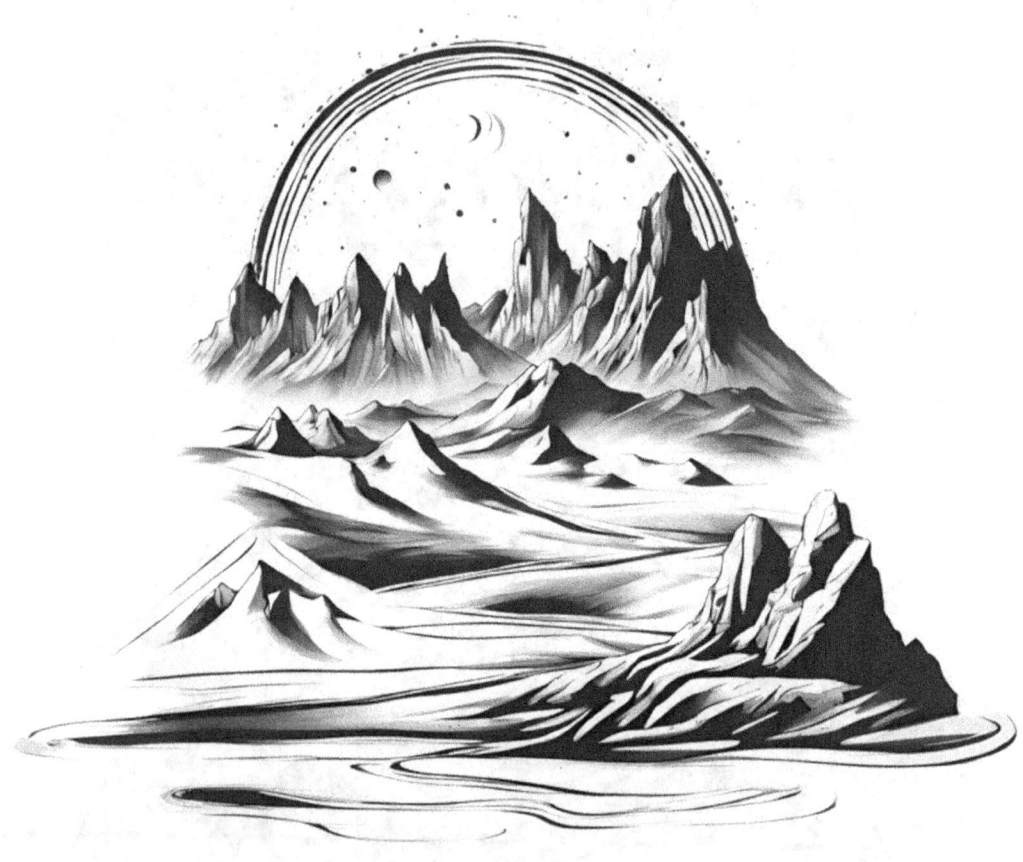

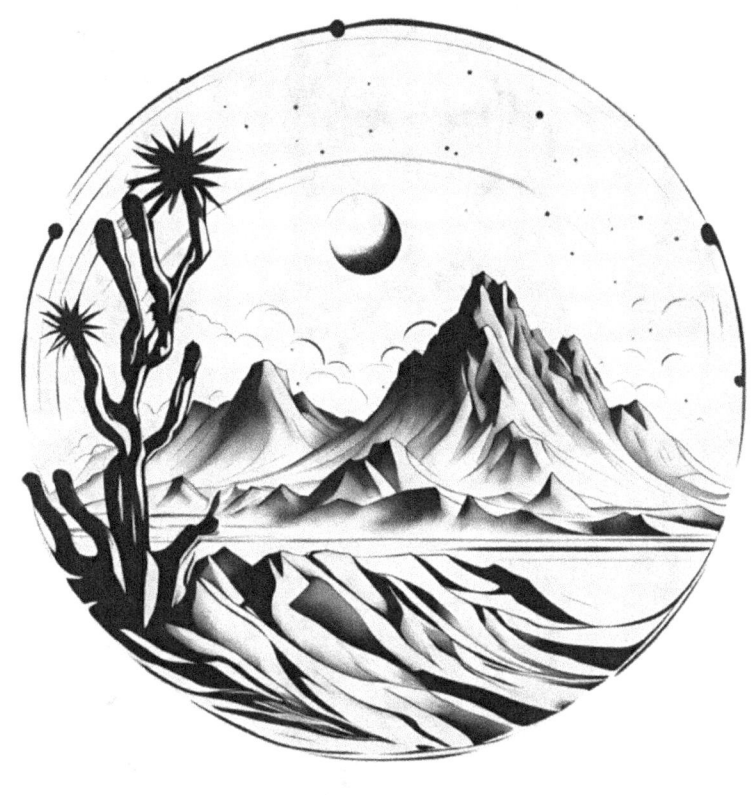
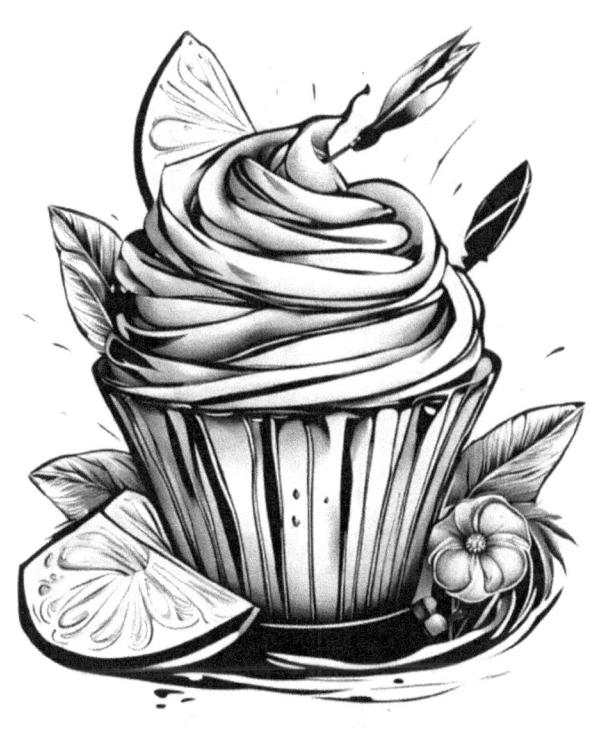

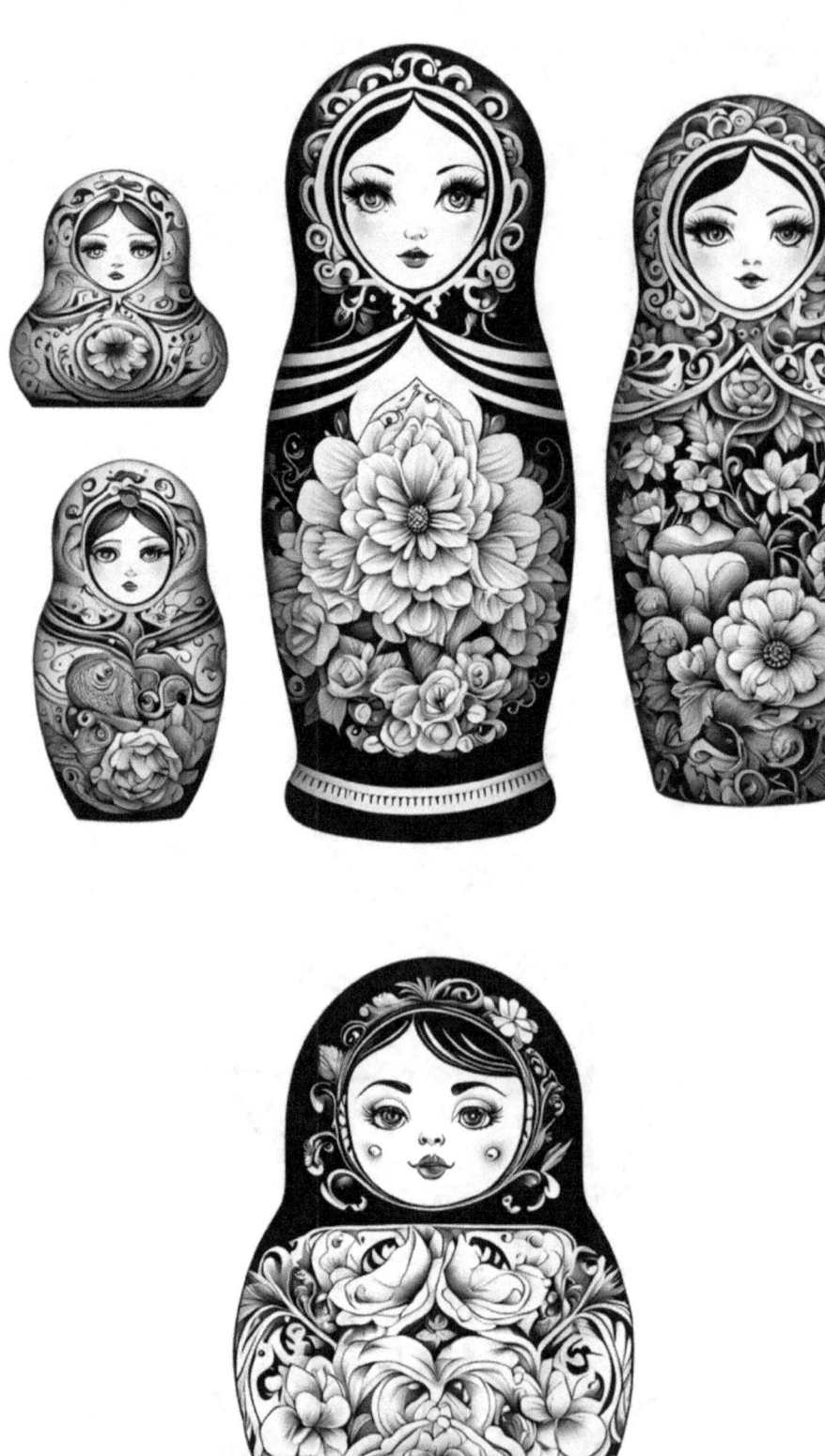

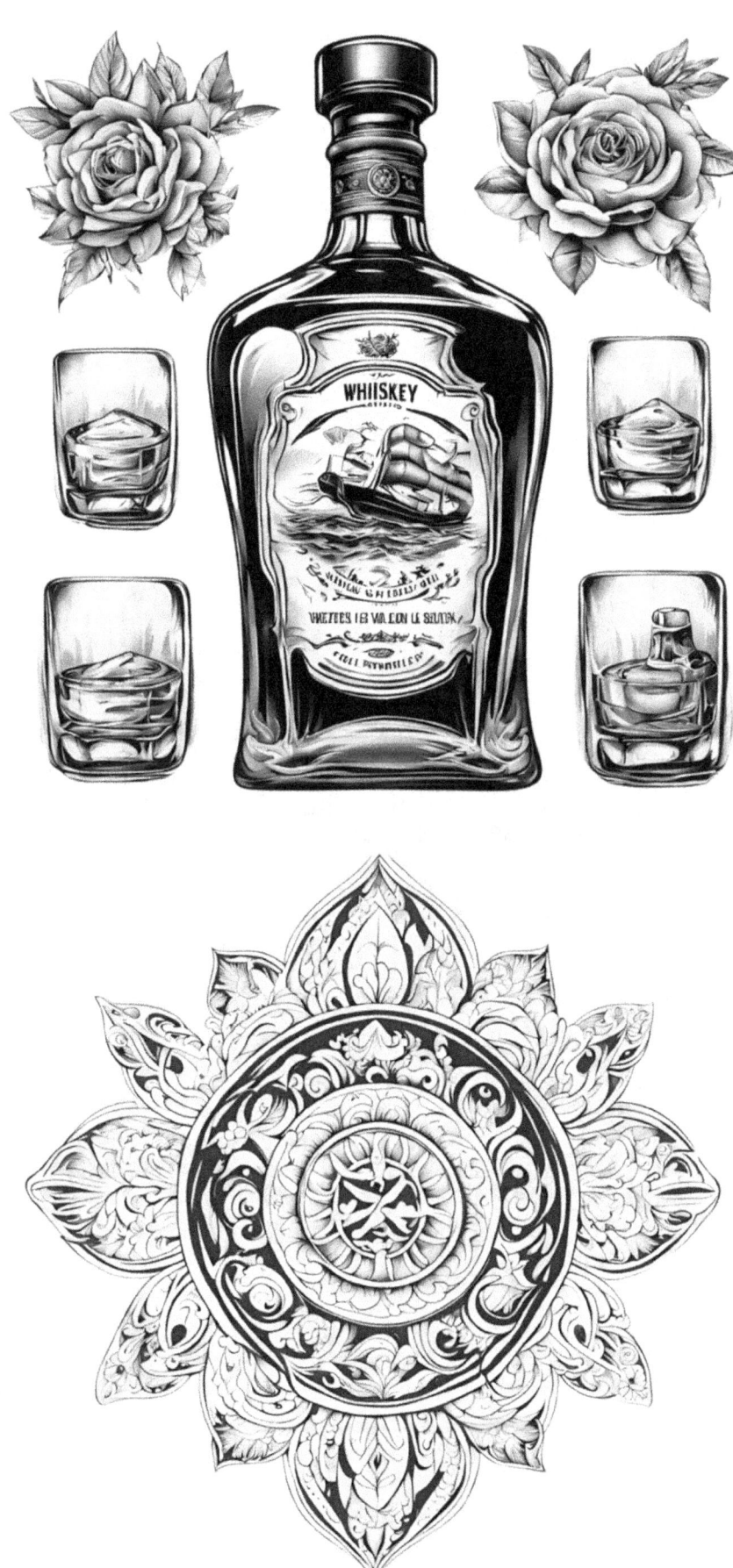

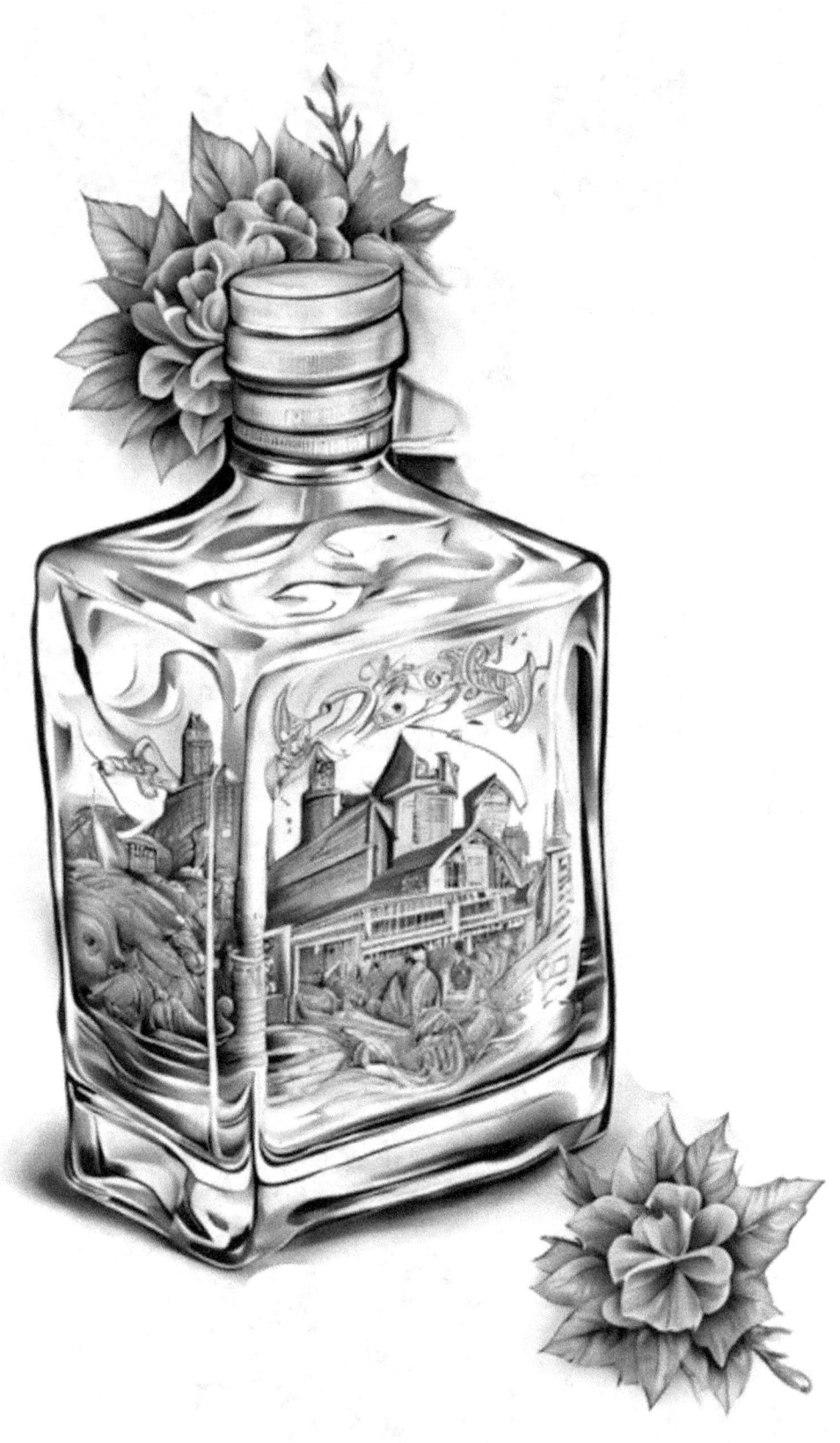

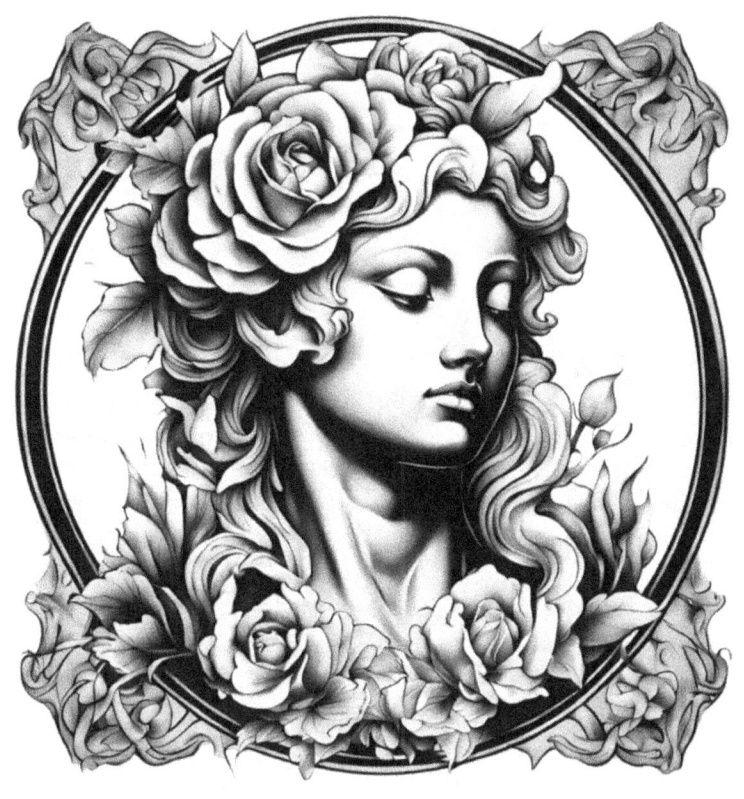
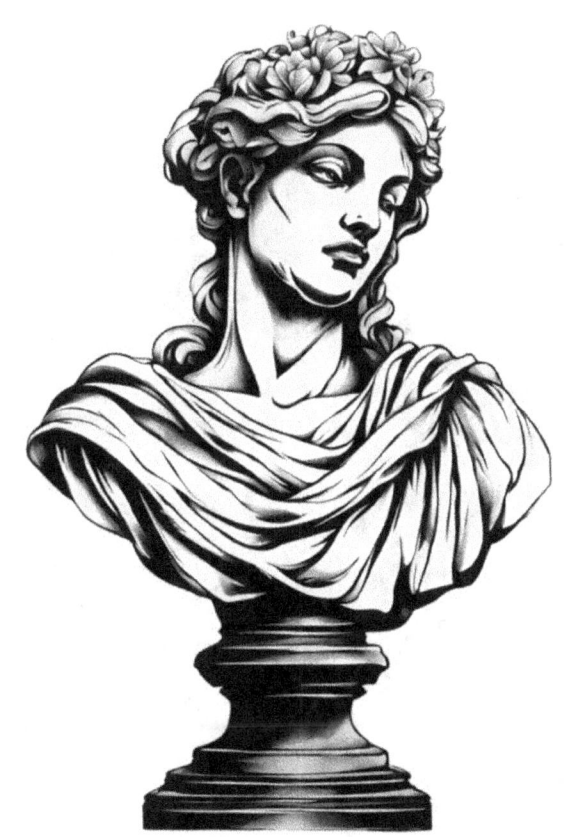

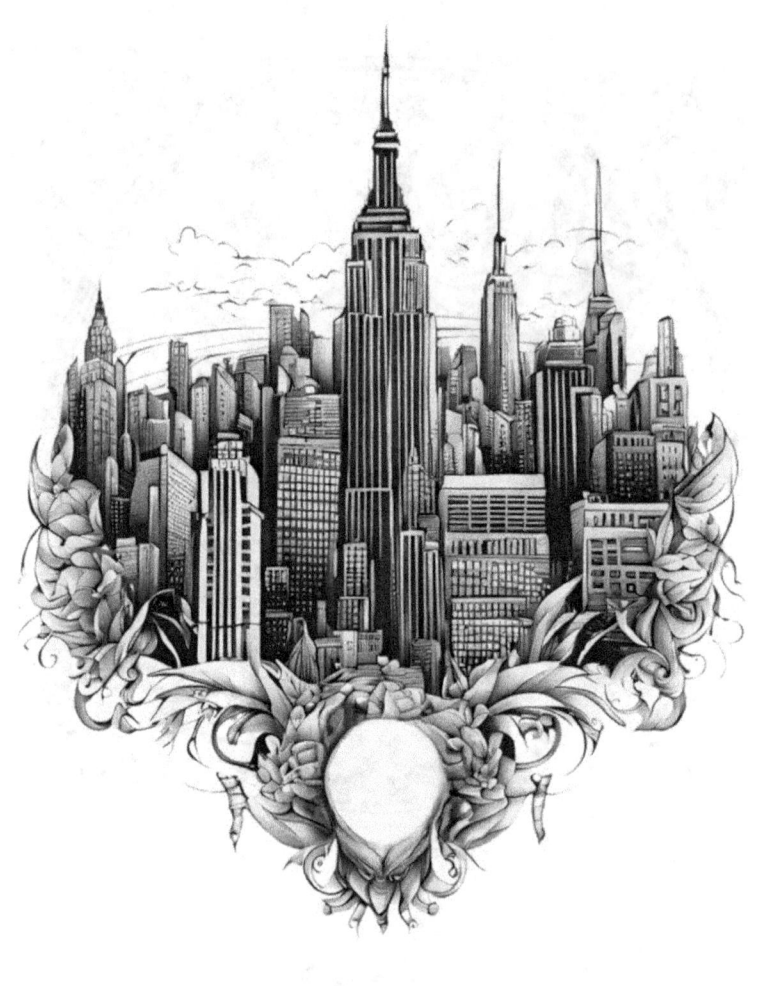
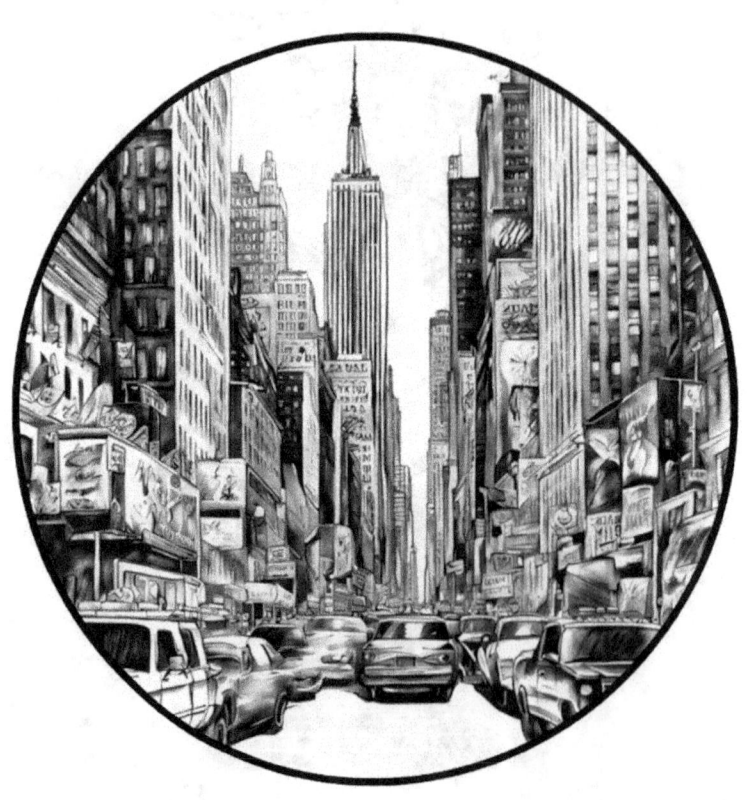

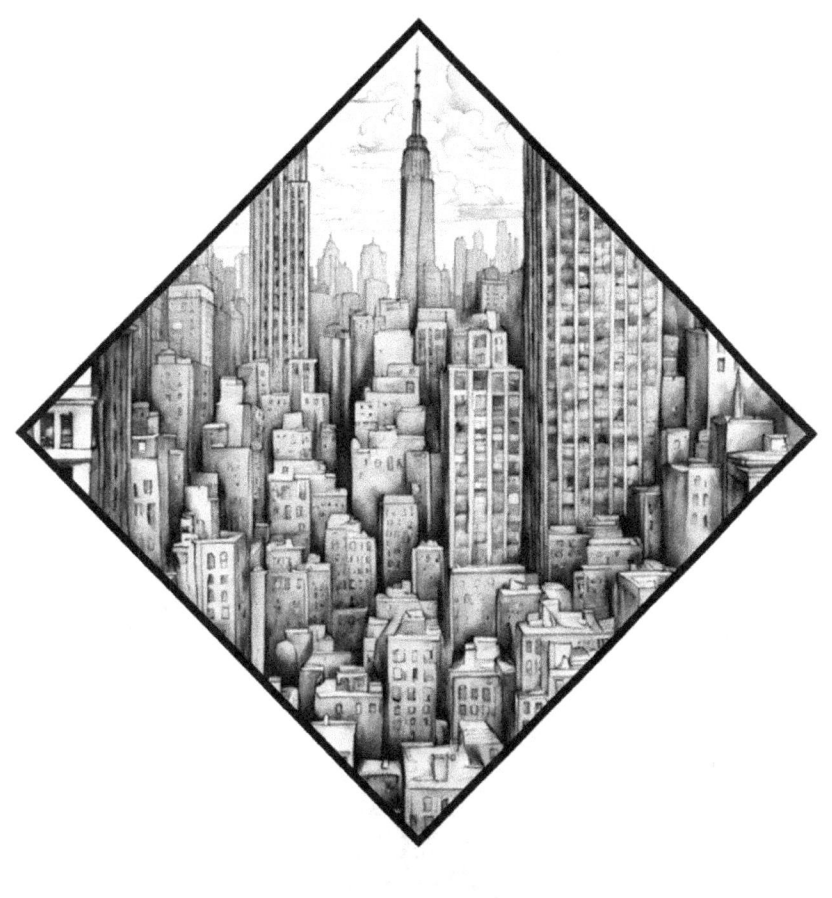
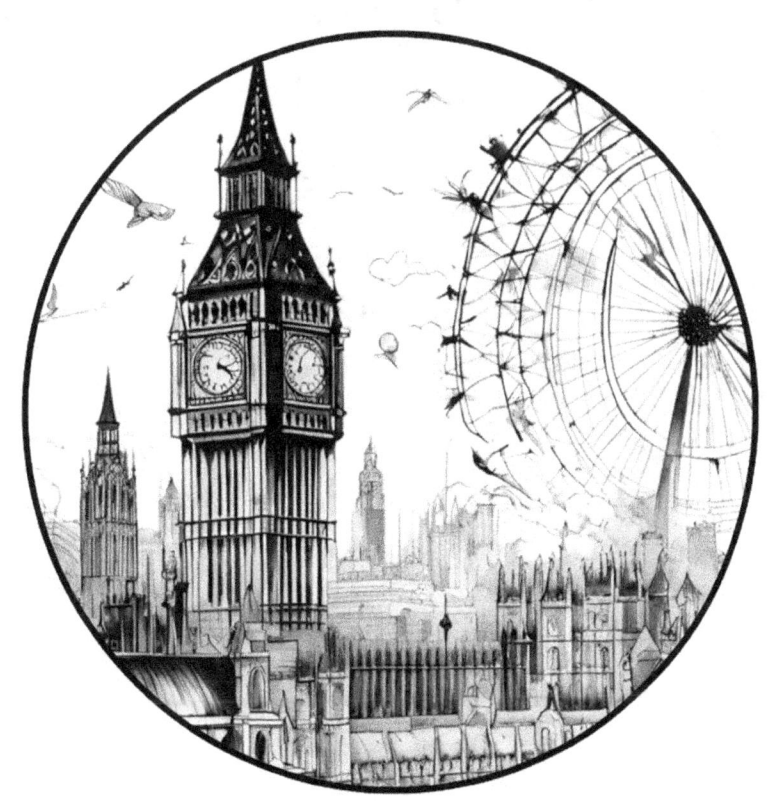

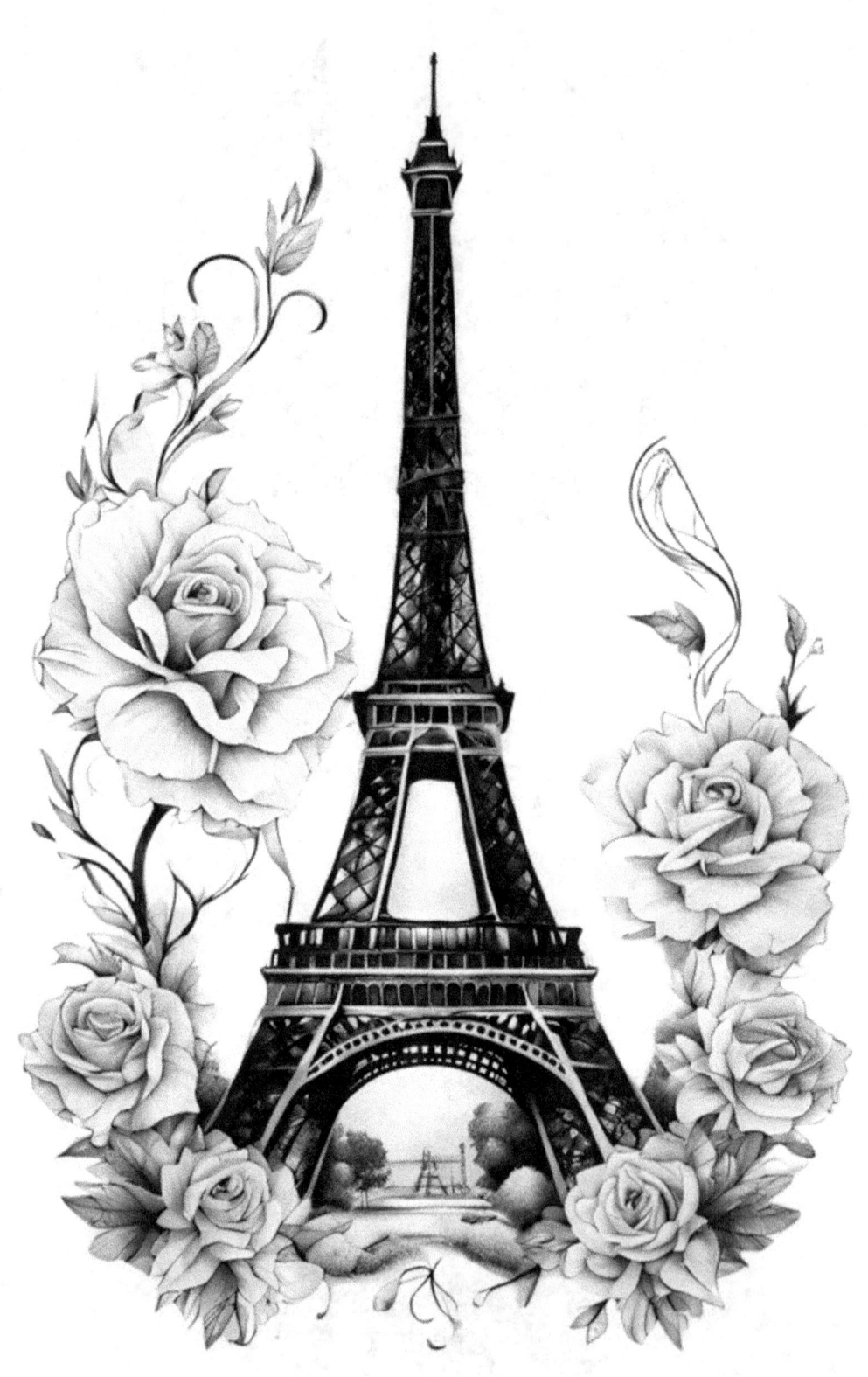

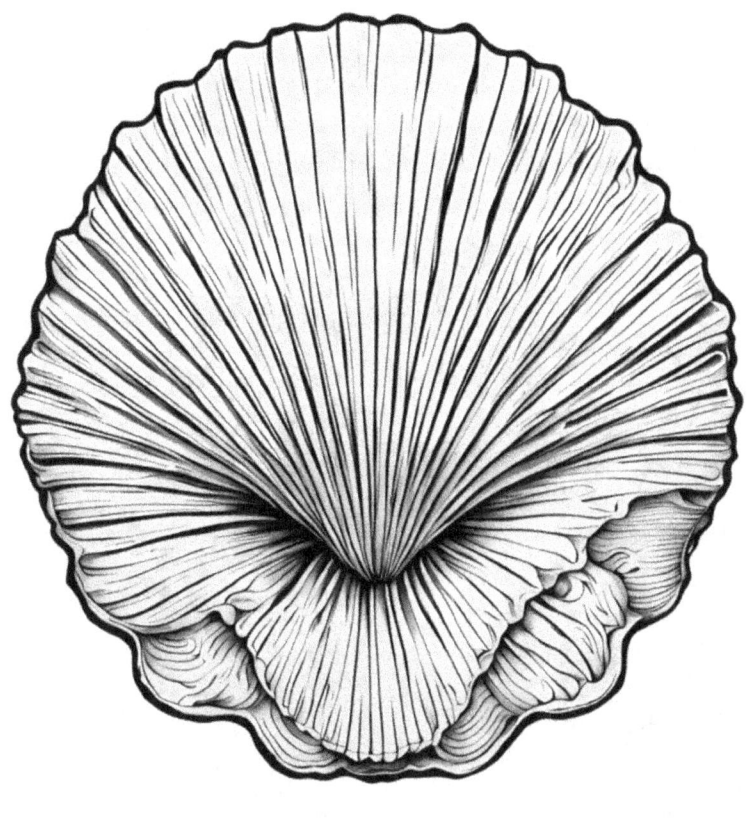
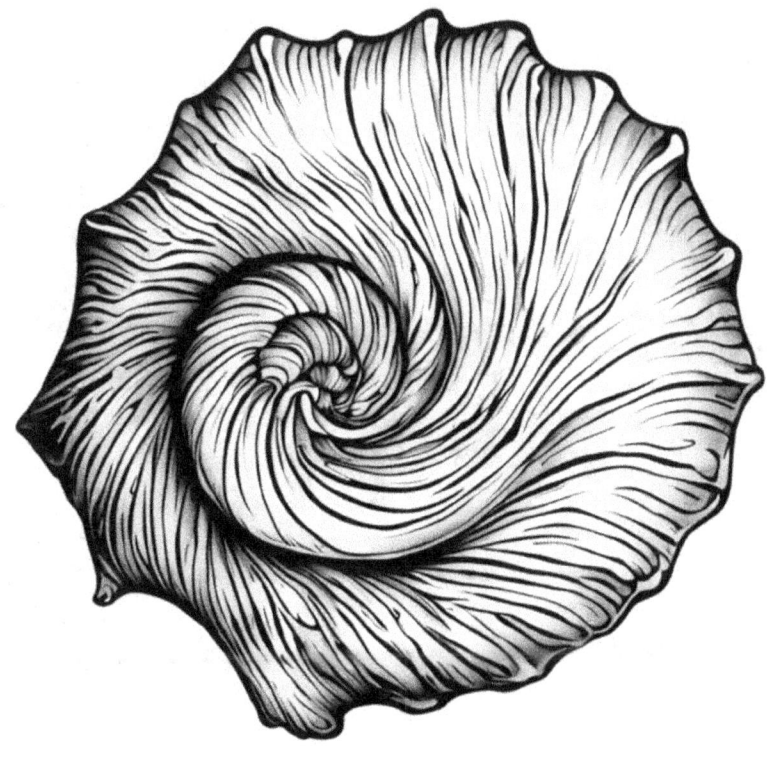

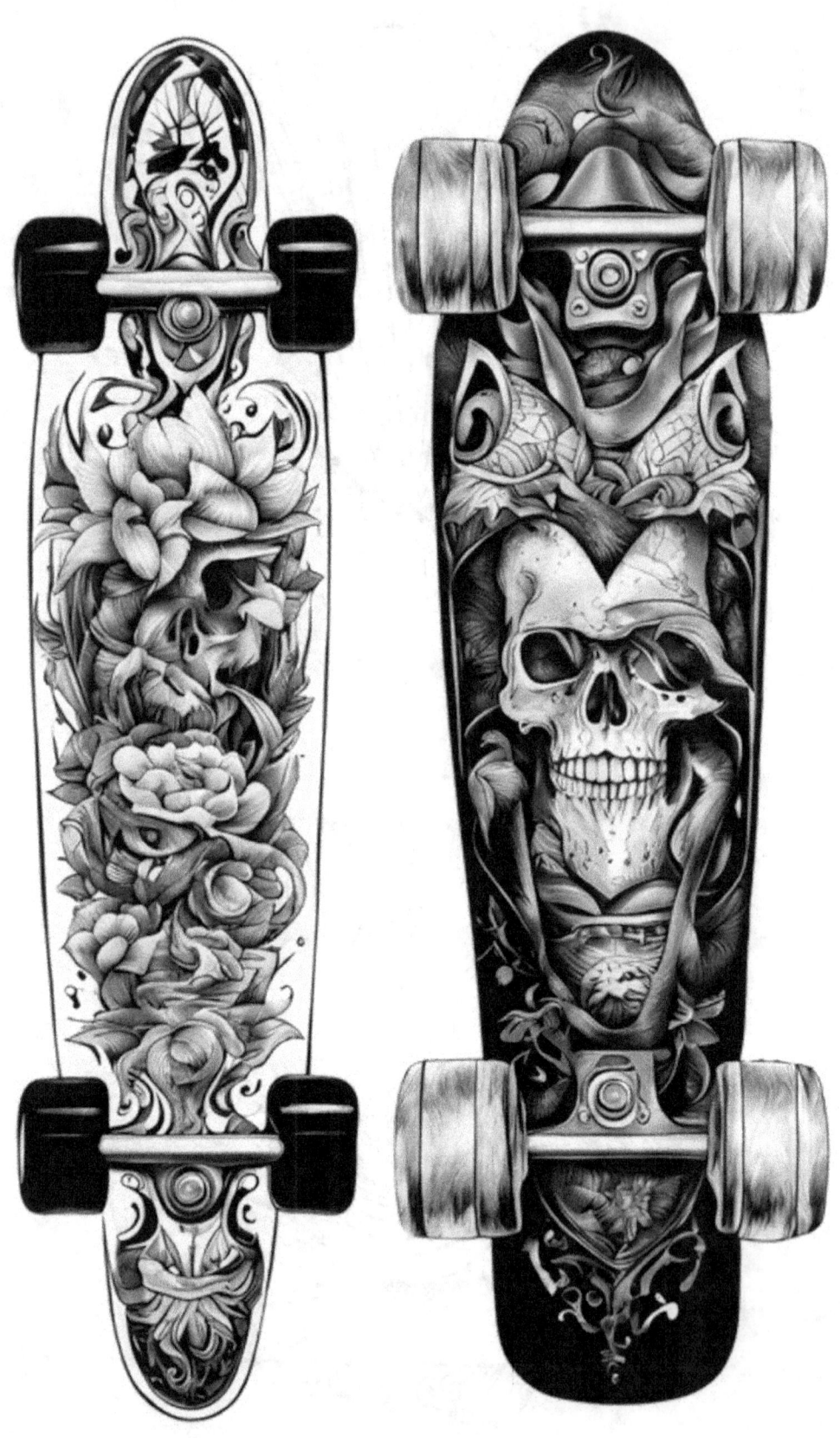

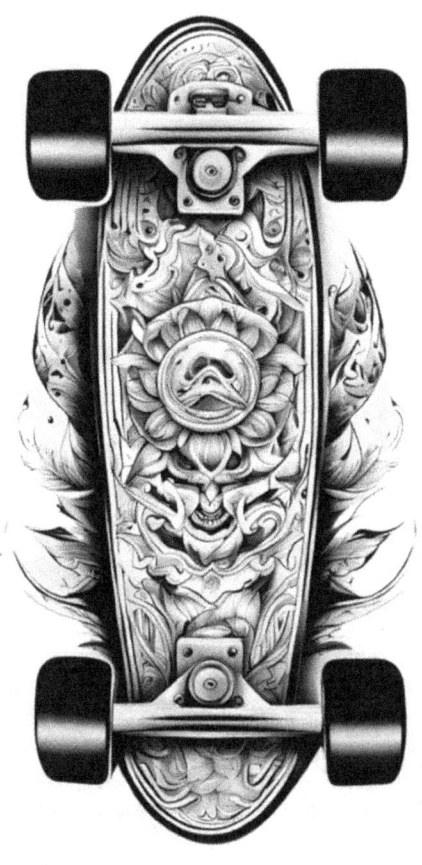
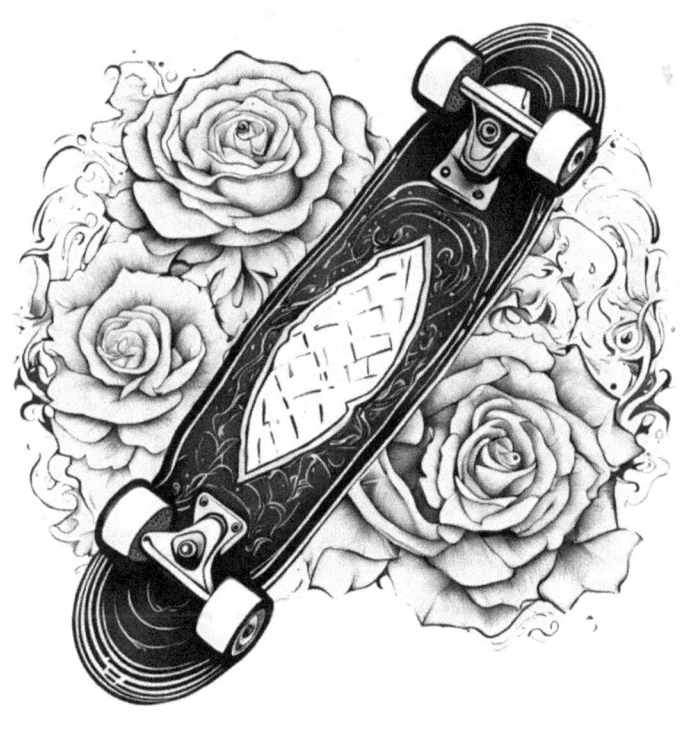

169

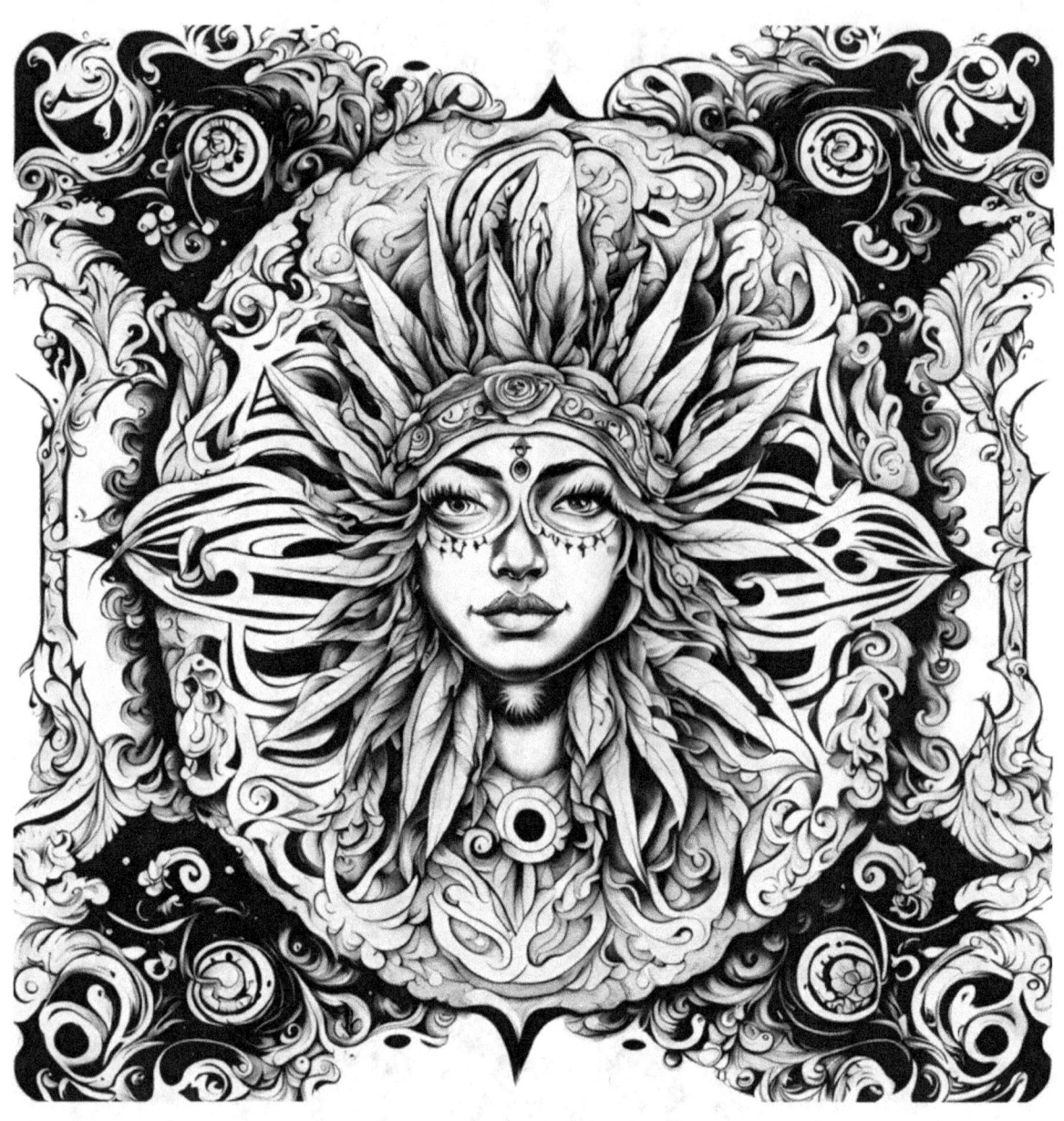

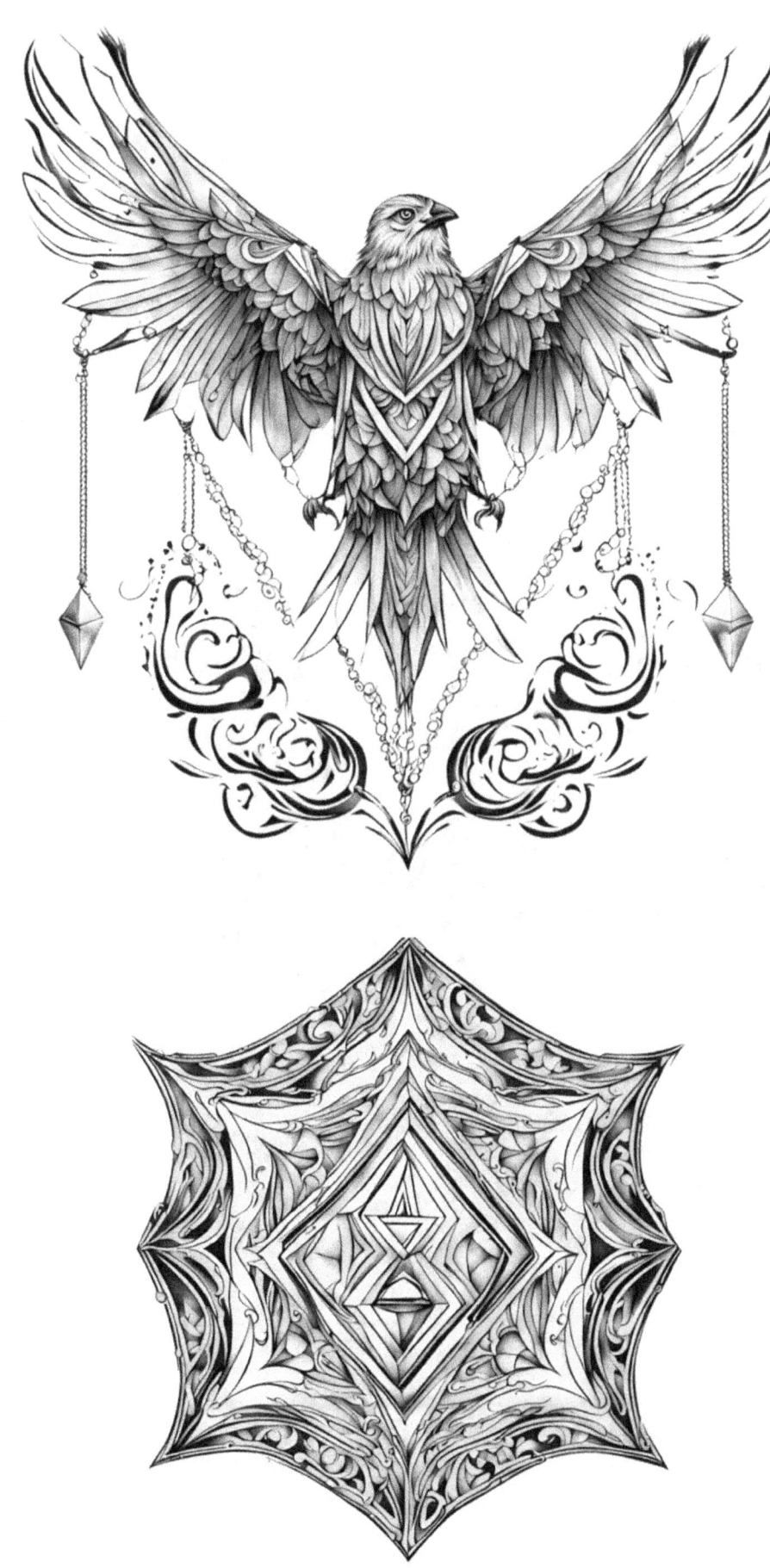

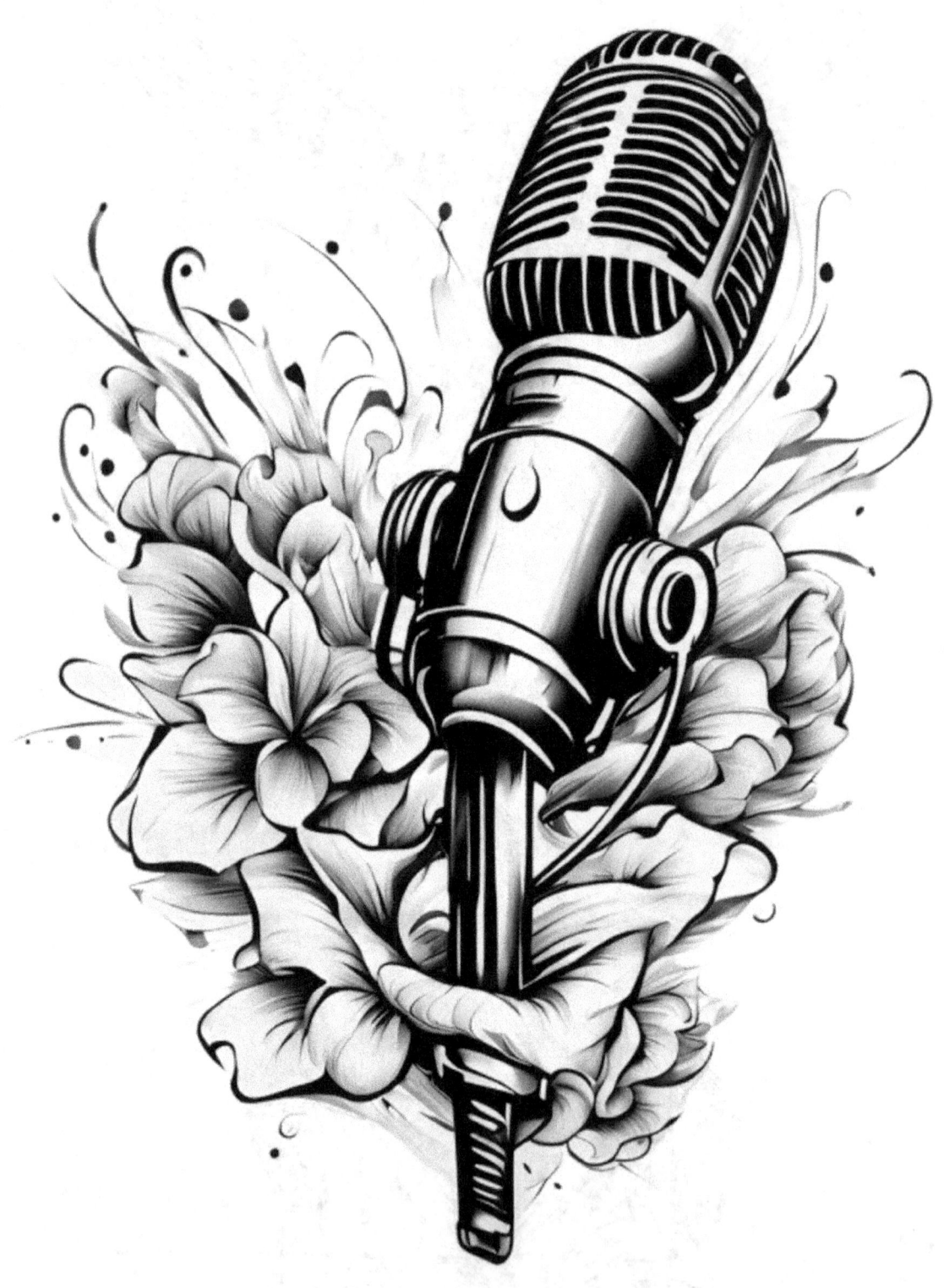

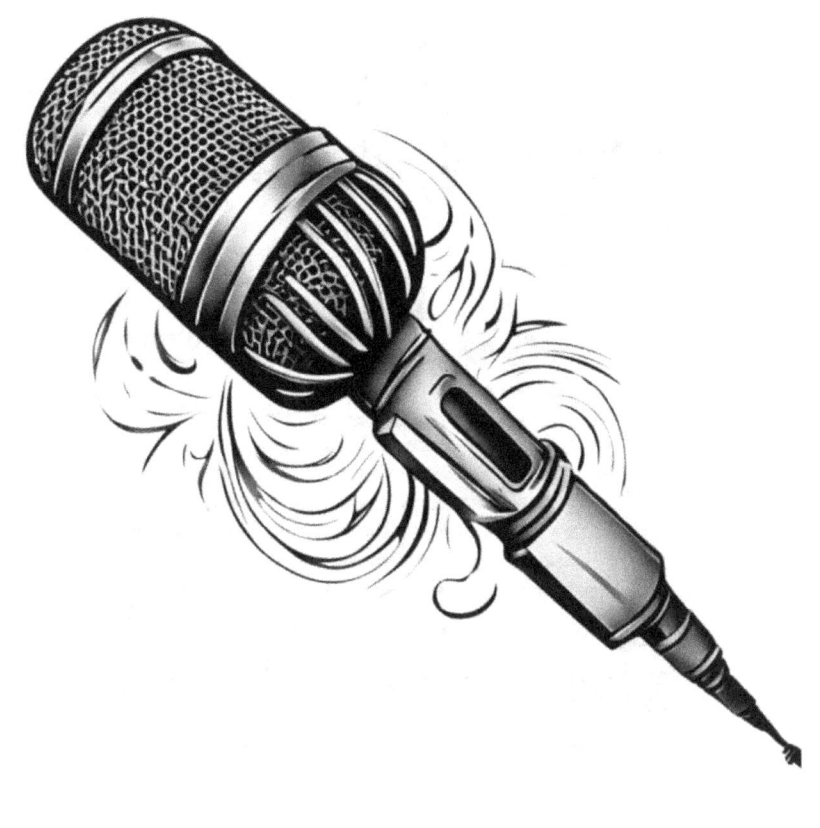
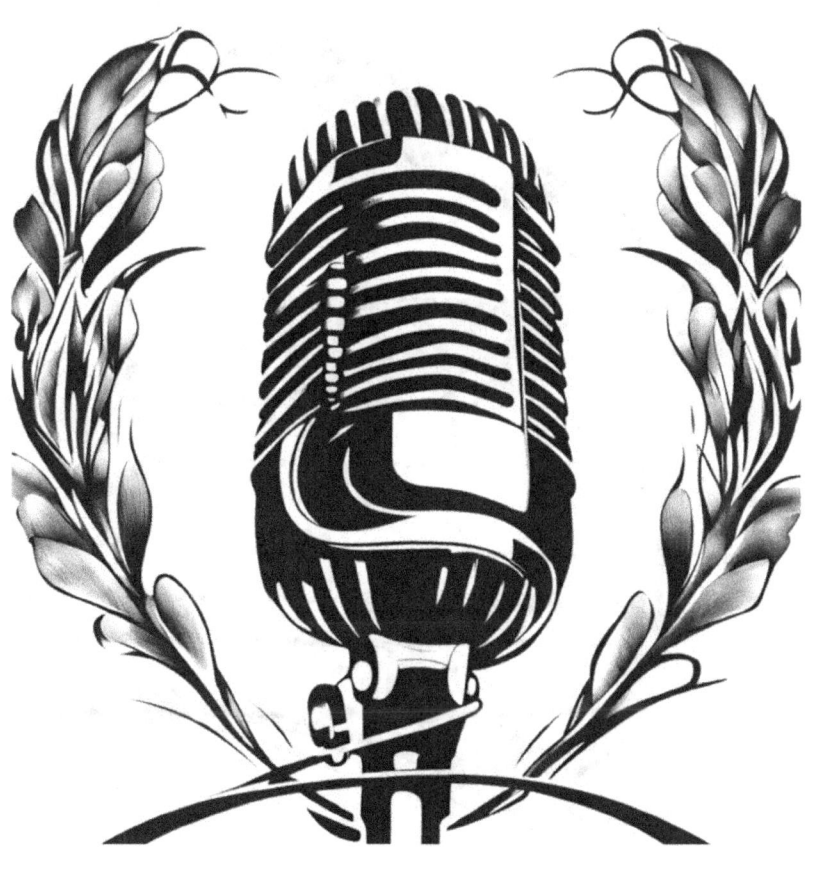

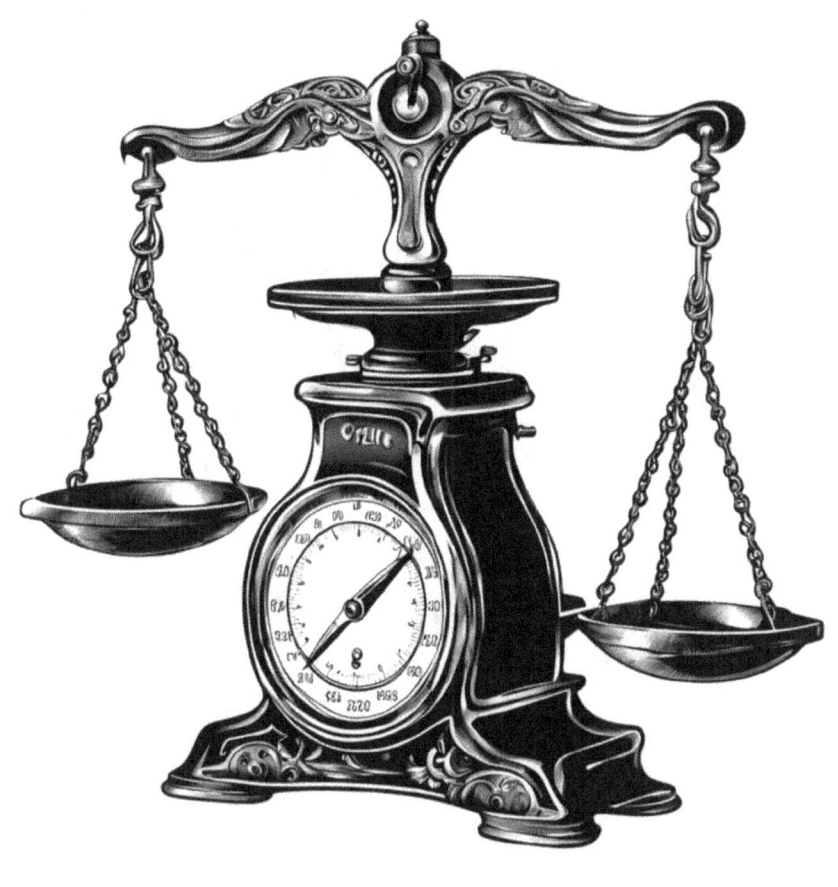
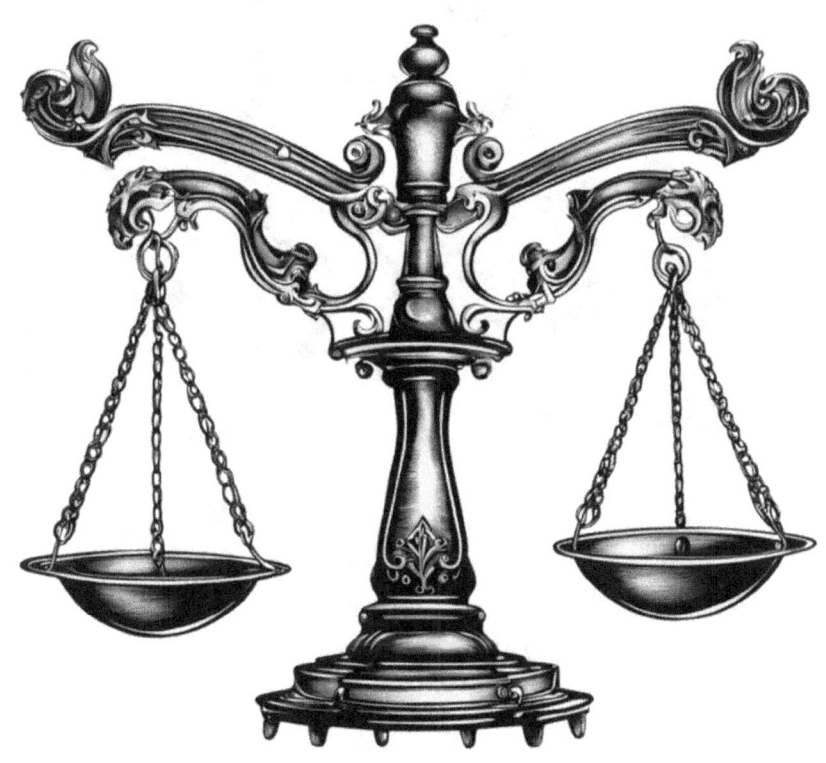

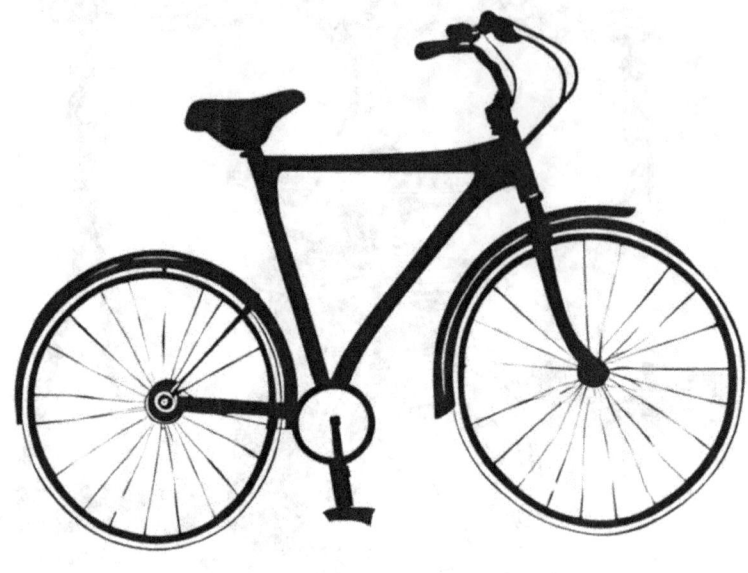
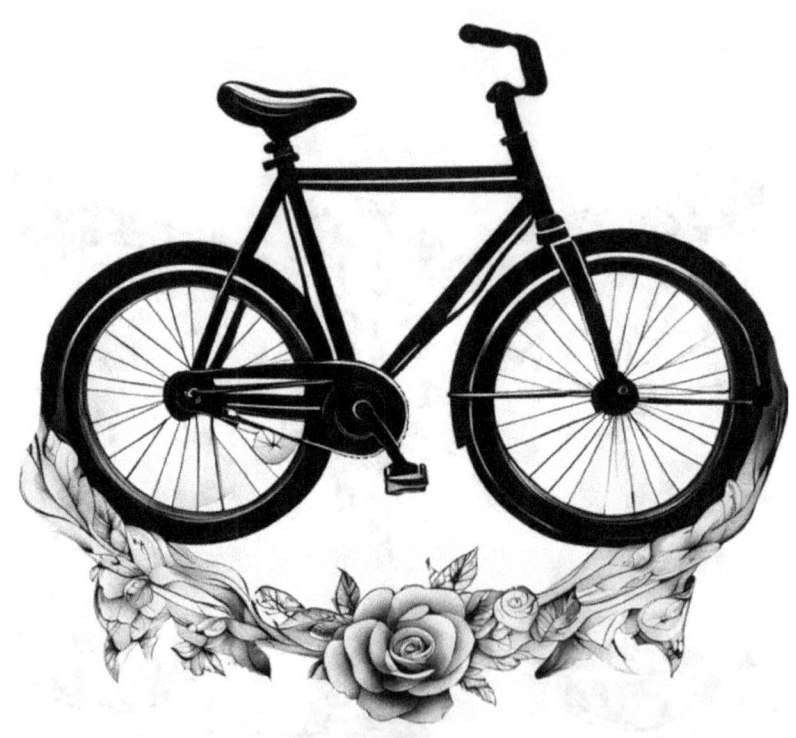

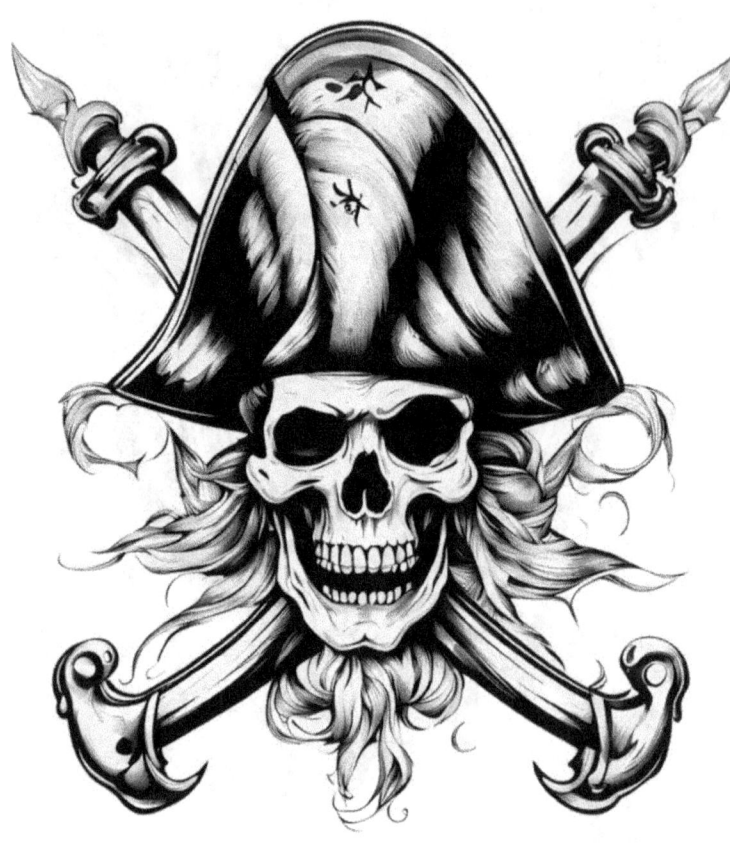
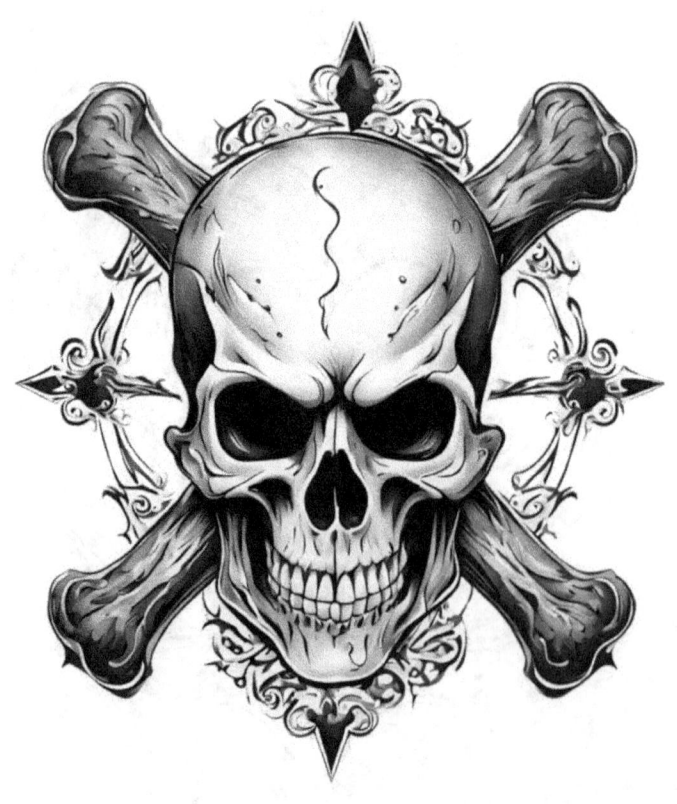

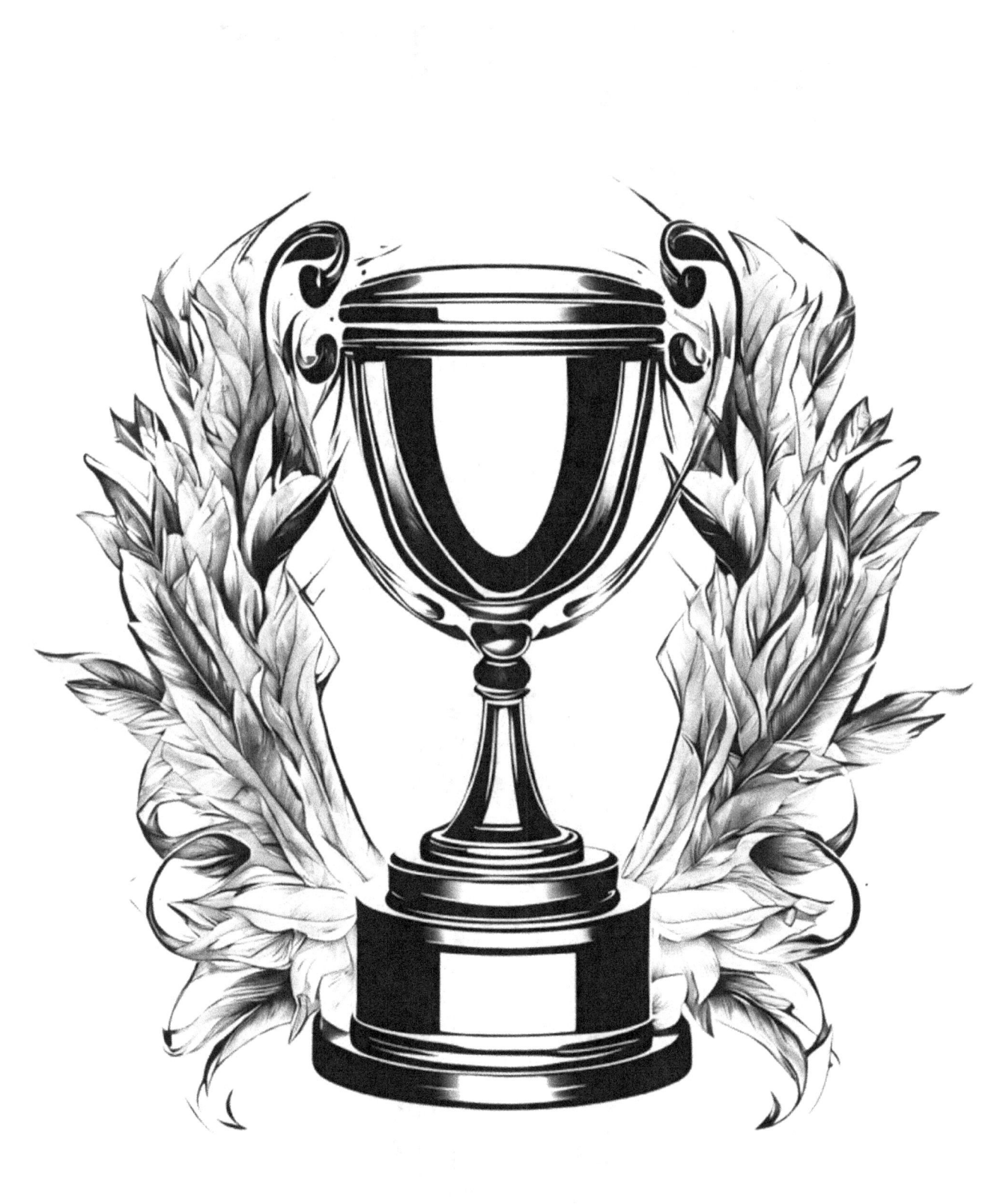

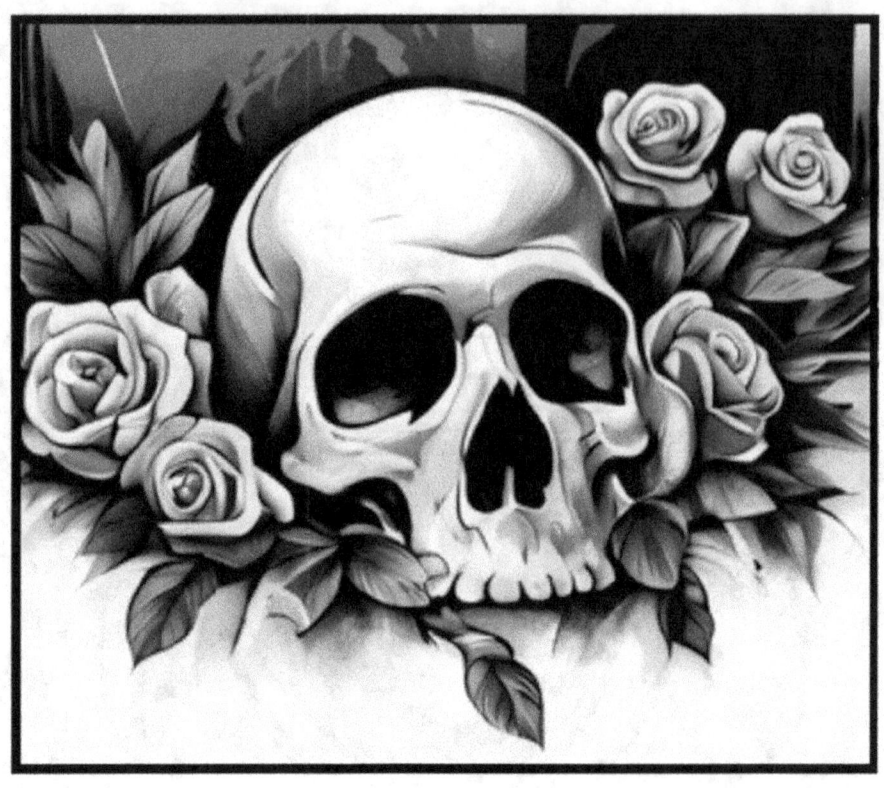
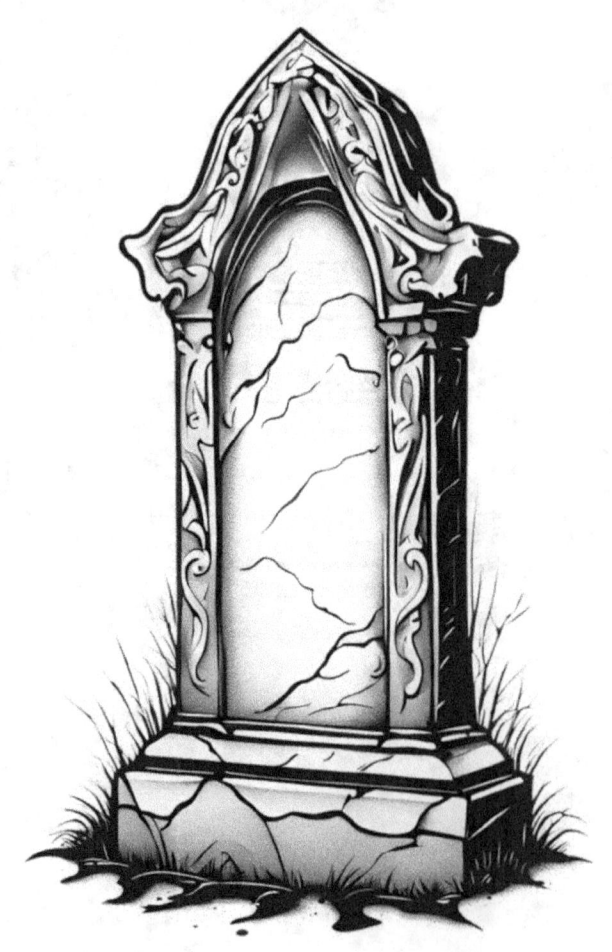

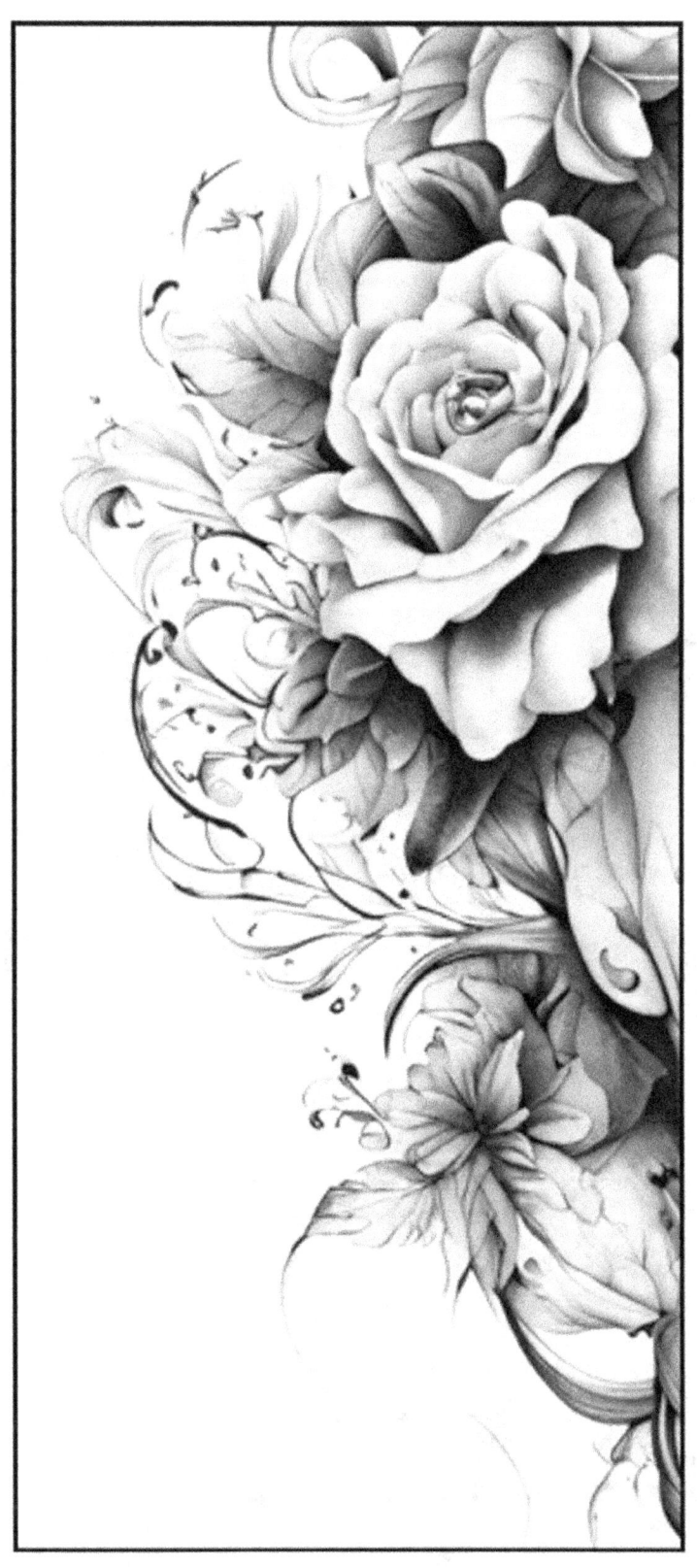

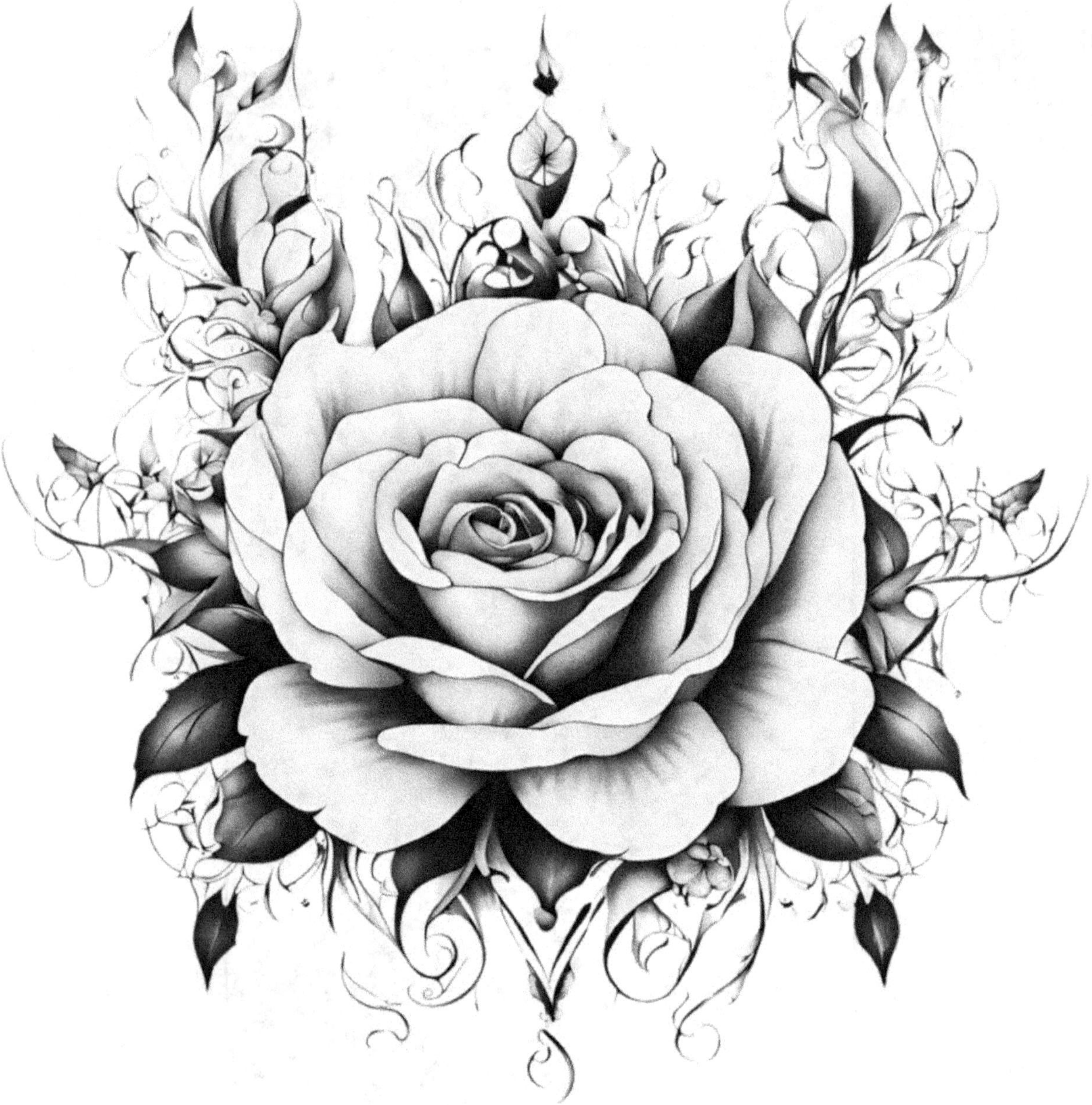

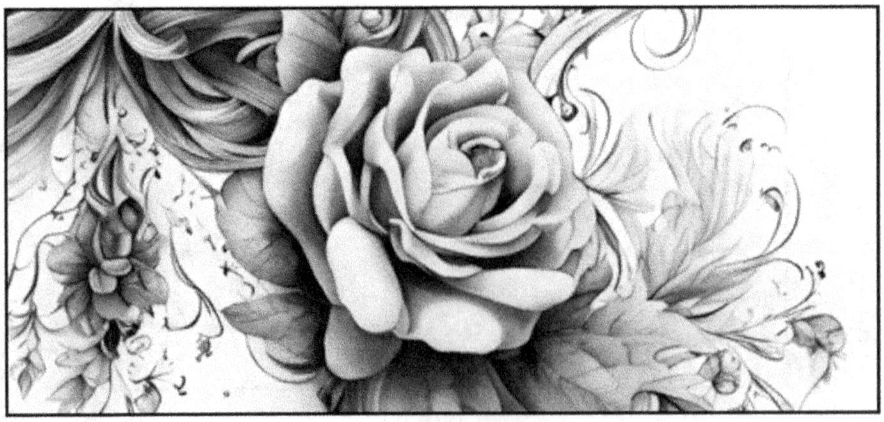

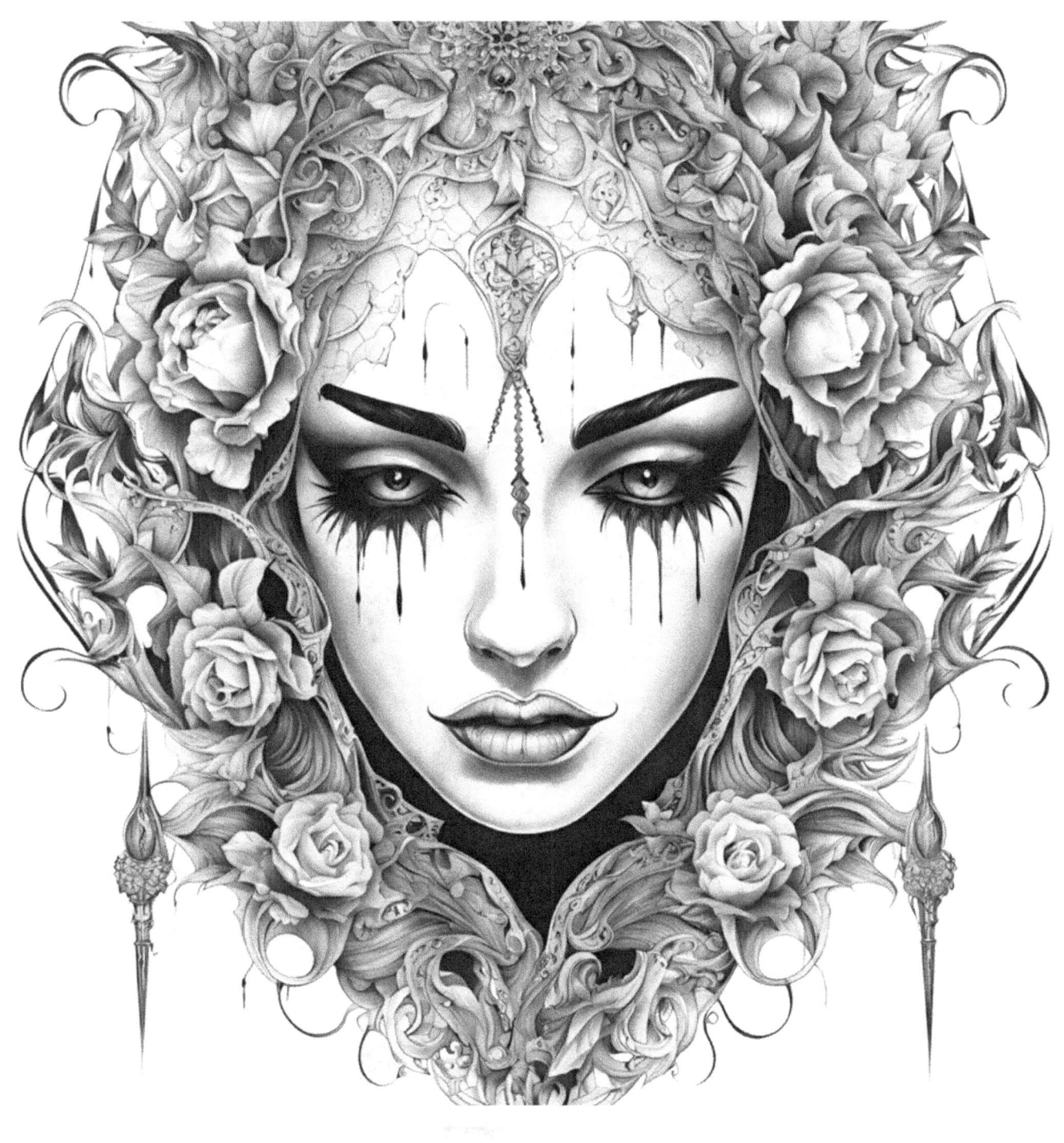

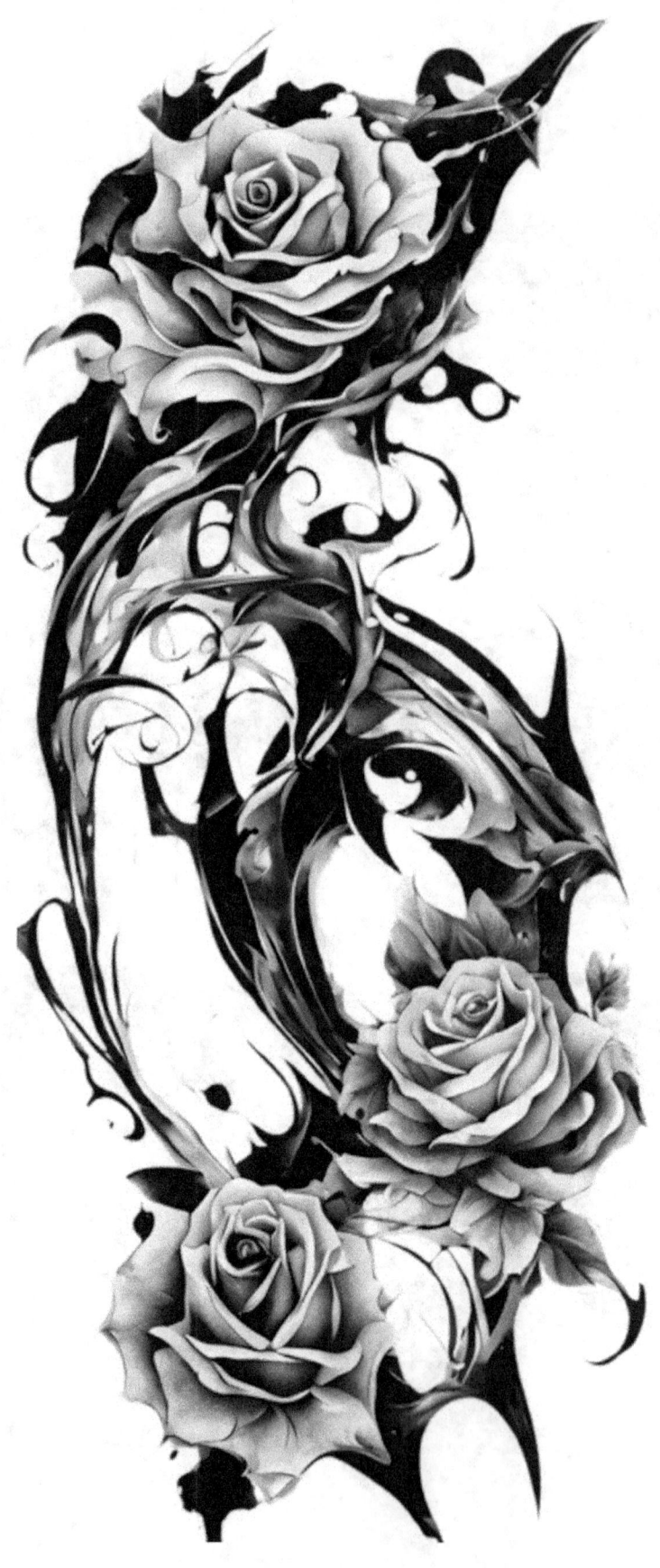

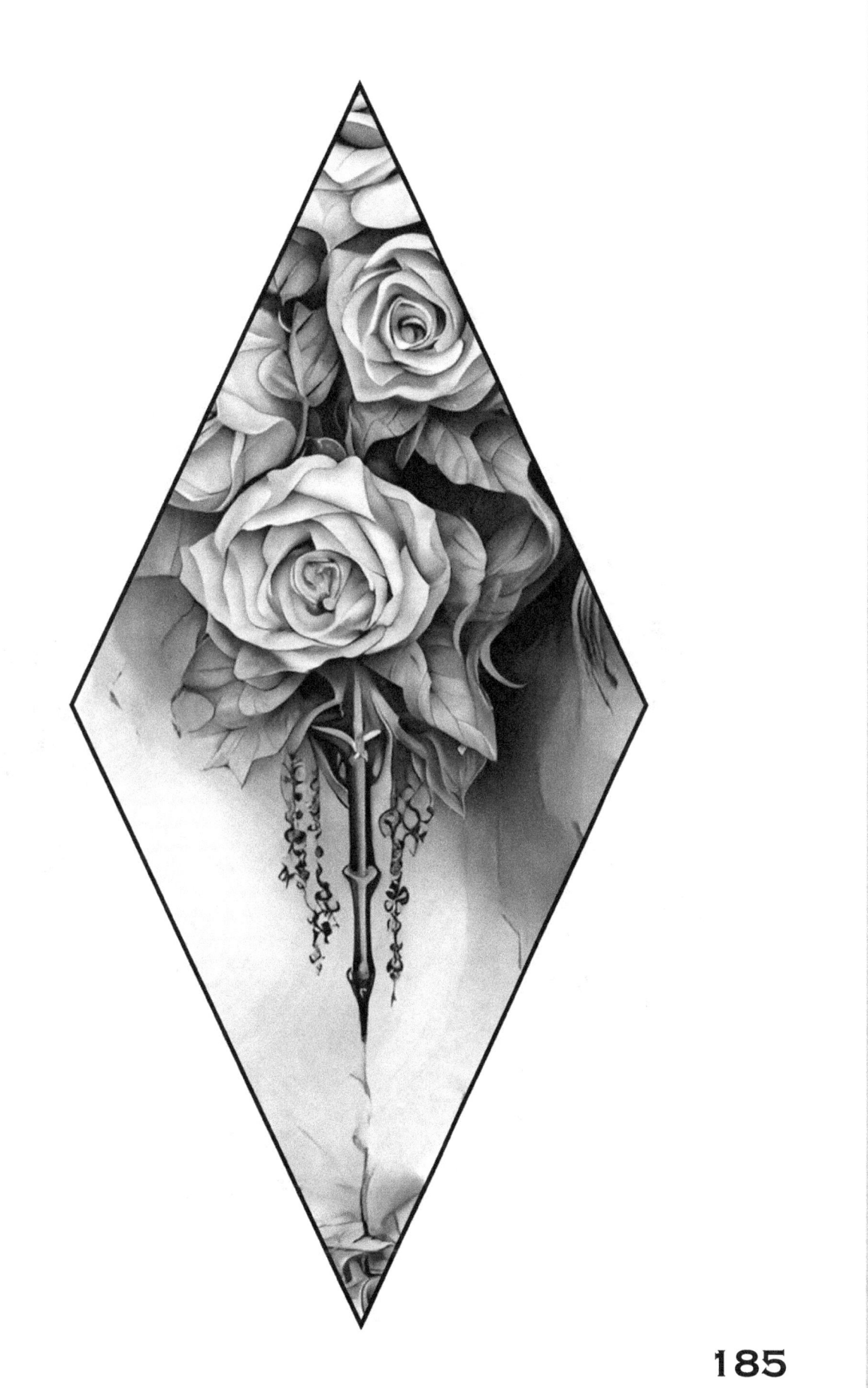

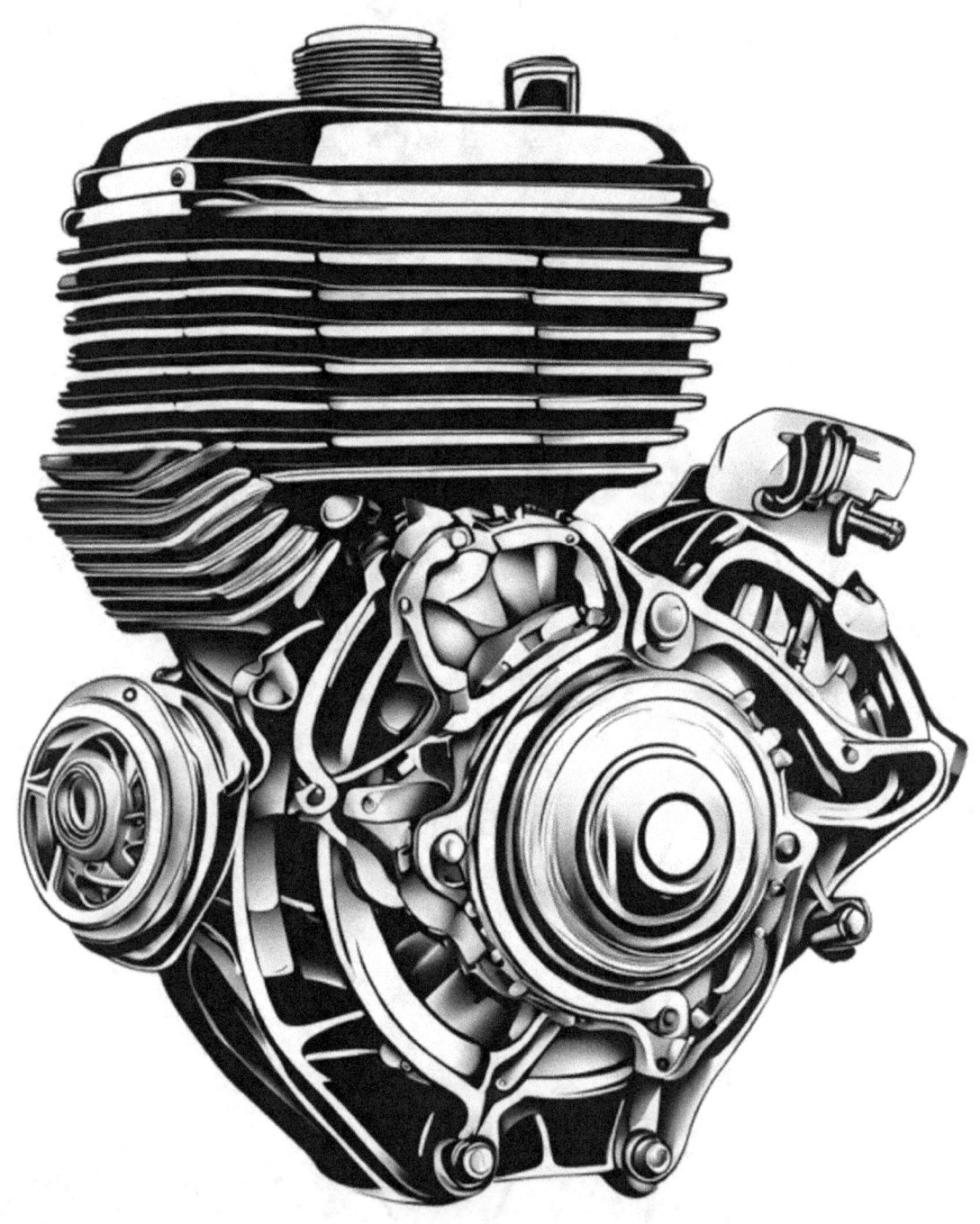

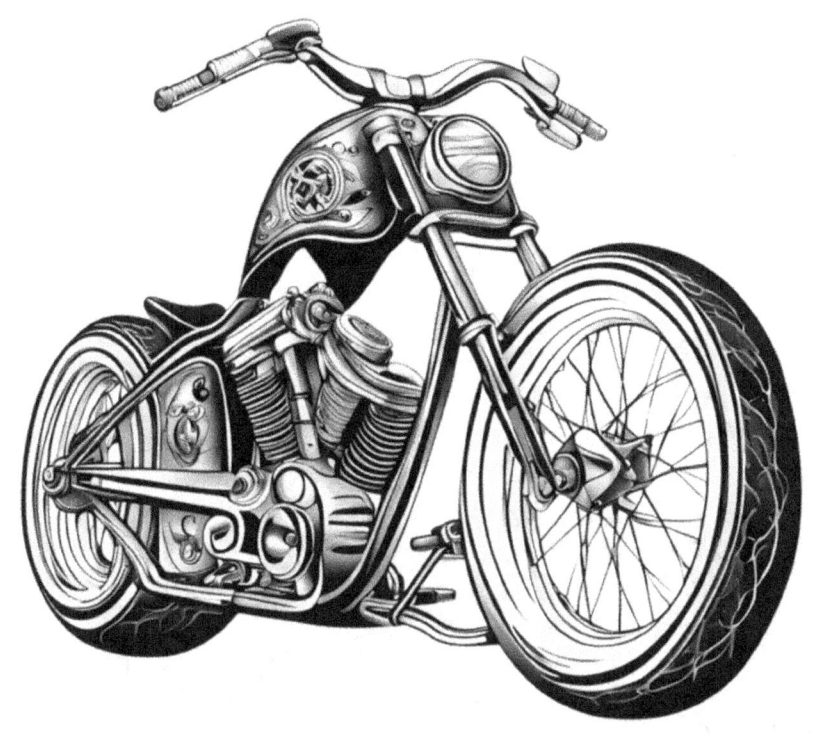
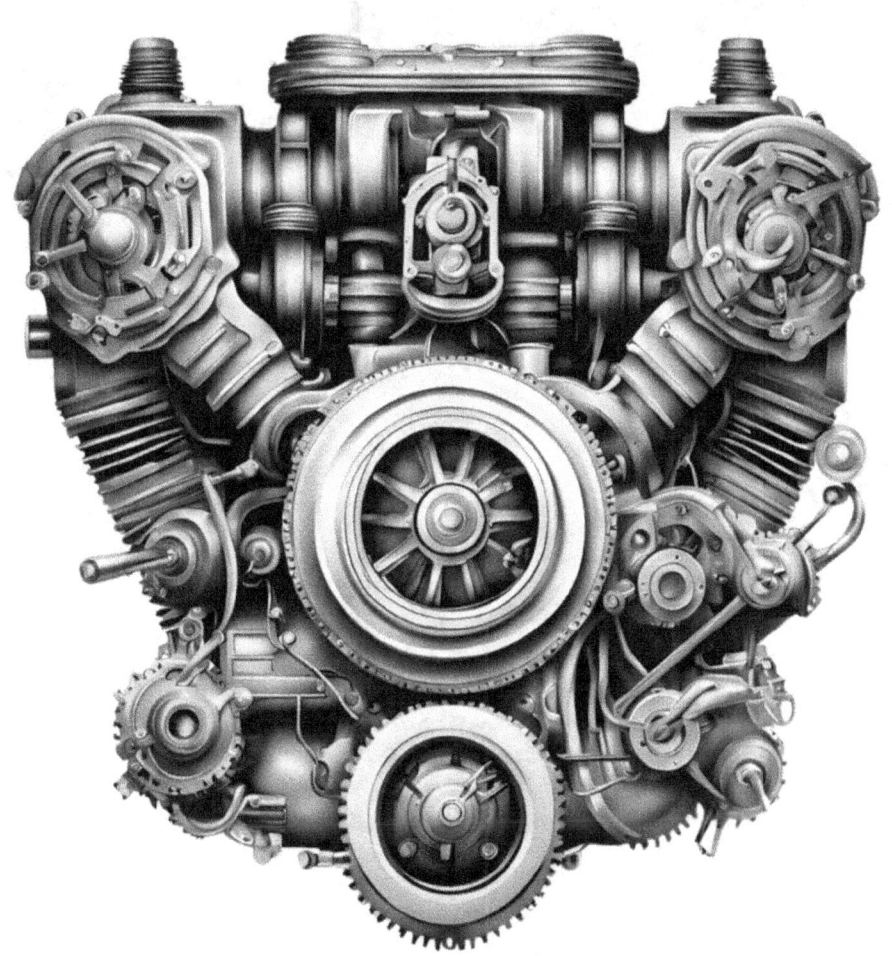

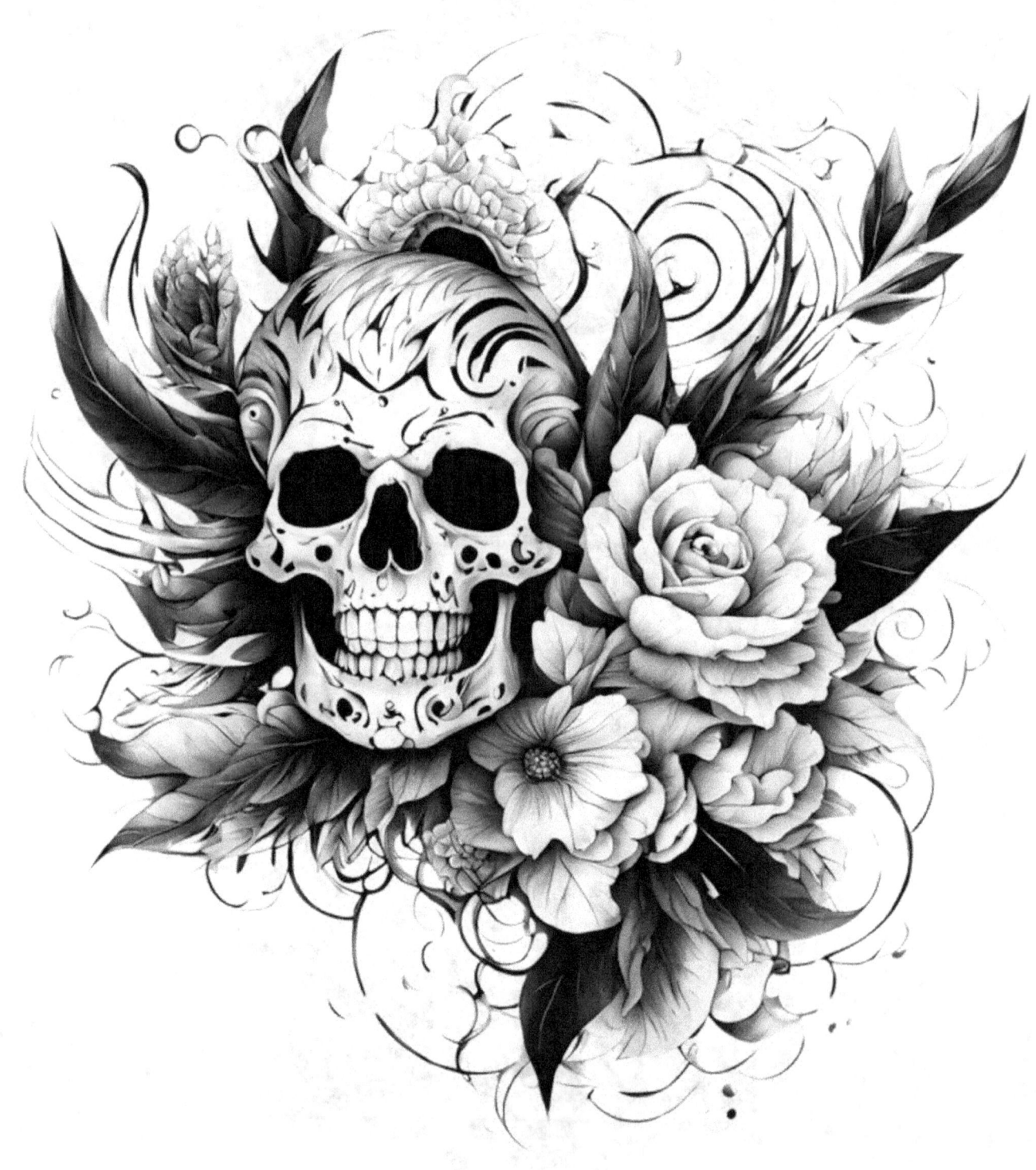

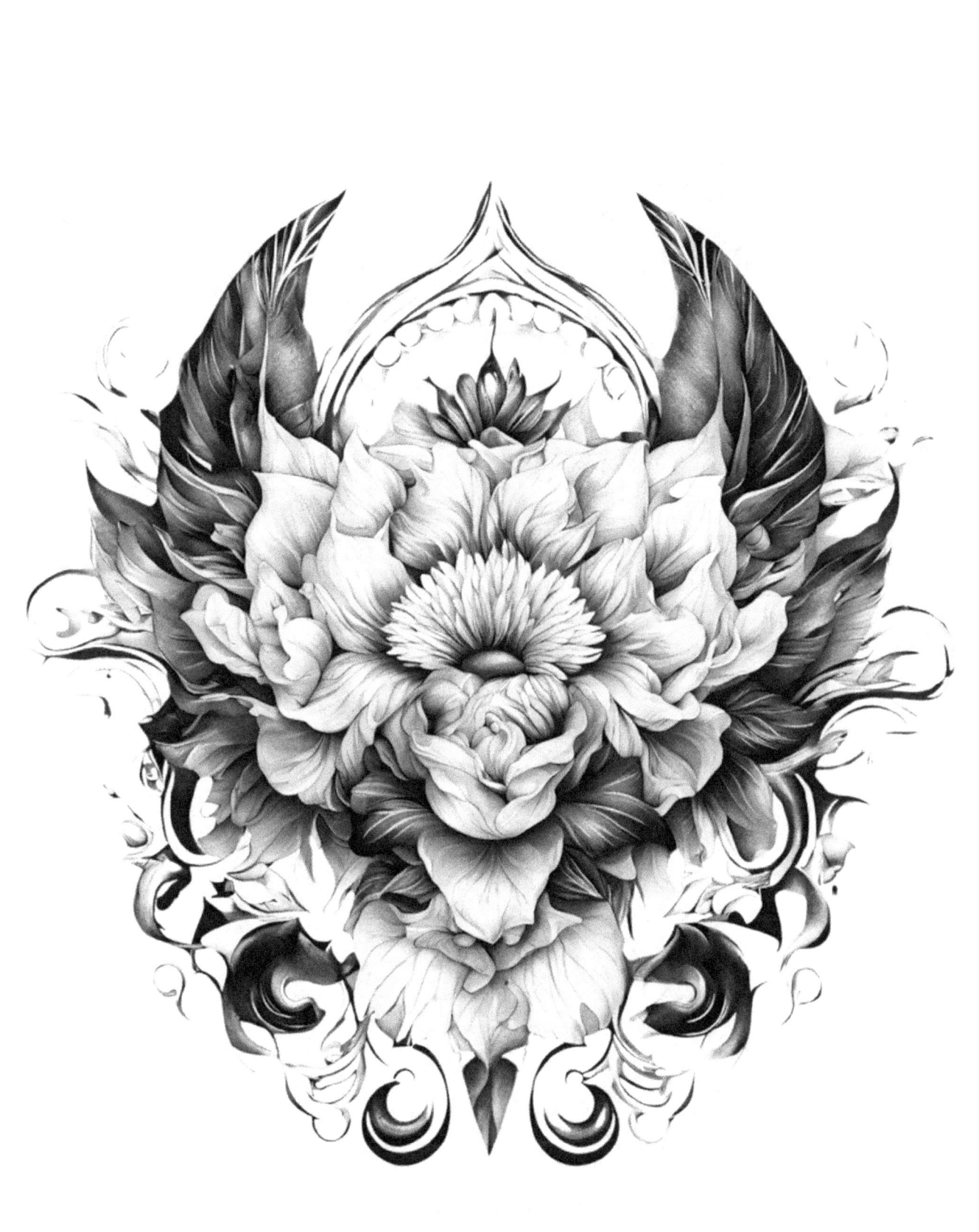

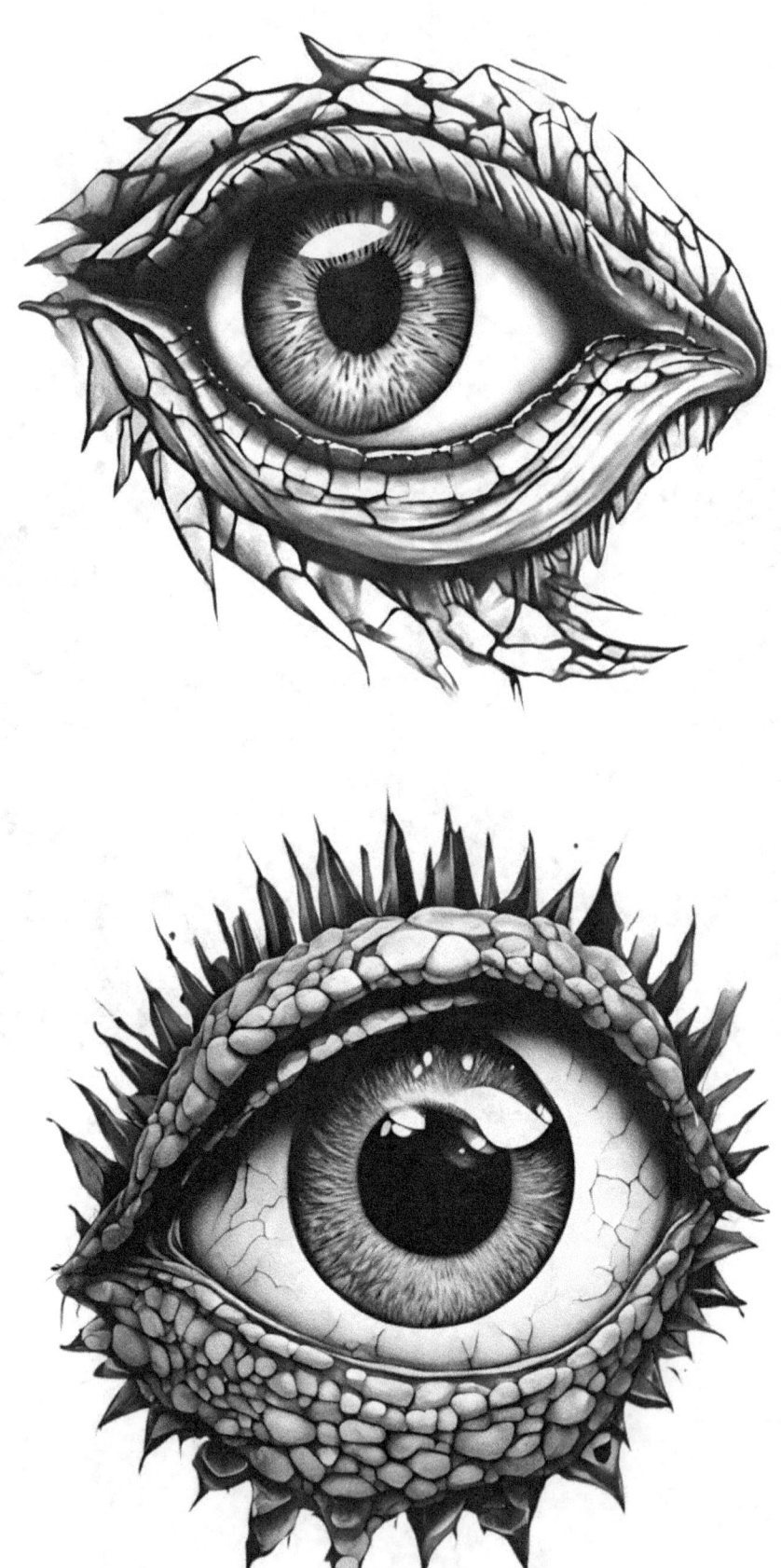

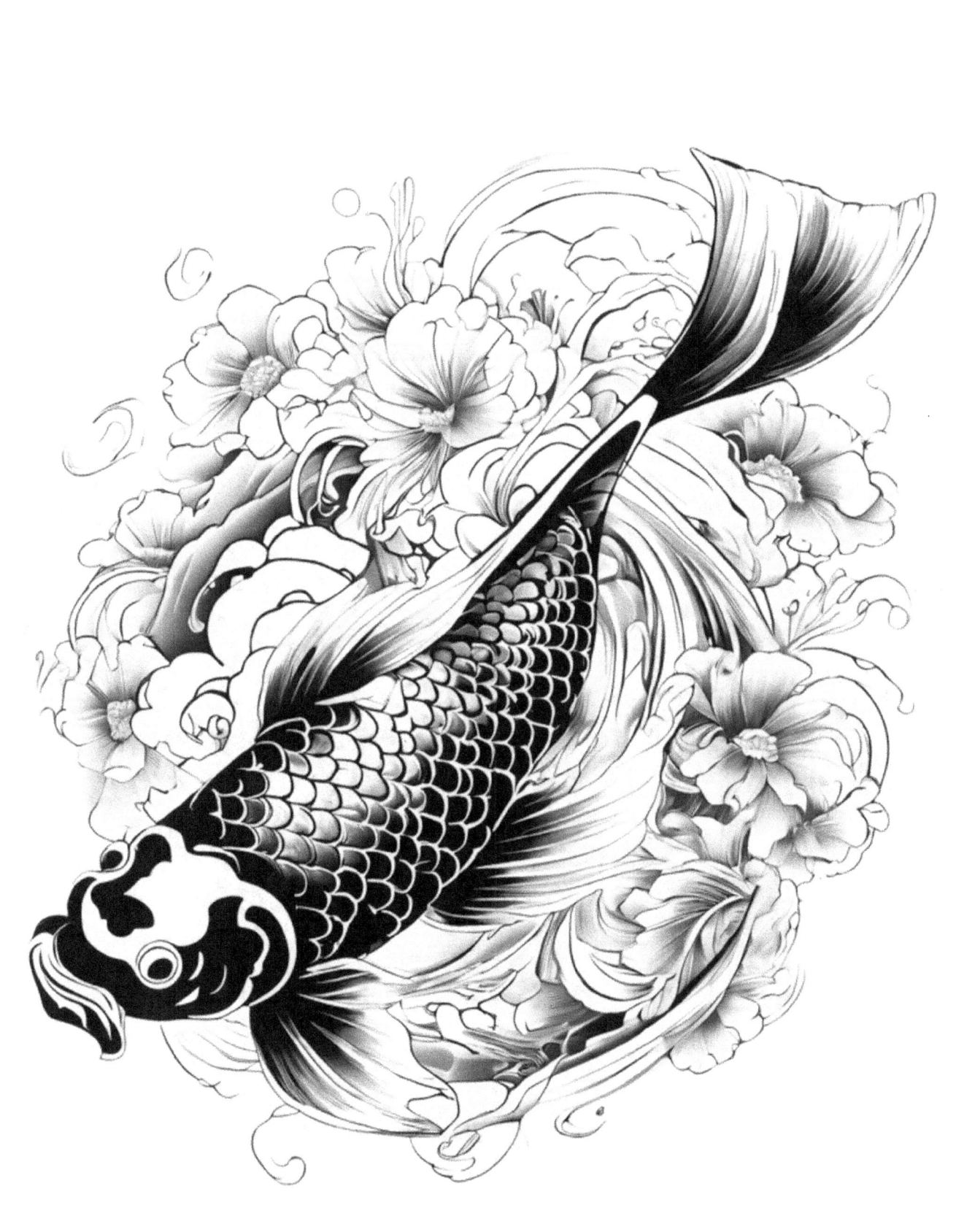

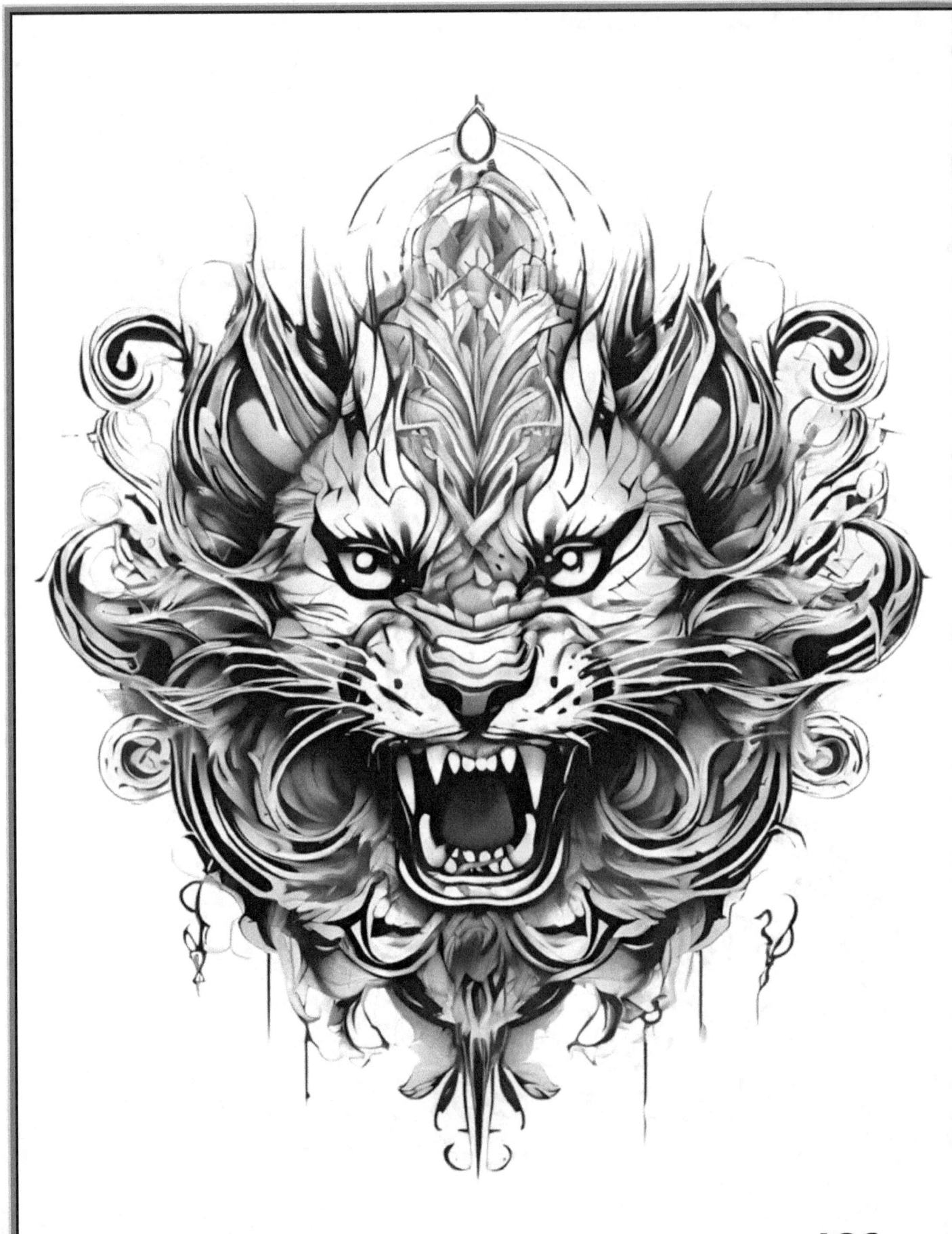

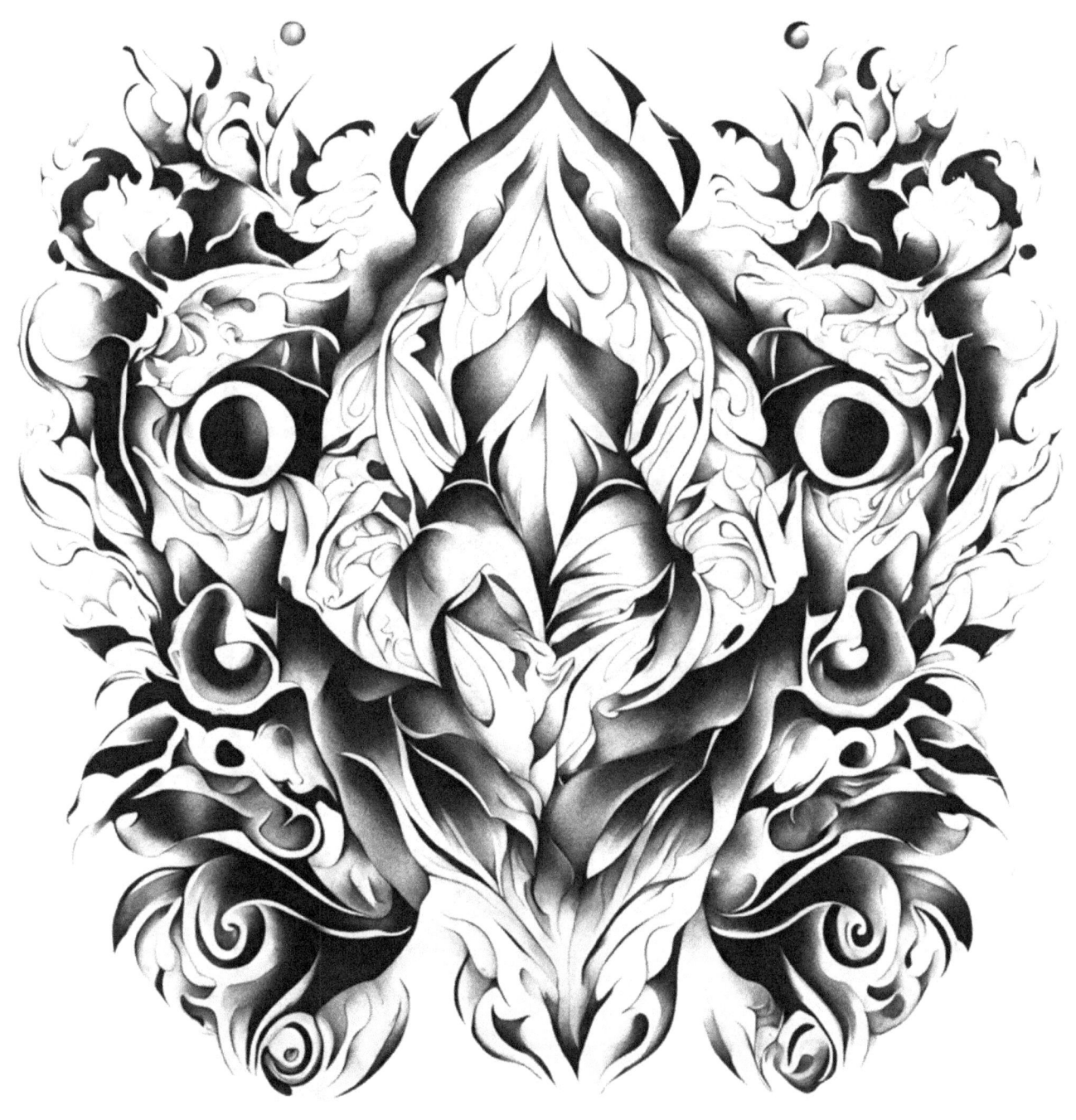

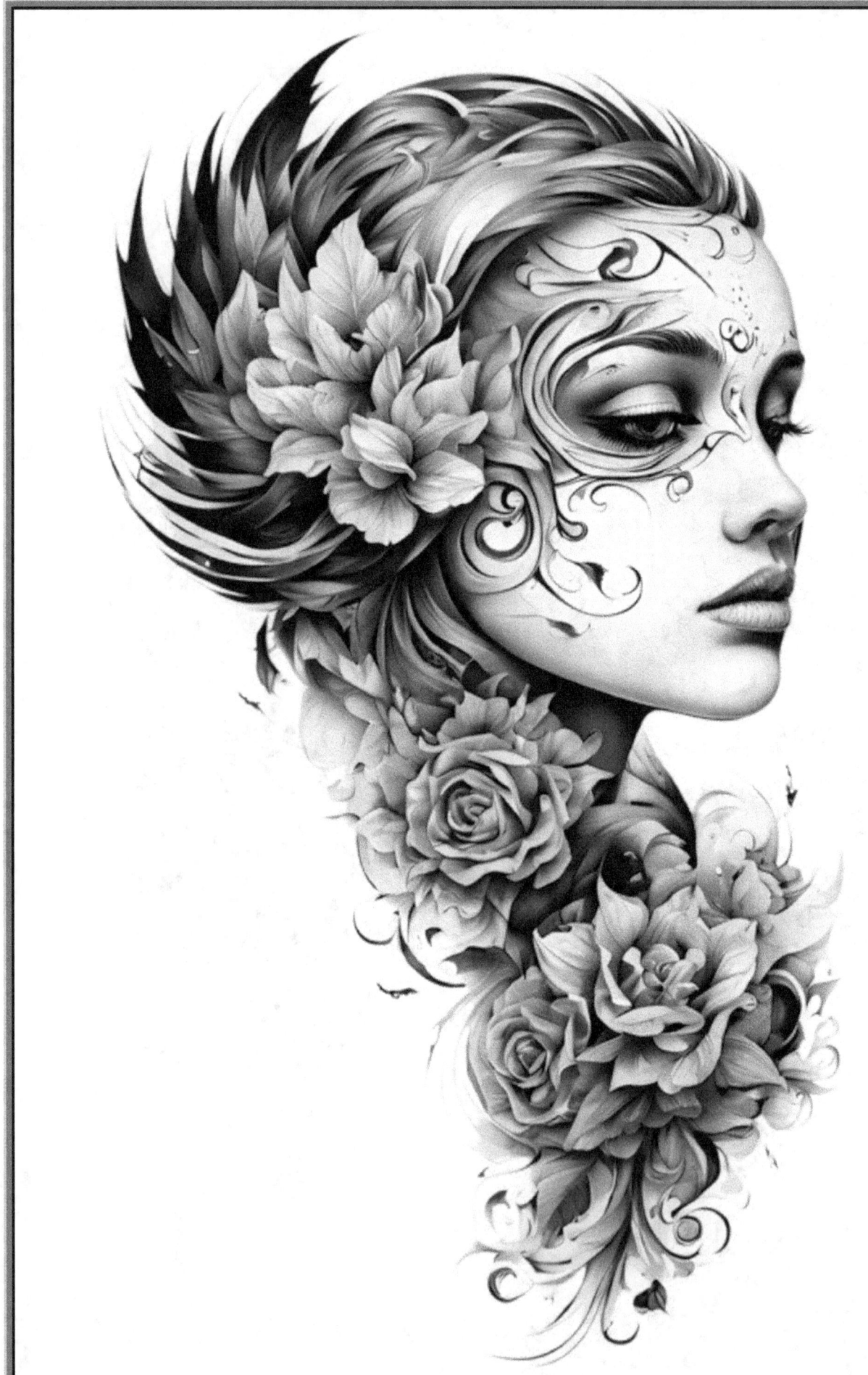

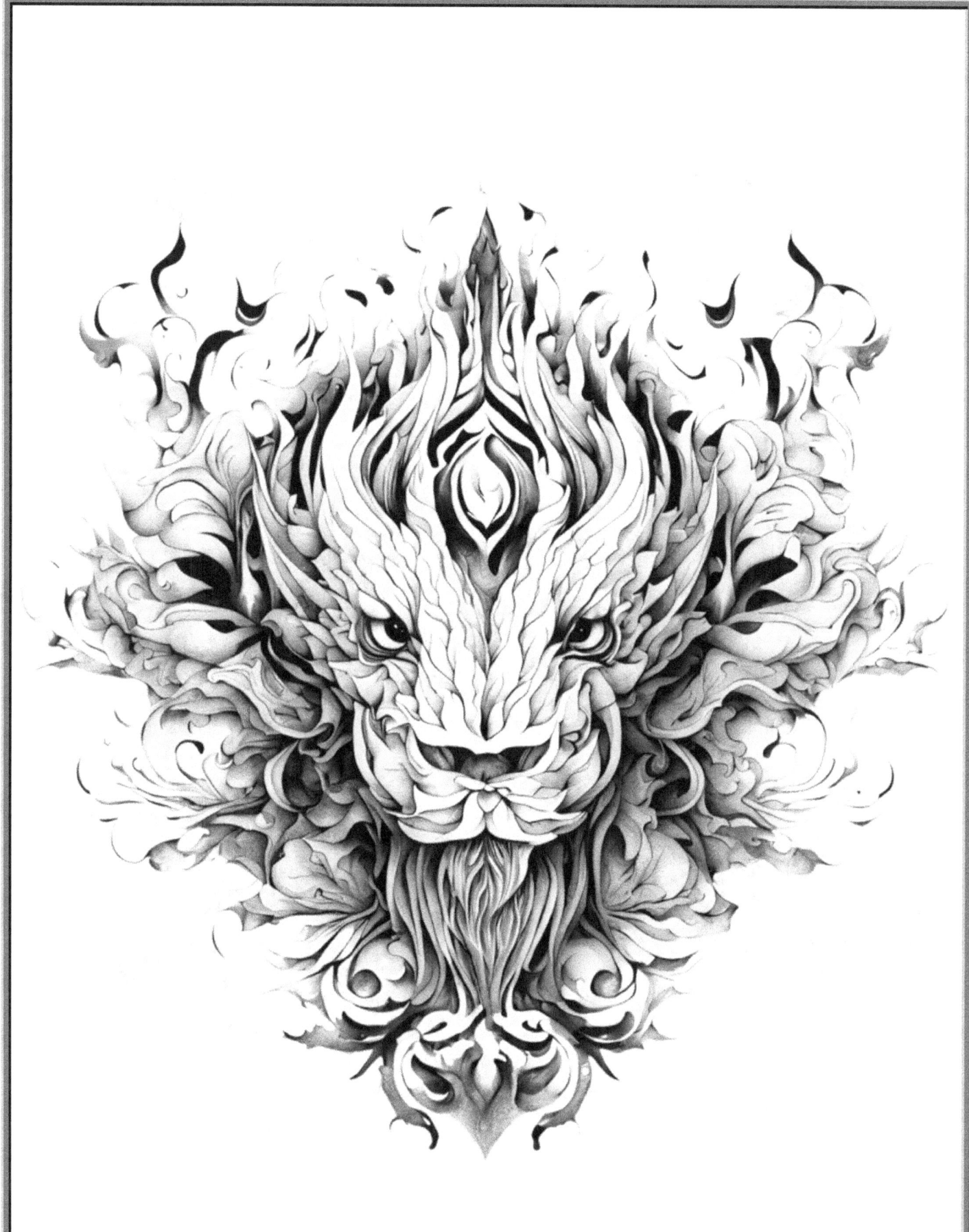

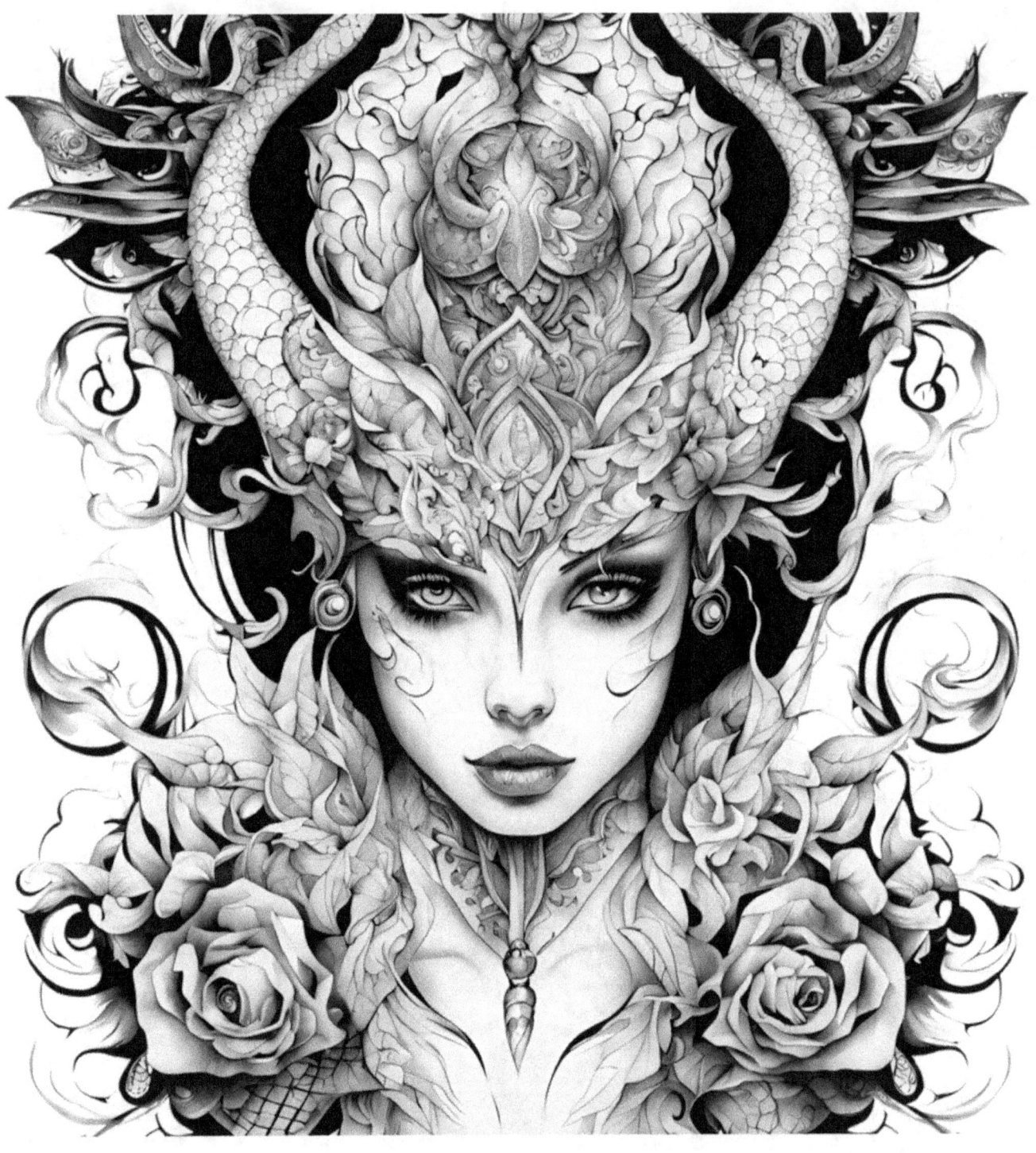

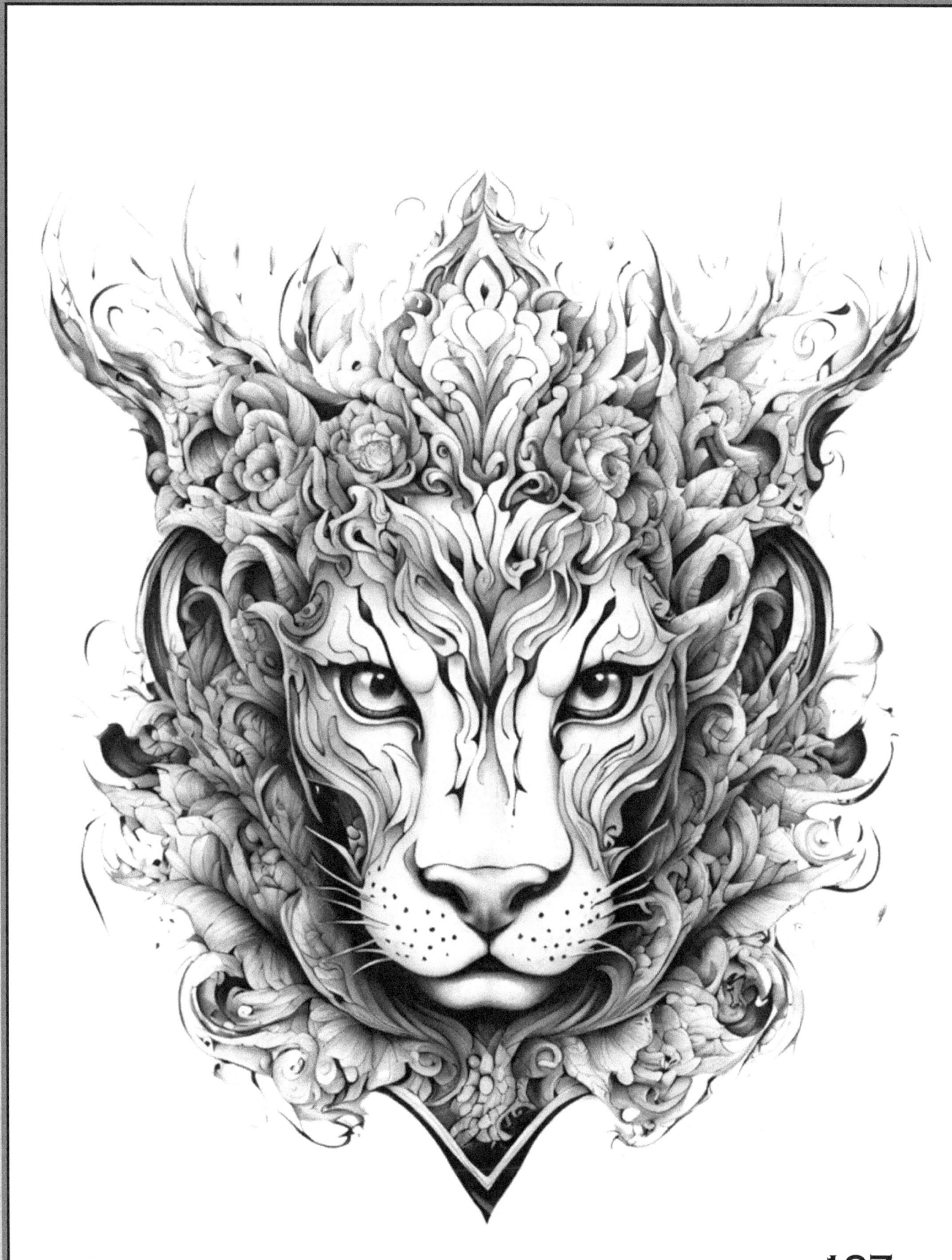

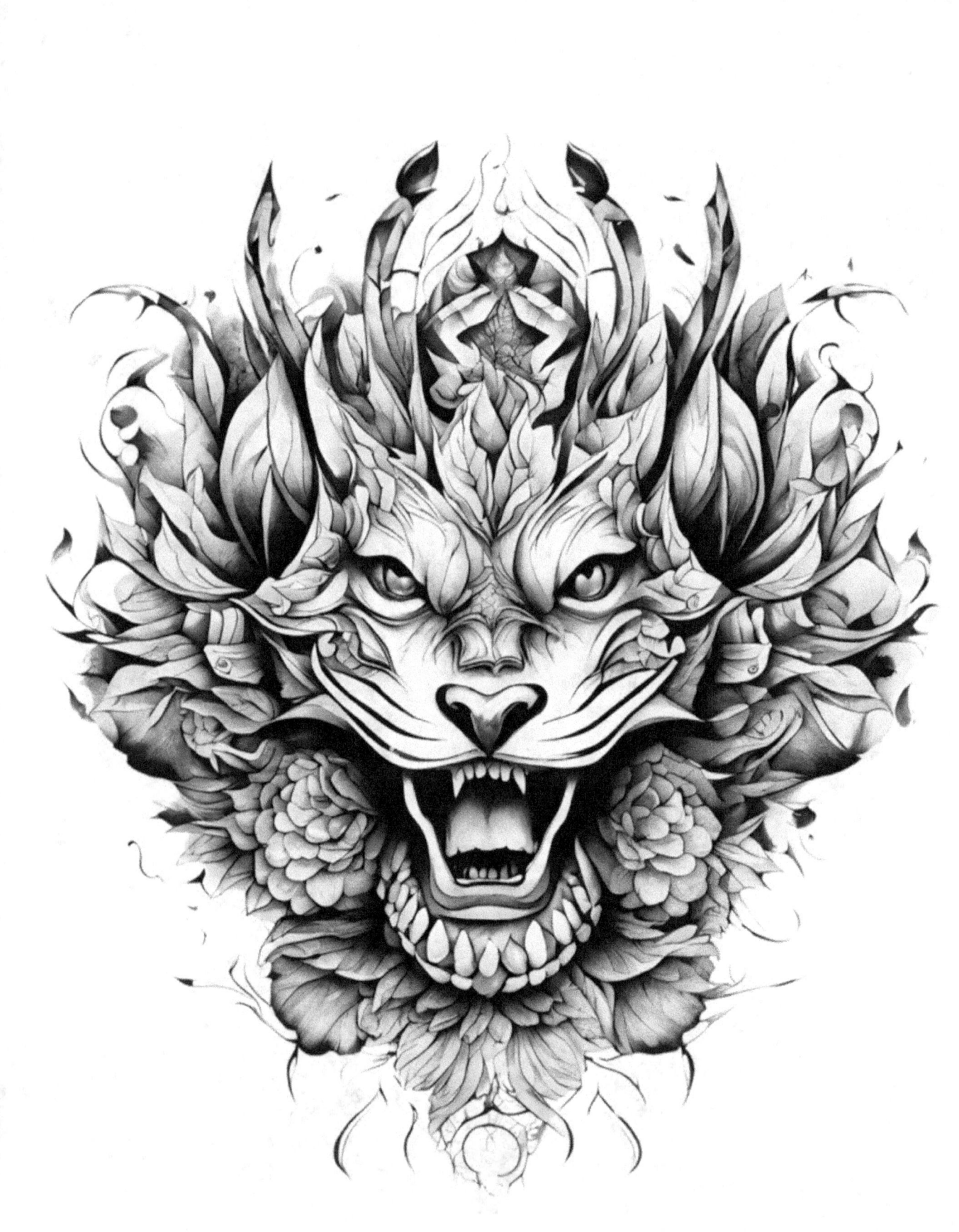

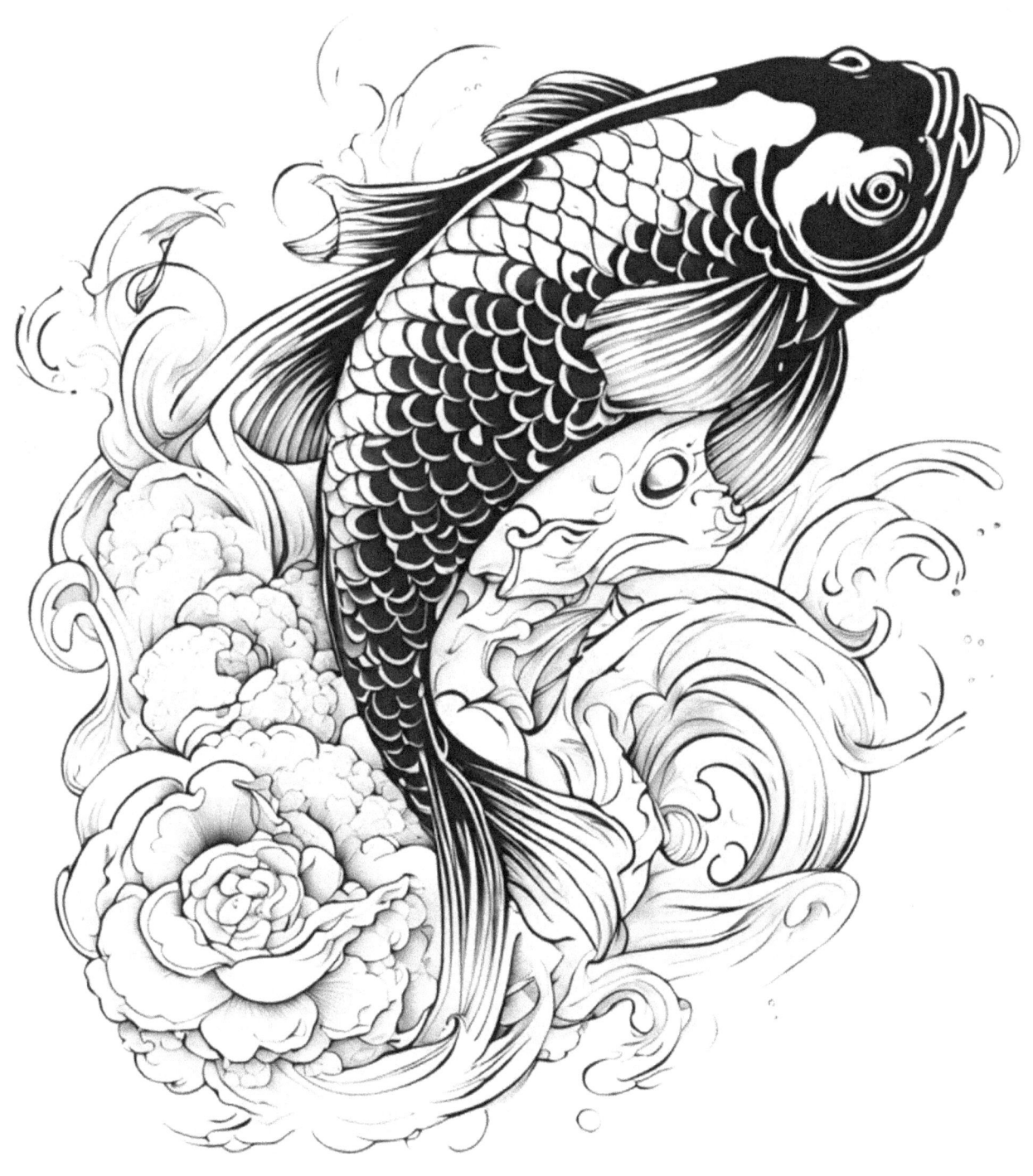

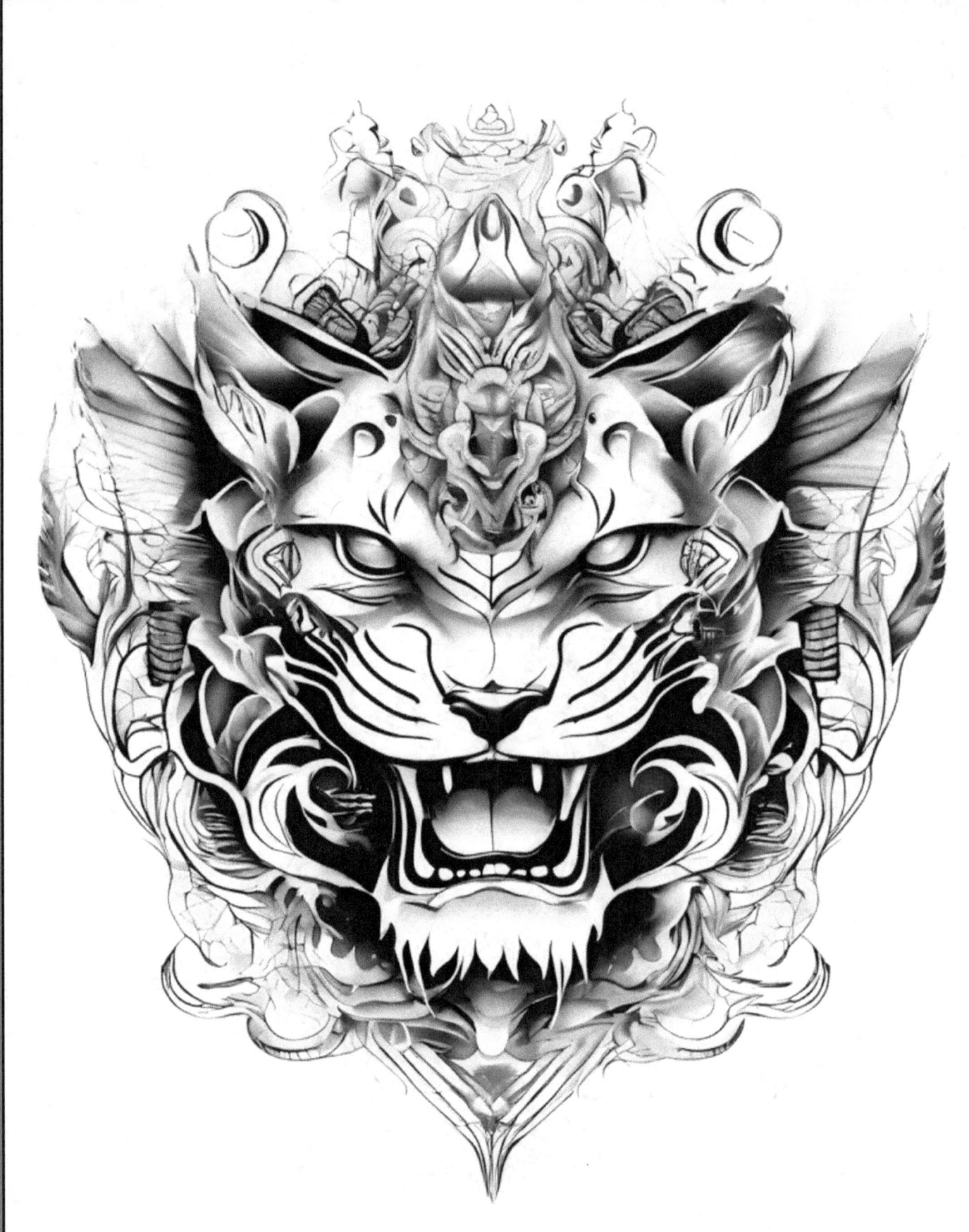

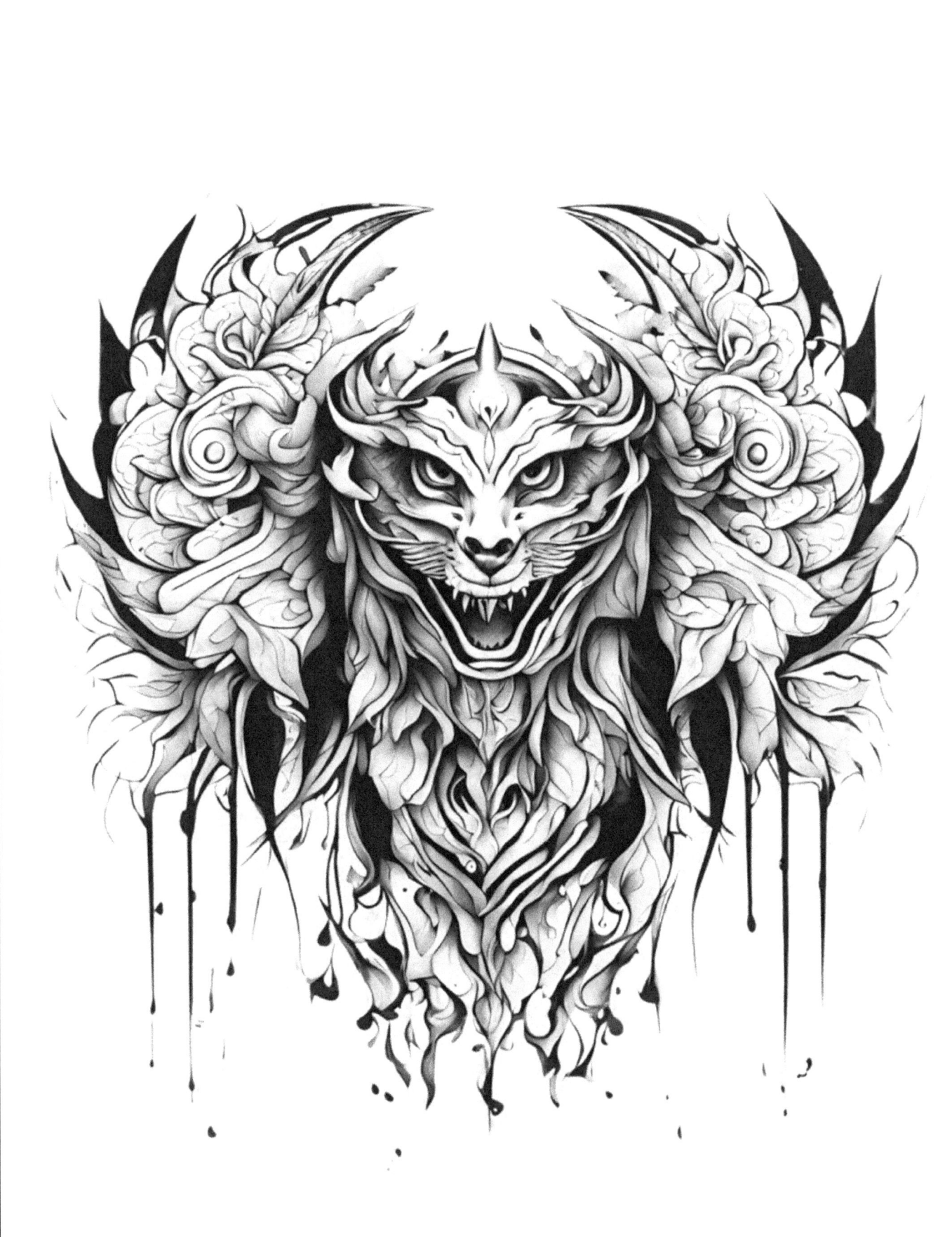

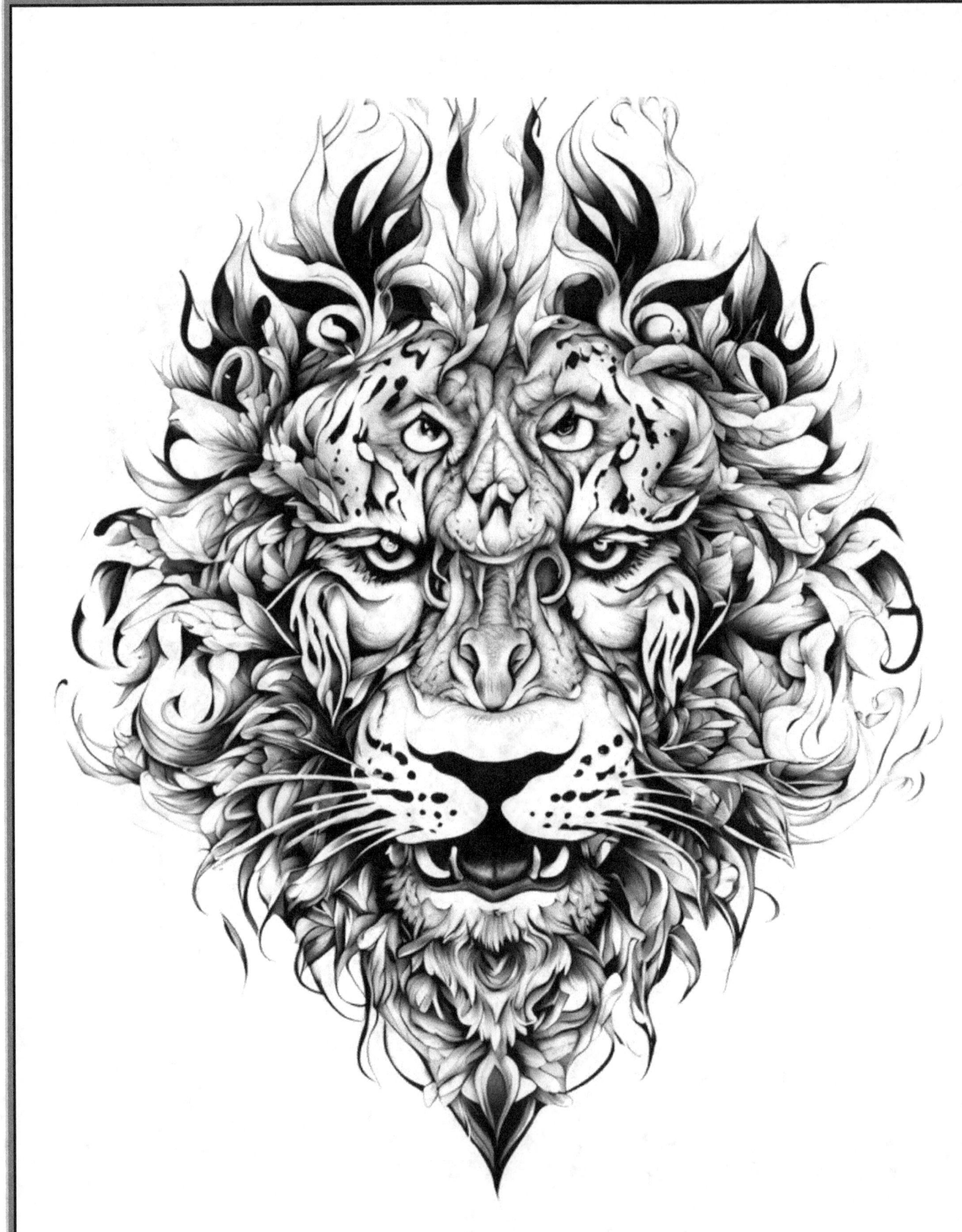

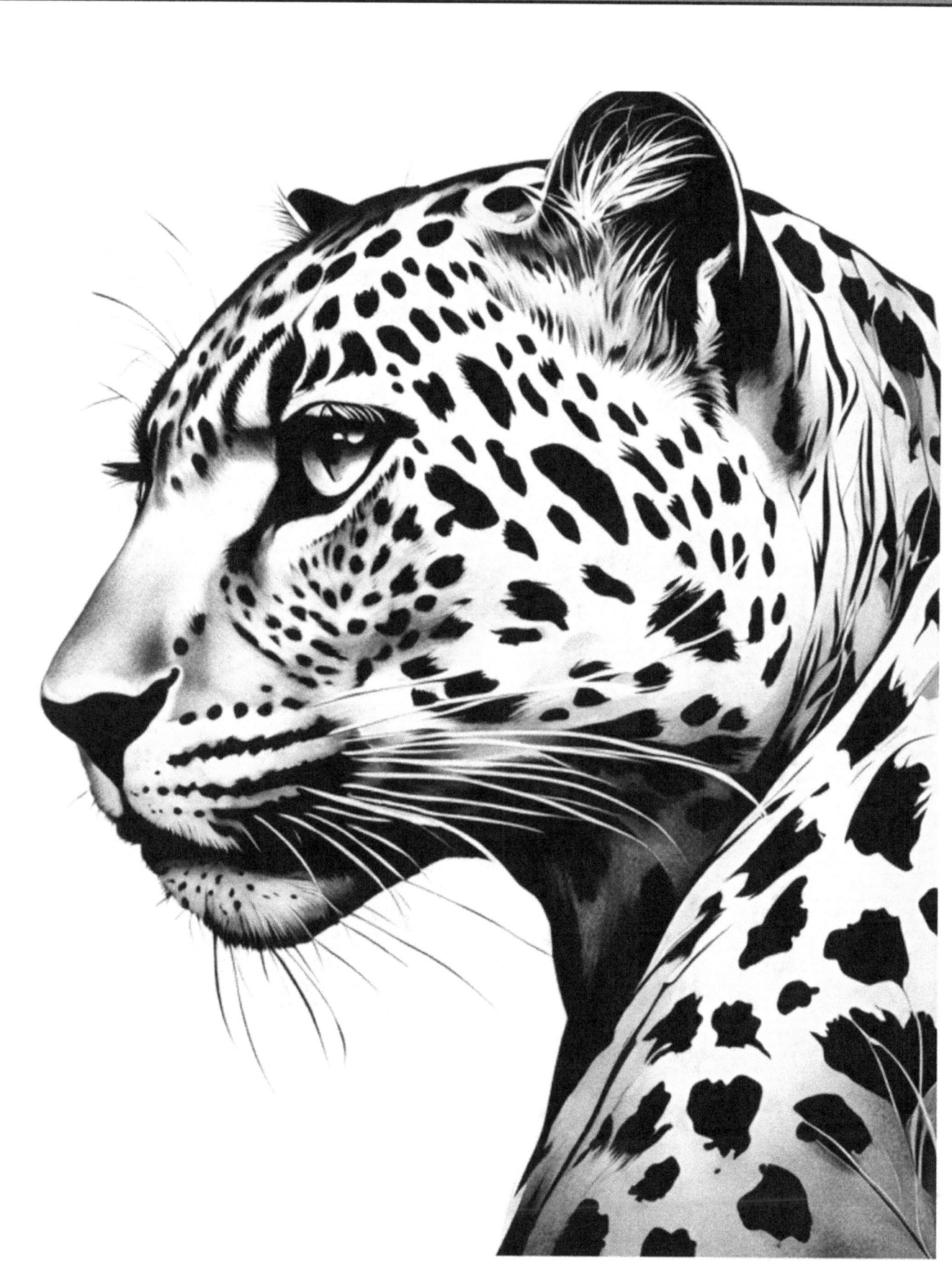

203

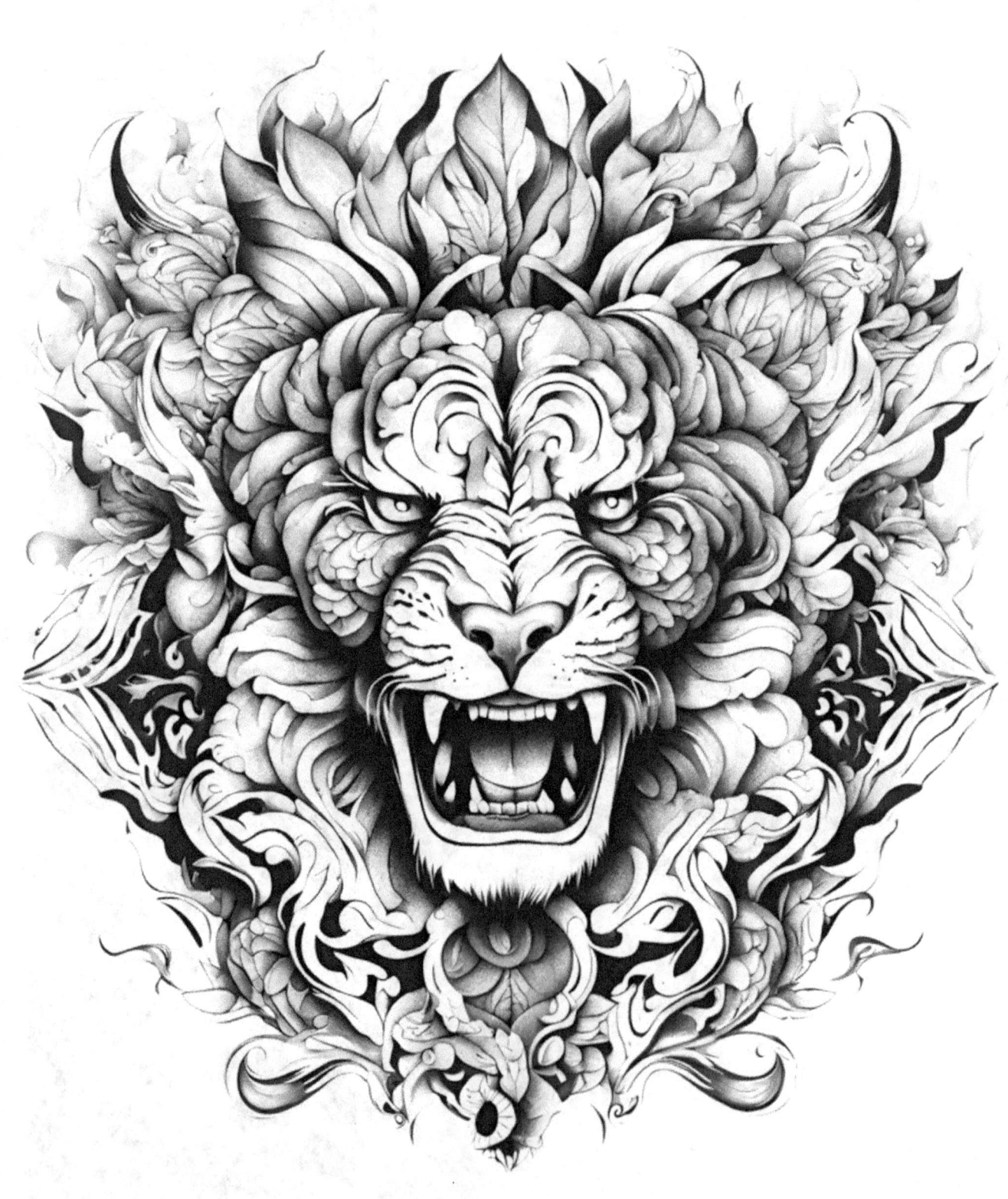

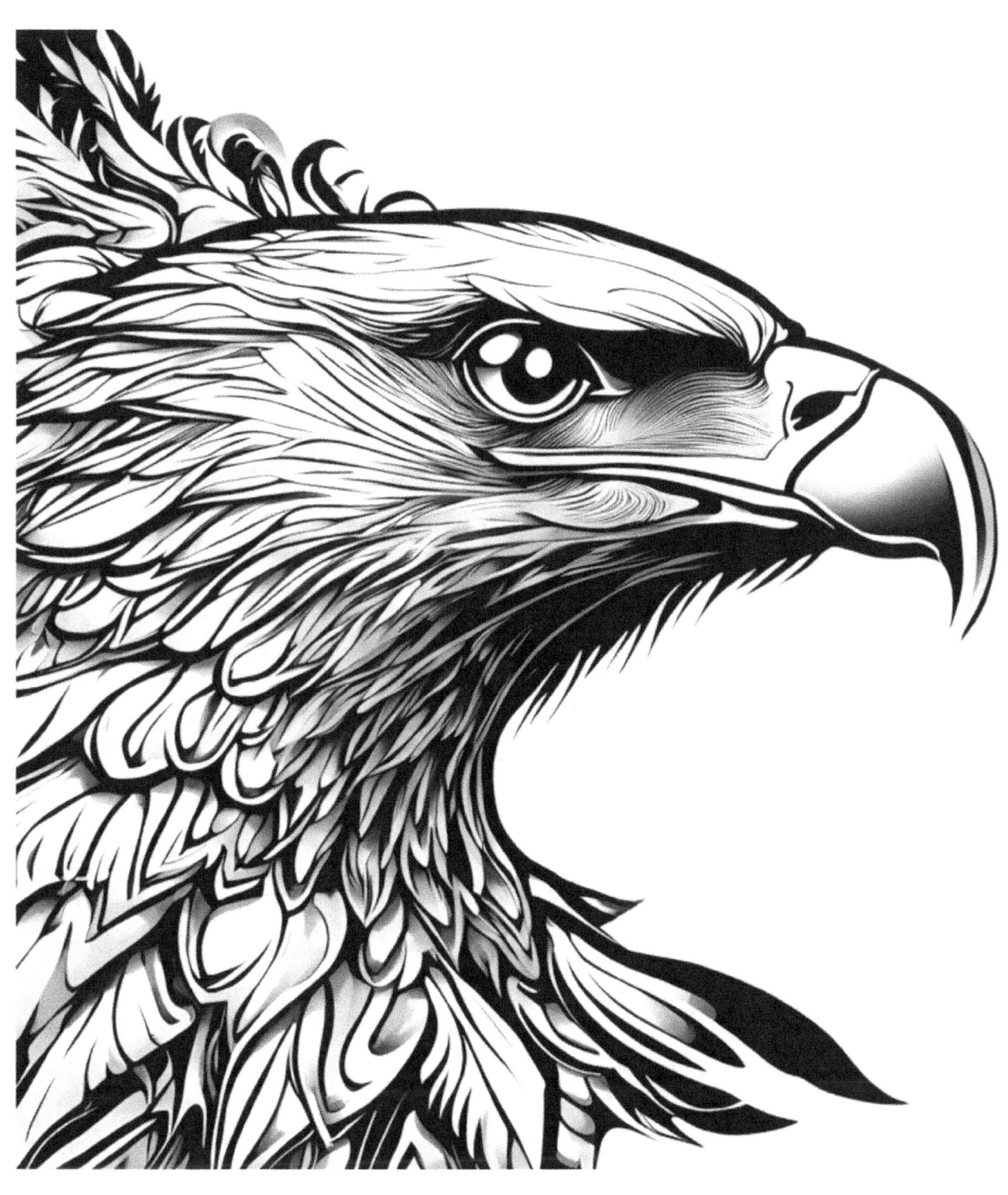